Babysitter

Babysitter

An American History

Miriam Forman-Brunell

New York University Press • *New York and London*

NEW YORK UNIVERSITY PRESS
New York and London
www.nyupress.org

© 2009 by New York University
All rights reserved

Library of Congress Cataloging-in-Publication Data
Forman-Brunell, Miriam, 1955–
Babysitter : an American history / Miriam Forman-Brunell.
p. cm.
Includes bibliographical references and index.
ISBN-13: 978–0–8147–2759–1 (cl : alk. paper)
ISBN-10: 0–8147–2759–X (cl : alk. paper)
1. Babysitting—United States—History—20th century. I. Title.
HQ769.5.F67   2009
649'.10248—dc22   2009005920

Manufactured in the United States of America
10 9 8 7 6 5 4 3 2 1

Contents

Acknowledgments

I was a teenage babysitter. Yet my scholarly interest in babysitting stemmed from a previous book on the history of dolls in the lives of American girls. I had been intrigued by anecdotal evidence of girls who had purchased dolls with money they had earned pushing carriages as "baby-walkers" or "baby tenders." These early twentieth-century babysitters proved to be just as business-minded as a group of plucky preadolescents I happened to encounter at the end of the century who confidently charged parent-employers by the number of children they cared for. I first began investigating the history of babysitters under a grant from the Princeton University Committee on Research in the Humanities and Social Sciences. I continued this project with support from the Center for Research on Women at Wellesley College and a Faculty Research Grant from the University of Missouri-Kansas City. The University of Missouri Research Board's generous grant enabled me to spend an entire year researching and writing.

Piecing together the history of those who "minded the baby" earlier in the twentieth century with those by its end was made possible with additional assistance. Colleagues in the Department of History at the University of Missouri–Kansas City, especially Dennis Merrill and Louis Potts, as well as Jim Durig, a former dean of the College of Arts and Sciences, saw in this project something worth supporting. Andrew Bergerson, Gary Ebersole, Jane Greer, and Lynda Payne read chapters and offered cogent critiques. My thanks to my colleague Kristi Holsinger, in the Department of Criminal Justice and Criminology, for helping me to better understand the emergence of the delinquent babysitter.

Numerous librarians, archivists, and other experts located all kinds of wonderful sources. Cynthia Churchwell, the former social sciences reference librarian at Miller Nichols Library, who conducted an expert library search, uncovered newspaper articles and other sources. Chuck Haddix, director of the Marr Sound Archives at the University of Missouri–Kansas City provided helpful audio-technical assistance (for which I gave him a 45 rpm of the early 1960s hit "Baby Sittin' Boogie"). Marilyn Carbonell, then assistant director for collection development at the Miller Nichols Library at UMKC, permitted me to borrow back issues of popular periodicals. Music/media librarian Laura Gayle Green sent babysitting lyrics my way. Images from magazines were expertly photographed by Sherry Best, assistant professor and curator of Visual Resources. Sherry worked closely with Kelly Pangrac, document delivery librarian of the Kansas City Missouri Public Library, who generously loaned volumes of bound periodicals. Librarians at this library saved me countless hours collecting books about babysitting from branch libraries. I am especially grateful to Elizabeth Forbes and Marie McDermed at the Plaza branch library for locating a number of hard-to-find titles. I appreciate the help provided by Jeremy Drouin, the special collections librarian at the Kansas City Public Library, who provided a reproduction of the cover illustration of *Henry Reed's Baby-Sitting Service* included in this book. The Norman Rockwell Family Agency generously provided permission to reprint Norman Rockwell's *Babysitter* illustration, which graces the book's cover. The image, which first appeared on a 1947 *Saturday Evening Post* cover, poignantly captures the perspectives of babysitters and their bosses privileged in this study.

Liz Bezera, associate director for Information Services at the Emerson College Library, provided me with a photocopy of the only master's thesis on babysitting, as well as permission to cite it. Sherl Casper, a reporter and one of my graduate students, found many useful newspaper articles published in the *Kansas City Star*. Tok Thompson, archivist at the University of California at Berkeley Folklore Archives, facilitated the retrieval of over two hundred babysitter urban legends. My thanks to Simon Bronner for putting me in touch with Rachel Wolgemuth, archival assistant at the Center for Pennsylvania Culture Studies, who sent me another dozen babysitter legends. Jan Harold Brunvand aided my understanding of the fascinating world of urban legends. My thanks to Linnea M. Anderson at the Columbia University Archives and Mary Degenhardt at the Girl Scouts of the U.S.A., who gave me many handbooks and other materials related to babysitting.

The Internet provided me with access to a treasure trove of materials that regularly and repeatedly turned up on eBay. I quickly learned how to "snipe" after being painfully outbid in an early attempt to acquire Barbie's babysitting accessories. Extant magazines, manuals, movies, and many other sources of evidence that appeared on eBay and on other sites made visible the history of an uncharted field. D. Michele Maki opened my eyes to Little Lulu cartoons and comics, and Janet Smith opened my ears to the many babysitting episodes that aired on radio programs. Andrea Lorimer generously included infant care pamphlets along with the 1950s Gerber Baby Sitting pamphlet I purchased. I am also very grateful to Laurita Ferry and her late husband, Clint, for rescuing and transferring files and for keeping my many laptops in tip-top condition over the course of this long project.

When I first began this project in the early 1990s, the number of scholars working on the history of girls could be counted on one hand. By the end of the decade the field had flourished. Sherrie A. Inness, who focused early scholarly attention on the fledgling field, introduced me to the pioneering work on "girls' culture" by up-and-coming scholars. Kelly Schrum's foundational scholarship, careful reading of my chapters, and pieces of evidence she sent my way shaped my understanding of how girls and their subcultures related to babysitters and their employers. Joe Austin, responsible for showcasing the work of youth studies scholars, and Ilana Nash, who examined teenage girls in popular culture, contributed immensely to my understanding of generations of female adolescent babysitters' subcultural principles and practices. I am especially indebted to the many other scholars, such as Leslie Paris, who, over the course of this project, brought the study of children from the margins into the mainstream. Steven Mintz's outstanding work on the history of boys, girls, and the American family provided me with the firm foundation and solid structure upon which this study is built.

The direction of my research was often influenced by my students, whose questions and insights derived from the memories of babysitting they also shared. A number of my students who worked as research assistants uncovered priceless material used in this study. Melissa Hardin spent a summer tracking down magazine sources at the Library of Congress and manuscript material at the National Archives. While still a graduate student at the University of Missouri–Kansas City, Jane Dusselier amassed enough first-rate primary sources to keep me going for years. She was followed by Greta Kroker, who proved to be particularly helpful locating babysitter movies in the days before they became more readily accessible on the internet. While still undergraduates, Angela Lupton and Lisieux Huellman were among my most capable and meticulous researchers who brought me bundles of wonderful articles. Laura Bart, a history graduate student at the University of Indiana, copied valuable sources in the Sylvia Plath collection at the Lilly Library.

Yet if it were not for Mary McMurray—research assistant par excellence—this book would never have been finished. It was she who fixed my footnotes and compiled the comprehensive bibliography of primary and secondary sources used in this study. I cannot thank her enough for the many long hours she spent engaged in the more tedious and less entertaining aspects of this project. The intelligence, diligence, reliability, compassion, and quick wit of this talented young historian-in-the-making enabled me to complete this project.

I also owe thanks to the many commentators, panel members, and audiences at the 1996, 2002, and 2008 Berkshire Conferences on the History of Women; the 2007 American Anthropological Association Conference; the 2006 American Studies Association Conference; the 2003 Midwest Popular Culture/American Culture Association Conference; the 2000 and 2003 Biennial Meetings of the Society for the History of Children and Youth; the 1999 International Interdisciplinary Congress on Women at the University of Tromso in Norway, and the 1999 "Notions of Women and Gender" forum at the University of Missouri–Kansas City. Numerous women (including Sharon Nathan, Liz Wilson, and Cheryl Lupton) shared sources and stories about their babysitting experiences that made possible a unique sitter-centered perspective that often challenged adults' top-down view. Pseudonyms have been used to protect the confidentiality of other babysitters.

I owe many thanks to those others who not only believed in this project but also helped shape it along the way: Bob Brugger, Deirdre Mullane, Vik Mukhija, Karen Wolney, Brendan O'Malley, and the historian, and my former teacher, David Nasaw. I especially owe my appreciation to my editor, Debbie Gershenowitz. Her capable editorial assistant, Gabrielle Begue, tracked down permissions, handled images, and managed the manuscript. I am grateful to this future book editor and to the interns, Julia Pentz and Stephanie Zimmerman, who also assisted with illustrations. And finally to Despina Gimbel: many thanks for catching all the dangling modifiers.

It is not often that babysitters are given thanks in acknowledgments though they probably should be. This project could not have been written if not for the many who provided outstanding child care for my children. At Princeton University Melissa Hardin was not only a crackerjack researcher but also a terrific babysitter who gave my then baby son his first introduction to teen culture and college life. I am indebted to Ingrid Kondos, who opened her home first to Perry and then to Zoë. Ingrid made them delicious home-cooked (organic, Swedish, and Greek) meals and hand-knit sweaters. In Kansas City, Susan Erwin and her daughter Tracey, were our most favorite "steady sitters." The "Garner Twins"—Amelia and

Suzanne—were terrific mother's helpers to me and playful companions to my children. My long overdue thanks as well to Mrs. Adorno and Aunt Rose, who took care of me when I was a little girl in the late 1950s and taught me to appreciate what goes into being a great babysitter. My fond thanks to Douglas Gellman, the imaginative toddler I liked the most when I was a teenage babysitter.

To family, I thank you all for your help, love, and support. I so deeply appreciate Barbara Berg and Arnie Schlanger for everything and especially for being there when it counted most. My warm thanks to my sister-in-law for her hospitality. Colette Josephson made it possible for me to spend days researching at the Library of Congress. The inspired conversation of my Swedish *kusiners*, Nancy Miller and Kaj Schueler, and the very tasty food they prepared, also supplied me with the energy and eagerness to write. I am especially grateful to my father, John Formanek, who was not only a babysitter in his youth but also married one. My mother, Ruth Formanek, inspired me to live the life of a scholar filled with important books, spirited conversation, deep conviction, great food, long walks, and good humor. I learned how to write from her careful editing. My children, Perry and Zoë, have been fellow travelers to libraries where I researched and they played, and to conferences where I presented papers and they played some more. They shared my enthusiasm for the engaging songs, movies, and toys with babysitting themes. They learned the words to "Babysittin' Boogie" and watched nearly as many sit-com episodes and full-length movies about babysitting as I. They have also been great "sittees" who only once challenged the authority of a sitter, and she was kin. Finally, many pets in my life have come and gone while I have labored on this project. My cat, Simon, often interrupted my writing for a snuggle. I so miss those moments now that he is gone.

While initially my husband had to be convinced that this topic was bookworthy, thereafter he never stopped urging me to think about babysitting dynamically, combining the historical with the psychological. He has been a great listener, an insightful reader, a terrific editor, and, in many ways, my coauthor of this book. It is to Claude, whose love and humor has sustained me for more than a quarter of a century, that this book is most lovingly dedicated.

Introduction

"A good babysitter is hard come by," explained a reporter on *CBS News* during the summer of 2007.[1] A year earlier, a mother blogged that "babysitters seem to care nothing about kids and charge $16 an hour to watch TV and text message their boyfriends."[2] And then, of course, reported *Living Safely* magazine in the 1990s, there were the "horror stories: parents arriving home to find their sitter has thrown a party, or gone to one. . . ."[3] Intrinsic to such typical complaints is a longing for the golden age of babysitting when teenage girls were both pleasant and plentiful. Yet the view that babysitters today are hard to take and even harder to find is not new. In a letter to "Dear Abby" in 1969, one woman described the batch of hungry sitters "who ate the fridge to the bare walls" and disparaged the one with "the gall" to raid the "deep freeze."[4] What is unknown to these recent observers is that a prior idyllic age of babysitting is more apparent than real: distressed parent-employers have suspected their sitters of doing wrong ever since the beginning of babysitting nearly one hundred years ago. In fact, parent-employers have been complaining about babysitters since the advent of the "modern" American teenage girl, a debut that coincided with the creation of babysitting, the job that defaulted to white, middle-class, female adolescents by virtue of their sex, race, class, and age.

Though researchers have dated anxieties about babysitters to the expansion of babysitting after World War II, babysitters had already earned considerable notoriety by then.[5] It was during the 1920s—when babysitting was just in its infancy—that one parenting guide first urged mothers not to hire "high school girls" who trundled "babies about to hockey games, basketball practice, and [engaged in] street-corner flirtation."[6] As the "babysitter" gained ground during the Great Depression (when the word was originated though rarely used), advisers focused on the unkempt clothing and garish cosmetics of female adolescents suspected of preferring their "crowd" of friends to the kids in their care. Then, despite attempts to make scandalous V-girls into patriotic babysitters during World War II, *Newsweek* reported that a veteran and his wife arrived home after an evening out only to find their "bobby-soxer" babysitter dancing with friends and their toddler teething on marbles.[7] Represented as villains who have caused danger, and as victims who have courted it, in the innumerable stories adults have been telling for almost a century, babysitters have ostensibly damaged property, ruined marriages, and destroyed families.

Though most often babysitting proceeds without a serious hitch, the problems associated with it have been widely and sometimes wantonly exaggerated on many levels, from the conversational to the cultural. In movies (popular, pornographic, made-for-TV, and horror), newspapers, magazines, music, television, cartoons, teen fiction, sit-coms, comics, manuals, urban legends, toys, and other sources upon which this study draws, babysitters have been deemed harmful rather than helpful. The omnipresent babysitter has been notorious for sneaking her boyfriend in the back door, talking on the telephone, sitting glued to the TV, eating her employers out of house and home, and neglecting the children while paying too much attention to the man of the house.[8] This deceptively simple stereotype of the unruly babysitter expresses the anxieties of parents as well as the concerns of the culture about teenage girls. Left to do as they please, girls will recklessly transgress the essential boundaries between private and public, family and community, labor and leisure, childhood and adulthood, girlhood and womanhood, love and lust, reality and fantasy, culture and chaos, yours and theirs.

But are teenage girls who babysit really mischief makers, home wreckers, husband stealers, child abusers, kidnappers, thieves, and whores, as they have been variously imagined? What accounts for the deeply ingrained sitter stereotype encoded in the many anecdotes and parables that parents routinely hear from one another and see in the mass media? Why hasn't the babysitter earned distinction instead of eliciting dread? What has she meant to adults and, just as importantly, to the generations of girls who babysat? The first aim of this book is to interrogate adults' assumptions about teenage girls they suspect of jeopardizing the safety of their children, the security of their homes, and even the sanctity of their marriages.

In this social and cultural history I argue that what adults' enduring anxieties about babysitters reveal is unease about the far-reaching gender and generational changes that gave rise to the "modern" American teenage girl, whose emergence coincided with the creation of the babysitter in the 1920s. Thereafter, the babysitter's highly charged position as a youthful stranger overseeing children within the privacy of the American home made the babysitter a lightning rod for the expression of adults' profound uncertainties about the unprecedented possibilities of teenage girls. For nearly one hundred years the babysitter has stood at the indeterminate boundary between adults' unresolved dilemma over the benefits of female adolescent empowerment and the threat of girls' independence. I also argue that in an ongoing attempt to resolve conflicts over the nature of girlhood, babysitting has functioned as a primary site for girls' social rehabilitation. Since the emergence of babysitting early in the twentieth century, the acculturation of girls in the utilitarian aspects of babysitting has furthered an essential and enduring ideological endeavor: to allow girls a modicum of independence while reinforcing the domestic and maternal imperative.

While no American worker has been more consistently disparaged than the iconic self-absorbed babysitter who studies her fingernails instead of cuddling the kids, this book also aims to document babysitters' subjectivity as well as their subjection by making historically visible the job that served as the ambiguous gateway to female employment and young womanhood throughout the twentieth century. Though overlooked as historically significant for most of the century, babysitters appear as helpful, contented, and grateful workers in recent syntheses on the history of children and youth.[9] In truth, since the beginnings of babysitting, girls have expressed more ambivalence than enthusiasm about their designated social role. This history sheds light on the perspectives of girls whose lives were shaped by the reality that, throughout most of the century, babysitting was the only job available to girls. The less often heard stories about babysitting that have been a part of girls' everyday lives include persuasive complaints about impetuous, irresponsible, insensitive, and unappreciative employers. Girls' stories—which go back to the earliest days of babysitting—go far toward explaining why teenage girls have been leaving the field of babysitting ever since it first emerged.

While babysitting has served as the main port of entry for female employment, it has always been much more than just a casual part-time job for girls or a solution to the everyday needs of ordinary parents. On a social and cultural level, babysitting has aimed to reconcile a dichotomy that grew more conspicuous over the course of the twentieth century. Girls increasingly negotiated between adolescent self-assertiveness, rebelliousness, sexual experimentation, and autonomy on one side, and feminine self-sacrifice, compliance, sexual restraint, subordination, and dependence on the other. By providing girls with a part-time job that enabled them to attain semiautonomous status—outside of their own family but within the bosom of another—experts, educators, and other adults hoped to regulate girls' behavior and neutralize the threat they posed. Applying Michel Foucault's theory of discourse to the history of babysitting enables us to discern the larger systems of ideas, attitudes, institutions, and practices of experts, educators, and employers who produced knowledge, constructed truths, defined social relations, constituted subjectivities, and established social power over teenage girls.[10] These adults together made babysitting into a discursive field.

The central perspective of this study is that babysitting is a cultural battleground where conflicts over girlhood—especially regarding sexual, social, cultural, and economic autonomy and empowerment—are regularly played out. Whether real or imaginary, the babysitter has long been a figure fraught with contested meanings about girlhood that have both distorted adults' perceptions of female adolescents and vitiated girls' expectations of babysitting. Embodying adults' expectations and reservations about female adolescents, the babysitter has served as the quintessential symbol of the girl adults desire but have widely represented in American mass culture as dangerously disruptive.[11] Consequently, American parents who hired babysitters opened the door both to preconceived fantasies of daughterly devotion and to prepackaged fears of teenage transgression.

The ordinary and extraordinary problems associated with babysitting stem from elemental struggles over contending notions of girlhood first set into motion during the 1920s by changing ideals and conventions. Tracing the history of babysitters over the course of the twentieth century reveals that generations of parent-employers unknowingly drew upon a succession of historically constituted stereotypes of female adolescents that typically framed their conceptions of the girls they employed. As the archetypal teenage girl, the babysitter embodied the full range of a long-standing and wide-ranging critique of female adolescents as self-absorbed, unpredictable, irrational, irresponsible, unreliable, inscrutable, disorderly, unstable, irresistible, uncontrollable, consumeristic, pleasure seeking, and money hungry. Not wholly aware of the disparaging stereotype of teenage girls that gave form to their fears, generations of parent-employers consecutively cast babysitters as pleasure seeking in the 1920s; frivolous shoppers in the 1930s; street-walking Victory Girls during World War II, and rabble rousers after the war. As the expansion of girls' youth culture accelerated over the course of the second half of the twentieth century, the babysitter continued to serve as an object of adults' fears and fantasies about female adolescents run amok. Babysitters were culturally typecast as irreverent "bobby-soxers" in the 1950s; energetic and arousing in the sixties; in dire need of violent restraint during the 1970s, and double-crossing teenage villains and plucky preadolescent "Super Sitters" during the 1980s. By the end of the century, girls were seen as "Quitter Sitters."

Whatever form teen transgressors have been made to assume in the cultural imagination, girls' own notions of girlhood have vied with adults' for dominance since the birth of modern American female adolescence in the 1920s. Laying the basis of what would follow, the quest for social, cultural, and economic autonomy and empowerment—hallmark of adolescence— found repeated expression in girls' culture, the ongoing and variously shifting principles and practices that generations of teenage girls created and inadvertently carried with them to the neighbors. While babysitting brought adolescents and adults into closer proximity, however, antithetical beliefs about girlhood set them further apart. As a result, played out in the embattled field of babysitting and embodied in the contested representations of babysitters have been intergenerational conflicts over what it means to be a teenage girl.

While the babysitter has provided a way to talk about what girls should be and should not do, this study of babysitting provides a unique historical lens through which we can more clearly discern the history of adults' attitudes about girls, as well as the methods devised for dealing with teenagers. In order to correct girls and contain the influence of their youth culture, generations of adults utilized a wide variety of sources and devised a diversity of strategies. Embedding a shifting rationale for babysitting in everything from textbooks to toys, adults tapped girls' desire for independence, which they also defused and reused for their own child-care needs. Or so adults thought. Though babysitting served as a method of socialization, adults proved to be as ineffective at stemming the tide of girls' culture as they were in halting the decline of babysitting. Legions of experts who consistently packaged babysitting as an opportunity for female self-sufficiency sought to make selfish girls selfless. Yet babysitters, frustrated by the limitations of the unregulated job that made them vulnerable to economic exploitation and sexual abuse, eventually left babysitting and parent-employers in the lurch.

Major Themes in the History of Babysitting

Typecast as a home wrecker and trivialized as a caretaker, the babysitter is more complex and consequential than one might initially suppose. In fact, her history is rife with conflicted expectations and complicated interactions between generations who vied for the cultural dominance of girlhood. This study amplifies the underlying issues that have long dominated and distorted our perceptions of the babysitter; it is no coincidence that these also shaped American life in the twentieth century. Discernible in assorted variations of the babysitter that emerged, developed, and recurred are such major themes as (1) the anxieties of adults roused by changing notions of gender and sexuality; (2) the rise of the teenage girl, the expansion of youth culture, and the concerns these provoked about girlhood; (3) the social meanings of vocational education and mass culture entertainment; and (4) the consistently ambivalent standpoint of generations of babysitters upon whom parents have all depended.

The Power of Parental Anxieties

Long before middle-class teenage babysitters became the object of parental scrutiny and criticism, "common servants" who managed the home and minded the children for middle-class parents had been widely regarded as "a little better than idiots."[12] Victorian ideals about family life, gender roles, childhood, labor, leisure, and sexuality shaped the perspective of middle-class employers who looked down on the working-class women they regarded as cultural inferiors. While advisers had little to say that was not disparaging about servant girls between the Civil War and World War I, the hope that "ignorant" domestics could be trained to be better ones had led the American Medical Association to publish *The Systematic Training of Nursery-Maids* (1887).[13] Another late-nineteenth-century guide, published the same year that saw the establishment of the American Pediatric Society, informed mothers to carefully choose a nurse-maid who "should enjoy good health; her skin should be clean, and she should be full of animal spirit, not languid and moping."[14] The low regard that employers had for their working-class servants also found expression in the popular culture of the time. J. M. Barrie, who cast the nanny as a dog in *Peter Pan* (1911), consigned Nana to the doghouse for her dereliction of child-care duties.[15]

The study of the medical, psychological, educational, and social aspects of children's lives by late-nineteenth-century pediatricians, psychologists, mothers, and teachers led reformers to place children at the center of their concerns by the turn of the century. The establishment of the new fields of pediatrics and child psychology were followed by the formulation of the National Congress of Mothers (soon to be renamed the PTA) and the U.S. Children's Bureau. The centrality of children that increased the focus on caretakers led the Children's Bureau "to speak a word of warning as to nursemaids" in *Infant Care*, the pioneering pamphlet published in 1914. "One has only to visit the parks of any city on a pleasant day to note the instances of carelessness on the part of nursemaids toward the babies in their charge."[16] In the decade before middle-class girls challenged bourgeois codes, conventions, and customs, working-class girls who sought out casual yet intimate acquaintances with young men were the first generation of American girls to openly defy the gendered ideals of the declining Victorian order.[17]

Rising expectations about motherhood—which accelerated during the 1920s, intensified after World War II, and soared beyond the grasp of women during the 1980s—further drove mothers to scrutinize those hired to take their place. With mothers believing—at some level—in dominant ideals of motherhood, babysitting became a magnet for anxieties about maternal adequacy that spurred exaggerated fears about teenage girls' expanding social, cultural, and sexual independence and authority.[18] Reflecting the angst-ridden flux in gender roles for females, different representations of babysitters arose in which the babysitter cunningly shifted between wage earner and dutiful daughter, child-care provider and housekeeper, maternal surrogate and stand-in wife, submissive lover and destructive bitch.

Though it was chiefly men who created the babysitter characters who appeared in novels, short stories, movie scripts, and other works, few, if any, ever explained the desire or hostility that fueled their depictions. Changing notions of masculinity during specific historical moments provide windows into the frustrations, fascinations, and fears of men about adolescent babysitters. Beginning during the Depression and emerging with full force in the years after World War II, for example, was a masculinity crisis that stemmed from the convergence of changing ideals about womanhood and adolescence. Sardonic portrayals of women generally, and satirical characterizations of babysitters specifically, conveyed male anxieties about all females pushing their claims for independence. In popular magazines men ridiculed both babysitter unions brought into being by a residual wartime gender ideology that valorized women wage earners and the developing teen culture that empowered adolescents. American men cultivated a perception of teenage babysitters as militants during the late 1940s and as miscreants during the 1950s,[19] thus expressing their fears about the decline of paternal authority and aiming to reassert patriarchal power as the country edged into the age of domesticity.

During the 1960s female adolescents' claims to sexual independence led babysitters to become objects of masculine desire in often leering fantasies in magazines and movies. The pleasures and perils of the sexual revolution and the counterculture were manifested in babysitters who were widely and blatantly eroticized in everything from pornography to high culture. The rising female authority and declining male dominance led to raw depictions of teenage babysitters subdued by their horny employers. Acting out the ambivalences of men who were both stimulated and scared by the sweeping social changes that accelerated during the 1970s, mainstream culture conscripted the services of male maniacs who sought to contain girlhood autonomy, sexual and otherwise. Babysitting became a particularly violent site of struggle between mad men and independent girls during the 1970s, when maniacs in urban legends and horror movies set their sights on babysitters.

Anxieties about the changing role of men as heads of the American household—a persistent motif in the history of babysitting—had first emerged during the Great Depression. Adults during the 1930s felt uneasy about family disruption and the altered patterns of power caused by men who lost their jobs and women and girls who held down the fort. During World War II, working women and their employed teenage daughters ignited a wartime panic about the family, fatherless for the duration. Years of deprivation, compounded by Cold War anxieties, caused marriage and family to be seen as the most important source of self-fulfillment and security.[20] But rising rates of working mothers reignited fears about the impact that their absence from the home might have on the well-being of the postwar family. Experts who promoted the "togetherness" ethos pointed to men's declining authority, wives' abdication of motherhood, and the shift of child-rearing duties onto others as major causes of family decline.

At this time, the cultural anthropologist Margaret Mead observed that "the self-contained little family is only made possible by the sitter—an outsider paid to come into the home and maintain it as a going concern."[21] But instead of earning recognition for the role she played in sustaining families, the babysitter, who was only a bystander witnessing the long-term changes that had been reshaping American family life since the

1920s, became scapegoated in discourses about its destruction. "To many," reported the *Journal of the National Education Association* in 1951, "baby-sitting heralded the breakdown of the American family."[22] Converging on the babysitter were the worries of parents about rising rates of working mothers and a changing social and sexual system. From the 1960s onward, anxieties about motherhood, fatherhood, and girlhood were projected onto the sexualized sitter who seduced male employers and imperiled their families in popular and pornographic narratives.

The Rise of Girls' Teen Culture

Situating babysitters within broader social and cultural contexts reveals how the emergence of the teenage girl in the 1920s set into motion a collision of ideas about girlhood. Yet failing to resolve the contradiction between teenage girls' desire for personal freedom and adults' expectations that they stay close to home, the compromise to babysit set the stage for enduring conflicts between girls and grownups. Through a process of ongoing negotiation with dominant ideals, generations of girls defined their own notions of girlhood within the self-styled subcultures they created, with their own distinct beliefs, meanings, behaviors, and rituals.[23] Though socializing institutions reinforced the gender order, high schools also played a principal role in the incubation of girls' youth culture, which flouted prevailing social conventions and furthered generational estrangement.[24] Drawing girls into the labor market as workers and into the marketplace as consumers, the teen culture that emerged during the interwar years accelerated during the war and expanded in the postwar period. By the 1950s, suburbanites who looked to babysitters to uphold their values looked down on girls' culture. While youth culture drew—not unusually—upon African American and lower-class cultural performances, upwardly mobile working-class adult suburbanites aiming to be (but were not yet securely) middle class perceived teen culture as a threat to their aspirations.[25] Nor were they unusual. Youth cultures typically strike grownups as offensive, inferior, and threatening to middle-class ideals, especially regarding gender.

What triggered adults' apprehensions about babysitters in particular was their perception of the youthful social practices that girls brought with them when they babysat.[26] For instance, sitters made unauthorized use of record players and telephones and conducted "raids" on refrigerators, according to their suburban bosses during the fifties. What gave meanings to adults' personal experiences were "public perceptions and understandings of teen girlhood," explains Lorraine Kenny in *Daughters of Suburbia: Growing Up White, Middle Class, and Female* (2000), a study about teenage troublemakers.[27] The sitter certainly reinforced dominant perceptions, confirmed cultural prejudices, and reinforced fears by committing misdeeds in anecdotes, parables, legends, movies, novels, cartoons, sit-coms, and news stories. Assuming such occurrences to be both excessive and pervasive, parent-employers sought out boys, venerated as babysitters in the popular culture despite broader fears about antisocial behavior and homosexuality. In fact, from the Great Depression to the new millennium, male sitters were consistently portrayed as models of masculine identity for impressionable little boys threatened by feminized suburbs and female-headed households.

Presuming that as "females" girls naturally possessed innate abilities and desires to mother, what adults found troubling was the unpredictable, irresponsible, irrational, and independent behavior of teenage girls and their oppositional cultural styles. Not only did they ostensibly fail to meet the needs of parent-employers for child care, but girls also seemed to buck the cultural imperative to socially reproduce "good" gender, class, and racial values. Instead of maintaining social order, seemingly unruly middle-class girls threatened the future of motherhood, the family, and middle-class culture. That it was white girls especially who inspired fear is made clear by the overwhelming abundance of Caucasian, middle-class, female adolescents who cornered the babysitting market in the popular culture. The iconic sitter's "whiteness" mirrored the reality of the historical labor force where, other than caring for kin for no pay, babysitting among Hispanic, African American, and Asian girls was limited.[28] Yet critiques at the core of popular and pornographic narratives about rotten babysitters exposed a particular discomfort with the archetypal "girl next door."[29] As the quintessence of female adolescence, the babysitter acted out the struggle between normalizing American girlhood as white, middle-class, and suburban and pathologizing it.

Babysitter Training and Girlhood Socialization

Attempting to transform the widely imagined disruptive teen into a disciplined sitter has been the underlying (albeit unstated) purpose of babysitter training, an acculturation that has taken place across a vast discursive domain that spans from classrooms to comic books. A major motif in the history of babysitting is the effort to limit girls' assertion for social equality. The constraints placed on girls have been obscured by experts' and educators' apparently well-meaning intentions to help them. For instance, the seemingly sensible advice about clogging up the telephone with long "gab fests" that was included in manuals, pamphlets, and educational movies also served to modify the behavior that kept girls from satisfying the needs of parents and society.[30] Though experts in the 1920s dismissed girls as child-care providers, those thereafter sought to restrain, retrain, and redeem teenage girls by binding them to babies. Advisors and educators did so by earnestly constructing various versions of an ideal sitter who combined idealized feminine standards with girls' more independent goals: competent yet compliant, sensible and sensitive, responsible and responsive. Whether experts promoted babysitting as "patriotic" in the 1940s, as "professional" in the 1950s, or as a "business" since the 1980s, the construction of gender identities that diluted girls' opposition to restrictive ideals operated as a practical undertaking with a conservative goal: to combine female adolescent autonomy with feminine accountability.[31]

That experts and educators increased expectations but not social status or wages led generations of babysitters to feel discouraged and disgruntled. With the inexorable exodus of teenage girls from the field by the 1980s, preadolescent girls became the focus of educators who established national training courses, experts who published handbooks, and authors who wrote lots of preteen fiction about babysitters. One of the most influential was Ann M. Martin, whose enormously popular Baby-sitter's Club book series and its innumerable commercial spin-offs disseminated, popularized, commodified, and neutralized Girl Power ideals for preadolescents coming of age. Adults sought to acculturate young girls into superlative sitters by valorizing the "Super Sitter" ideal that stood in sharp contrast to the villainized teenage "Other" who appeared around the same time. Projecting intense antifeminist anxieties about the hazards of female empowerment, teenage babysitters were murderous in movies made for television. Yet the culturally constructed "Super Sitter" assuaged parent-employers' anxieties by harnessing the energy of preadolescents who replaced sexually centered teenage girls.

Little Lulu, the cartoon character in *Operation Babysitter* (1985), was one of many fictional representations of the newly exalted preadolescent girl who populated the imaginary suburban landscape in the 1980s.[32] The first time she had been hired to babysit was in another cartoon made forty years earlier when wartime teenagers had shown less interest in caretaking than in carousing.[33] But the postwar ethos that sheltered children within the nuclear family had rendered preadolescent girls like Lulu economically useless. While child-care advisers in the 1950s warned parents not to hire a babysitter who was "younger than her midteens," those in the 1980s did an about-face and promoted the preteen instead.[34] At a time when women were bombarded with a newly formulated standard of unobtainable maternal perfection, preadolescent "Super Sitters" aided "Super Mothers" stressed by the conflicting demands of careers and kids.[35]

Recognizing that girls' desire for autonomy and empowerment could be managed toward productive ends, adults consistently sought out new methods to contain girls by using other controlling narratives. While a doll that could sing and tell stories was advertised as the "National Babysitter" in the late 1940s, this study shows that the making of real babysitters took a lot more than a little marketing.[36] Entertaining movies, sit-coms, toys, games, urban legends, and novels that featured babysitters also served didactic purposes. Though depictions shifted somewhat over time and across media, imagined sitters who threatened family stability, marital bonds, children's well-being, and community cohesion always did so in remarkably consistent ways. Numerous stories in magazines, movies, and fiction shared a cast of characters, dominant themes, and narrative structures that managed girls' femininity by mediating between embattled notions of girlhood.[37] Consequently, babysitting was represented as a formative coming-of-age ritual for girls faced with two paths: the conventional course deeply rooted in traditional gender customs and standards adults hoped they would follow and the illicit one they feared girls would pursue. The senseless girl transformed into a level-headed one over the course of a sitting stint modeled the version of girlhood adults applauded.

Utilizing many of the same tropes and probing similar themes, stories about babysitters contributed to a larger encompassing dialogue about how to harness the carefree teenage girl and prevent her from becoming a careless woman. Set in clear stories about the problem of the teenage girl, the babysitter was compelled to negotiate between self-indulgence and selflessness, defiance and deference. Made to play out the gendered conflicts between autonomy and accommodation, liberation and submission, the edifying babysitter aimed to teach real girls to recast themselves in better roles. While in young adult fiction, babysitters struggled between empowerment and acquiescence, in bare-boned pornographic narratives, sitters moved back and forth between extreme dominance and total submission. In addition to education and entertainment, other methods utilized to transform girls' behavior included coercion, condemnation, and retribution. The maniac who first materialized in order to punish disobedient sitters in the 1960s proved to be an especially sinister and long-lived taskmaster. His favorite weapon to punish, intimidate, and victimize remained the telephone that is the classic marker of girls' liberation. In the end, however, all the babysitter stories that artfully informed imaginations and shaped impressions by educating and entertaining, terrifying and titillating, eliciting and expressing, failed to satisfy the needs of grownups or girls.

Sitters' Standpoint

Stories about babysitters are essentially conservative myths that reinforce gender and generational hierarchies by cementing dominant power relationships between males and females, adults and adolescents, and employers and employees. Yet compelling narratives about powerful babysitters did not always succeed in bringing about compliance. Girls' alternative readings were made possible by the ambiguities that often characterized portraits of babysitters in the mass-culture entertainments aimed to attract female consumers. A major theme in the history of babysitting is the way in which generations of babysitters used their social power as girls—and the girls' cultures they forged—in order to reconstitute the social meanings of babysitting and to contest it as a site of feminine socialization. The babysitters whose experiences are represented in this book demonstrate that despite the repressive potential of mass culture and feminized labor, girls often challenged the hardships posed by the unstructured and unregulated nature of the field. Though girls' culture has historically reinforced traditional feminine ideals, it also provided babysitters with the authority, resources, and opportunities to negotiate the demands of the job and optimally reap its benefits.

Eager to make money rather than to mommy, generations of girls who understood the stakes used this feminized form of labor for their own proto-feminist purposes. Babysitters formed unions, issued manifestos, wrote contracts, negotiated working conditions, lobbied for raises, and, very importantly, largely eliminated housework from babysitting. When employers stood in the way of their goals, girls' opposition was played out in the semiprivate space of neighbors' homes, where they put their own subcultural principles into practice.[38] Drawing upon the language and values of their subculture, girls expressed their disdain for "wadders" (of cash) and "hour splitters," those employers who underpaid sitters but overindulged their own "brats." In the 1950s, babysitters' desire for social, economic, and cultural independence was incompatible with what they derisively called "bratting." Babysitters also resisted abuse by turning down job offers from employers who were "creeps" and fortified themselves against unknown crank callers, repulsing them with ear-shattering whistles and noise-blasting radios. For the vast majority of seemingly polite babysitters, their compliance masked underlying complaints about the job that has been at odds with girls' goals for themselves for generations.

Spotlighting the Sitter

While the teenage girl has been the focus of many books, especially of late, the babysitter has been the subject of none. That is surprising given the insights of observers who long ago recognized the long-term significance of babysitters to American society and culture. Though the word "babysitting" had yet to be included in dictionaries in 1948, *The Saturday Evening Post* already proclaimed babysitting to be a "key industry."[39] By 1949, the *New York Times* exclaimed that "[t]he person whom you employ to take care of Junior while you are out is important enough to rate a book!"[40] As the baby boom swelled and suburban developments sprouted, the newspaper further declared that the babysitter had become an "American institution."[41] Affirming that "the sitter is a prominent figure in our culture," the paper explained in 1960 that

> Should she vanish, millions of couples would prowl their apartments and ranch houses on Saturday nights like caged tigers. Movie houses and bowling alleys would close, Chinese restaurants and pizza parlors go bankrupt, gas consumption and toll collections plummet, and the crew-neck sweater and Bermuda shorts industries decline for lack of solvent teen-age customers.[42]

Though it was not until 1980 that a team of psychiatrists launched the first academic study of babysitters, scholarly inquiry about "one of the most familiar figures in our culture" is still meager more than a quarter of a century later.[43] Despite her increased workplace surveillance and sensationalized appearances in the media, the babysitter has remained nearly invisible to scholars.[44]

Though ubiquitous in conversation, communities, and culture, the babysitter has eluded serious examination.[45] Caregivers, especially mothers, have captured the recent attention of historians, sociologists, economists, psychologists, and others; these scholars have nevertheless overlooked babysitters in the invisible economy that meets critically important needs, especially mothers'. The noticeable absence of the babysitter in the historical scholarship is partly due to definitional, ideological, and methodological challenges. The term "babysitter" is a rather ambiguous term used to describe nonfamily as well as family members, those who are paid as well as those who are not, adults as well as youth, work that is institutionally based or takes place in the home. For the purposes of this study, "babysitter" refers to nonfamilial child-care providers who work on a temporary basis for pay, typically in the home of their employer. Because quantifying babysitters in the population presents another challenge—it is impossible to count them—I have, wherever possible, drawn upon statistics reported by newspapers and magazines and compiled by institutions and organizations. Yet due to the part-time nature of the work that is sometimes unpaid (as is often the case when older siblings are left in charge of younger ones), there is ultimately little empirical data on babysitters.

Babysitting also inimitably complicates such standard categories as production and consumption, labor and leisure, vocation and socialization, preadolescence and adolescence, and reality and fantasy. Because babysitting takes place in the informal economy and in the realm of the imagination, distinguishing fact from fiction poses particular challenges. In order to make sense of the babysitter's multidimensional meanings, this study by necessity has crossed disciplinary boundaries (history, literature, media), combined tools of analysis (age and gender), and overlapped the borders of historical fields (gender and youth).

Over the last fifteen years historians as well as scholars in other fields have skillfully mapped the changing worlds of female adolescents.[46] Thanks to their path-breaking work we now know a lot about the social and cultural dimensions of female adolescents' lives, especially as students and consumers. Yet what remains to be explored is the correlation between changing notions of girlhood and girls' possibilities for economic autonomy, as well as the impact that girls' income earnings had on notions of girlhood. To that end, this book focuses on the babysitter in order to examine the meanings that girls' cultural and economic production had on the adults who employed, educated, advised, acculturated, and imagined them. By illuminating the history of babysitters in fact and in fiction, this study sheds light on the interconnections between the representation and the reception of girls as workers, as consumers, and as producers of their own subculture.

This work is aimed at those interested in the history of teenagers and children, youth culture and popular culture, vocational training and labor history, parenthood and family life, women, gender and, especially, girls. In addition to academic readers, this book also aims to reach a broader audience, including the many who were cared for by babysitters, worked as babysitters, employed babysitters, and were parents of babysitters. It is my hope that parent-employers in particular might better understand what automatically stirs them to suspect the sitter when something—however small—goes awry. For nearly a century adults' fears and fantasies have distorted the lens through which they have perceived girls and have tried to make sense of them. The result has been a cultural figure more reviled than revered. Yet by foregrounding the babysitter in American culture and documenting the historical experiences of babysitters from their point of view in the chapters that follow, this work aims to provide a clearer vision of the cultural concerns and a more accurate accounting of the formative work experience of the majority of American girls who came of age in the twentieth century.

Chapter 1 of this study traces adults' emerging apprehensions about hiring female adolescents to "mind the children" from the beginnings of babysitting in the 1920s to the doorstep of its expansion in the mid-1940s. What fostered unease during this early period was the simultaneous development of both teenage girls' "modern" beliefs and the behaviors that openly challenged traditional ideals and gender norms. Those who wore makeup and donned teen fashions, talked on the telephone and entertained friends while babysitting during the Great Depression provoked female employers to complain and experts to constrain girls' cultural practices. As girls' new brassy behaviors further challenged standards of respectability during World War II, experts' moral panic led them to reassert order by reminding girls of their patriotic duty to the nation's children. Experts endorsed conservative notions of girlhood that satisfied the needs of parent-employers and the dominant social order, but minimally influenced teenage girls who—as would always be the case when opportunity knocked—left babysitting to others.

In the years after the war, the convergence of residual beliefs in female empowerment and youth culture's claims to autonomy gave rise to reformist babysitter unions. Chapter 2 examines the rise of unions from the perspective of the babysitters who established them, the women who supported them, and the men who perceived teenage babysitters as insurgents. The social changes that diminished male authority, increased female autonomy, and expanded girls' culture, led men to satirize teenage babysitters in print, pictures, and movies.

Chapter 3 examines the widening cultural gap between adults and adolescents in the postwar suburbs where babysitting took root during the 1950s. Against the backdrop of restratifying gender ideals shaping the expectations of parent-employers, "bobby-soxer babysitters" were widely caricatured as irrepressible, irreverent, insatiable, incapable, and unreliable. Anxieties about the challenges girls posed to the ideology of domesticity and generational norms led employers to suspect babysitters of overstepping their bounds. While not as wild as adults believed, teenage girls in the process of challenging older notions, constructing new identities as teenagers, and creating an oppositional youth culture, widened the gap between themselves and adults. Colliding with adults' notions were girls' beliefs in gender fairness, which shaped their views about babysitting, their bosses, and the work culture rituals devised to both resist and adjust to the job they called "bratting."

Chapter 4 examines how parents caught between their growing fear of adolescent girls and their increasing need for them sought out the sitting services of other adults—grandmothers, neighbors, mature women—and of teenage boys, widely presented as upstanding, trustworthy, reliable, and responsible. In an effort to stop girls from raiding the fridge and jitterbugging in the living room, experts and educators employed a variety of educational methods aimed at making bad babysitters into better ones. At the same time that nation-wide programs sought to harness girls' autonomy, new legislation restricted babysitters' rights as employees in states like New York.

Chapter 5 explores how the profound social transformations of the 1960s that developed along lines of gender and age came together in the icon of the babysitter who spoke the language of resistance but discouraged girls' rebellion. Instead of popular magazines and training materials, commercialized girls' culture aimed to make unruly girls into obedient babysitters. Representations of boisterous babysitters in sit-coms and vocational movies reflected, reinforced, yet also retarded girls' growing social and cultural empowerment. So did cautionary urban legends about self-indulgent babysitters causing and encountering catastrophes. The most enduring of these allegedly "true" stories was the one about the babysitter victimized by a male murderer because she did not do as commanded and "check the children."

Chapter 6 examines how anxieties about the profound social changes of the 1960s that upended traditional ideals and customs found expression in the intense relationship between the male maniac and the sexy sitter. As a representation of "the sexually active girl" of the era, sitters eroticized in soft porn and popular culture exacerbated fears of teenage girls as dangerous. Escalating anxieties about gender disorder led to the victimization of babysitters by maniacs who migrated from cautionary tales to horror movies in the 1970s. Babysitting became a site of powerful conflict between the babysitter trying to achieve economic, social, sexual, and cultural autonomy and male monsters seeking retribution for the diminishing of male privilege. Soaring rates of female employment and divorce coupled with plummeting birth rates generated a mixture of fright and yearning in adult men who needed babysitters and felt unnerved by them.

Chapter 7 contrasts representations of teenage killer sitters in mostly made-for-television movies with, the preadolescent "Super Sitter" in handbooks and novels like the Baby-sitter's Club book series. Cultural anxieties about the impact of feminism, especially on teenage girls who increasingly abandoned babysitting for service-sector jobs during the 1980s, fueled fears about the autonomy and authority of teenage girls. To generate enthusiasm among preadolescent girls, manuals and magazines from *Women's World* to *Weekly Reader* promoted the "Super Sitter" ideal. In contrast to berserk babysitters who harmed families were representations of helpful preadolescents. The establishment of Safe Sitters, Inc., and other babysitting training programs taught girls vocational skills and nurtured domestic sensibilities by channeling some aspects of Girl Power and containing others. Unlike transgressive teenagers in movies, perky preadolescents ideally combined empowerment and accommodation into a social identity that was to be more endearing than dangerous.

Chapter 8 demonstrates that in contrast to fictionalized girls' unequivocal enthusiasm about babysitting in the hundreds of saccharine stories published since the 1980s, preadolescent and adolescent girls toward the end of the twentieth century voiced many of the same complaints as previous generations. Still committed to pursuing their personal independence, babysitters objected to the unregulated and unstructured working conditions that exposed them to out-of-control employers and children who acted out. By the end of the century, girls with greater self-esteem, growing individualism, higher aspirations, more extracurricular activities, and new job options abandoned the field of babysitting that had been the leading form of female adolescent employment for generations.

The final chapter reveals that the babysitter continues to serve as a vessel for anxieties about gender and generational changes still in the making. As adults project—rather than introspect—about the meanings of the stories they hear and pass along, babysitting continues as a site of conflict and control. While real babysitters are even harder to come by today than they were in the past, new ones have steadily appeared in the popular culture created by young women. Their creative reappropriations of the iconic babysitter in recent folk and rock music reveal that, while girls still routinely give up babysitting, the sitter remains a fertile symbol of the struggle over girlhood autonomy and empowerment.

1

The Beginnings of Babysitting

Steer clear of "high-school girls" who "take charge" of children, warned the authors of *Wholesome Childhood* in the mid-1920s, more than a decade before the concept of the "babysitter" and suspicions about her became widespread.[1] That active and athletic girls attended sports events and flirted with men on street corners, especially in front of the innocent babies they trundled about, led the authors of this new child-rearing manual to disparage adolescent girls and to dismiss them as acceptable child-care providers.[2] This early critique of babysitters signaled the emergence of a struggle over girlhood between adults and the first generation of American teenage girls whose "modern" beliefs and behaviors now openly challenged established ideals about what it meant to be a girl. The experts' emergent estimation of female adolescents as a social problem would lead to the soon-dominant evaluation of girls as bad babysitters.

In this chapter I argue that what led these child-care experts to issue their caution was the convergence of anxieties about the generational and gender changes that were reshaping girlhood. In the years after women won the right to vote, worries about female autonomy filtered throughout American culture and society. Many adults felt unsettled by the "modern" customs and values spreading rapidly among young women and trickling down to high school students. In the private as well as in the public spheres, girls had begun to contest the reigning ideal of female innocence in highly visible ways. By wearing makeup, reading popular magazines, attending movies, and "petting" at parties and in automobiles, teenage girls in the process of creating a commodity-based youth culture challenged traditional gender ideals and redefined female adolescence.[3] In the process of forging their own social identity, however, girls also fueled adults' ire.

Though it would still be more than twenty years before babysitters would become familiar figures in American communities, culture, and conversation, evolving perceptions of girls as unpredictable and their teen customs as unfathomable shaped adults' fears about those they relied on to babysit. During the 1930s, adults' critical assessments of girls abounded as youth culture widened, babysitting spread, and traditional gender conventions weakened. To employers and the experts who advised girls during this period of profound social disruption, babysitters' skimpy clothing and other staples of the girls' teen culture that flourished in American high schools signaled disrepute and disorder. The fear that teenage girls threatened the future of American family life led experts to establish a blueprint followed by succeeding generations: to provide girls with advice that appealed to their desire for autonomy yet affirmed their femininity.

The numbers of increasingly "sassy" teenage girls widened the cultural conflict between adults and adolescents at odds over what it meant to be a girl. Because many felt taken advantage of by parent-employers who overworked and underpaid babysitters during the Depression, girls sought out other jobs during World War II. Influenced by the proliferation of homefront teen culture that advanced the transformation of girlhood in ways that further unsettled adults, girls mingled with girlfriends and male acquaintances rather than "mind the children." Anxious to restore gender conventions and generational codes disrupted by the war, educators and experts reached out to girls. Though adults promulgated babysitting as patriotic, high school girls on the home front nevertheless left "child minding" to those in elementary school.

The Challenges of Motherhood in the 1920s

The 1920s was a new era for women voters but not for mothers with young children. Following the passage of the Nineteenth Amendment, which gave women the right to vote, everyone from experts to advertisers promoted the traditional notion that self-fulfillment for women could only be found in caretaking, consumption, and cleaning. That the percentage of wives between the ages of twenty and thirty-five who worked for wages increased stirred anxieties about the independence of women. Marriage expert Ernest Groves was not alone in expressing his opinion that "when the woman herself earns and her maintenance is not entirely at the mercy of her husbands' will, diminishing masculine authority necessarily follows."[4] Fears about the future of the family gave rise to the glorification of motherhood, an ethos that was rife with expectations and riddled with frustrations for mothers. On the one hand, middle-class wives living in the newly established "streetcar suburbs" that sprang up on the fringes of American cities enthusiastically purchased up-to-date electrically powered household appliances.[5] On the other hand, housewives ended up spending more time inside their Cape Cod bungalows than outside them. Even though advertisements promoted electrically powered washing machines, irons, and vacuum sweepers as "time saving," rising standards of cleanliness and the exaltation of housework meant that mothers spent twice as much time completing household chores as their grandmothers.[6]

Although the size of the American family decreased from 3.6 children in 1900 to 2.4 by 1929, mothers also spent more time raising their children. The era's experts urged mothers to practice more intensive and extensive child-rearing procedures. Many mothers followed the narrow and repressive practices of psychologist John B. Watson, who pioneered the theory of behavioral psychology that sought to rigidly standardize the habits and behaviors of children.[7] Along with children, mothers were also bound to minute-by-minute schedules of child care. Competing notions based on Freudian theories and the pioneering research of psychologist and pediatrician Arnold Gesell also produced a new vigilance about children's psychological development. Being charged by experts with shaping the personalities of their little ones and by advertisers with expressing their love through cleanliness added to mothers' already heavy load.

Mothers' full-time responsibilities to the child-focused family and suburban home mounted just at the time when recreation acquired a new cultural primacy. A broad acceptance of play in the social and psychological lives of all Americans led to the widespread availability of new leisure activities, commercial amusements, and playthings. For children, new notions of play meant an unprecedented number of toys, games, and fun-filled activities.[8] But mothers seeking to enjoy their leisure were often taken to task by advertisers and experts for shirking their maternal responsibilities. For example, the coauthors of *Wholesome Childhood* (1924) criticized middle-class mothers who were "prone to hire young girls to take charge of their little ones, every afternoon, so that the mothers may play Ma Chiang, run into the near-by city, shop, gossip, or even sew, bake, and clean house to their hearts' content, with no children on their minds."[9]

In fact, finding someone to mind the children and clean the house had become a serious problem for middle-class housewives by the 1920s. Hiring a nurse or governess with "both the cultural background and the wholesome personality needed" was not easy, explained Ernest and Gladys Groves in *Wholesome Childhood* (1924).[10] Simultaneous with the expansion of the middle class was the further contraction of white, working-class household workers. Conditions for middle-class mothers in need of household assistance worsened as new immigration restrictions limited the availability of replacements and native-born women sought better employment opportunities.[11] Many middle-class mothers compounded their own problems by refusing to hire African American women, who increasingly dominated the field of housework, and by relocating too far away for most day workers to commute from cities to suburbs.[12] Consequently, middle-class mothers had no choice but to follow the Groves's advice that they take care of their own babies.

Previous generations of mothers had relied heavily on girls (and sometimes boys as well) to help with the children. In colonial New England Puritan girls had little choice but to take care of younger siblings. On southern plantations, enslaved African American children—girls as well as boys—were forced to attend to younger children—both free and unfree. Adolescent girls from middle-class Victorian families facing financial hardship cared for cousins or worked as governesses attending to the children they tutored.[13] Working-class children in the urban Northeast looked after siblings as well. By the turn of the century, a new generation of immigrant girls (dubbed "Little Mothers" by reformers) cared for siblings on front stoops, sidewalks, and city streets. Simultaneously, girls not yet in their adolescence pushed perambulators for well-to-do mothers.[14] More like babysitters today, these "baby tenders" and "baby-walkers" shared in the consumer culture that flourished at the turn of the last century. As middle-class notions of children as "emotionally precious" rendered girls "economically useless," "Little Mothers" and "baby tenders" soon vanished from the cityscape.[15] That concepts of childhood were changing along with notions of girlhood would give rise to an increasingly dominant view: adolescent-aged girls with "little conception of the needs of small children" posed a danger to both.[16]

High School Girls "Taking Charge" in the 1920s

The vast majority of middle-class girls did not look to babysitting for their "spending money." For their discretionary income most relied on the weekly allowance doled out by parents who did not generally encourage their daughters to work for money. Only 9 percent of the hundreds of high school girls in Muncie, Indiana, surveyed for the sociological study *Middletown* (1929) earned all their own spending money. Just 5 percent earned money and got an allowance.[17] Most parents hoped that if they provided daughters with spending money, girls would regulate their consumer desire and control their spending habits.[18] But increasing numbers of teenage girls who went to the movies, bobbed their hair, or bought makeup, cigarettes, magazines, and "waistless" dresses liked to spend their allowance on things "teenage."[19]

While the topic of babysitting was too new to elicit much comment, adults already had lots to say about teenage girls in the process of contesting conventional notions. Girls' own parents were among the many adults who grumbled about the growing insolence and independence of the younger generation, which pushed feminine respectability beyond traditionally acceptable borders. Unlike generations of female adolescents before them, those from middle-class families insisted on going out at night during the week and on weekends. Frustrating their own parents as well as others needing someone to "mind the children," girls made it plain that they had neither the time nor the inclination to sit at home or at the neighbors'.[20]

For girls exuberantly exploring their autonomy and mobility, the flourishing of a new social morality and consumer culture, the ascendance of peer influence, and the erosion of parental authority nurtured their interest in buddies, not babies. Modern girls who shunned decorum and domesticity now found "dull" the traditionally gendered activities of "helping their own mothers" and "doing for others." So did Ella Cinders, the comic strip character who debuted during the middle of the decade. Though a domestic, she eschewed the endless housework that was expected of her with the moxie that was characteristic of adolescent girls, who also enjoyed the 1926 movie comedy *Ella Cinders*.[21] Sporting a dutch-bob haircut, speaking slang, and creating havoc in the movie, Ella Cinders nevertheless babysat for the neighbor's children in order to raise the three dollars she needed to enter a beauty contest and win a Hollywood career.[22]

Instead of spending their free time helping out at home, many teenage girls routinely spent half their evenings out with friends.[23] According to a 1929 study on the interests of high school girls published in the *Journal of Home Economics*, girls made "[p]ersonal appearance and self improvement" and the attentions of boys and their school "crowd" the focus of their lives.[24] The heterosocial world that flourished in high schools, where adolescents shaped each other's tastes and shared styles, facilitated girls' sexual expression and experimentation.[25] At high school, now attended by the majority of adolescents, girls also explored their independence and asserted their individuality.[26] Increasing to include about half of all American youth by the late 1920s, high schools became incubators for the innovative teen principles and practices that defied the vestiges of Victorian girlhood and defined "modern" female adolescence.[27]

While earlier in the century experts had hoped that high schools would keep youth off the streets, they came to realize that educational institutions had not successfully prevented the spread of contaminating influences. Their thinking had been based on the turn-of-the-century theory that adolescence was a turbulent period characterized by emotional intensity, lability, impulsivity, and conflict. This notion had been put forward by American psychologist G. Stanley Hall. In *Adolescence: Its Psychology and Its Relations to Physiology, Anthropology, Sociology, Sex, Crime, Religion, and Education* (1904), Hall recommended that adolescents be corralled in schools and cut off from temptations that might exacerbate their biological inclination toward storm and stress.[28]

High school students' precocious embrace of sexuality, individuality, and independence led parents, teachers, social workers, probation officers, psychiatrists, psychologists, educators, legislators, police, judges, and administrators to condemn "incorrigible" girls and contain their resistance. In places like Muncie, Indiana, parents upset with the new morality complained about girls' immodest attire and poor manners. Many adults expressed their disapproval of adolescent girls who imitated college-age "flappers" starring in popular movies as vamps, not virgins. While progressive-minded adults more readily accepted the emergence of the spread of "sexual liberalism," the affirmation of heterosexual pleasure, sexual satisfaction, and personal happiness, those with more conservative ideas perceived girls' new social and sexual freedom as a threat.[29]

Though most adults generally approved of girls' "healthy" pursuits like swimming, cycling, tennis, and field hockey, many strongly disapproved of girls' other new passions and pastimes, such as the recent practice of double-dating at movie theaters, amusement parks, and ice cream parlors.[30] Ernest R. Groves, a prominent family sociologist and an avid promoter of courses on marriage education, warned mothers against girls who wheeled "babies about to hockey games, basketball practice, and [engaged in] street-corner flirtation."[31] They made unacceptable caretakers. Female adolescents were just beginning to be seen as a growing threat to children believed to be in need of responsive and responsible caretakers, not impetuous, self-interested, and promiscuous ones.[32] Groves concurred with other proponents of the study of child development who viewed children as vulnerable beings who needed to be physically and psychologically protected from an ever-growing number of threats to their mental health and physical well-being.[33] Influenced by wider fears about youthful flappers' rejection of middle-class manners, morals, and gender conventions, he warned mothers to avoid hiring pleasure-seeking "high-school girls who take charge of little ones."[34]

Adults who perceived girls' saucy deportment as a threat failed to understand that beneath the flaunting were fears. Assertive girls might have appeared confident, but that did not mean that they welcomed sexual experimentation with open arms. While adults worried about the new social climate, girls protected themselves from unwanted pregnancies by limiting sexual behavior to kissing and "petting." Though "dating" was unsupervised, girls effectively confined their sexual side to forms of physical intimacy that were typically respected by peers. Rates of premarital intercourse jumped to around 50 percent among adolescent girls, but that generally occurred between those couples intent on marrying.[35]

Inviting a boyfriend to join them while babysitting had yet to enter the activities of babysitters. But that did not stop the Groveses from criticizing high school girls. However brief, the harangue about babysitters enjoying the new sexual freedom reshaping girlhood, it would only be the first of many that would express adults' anxieties about adolescent girls, who were just beginning to set themselves apart from their elders and their outdated conventions. Though babysitting was still in its infancy by the end of the 1920s, the threat of female adolescents' challenge to traditional female roles and feminine respectability had already set into motion a gendered and generational rupture that would only widen as the field of babysitting expanded over the next decade.

The Spread of Girls' Culture and "Child Minding" in the 1930s

Despite girls' overall indifference to babysitting and adults' increasing reluctance about adolescent girls during the 1920s, the field of babysitting gained considerable ground during the Great Depression. According to the author of *American City* (1937), who is credited with first using the term "baby sitter" in print, teenage girls in Minneapolis, Minnesota, hired "out for twenty-five cents an evening as 'baby sitters' when the family wants to go to the movies."[36] Mothers sought out babysitters, especially after birth rates began to rise toward the end of the decade. Increasingly confident that hope was on the horizon and that girls could play an integral role, mothers called girls like Ilene Fairbanks to ask, "Will you come over and stay with the children?"[37]

That the pool of babysitters swelled during the Depression was due to unstable and/or inadequate family finances that had diminished allowances for teens like Irene. After her father died and money was tight, the fifteen-year-old began to babysit every Friday and Saturday night for families in Southern California.[38] Prevented from competing with adults in the job market, 750,000 girls of high school age became "mother's helpers," "neighborhood helpers," "child minders," or "baby sitters," the latter term having been coined by now, though it was rarely in circulation.[39] The rising number of teenagers relative to the population, their unprecedented attendance in high schools, and the spread of the commodity-based youth culture also contributed to the rise of babysitters. The new beliefs and behaviors of teenagers set into motion during the 1920s continued to broaden throughout the 1930s despite the exigencies of the economic crisis that affected the nation. American high schools provided ample opportunities for three-quarters of all adolescents to exchange information about fast-changing fads. Students like Irene fueled the consumption of specific goods and gadgets that became the hallmark of adolescent girlhood.[40]

As the position of teenage girls as a distinctive cultural demographic solidified and their visibility increased, however, so did anxieties about the practices that girls carried with them when they babysat.[41] While historians of childhood and youth acknowledge that many increasingly independent girls turned to babysitting as youth culture took shape, they have overlooked the conflicts that

took place between girls' and grownups' colliding notions.[42] Marketers enticed girls to shop for teen styles ("campus fashion") with the money they earned from babysitting, yet other adults during this period of belt-tightening looked askance at teenage girls' frivolous purchasing and needless preening.[43] Adults objected to the fact that while many families could not afford the basics, girls shopped for their own selfish pleasure.

In particular, girls' involvement in beauty culture made adults hot under the collar. The rise of bathroom mirrors, the decline of disfiguring facial diseases, and the expansion of beauty culture enabled adolescent girls to spend more time experimenting with their appearance. Because parents often opposed their daughters' immodest use of makeup, girls waited until they went to a friend's house or to babysit at a neighbor's before unleashing their cosmetic craving. But because middle-class women still associated nail polish with prostitution, many deemed painted nails to be "vulgar."[44] In addition to parents and teachers, "most" female employers also "object to colored nails and too much lipstick while you are on duty," the *Woman's Home Companion* informed girls. (That magazine, along with the *Ladies Home Journal*, aimed to reach and direct the rapidly expanding teenage girl market.)[45]

Whether it was girls' own parents or someone else's, adult opposition to the goods girls purchased and the beauty rituals they practiced revealed that the flare-up was more than skin deep. A makeup-wearing girl symbolized sexuality to many adults anxious about the institution of marriage at a time when many had fallen apart and others were being indefinitely postponed. Yet to girls challenging sartorial customs and sexual codes, makeup was not evidence of sexual improprieties but instead a means of shaping one's identity in ways that were accepted by and attractive to peers. Fundamental to the teenage girls' culture that spread from cities to towns was being popular and looking pleasing. Style served as a critically important nonverbal form of expression and communication for girls cautiously negotiating between their need for conformity and their desire for individuality.[46]

In the years before the term "baby sitters" was coined, it was the job of "child minders" and "neighborhood helpers" to "mind the children." M. C. Steffens, "Mother's Helpers: A Few Rules," *Woman's Home Companion*, October 1937, 56. General Research Division, The New York Public Library, Astor, Lenox and Tilden Foundations.

The spread of teen culture that fueled the field of babysitting also stoked adults' suspicions that teenage girls were increasingly taking their cues from the "crowd" and not the children they were hired to watch.[47] Female adolescents declared their generational independence at the same time that children were increasingly seen as helpless by middle-class mothers whose child-centered child-rearing notions spread throughout the decade. Sounding a lot like parent-employers today, those during the Depression objected to the fact that while some girls invited friends over for the evening sit, others spent the evening chatting on the telephone. Though fewer than half of all American households would even have a phone on the eve of the war, those who already did typically located them in public areas of houses, such as foyers, kitchens, and living rooms.[48] Babysitters who took advantage of a house with a phone, or just one emptied of adults, in order to talk with friends irritated employers who expected them to be "all ears."[49] And girls who rang up their friends also ran up the phone bill, further irking parent-employers living in a culture of thrift. Cutting back on the telephone was one method of economizing that enabled Depression-era families to shift their resources and preserve such pleasures as a night out.[50]

To employers, parents, teachers, and other adults, blabbing babysitters already typified what they did not like about teenage girls. In Muncie, Indiana, middle-class parents complained about their adolescent daughters' unbecoming speech as well as their unattractive dress and disagreeable behavior.[51] While new representations of female adolescents in popular movies spread teen culture among a wider audience, stereotypes of girls as disruptive reinforced adults' apprehensions.[52] Parents objected to girls who imitated scandalous movie stars they admired and incorporated musical styles they adored. In fact, music was a particularly contentious issue among adults increasingly worried about the inroads it made into girls' teen culture.[53] The media's broader focus on the dress, language, tastes, and energetic dancing styles of teenage music fans fueled fears about the unmanageability of youth and their seeming rejection of adult responsibilities. While nationwide media reports about the raucous crowds at Benny Goodman concerts hastened the development of teenagers' flamboyant generational identity, dancing energetically to "swing" music also kindled concerns that teenage girls had abandoned decorum.

Child Tenders: Models of Youthful Manhood

This would be the first of many times when adults' concerns about dis-orderly teenage girls and their disreputable behavior would lead to the employment of male "child tenders," one of the many terms in use in the years before "baby sitter" became widespread. Among the one million adolescent boys who were unemployed during the Depression were those like Lowry and his buddies. When they were not "running errands, mowing lawns, shining shoes, carting groceries, and returning soda bottles," they washed dishes, mopped floors, and tutored Junior.[54] Youthful breadwinners charging fifty cents for four hours (a quarter for overtime) became saviors to distraught mothers and weary housewives unsatisfied with neighborhood girls.[55] One woman hired Lowry because she believed that boys were more willing and better able to lighten the load of busy mothers. In her eyes, Lowry was not only responsible but considerate as well. Once when Lowry was unavailable he asked his employer

> if we would like him to get Eddie for us. Maybe we would, but who was Eddie? Well, Eddie was Lowry's pal and he also "minded" children. So we had Eddie. Came an evening when neither Lowry nor Eddie could come—so how about having Murray? And who, pray, was Murray? Why, Murray was Lowry's brother, also a child tender with a long unblemished record. So we had Murray.[56]

In glowing descriptions in *Parents Magazine*, there was nothing that boy helpers like these could not do, and what they did they always did well.

In fact, experts informed mothers that "[i]f the idea of a young man as a sitter is new to you, give a thought to the hero worship a little boy accords his not-so-elders."[57] Providing young sons with a laudable male "child tender" became especially important during the Great Depression because many Americans at the time were losing faith in fathers. That many unemployed and underemployed fathers could no longer provide for their families generated anxieties about the foundation of masculine identity, the stability of the family, and the future of the nation. That fathers stayed at home with the children while mothers went out to work generated concerns which found expression in the popular culture. In *Melodie Trail* (1935) Gene Autry babysat while working as a ranch hand. But according to Depression-era humorist Robert Benchley in "The Vanishing Father,"

Fathers today are a craven lot when it comes to appearing in public as a parent. They try to wheel the baby-carriage up side streets and, if they are caught leading a toddler along by the hand, they try to make believe that they are minding the child for some strange woman who has just disappeared. I have even seen a father hurriedly slip a cigar into his son's mouth at the approach of friends, hoping that they will think he is out with a midget business acquaintance.[58]

Other men too humiliated by unemployment got depressed or deserted the family. Though many at the time feared that the demise of manliness disheartened boys who "took to the road" instead of staying at home, child-rearing experts believed that male child minders would actually restore boyhood.[59] While husbands helplessly sank into despair at the loss of their position at work and place in the home, boys were up to the task, *Parents Magazine* reassured readers. "There is real stuff in these lads— the kind of stuff that makes fine men. They know that no work, however humble, would lower them; rather they would elevate the job to their own level. No feeling of inferiority disrupts their calm assurance because they do it."[60]

Babysitting: Cure and Conflict

As the cultural differences between girls and adults became more conspicuous, however, babysitting emerged as a site for the social rehabilitation of girlhood. In addition to their injunctions against cosmetics, experts also advised that girls replace the teen fashions employers frowned upon. While advisers neither admonished nor advised boys about how to better their performance or improve their personality, they suggested that female babysitters replace image-shaping fashions with a "clean, neat, and wholesome" look.[61] In order to make teenage girls more ladylike, experts encouraged girls setting their own standards to instead "dress neatly," "keep your hair and hands clean," "keep your clothing clean and pressed, [and] your shoes and stockings neat."[62]

The advice that experts provided aimed to discipline girls' bodies and behavior according to approved rules of appropriate feminine conduct. In an effort to teach babysitters a work ethic that would appeal to the values and habits of middle-class employers, experts urged girls to "be prompt and dependable." Along with parents who tried in vain to reinforce the generational respect adolescents contested, experts told babysitters to "listen attentively and cheerfully accept your employers' instructions no matter how different her methods." In order to rid their speech of slang, the subcultural language adults found both irreverent and incomprehensible, girls should "[a]lways use the best grammar you command and be critical of your choice of words." Overall, sitters were encouraged to monitor themselves more than to manage children.[63]

To attract girls to babysitting, however, advisers framed it as a way to gain more independence. Babysitting, they claimed, would provide skills in whatever career girls might choose. The belief that a girl should pursue her own calling was a consequence of the erosion of the financial position of fathers and would-be husbands. The notion that girls' economic autonomy was more of a temporary answer than a permanent solution, however, can be seen in the mixed messages aimed at girls during the 1930s. Straddling competing ideals for girls, *The American Girl* magazine glorified professional women for their economic autonomy and featured standard prescriptions of gendered behavior.[64] Among other publications, the Camp Fire Girls' *Everygirls* magazine also provided girls with a wide-ranging selection of future possibilities that included homemaking, as well as mountain climbing.[65] Reflecting the apprehensions of adults about girls' economic independence, experts framed the rationale to babysit along similar lines. Rather than endorsing girls' independence, experts rationalized that babysitting was a vocational skill useful for "child minding" in the present and homemaking in the future.[66] It was a one-size-fits-all rationale that future generations of experts would utilize in their efforts to attract the largest number of teenage girls to babysitting and minimize their opposition to prevailing girlhood ideals established by adults.

The Problems of Child Tending

Despite the upbeat tone of the overall message, one sympathetic reporter maintained that girls deserved "a better introduction into the business world" than "child tending." Because the employment methods of employers were often "arbitrary," "inconsistent," and "inexact," the girls she interviewed for an article published in *The American Home* magazine found babysitting more disagreeable than desirable.[67] Babysitters were expected to do much more than just "mind the children," though the rising social value of children was putting an end to child labor nationwide. As politicians, reformers, and educators in the thirties redefined childhood as a "stage of life protected from adult responsibilities," mothers piled "all sorts of additional duties" onto babysitters.[68] Passage of the Fair Labor Standards Act (1938) restricted those under the age of seventeen from employment, but babysitters were nevertheless expected to wash dishes, mend clothing, and iron while "minding the children."[69] Adolescent girls were punitively excluded from the new social value of childhood. Many Depression-era mothers who revived domestic skills and stretched resources "made do" by shifting household chores onto the shoulders of younger helpers.[70] Sometimes employers made girls wash the "supper dishes" and "mind the children" of several families. Though the occasional magazine article advised mothers to provide helpers with clear instructions, the meager advice did little to halt the spread of employment practices sitters found "exasperating."[71]

The many problems of babysitting led *The American Home* magazine to rhetorically ask parent-employers if they provided the young girl who "stays with the children with adequate instructions, paid her promptly for the number of hours she worked, and saw that she got home safely? If you don't, you should be ashamed, too!" By failing to provide emergency telephone numbers, as well as instructions about meals and medicine, bedtime and bottles, covers and colds, fifteen- to eighteen-year-old girls were routinely "treated as no adult would treat another adult." Parents also underpaid girls for the anticipated amount, not the actual time spent babysitting. Haven't girls "the right to expect more pay for a six-hour period than for a four-hour evening?" Sometimes parents failed to pay even a penny. Despite their promise to pay up the next day, "'tomorrow' was often forgotten." Though babysitting was still in its infancy, *The American Home* magazine declared that the treatment of "child-minders" by parent-employers had already become a "shameful American custom."[72] Failing to adequately resolve the contradiction between teenage girls' desire for personal freedom and adults' expectations that they stay closer to home, the concession to babysit had set the stage for an enduring collision between girls and grownups.

Sitting on the Home Front: The Contraction of Babysitting

During World War II, adolescent girls like my mother, Ruth Lowenstein, a recently arrived Jewish refugee from Bingen, Germany, babysat for mothers so that they could shop for groceries, run errands, go to the movies, or go out to work.[73] A rise in births that began during the late 1930s and surged during the war accelerated the demand for babysitters, especially among the 1.5 million working mothers with children under the age of

The second rule would be,
the children is going to inclu
dren's supper dishes.'" Katio
she was left one night with s
protested to her mother, "wh
'Can you do your home-wo
Franklins' new house'? They

Another protest may sta
couples leave their children t
expect the young girl to tak
anywhere. We'll sort them o
happen. It's not hard to im
yelling, the fights and the t
can separate and quiet these
plete disruption of their rout
and to the girl who receive

That pay is another distur
and their own mothers—if tl
six-hour period than for a fe
most home-coming parents s
involves no time limits for t
we wish," Katie and her frie
their purses and pockets an
have left, and will that be
tomorrow. 'Tomorrow' is of

Most important of all, th
tered clothes or a house t
o'clock—is the lack of a tele

capped by the
True, Katie,
the house next
pable." But wh
and when, and
have establishe

And now, a j
helpers. Do bri
out into the ni
need protection
with your thre
your daughter

*Ewing
Galloway*

Popular women's magazines that aimed to elevate Depression-era girlhood encouraged teenage "baby sitters" to dress neatly and behave nicely. Yet babysitters cared more about being treated fairly by demanding parent-employers. "An American Custom We're NOT Really Proud Of!" *The American Home*, June 1941, 102. General Research Division, The New York Public Library, Astor, Lenox and Tilden Foundations.

ten.[74] Though the money my mother earned was used to buy groceries, and not the gadgets that became the hallmark of girls' culture, babysitting provided her with the autonomy she sought. While many middle-class babysitters who earned twenty-five cents per hour spent it, along with their two- to three-dollar allowance, on movies, malteds and milkshakes, lunches, soft drinks, records, clothing, and other staples of wartime teenage girls, Ruth babysat so she could listen to the radio, smoke cigarettes, and spend time with her boyfriend—away from her mother, who disapproved of her independent behavior.[75] That Ruth brought a boyfriend along while babysitting reflected a wartime practice among girls who yearned for greater privacy than cramped wartime living quarters afforded.[76] Despite the benefits that babysitting afforded Ruth, however, she longed to spend time with friends.

Like other teenage girls during the war, Ruth also wanted to make more money. Despite the soaring demand for babysitters generated by the rising birth rate, girls turned away from Depression-era domestic jobs that had unfairly combined child care with housekeeping chores. Moreover, babysitters only earned twenty-five cents per hour as compared to the new minimum wage rate that paid forty cents between 1941 and 1944.[77] For teenage girls on the home front, wartime conscription, migration, and widespread occupational mobility generated many new employment opportunities.[78] Attracted by the "glamour jobs" they saw in the newsreels shown before movie features, many girls traveled from farms and towns to war production centers and camps.[79] Children as young as fourteen and fifteen years old got jobs after school or at night in Delaware, Florida, and other states that had relaxed age restrictions.[80]

While many girls worked after school, hundreds of thousands of teenagers dropped out of school so that they could work full-time.[81] Many found jobs in war factories, soda fountains, and department stores. Girls were so eager to move out of typical "children's occupations" such as babysitting, errand running, and housework that their employment rates made up the "largest proportionate increase of any one group."[82] By 1944, there were nearly five times as many girls at work than in 1940.[83] While the proportion of girls who worked in wholesale and retail businesses had hovered around 7 percent in 1940, by 1943, those who worked in ten-cent stores, drug stores, groceries, and other businesses increased to 54 percent.[84] As for sixteen- and seventeen-year-olds, they left trade and service jobs for employment in the mechanical industries and the manufacturing sector, where they increased their participation from 38 to 53 percent of the work force.[85]

Faced with a scarcity of babysitters brought about by girls who took jobs that paid more than babysitting, millions of mothers turned to their own parents for help with the children.[86] As one grandma explained, "I have had my house full of grandchildren for a month, and so have all of my friends whose children are off for war work of one kind or another."[87] Another told *McCall's* magazine, "I guess I'm not the only woman who's raising a second batch of children, now that the country needs the young women to make munitions."[88] While some referred to World War II as the "grandmother's war," not all grandmas were so willing to do their duty.[89] In fact, the fastest growing group of women workers were those whose grown children had already left home.[90] Many chose to serve in military and civilian hospitals, volunteer for the Red Cross, cook at canteens, and work ten-hour days in defense plants.[91] By the war's end, working women over the age of forty-five would increase by 20 percent and those over the age of thirty-five would constitute 50 percent of all working women.[92] Unlike older women, though, young mothers would achieve the smallest gains among war workers in part because of the difficulties they faced finding someone to "mind the children."[93]

Yet millions of young mothers left hometowns for jobs elsewhere during the massive wartime migration.[94] While some children were watched by grandmothers nearby and others were sent to live with relatives, many more were far removed from supportive kinship networks. Mothers who worked long shifts left their young children with neighbors.[95] Though the Lanham Act of 1943 funded three thousand day care centers, these accommodated only one in ten children of war workers. Moreover, many centers were not only overcrowded but ill equipped and understaffed.[96] Consequently, nine out of ten preschool and school-age children lacked regular, dependable care, much to the horror of newspapers and magazines that covered cases of extreme neglect. Though these were less frequent than one might have imagined from media reports, "latch-key" children or "8-hour orphans" were often left to fend for themselves in trailer towns, new housing developments, urban apartment houses, and rural homes.[97] Critics blamed mothers for neglect and reminded them about the importance of women's primary role. Despite the momentous social changes that led women into the labor force and seemingly eroded traditional gender ideals, many Americans continued to adhere to traditions.[98]

The Expansion of Girls' Culture:
Pleasure and Panic

Teenage girls during the war—as before it—were eager to get out of the house, earn money, and have fun.[99] Because war wages were high, young workers could now purchase what was available in the wartime economy. Girls influenced by teen fads and fashions bought clothing, records, and magazines, while also using their wages to increase their social independence.[100] In the months before the war, the American Youth Commission's *Time on Their Hands* revealed that American youth would eagerly trade their solitary leisure for more social recreations.[101] Once they had the chance to be free from parental surveillance, teenage girls beyond the reach of protective fathers delighted in their greatly expanded freedom.[102] The diminishing authority of parents, the relaxing of social restraints, the rising economic autonomy of adolescents, and the flourishing of teen culture facilitated girls' energetic exploration of new social, sexual, and emotional domains. Peers, not parents, accompanied wartime girls who frequented canteens and attended unsupervised "pantry parties" or concerts, where many smoked, drank, and danced the "Lindy Hop" and the "Suzie Q" to "Swing" music.[103]

As wartime girls challenged older notions and constructed new ideals, girlhood experienced the most sweeping transformations.[104] Changing social priorities and new opportunities energized girls and reinforced their increasingly assertive identity as "teen-agers."[105] Rejecting the idea that adolescence was a period of wholesome innocence, finger-snapping and jive-talking teenage girls embraced the emergent principles and customs of wartime teen culture.[106] Contributing to the solidification of girls' culture that had been building since the 1920s was the introduction of new girls' magazines. *Calling All Girls, Junior Bazaar, Deb*, and *Seventeen* (formerly *Stardom: Hollywood's Most Exciting Magazine*) nurtured girls' individual and collective identities and stimulated their consumer desire for the thriving wartime market in teenage products.

In the midst of wartime shortages, enterprising advertisers and department stores helped make girls into a unique market category by promoting girls' authority as shoppers for innovative and oppositional clothing styles.[107] For example, as a reflection of their vigorous assertions into male domains, girls wore blue jeans and oversized men's shirts. Though commonplace today, these items were important cultural markers of girls' growing resistance to conventional standards of girlhood. Girls shed domesticity and abandoned deportment by donning casual ware—ankle socks, saddle shoes, sweaters, and skirts—that proclaimed their generational affinity and allowed for greater personal freedom.[108]

Though teenage girls had been wearing socks since the mid-1930s, it was not until 1943 that the media branded teenage girls as "bobby-soxers." The saucy, slangy, female adolescent "bobby-soxer," closely identified with Frank Sinatra and soon featured in movies, periodicals, and Broadway plays, became the newly visible "national model" of teenage girlhood.[109] The *March of Time* newsreel "Teen-Age Girls," shown in more than fifty thousand neighborhood movie theaters, proclaimed that this new breed of female adolescent had become the "most noticeable group in the nation."[110] Some six million American "bobby-soxers" were more "noticeable" not only because there were more of them in the population but also because teenage girls flaunted their brassy cultural practices.[111]

While girls' appropriation of the clothing they reinscribed with new social meanings won the approval of peers, adults increasingly criticized girls for their lack of innocence and respect. Although adults found some aspects of wartime girlhood bemusing, they felt bothered by teenage girls' unfeminine appearance, wasteful indulgences, and distasteful behavior.[112] Although adults wholly disapproved of "Victory Girls" who engaged in indiscreet romantic liaisons with military men they met at "taverns, beer parlors, honky-tonks, nightclubs, dance halls, hotels, juke joints, bus stations, factory gates, and soldiers' camps."[113] In Little Rock, Arkansas, alone, reported *Reader's Digest*, six hundred "pickup" girls could be found loitering around bus stations and hotels.[114] Lurid news reports described the throngs of "uniform-struck" twelve-year-old girls who supposedly prostituted themselves.[115] Sensational accounts, such as this one published in *Recreation* magazine, that described the methods used by gangs of urban "patriotutes" to ensnare service men, stirred fears about the dangers of girls and the demise of girlhood.

These girls are from twelve to seventeen years old—and not the older girls, or the prostitute, but the high school and junior high school girl— and not necessarily in camp areas. They travel in crowds and bandy wisecracks with civilians and soldiers alike on street corners. They walk down city streets, six or seven abreast, breaking as they pass civilians, but holding on to each other's arms as they approach a soldier or a sailor, forming a very flattering net around him. As the walk progresses, the line gets shorter and shorter, as girl and boy pair off and leave the group. It's a childish, very effective get-your-man plan used by girls around fourteen and fifteen years old![116]

Graphic reports like this about high school girls ignited a moral panic among those who came to regard girls' social and sexual practices as a serious social problem, one that threatened the very foundation of American society. "If our daughters lose the desire to become homemakers, we shall lose our homes," anxiously explained the Ladies Home Journal.[117] Fearing the spreading of venereal disease by "Victory Girls," the U.S. military and Parents Magazine shared the perspective that "the whole structure of civilization may become undermined" by wartime "cuddle bunnies."[118] In its panicky assessment of "khaki-wacky" girls who challenged appropriate standards of femininity, Newsweek intoned, "The moral breakdown among teen-age American girls" was "the gravest home-front tragedy of the war."[119]

Teenage girls' scandalous disregard of traditional standards of feminine conduct especially troubled mental health professionals and public leaders. The task of getting the lawless to behave like ladies fell to the police in places like Omaha, Nebraska. While the police sometimes escorted prowling girls back home, they also arrested "runaways," teenage migrants, and girls still living at home for "disorderly conduct" and offending the "common decency."[120] Reader's Digest reported that the rates at which girls had been arrested in 1943 had "doubled in Dayton, Ohio, almost tripled in San Francisco, and almost quadrupled in Oklahoma City." Reports from cities and towns throughout the nation revealed similar patterns.[121] The soaring rates of delinquency among teens and psychological maladjustments among children led wartime critics to place blame on mothers.[122] Widespread fears that the erosion of parental authority had led to female adolescent promiscuity fueled charges of child neglect. This led to a confusion of official messages that summoned mothers to work to save the country at the same time that mothers were ordered to stay home and protect the family.

Criticisms and constraints also directed at girls did not dissuade them from pursuing their social and sexual pleasures. That was due in part to the fact that girls had come to believe that pundits and parents made "too big a deal" of staying out late and going to parties, according to girls polled by the Ladies Home Journal. While 40 percent of those under sixteen and 66.7 percent of those over sixteen admitted to "necking," 92.3 percent had not done so on the first date, and "never in public places." As to the activities that so alarmed adults, three-quarters of the twelve- to sixteen-year-old girls surveyed had never smoked a cigarette, and more than half had never tasted an alcoholic beverage. Though the sample was hardly scientific, it accorded with other surveys that showed that the vast majority of girls did not have casual sex with multiple partners, although they did prefer to "date" a number of boys rather than "go steady" with just one.[123]

In hindsight, it is clear that adults were anxious not only about the war but also about the lack of deference that characterized wartime female adolescence. Adults failed to see that, as was the case with previous generations, teenage girls had established their own regulatory customs that governed such behavior as smoking and placed peer-based limits on sex. Despite adults' fears about girls, the vast majority did not engage in promiscuous sex. In fact, instead of being sexual aggressors, many girls felt psychologically anxious. The Second World War had transformed the lives of teenage girls in ways that opened doors to both opportunities and apprehensions. Though wartime disruptions enabled girls to expand their horizons, migration and military service had left girls feeling vulnerable to death and danger. Along with other Americans, girls also felt stressed by the insecurities they faced trying to adjust to life on the home front.

New Roles and No Rules:
The "Hidden Army" of Patriotic "Baby-Minders"

Adults thought they knew what to do to ameliorate the social problems brought on by the war. Training teenage girls to babysit would get girls off the streets, provide them with socially acceptable public roles, and prepare them to assume important responsibilities as wives and mothers in the postwar world. Instituting a similar approach utilized by Depression-era experts, those during the war presented babysitting in ways that served to attract girls and acculturate them to an approved girlhood. By representing babysitting as a "war job," they presented the patriotic sitter as a wartime ideal that provided girls with a wholesome and helpful way to contribute to the war effort. Moreover, girls could demonstrate their national loyalty by babysitting in the same way that working mothers performed patriotism.[124] Consequently, guarding the home front as babysitters became the job of the Girl Scouts, who trained babysitters fifteen years old and up.[125] Protecting the "children of the nation" became the job of Wellesley College undergraduates who took courses in child care and worked in child-centered institutions.[126] Caring for the young children of war workers and training "new recruits" was the duty of "Junior WACs" who enlisted at the Worcester Girls' Club day care center.[127]

Saluting the nation's daughters, *Calling All Girls*, the leading girls' magazine of the era, urged them to do their patriotic duty by watching over the nation's youngest as babysitters.[128] Pleased with the activities of organizations, *Reader's Digest* enthusiastically explained that the high school Victory Corps, the YWCA, and other organizations had trained "youngsters for important work."[129] *Recreation* magazine suggested that "[i]f . . . minding that baby, or washing those dishes means that mother can be a nurse's aide, or in any real way increases her contribution to the war effort, then that [domestic] chore becomes a real war service."[130] And *Parents Magazine and Home Guide* tenderly opined about the Girl Scouts, "Fortunate indeed is the mother who has one of these carefully trained sitters to guard the home front in her absence."[131]

The *Ladies Home Journal* initially commended the teenage girls who had "given freely of their time," but then lamented their falling off during the second half of the war. Though the term had been recently coined, "babysitting" still earned little currency with teenage girls, who preferred jobs that paid better, provided higher status, and offered greater sociability. Thus teenage girls left child care to those much younger than themselves.[132] As a result, many fourth, fifth, and sixth graders regularly cared for younger children as "mother-aides" in places like Elmira, New York, a small city with a booming war industry. According to the *Journal of Home Economics*, after school and on Saturdays, it was not teenagers but younger children who worked in the homes of defense workers, as well as in "day nurseries."[133]

Recognizing this new reality led organizations like the Children's Aid Society to provide "complete courses in baby care to girls as young as eleven, twelve, and thirteen" in much the same way that toward the end of the century preadolescents would again become the focus of experts.[134] In contrast to methods of child care today, those enrolled in wartime classes learned how to puree vegetables, prepare sterile formula, and diaper, wash, and weigh a baby. Aiming to provide assurances to home-front mothers that young girls could make reliable babysitters, the *Woman's Home Companion* chronicled the wartime "baby course" education of preadolescent Dolores Rinaldi in a photographic essay that even little girls could comprehend.[135]

"Most young girls get a great kick out of minding babies, and, what's more, profit by the experience," explained the *Ladies Home Journal* optimistically.[136] And that was certainly how some girls saw it, how the media reported it, and how historians have recorded it. One junior high school girl said that she did not mind giving up her favorite activities because it meant that the men would be coming home sooner. When she babysat for more than one family at a time, that left "two more mothers available to work," she explained.[137] In a letter to General Douglas McArthur, a twelve-year-old Girl Scout from Wichita, Kansas, explained that she was helping the war effort "by taking care of small children so that the parents may work in war factories."[138]

While some young sitters felt similarly patriotic, others grew as jaundiced about babysitting as their older sisters. And, strikingly similar to prewar sitters, wartime girls complained that mothers rarely supplied instructions or left telephone numbers. Sometimes wages were paid in part, or not at all. "Staying with the children" still meant having to wash the dishes and do other household chores. That was because homemaking required nearly as much energy, organization, and patience as it had during the Depression. Inadequate housing, the rationing of foods (sugar, coffee, butter, vegetables, meat), the shortages of soap, gasoline, tires, and household appliances (and repairmen to fix them), inflexible supermarket hours, and other obstacles challenged the abilities of all American housewives. Cloth shortages even reduced the supply of diapers. Whether they liked it or not, sitters who picked up after the kids were forced to pick up the slack for laboring mothers working long shifts. One girl cared for five children (between two months and nine years old) from the late afternoon until early morning.[139] A junior high school girl took care of the children of war workers from 4:00 to 11:00 p.m.[140] And because the wartime shortage of sitters generated stiff competition from better-paying jobs preferred by teens, some mothers would leave a single young sitter in charge of all the children. According to the *Journal of Home Economics*, "two thirds of the girls in the [Elmira, New York] school system—most of them under sixteen—were regularly caring for children and were working late hours with inadequate pay."[141]

Recognizing the dispiriting reality of teenage girls on the home front, *Recreation* magazine reversed its earlier predictions about the value of training girls for child care. "Making a patriotic duty out of minding the baby, or washing the dishes, is a very good way to undermine all interest and enthusiasm about the war," the magazine concluded.[142] It was also a great way to undercut girls' interest in babysitting—and just at the time when parents of tens of millions of "baby boomers" would need someone to babysit.

Conclusion

The roots of grownups' anxieties about babysitters and girls' ambivalences about babysitting lie in the birth of modern American girls' culture. As we have just seen, the emergence of a distinctly female adolescent culture grounded in peer influence, things teenage, and freedom from adult supervision had been vexing adults since the 1920s. By the 1930s experts who sustained and supplemented earlier warnings used babysitting in order to both criticize and acculturate. Depression-era experts urged babysitters to adopt feminine strategies and standards acceptable to adults, not adolescents. As the cultural differences between female adolescents and adults became increasingly more prominent, babysitters were told to shape up by dressing down, listen "attentively," accept instructions "cheerfully," and avoid speaking in slang.[143] But experts' embryonic efforts at rehabilitating girls through babysitting or replacing them with juvenile father figures appeared to have had little effect on girls, whose unrestrained exuberance and high visibility marked wartime girls as agents of unsettling gender and generational changes. Experts tried to mold reprehensible "khaki-wackies" into responsible babysitters, but teenage girls who were "having a ball" on the home front left the patriotic responsibility of child care to more compliant little workers.

The subcultural principles and practices that teenage girls propagated in spite of the adversities of the Great Depression and the exigencies of World War II would prove to be of even greater concern in the postwar era. As children become the primary source of parental fulfillment, parents' rising expectations of caregivers would collide with their perceptions of the devil-may-care culture of teenage girls. It would be anxious fathers back from military service, more so than the mothers, who would criticize the crop of teenage babysitters. The gender and generational transformations that were fueling girls' redefinition of girlhood would unsettle these bewildered war heroes and complicate their view of babysitters, upon whom they would have to rely if they wanted a break from the kids and "a night out" with the wife. Positioned as a cultural phenomenon in the years after the war, the female adolescent babysitter would menace the imaginations of postwar men when they were most vulnerable.

2

Suburban Parents and Sitter Unions

"The way most of us make our money is by babysitting," explained a perky girl who spoke for many in the 1945 *March of Time* newsreel "Teen-Age Girls."[1] But by 1947, the sober realization that babysitting had become the only way middle-class girls could make money led some to seek out better ways of dealing with the new employment realities.[2] Drawing upon the rising authority of teenage girls' culture and the residual wartime support for female workers, teenage girls in high schools and colleges banded together and "fashion[ed] a set of rules," just as the journalist for *The American Home* had suggested before the war.[3] Taking advantage of the flux in gender roles and generational relationships in postwar America, teenage girls organized babysitter unions in the Midwest and Northeast. In the years before domesticity became the prevailing gender ideology, self-confident teenage girls tried to eliminate the labor abuses that had made babysitting both unprofitable and undesirable.

In addition to exploring the agency of teenage girls during the late 1940s, this chapter also examines the position of postwar mothers. Though they traded defense work for housework and war production for reproduction, the new emphasis on maternal devotion and "family togetherness" left many women with no real choice aside from full-time child bearing and rearing. Though the baby boom was only one year old, ministering to the needs of their little ones without assistance or relief from routines left many mothers suffering from "cabin fever." But with fewer teenage girls in the population by the late 1940s—a consequence of plummeting birth rates during most of the Depression—suburban communities faced a shortage of babysitters. Mothers hoped to benefit from the postwar conception of empowered girlhood that could be an asset in a youthful childcare provider expected to manage children. By supporting sitters' unions and forming alliances with teenage girls, mothers hoped to gain access to the services of a few.

But some husbands felt more conflicted than their wives about teenage girls who were so self-assured. Men wondered whether their own presumed obligation to oversee family life was being usurped by domineering women and pirated by demanding girls. This chapter also examines in gendered and generational perspective men's public objections to the high school girls who laid down the rules in union "manifestos," "codes," and "contracts."[4] Among husbands who had looked to the postwar home as a peaceful haven, there were those who bristled at teenage girls' activities and attitudes. Portraying teenage girls as obstreperous in the magazines men read, male authors criticized sitters for their upstart assertions. They satirized sitters who ruled out "a bit of dusting" and would not "lift a finger" outside their child-care "specialty."[5] The Saturday Evening Post caustically reported that the new field of babysitting was "dominated" by a militant minority of teenage girls who procured money from powerless parent-employers.[6] Magazines described demanding babysitters threatening to picket postwar suburban communities, the place where "baby boomers" outnumbered babysitters. Though the war had ended, a new battle at home over who was in charge had given rise to a new cultural figure, the subversive babysitter, who trespassed into the fretful imagination of white, middle-class husbands growing increasingly irritable.

The Pleasures and Problems of Domesticity

Women and men raised in economic chaos and political crises, and exposed to the Holocaust and the atomic bomb, looked to the family to provide them with stability, security, and self-fulfillment in the years after World War II.[7] Marrying in greater numbers and at younger ages than their parents and grandparents, young couples reversed (albeit temporarily) a 150-year-old demographic trend toward smaller families. Between 1946 and 1951, twenty-two million babies would be born into families averaging between three and four children.[8] Seeking to alleviate fears about economic, political, even nuclear forces beyond their control, millions of white, middle-class, and upwardly mobile working-class couples left cramped quarters in urban ethnic enclaves. Searching for safe neighborhoods and good schools, they purchased spacious single-family houses in newly established suburban communities. Based on the premise that the country's six million GIs should have "a home of their own," the U.S. government financed the social mobility of millions of parents with low-interest mortgages.[9] The number of single-family houses built between 1944 and 1946 rose from 114,000 to 937,000.[10] Thereafter, an unprecedented building boom of single-family homes spread from Long Island to Los Angeles.

Suburbia rapidly became a sanctuary for a new domestic ethos: women's primary responsibilities were to be the care of the children and the management of the all-electric suburban family home. Many women set aside educational opportunities and career aspirations for a husband, house, kids, and car, and felt satisfied with the choice they had made. Others, however, failed to find emotional fulfillment in household routines increasingly glorified in postwar advertisements, commercials, movies, and sit-coms. Although popular magazines often extolled the virtues of domesticity, they also represented it as exhausting and isolating.[11] Increasingly, housewives felt overburdened by the endless cooking, cleaning, chauffeuring, and child rearing. What mothers found particularly taxing was trying to accomplish household tasks while also tending to children's needs.[12] Even with such "labor-saving" appliances as washing machines and electric mixers, a suburban wife would spend more time doing housework than women in cities, women in the country, and mothers in the past.[13]

Many mothers yearned for a break from the highly demanding rituals that required them to be thoroughly and exclusively attentive to the needs and wants of their children.[14] In 1946, *Parents Magazine and Family Home Guide* had published "Time Off for Mother," a first-hand account of the problems that had begun, and would continue, to plague America's homemakers.

> If you are a mother of young children, you have probably wished many times for a certain amount of time each week that you could call your own—a chance to do your share of community work, to pursue an interest or talent or, perhaps, to find some way to add to the family income. And yet, in most communities today, it is either impossible to find anyone reliable enough to care for your children at regular intervals or the cost is more than you can afford. As a result, you probably have few opportunities to engage in any activity outside your own home.[15]

Mothers wanted "time off" to "play bridge, go shopping or visiting, or just put up their feet and take a nap." Many also hungered for a "night out."[16] Wives without a certain amount of entertainment, warned *Today's Woman* in 1946, "become bored, resentful, and dissatisfied."[17]

While my mother was a babysitter during the war, it was not long before she needed one. My parents joined other young adults who pulled out of cities and settled in suburban communities in the years after the war. While some parents would organize cooperatively run nursery schools,

these did not admit infants and toddlers. All the day care centers established during the war had closed down, and domestic help was limited.
Drawing upon the prewar child-care traditions that Dr. Benjamin Spock
typically eschewed in his ground-breaking postwar guide, *The Common
Sense Book of Baby and Child Care* (1946), he advised mothers to hire a
"maid," nurse, or "foster mother."[18] Anticipating that the problem would
not be resolved anytime in the near future, five hundred "career mothers"
in search of babysitters informed the New York Herald Tribune Home
Institute that it was nearly impossible for them to "get anyone alive and
breathing."[19]

Fortunately for many wives, husbands increasingly assumed a greater role
in child rearing.[20] Encouraging men to do so were experts who believed that
postwar family life would furnish fathers with the security they sought after
witnessing a decade of unemployment and another five years of wartime absence.[21] Observations of fathers by sociologists at the time led to the view
that children satisfied men's emotional needs where employment did not.[22]
Though this new ideal of "paternal engagement" might have encouraged fathers to take an active role in family life, few husbands, in fact, actually assisted in the kind of child care and housekeeping that would have truly alleviated their wives' labors. The sexual division of labor typical of postwar
family life charged breadwinners with bringing home the bacon, not cooking it (unless it was on an outdoor grill).

Postwar experts who encouraged young couples to enjoy their night
out assured them that their time together would make them into better
parents.[23] In its revised publication on infant care, the Children's Bureau
suggested that it was crucial for couples now to "resume outside interests and enjoy an evening together."[24] In fact, a "night out" was just what
the doctor ordered because having fun made "well adjusted" people have
"healthier" marriages.[25] One suburban wife explained to readers of *Parents
Magazine* that "frequent periods of fun and relaxation . . . strengthened
our love for each other, our children, and our home."[26] Parents put faith
in public testimonials that affirmed experts' claims. Compared to the new
vision of family life put forth by experts, kin and community wisdom appeared increasingly antiquated.[27] Consequently, more parents would follow the advice of experts who advised them not only to put a little dis-
tance between themselves and their parents but also to put some space
between themselves and their kids.

Along with their wives, husbands also looked forward to "a few hours
of freedom from their little darlings," despite the exaltation of family life

as a postwar ideal. Being able to go out for the night was increasingly possible because major social changes decreased the length of the work week and increased salaries.[28] Because disposable incomes would grow by 200 percent, and discretionary income for non-necessities would double after 1947, many middle-class couples could increasingly afford to go out and have fun.[29] Shifting from an ethos of rationing to one of recreation, ninety million Americans went to the movies each week between 1946 and 1948.[30] While the economic exigencies and social disruptions caused by the Depression and the war had curtailed leisure in the past, postwar parents faced fewer impediments to their recreation than had their parents' generation, or so they thought.[31]

Trouble in Toddlerville

"Many young couples [still] cannot afford to have any social life or relaxation because there is not enough money to pay for an evening out and for the baby sitter too, at the prevailing price," one contemporary explained to the *San Francisco Call-Bulletin* in 1948.[32] Out of the seven dollars that Mr. and Mrs. Richard Mutti of Burlingame, California, spent to go to a double feature in 1950, five dollars went to the sitter, who earned one dollar an hour.[33] The growing number who could afford to hire a sitter, however, faced what *Today's Woman* referred to as the "great baby-sitter problem."[34] As one mother tersely explained, "The trouble in our town is that there aren't enough sitters."[35] That was because baby boomers outnumbered babysitters everywhere, but especially in the new "servantless" suburban neighborhoods. "If you live in such a community," explained one disgruntled mother, "you know just what this means. It means no baby sitters."[36] The postwar demographic imbalance between babies and babysitters was a consequence of birth rates that had shifted radically over the preceding decades. More babies would be born in the seven years after 1948 than in the previous thirty years.[37] That birth rates had plunged during most of the Depression meant that by 1948 there were only about two million sitters available to care for the nation's "war babies," let alone the new bumper crop of "baby boomers."[38]

Adding to the population imbalance where it mattered were new suburban residential patterns where young couples with small children predominated. Consequently, in one "suburb of 9,000 homes there are 8,000 children only about one hundred of whom were old enough for high school; most of the rest were still in playpens."[39] Only fifty high school girls were available to babysit in Madison, New Jersey, a suburban community with a population of just under eight thousand in 1947. The high demand for sitters meant that Madison girls who wanted to work could have held two jobs at the same time.[40] "There are only a few dozen teen-age girls" and "thousands upon thousands of toddlers," explained one teenage babysitter about Levittown, New York, a 4,000-acre development.[41] "There are 15,000 small homes in the area and in those homes live 27,000 children, most of them toddlers. . . . Each of the 15,000 houses has an 'expansion attic' where bedrooms can be added as children arrive. And how they arrive!" While adults referred to Levittown as "Fertility Valley" and "The Rabbit Hutch," babysitters dubbed it "Toddlerville."[42]

Old college towns hardly fared better than newer developments. Though Wellesley, Massachusetts, was filled with co-eds, there were not enough babysitters to go around. The placement bureau at Wellesley College had received only forty-six annual requests for the "care of children" during the Depression, yet by 1946, the school agency received 882 pleas from parents for "babysitters." Because only 167 students were registered at the Placement Office, the staff spent hours telephoning students in order to try to satisfy the needs of numerous parents. But, unable to drum up enough sitters that year, the bureau decided to accept requests only "insofar as there are girls available to fill them."[43] Conditions only worsened in 1947, when the college bureau was inundated with even more calls from parents seeking sitters.[44]

Butch and Other Boy Babysitters

Finding a babysitter was easier if one was willing to hire a boy, as had mothers in the past. While earning his college degree under the GI Bill, which supported the higher education of veterans, my father worked as a babysitter. Ivy League schools even institutionalized babysitting for male college students. As one popular periodical explained, "When parents step out in Cambridge, a Harvard athlete steps in."[45] Undercutting male sitters at Yale University by ten cents, Harvard sitters charged fifty cents per hour before 7:00 p.m., when the rate dropped to thirty-five cents (on the naive assumption that the children would sleep). After midnight, the rate rose to fifty cents per hour.[46] At Princeton, male undergraduates organized the Tiger Tot Tending Agency, where, beginning in 1946, college boys babysat for the children of faculty members and married students for

In 1947, at Princeton University, as at other colleges, male students ran
babysitting services like the "Tiger Tot Tending Agency." *Princeton Alumni
Weekly*, published March 13, 2002. Princeton Alumni Weekly Archives. Princeton
University Archives. Department of Rare Books and Special Collections.
Princeton University Library. Reprinted courtesy of Princeton University Library.

thirty-five cents an hour.[47] Ann Rose Reed and her husband employed the
services of the Tiger Tot Tenders. "I remember one who was in training
for a bicycle trip through Europe and chose to ride back and forth to our
house in the country."[48]

At Columbia University, the football coach (himself a former babysitter) established a sitting service for his players, taking equal pride in their
perseverance on the football field as in their professionalism in the field of
babysitting. "We've had men play in a game on Saturday afternoon, sit with
a baby that night, and do a bang-up job both times."[49] A graduate student
at Columbia who was a former army major also took care of babies. With
the apparatus he rigged up from an assortment of "loudspeakers, old radio
parts, an amplifier and a broken phonograph," he minded seven babies simultaneously. Hooking microphones onto the cribs in seven apartments in
the veterans' housing project in Shanks Village, New York, he studied while
lying on his couch, above which were perched seven loudspeakers, each

"Minding the babies" reinforced rather than reduced the masculine identity of boys like Butch, who (unlike his sister) would be consistently described in the popular and commercial culture as a hard-working, ambitious, reliable, and inventive babysitter. Ad, *Life* magazine, May 1947, 4.

marked with the name of the baby in his care. Every thirty minutes he also made the rounds to check on the children while their parents were out.[50]

That these fellows were willing to babysit and that mothers were willing to hire them was only partly due to demographics. As before and after the war, boy babysitters received strong support. To the nation's electric light and power companies, Butch the babysitter, an all-American boy featured in a full-page ad in *Life* magazine, exemplified the masculine qualities that defined the national character in the postwar era. "He's American business—in miniature."[51]

In a 1948 episode of the *Aldrich Family*, babysitting took place within a male network of fathers, sons, brothers, and buddies although the enormously popular NBC radio program promoted traditional family values.[52] Though initially hesitant about babysitting for the Ferguson baby because he had a date, hapless teenage Henry Aldrich nevertheless honored his commitment. He was able to do so because he got lots of help caring for the six-month-old baby boy. Henry's younger brother, his friend Willie (a self-proclaimed babysitting "professional"), and even his own father came to Henry's aid.[53]

Sheltering Grade School Girls

Though preadolescent girls could have helped alleviate the shortage as they had done during the war, those under the age of twelve were increasingly less likely to be hired to babysit. While wartime babysitters had been encouraged to do their duty on the home front, postwar experts steadily raised the minimum age. In 1947 the *Woman's Home Companion* explained that anyone below the age of fourteen was now considered too "risky" to hire.[54] Such was the case because "[m]ost children under fourteen do not have the wisdom to handle an emergency," explained Dr. Josephine H. Kenyon, director of the Baby Center, in 1949.[55] Other pediatricians and experts argued that "fifteen is the rock-bottom minimum" age for babysitters.[56] As a grade school sitter in the cartoon *The Baby Sitter* (1947), Little Lulu had clearly become a sitter of the past, not a symbol of the future.[57] While regarded as useful during the war, grade school girls were rendered economically worthless after it as the importance placed on children's productive labor gave way to children pretending to work while playing.[58] Suburbanites who anxiously sought to shelter their children from a threatening world provided their daughters with baby dolls that reinforced the postwar domestic ideology. Little girls could only practice babysitting with their own dolls or with the one advertised as the "National Babysitter." Produced between 1946 and 1948 by Violet Lee Gradwohl (founder of the Terri Lee Sales Corp.), the doll, which came with a recording of "Dolly's Lullaby" by Toni Harper with Eddie Beal and his Sextet, could ostensibly sing songs and tell stories. While child expert L. Emmett Holt Jr. would reiterate the advice that remained dominant until the mid-1980s, girls "younger than [their] mid-teens" sometimes sought out jobs as "wheelers," pushing baby buggies up and down suburban streets.[59] Speaking for other girls between ages seven and eleven, Janet explained that working as a "wheeler," was "more fun than dolls." That some babysitters were younger than their mid-teens led the *Boston Globe* to ask, "Who Is Baby Sitting for Baby Sitter While Baby Sitter's Baby Sitting?"[60]

Responding to the problem at hand, community organizations sought to shore up the shortage in personnel. During the 1947 Christmas season, several organizations established sitting services so that women could shop for holiday gifts.[61] The New York Young Women's Republican Club provided sitters, as did their rivals, the Democratic party. Armed with handbooks, teenaged Girl Scouts offered child-care services on Election Day so that mothers could get out and do their civic duty.[62] A variety of cultural institutions also offered their services to patrons of the arts. While the Buffalo Philharmonic arranged sitters for its season ticket holders, unoccupied actors took care of children at the Greenbush Summer Theatre in Blauvelt, New York.[63] Religious institutions also stepped in so parents could step out. The Roman Catholic Church in Rochester and the Vincentians in Brooklyn offered sitting services so parents in New York could attend mass.[64] Volunteers staffed a "baby-sitter corner" at a Park Avenue dental clinic.[65] In New Rutherford, New Jersey, a nurse watched the kids while Bergen County mothers shopped.[66] In San Francisco, the Park Bowl Alley hired babysitters two nights a week so that members of the women's teams could bowl.[67]

Despite the efforts of community businesses and organizations, housewives still were unable to make definite plans. Many would answer the occasional R.S.V.P. with a tentative, "I.W.C.G.A.S. (If We Can Get A Sitter)."[68] Sitterless couples could easily find themselves in the position of having to cancel their plans.[69] When that happened, sometimes parents loaded up the family station wagon and drove to a drive-in. While children were sometimes brought along on "tiring and inappropriate expeditions," at other times parents just "stayed home" and watched TV instead.[70] By 1948, television became a real alternative for one hundred thousand American families. Despite the new forms of entertainment, however, one sufferer from "cabin fever" explained sorrowfully that "I've had two kids in the last two years . . . and I've only been out twice in all that time."[71]

Although the cover illustration on *The Saturday Evening Post* in 1953 was entitled "New Baby Sitter," she was conspicuous by her absence. Forced to entertain in their living room because of the shortage of sitters was a couple and their friends all dressed in evening attire. The group mingled alongside the baby who lay in regal splendor in a bassinette draped with a flowing white bed skirt. Conveying the centrality of children in the lives of postwar parents, the grey-colored changing table (which matched the mother's silvery gown and complemented the father's grey suit) dominated the living room space and pushed the party of adults to the side.[72]

"Sitter's Rights": A Militant Minority

Although there were not enough babysitters around, the *San Francisco News* reported in 1946 that "[n]o accurate history of these peculiar times can be written without a full chapter on baby-sitting, a social phenomenon which has had more impact on the American family than anything since Selective Service."[73] Just one year after the war, babysitting had become the "No. 1 money-making endeavor."[74] According to a survey conducted in the Los Angeles schools, 90 percent of junior high girls worked as babysitters by 1948.[75] Babysitting had become the key source of employment for teenage girls following a job contraction that was more severe than that faced by male youth and women workers after the war.[76] By 1948, all children under sixteen would be largely absent from the paid labor force.[77] "It was the only way I could make money," explained Sally Wilcox about babysitting during her adolescence.[78] Changing social realities and new cultural standards forced girl workers to shift the site of their service from the public economy, where they were no longer wanted, to the private household, where they were desperately needed. Assuming that girls were as despairing as parents led one journalist in 1949 to report that three-quarters of all high school girls in public and private schools in Washington, D.C., were "willing and eager to take their books to someone else's home and sit with the children for 25 to 50 cents an hour."[79]

In fact, fourteen-year-old Sylvia Plath had been in an "excited state of anticipation" as she walked up the front steps of the house where she was to babysit in her home town of Wellesley, Massachusetts, in 1946. In the years before she became a magazine writer, published poet, and novelist who critiqued postwar notions of girlhood and womanhood, Sylvia agreed to care for two boys one Sunday afternoon. Sylvia had imagined that the boys would listen to the *Shadow* or some other popular radio program, while she would "sit down and read all the magazines that were in the house."[80] Like many other girls at the time, she was an avid reader of popular periodicals.

But Sylvia's fantasy was met with frustration that day. The boys in her care turned out to be less interested in listening to the radio and more interested in hearing Sylvia read stories out loud. "I read until my throat ached; I read everything from *The Grasshopper Man* to *Betty Grable and Her Life History*; and still they brought me more and more books. Finally when they wanted me to sing a songbook from beginning to end, I put my foot down."[81] Because Sylvia was unfamiliar with the kitchen, its utensils, and cooking, supper became an insurmountable challenge. It was a "near-catastrophe" when the popcorn "burst into flames" and filled the kitchen with "billows of smoke." Then, the boys jumped on top of her while playing "Kill the Bear." Sylvia Plath's first babysitting experience turned her into a self-described "cynic," who found little endearing in children's "charms." That day, Sylvia realized that "little children are bothersome beings that have to be waited on hand and foot, who are generally around when not wanted, and who are, all in all, a nuisance."[82]

Shaped by the expansion of the subculture that had continued to embolden female adolescents after the war, Sylvia was joined by other girls who shared their dislikes about babysitting with each other and with adults willing to listen.[83] "Sitters groused that they were being worked to the bone for a few shekels," explained one reporter.[84] "Sixteen-year-old Alice Turner was still 'sitting' at the same [twenty-five cents per hour] rate she has been charging for two years," reported the *Boston Globe*. That rate was acceptable to Alice, but only because the children were already "out of the diaper class," went to bed early, and no longer needed bottles. But another family Alice worked for had three children all under the age of two. According to her, "There's practically no chance there to study or even sit down during the evening."[85] Alice thought her employer "ought to pay extra rates." Low wages combined with increased household demands led sitters to complain about having to mind the children and "do light laundry, wash supper dishes, help Grandma upstairs, and walk the dog," explained *American Magazine*.[86]

When students at the West Branch High School in West Branch, Michigan, complained about the problems they faced as babysitters, their homemaking teacher suggested that they form an "agency for baby-watching," compile a list of "do's and don'ts," and establish "a standard wage scale."[87] Acting on her suggestion, they formed one of the nation's first babysitters' unions.[88]

Babysitters in New Jersey also established a union in which they drew up a "uniform set of working conditions."[89] While it remains unknown who or what inspired girls in New Jersey to organize, we do know that many Americans were demanding their rights.[90] For instance, National Student

A weekly business meeting of the West Branch, Michigan, babysitter union.
Barbara Stanton, "Baby Sitters United." *Woman's Home Companion*, March 1947,
151. General Research Division, The New York Public Library,
Astor, Lenox and Tilden Foundations.

Association activists, also unwilling to cast aside their specific wartime
gains, penned a Student Bill of Rights at the University of Wisconsin.[91] So
were workers who struck for higher pay and improved labor conditions.
And at the University of Virginia, college girls organized a babysitting association.[92] "In many colleges, with typical student vigor, unions have been
organized to negotiate raises and guarantee minimum rates for baby sitters,"
explained the *National Magazine for the Young Women's Christian Association* in 1947.[93] As we have seen, schools had been functioning as the locus
of group identity and the central arena of youth culture for decades.[94] These
institutions provided fertile ground for the development of peer societies
in which adolescents inspired and influenced one another.

On college campuses, as well as in high schools, adolescent girls and
young women congregated, complained, and, occasionally, organized.
Whether they were in high school or college, in Michigan or Massachusetts, self-confident babysitters sowing the seeds of wartime employment
drew up "manifestos" and "contracts" that sought to improve postwar labor conditions. One of the most pressing issues concerned wages. In West
Branch, Michigan, the sitters required that "[p]arents pay a standard wage
for sitting: twenty-five cents an hour until four P.M.; thirty cents an hour
until midnight; thirty-five cents an hour after midnight."[95] In Newton,

Massachusetts, sitters stipulated an hourly rate of twenty-five cents before midnight and thirty-five cents thereafter. They also wanted fifty cents per hour for "overtime" (the period after which sitters were expected home). Sitters in Leonia, New Jersey, wanted thirty cents an hour before midnight and thirty-five cents an hour after midnight. They also ruled that "[p]arents agree not to ask sitter to work after eleven P.M. on school nights nor after two A.M. on Saturdays."[96]

Sitters everywhere were also united in their verdict against housework, the drudgery they aimed to eliminate.[97] Self-assured teenage girls who did not conceive of themselves as domestics refused to wash the dishes. The *New York Times* reported that because women often linked child care with light housekeeping, the "uniform set of working conditions" spelled out by the New Jersey union specified that sitters would "not wash dishes except by special arrangement."[98] In West Branch, Michigan, sitters got their employers to agree "not to ask sitter to do extras like cleaning, scrubbing, or cooking—without arranging beforehand for a higher wage scale. For example, a parent must shell out fifteen cents extra if sitter does the dinner dishes."[99] Emphasizing the seriousness with which girls regarded the issue of domestic chores, the *Woman's Home Companion* explained that "[t]eens blacklist families who demand scrubbing and cleaning at sitters' rates."[100] More likely than an official blacklist, though, was the informal sharing of information among girls who cautioned each other about employers who expected housework.

Out to improve other labor conditions as well, babysitters in Leonia, New Jersey, required that employers also provide "adequate heat."[101] Wartime rations and postwar inflation still led some parents to keep thermostats turned down too low for comfort. Sitters also made it clear that for the job to be acceptable to them, it had to include refreshments, a desk, a telephone, and a radio, the principal form of entertainment for youth, who often listened to teen-targeted programs.[102] And because many teenage girls did not want babysitting to interfere with their social lives, a "red-hot issue" among sitters was the right to invite friends over. High school girls in Leonia, New Jersey, agreed not to entertain friends while on the job, but visits from girlfriends and boyfriends were even written into the Massachusetts sitters' code.[103] The girls in Madison, New Jersey, who wanted to combine babysitting with boyfriends, earned the support of their high school dean, who explained that "[s]o long as the b.f.'s don't arrive till the children are asleep, don't make too much noise, and leave by ten o'clock," having boyfriends over was acceptable.[104] Many girls had experienced a modicum of independence during the war and were unwilling to surrender it in peacetime.[105] Nor did it seem that they necessarily had to. Whether it was the permissive patterns of wartime babysitting or sheer desperation for a babysitter, there were some parent-employers who apparently accepted "sitters entertaining beaus," reported *American Home* in 1947.[106]

Common Cause: Housewives and Babysitters

In addition to teachers, there were other women who assisted babysitters in their efforts to establish organizations of one kind or another.[107] A Pennsylvania mother organized the Beta Sigma Phi Baby Sitting Club, in which the "girls set up their own rules and rates."[108] In suburban Boston, high school girls were "organized by" the Auburndale Woman's Club.[109] In Boston, Mrs. Harold Carnes presided over a roster of around thirty girls who were members of a babysitters' club.[110] By helping to organize sitters, many mothers probably hoped to increase the possibilities of finding a babysitter so that they could get out of the house.[111]

Looking back in 1951, the *Journal of the National Education Association* reported that the "students organized 'unions,' agreed on a scale of prices, and set up employment bureaus."[112] While little is known about babysitter unions (there are no babysitter archives), it seems that all had "agreements" that protected the interests of babysitters. The Auburndale babysitters' club in Massachusetts had a "fixed 25 cents an hour minimum; 35 cents for sitting after midnight; and a 'penalty' rate of 50 cents an hour if the parents promised to be home by 11 and didn't make it," reported the *Boston Globe*.[113] Another "club" agreed to wash, bathe, and put the kids to bed for "30 cents an hour till 11 pm and 35 cents thereafter (a rate that did not include dishwashing)." Sitters in that organization also required that parents provide adequate heat, desk space, transportation (if dark), and notification if they planned to return home later than expected.[114]

Writing articles under such titles as "Sitter's Right" and "Baby Sitters United," female journalists (who were perhaps themselves former babysitters) expressed particular sympathy toward sitters. Describing the development of one union, the *Woman's Home Companion* reported that babysitters had "rights" to an agreed-upon rate of pay; an agreement about the nature of the work; a "comfortable space" to do homework; "refrigerator rights," etc. What sitters had a "right not to do" were the dishes, unless extra wages were negotiated.[115] Photographs and captions also made it clear that female employers should aim to satisfy their sitters. "It is mother's job to make sure sitter knows. . . ."; "Before teen comes to sit, Mrs. Mack settles on rate of pay. . . ."; "It's a long evening's work so Mack provides. . . ."; "Mrs. Mack understands youngsters' big appetites, gives sitter refrigerator rights. . . ."; "Under the phone go written instructions. . . ."[116] Though this added to mothers' domestic burdens, unionized sitters were presented as a possible source of help for suburban mothers.

That mothers and girls worked together to establish sitting organizations earned the praise of women's magazines that commended the cooperation.[117] The headline "Baby Sitters United" not only described the alliance of sitters but also referred to the partnership between employees and employers. The *Woman's Home Companion* enthusiastically supported the Michigan union's efforts at seeking out the advice of mothers, commenting that for the "first time mothers and sitters were trying to help each other."[118] That kind of intergenerational conversation also occurred in magazines that courted teenage girl readers with accounts that emphasized the common cause of babysitters and their female bosses.

In an effort to interest girl readers and inform them about babysitter unions, the *Woman's Home Companion* concluded that "[t]he rules of the West Branch union make a very fine check-list for any lass who earns her pin money minding babies. And if you find the going a bit rugged in your town, a sitters' agency might be what you and your fellow-watchers need to put the job of baby-sitting on an organized businesslike basis."[119] To the journalist who observed one union in action, though, it seemed more like a genial sorority than a somber business meeting. "Monday evenings the union meets at Marilyn's [the business agent] house. They thrash out problems about their work and wind up with a gab session about dates, school clothes, and general frivolity. Dues are two bits a month and any surplus, after running expenses, is blown on a party."[120] Though not openly disparaging, the description hinted at an undercurrent of disapproval about the teenage girl and her subcultural practices, that first emerged among men in postwar America, as we shall see.

The "Youngest Profession": Female Sexuality and Male Anxiety

In contrast to the more understanding tone of the *Woman's Home Companion* and other women's periodicals that portrayed babysitters as helpful was the antagonistic position of weekly variety magazines. Though *The*

Saturday Evening Post was a "family" magazine, the conservative, middle-class publication reflected the anti-union outlook of employers. Perceiving sitters' unions as hot beds for radicals, *The Saturday Evening Post* described the Michigan union as "one of the most militant." The problem of radicalism was not confined to one union in one state, however. The periodical went on to describe babysitting as "a craft dominated by a militant minority of high school girls extracting $750 million a year" from parent-employers. The sarcasm of a subheadline, "The Union Sits on Unfair Parents," elicited sympathy for those forced to submit to the unjust demands of this new generation of wily babysitters who defied the authority of their betters, elders, and men. When asked about the union's goals by the reporter for *The Saturday Evening Post*, the impertinent fifteen-year-old business agent purportedly "sassed" rather than "stated" the organization's aims.[121] And that was only the beginning.

While women's magazines generally emphasized cooperation, periodicals with a solid male readership typically stressed conflict between argumentative babysitters and their irritated bosses. According to an article in the *Christian Science Monitor,* male employers often felt "needled and nettled" by assertive babysitters.[122] In other magazine articles, girls' aggressive usurpation of fathers' authority supposedly occurred with great regularity, especially in regard to young sons. In print and in pictures, concerns about girls' treatment of "Junior" emerged more often than they did about girls' treatment of "Jane."[123] The fifteen-year-old president of the West Branch, Michigan, sitters' union was purported to have said in her "no nonsense" way, "[w]e require full disciplinary authority. If Junior needs a spanking, he gets it."[124] While some fathers might have agreed with the union executive's methods of discipline, they would surely have bristled at her (mis) appropriation of their paternal prerogative. Reflecting the same sentiments expressed elsewhere, one male commentator for the *San Francisco News* explained that "[t]here was a time when the home revolved around father's ability to earn, but so deeply has baby-tending bitten its initials into the psychology of the family that now the home revolves around the babysitter."[125]

Perhaps seemingly powerful babysitters had tapped the social anxieties of men unsettled by the flux in gender ideals. According to experts who made the reintegration of fathers the focus of their attention, many post-war husbands and fathers felt as unsure of themselves as had men before the war.[126] War service, it seemed, had failed to fully restore notions of manhood that had disintegrated during the Great Depression. Lingering fears about the world war that mingled with looming apprehensions about the Cold War roused concerns among men about whether they could adequately protect the family (and the nation) from danger. *The Best Years of Our Lives* (1946) and other popular movies of the period reflected the persistence of fears about male insignificance, especially in the face of increasingly independent wives and daughters. Though women had been expelled from the labor market right after the war, their steady reentrance by 1947 further stirred fears about women's growing autonomy.[127] In San Francisco, the police searched for a 21-year-old housewife who hired a fourteen-year-old sitter to mind her three children "while she led a gay life downtown with men other than her husband."[128] In Boston, probate court judge Robert G. Wilson Jr. admonished the many wives who appeared before him in divorce cases for their excessive reliance on the "hired watchers." From his side of the bench, it was clear that mothers who left their children in one city in order to get a job in another, came home intoxicated in the middle of the night, or fed babies nothing but milk and water were neither fulfilling their roles as mothers or wives.[129]

Unusual among men was the judge who publically praised babysitters for their dedication to children. More often, men's fantasies about babysitters were colored by a discourse about the independence of the female adolescent. One employer shared his fears about a militant babysitter who allegedly threatened his freedom and his family. After Betty Ann informed him that she had a "monopoly on sittership" at their Kansas address, the fifteen-year-old intimidated him. She left him feeling that it would be "un-American and immoral" to hire anyone else to babysit. He imagined the "condescending" teenager protesting "outside the gate with a picket sign if we called in a [sitter] scab."[130] In this age of conformity when Americans of all ages were encouraged to fit in, babysitters who challenged the gender order stood out. Such was the case among the babysitters purported to have said, "Beyond washing dishes for 15 extra cents, we won't lift a finger outside our specialty." Along with other popular magazines, *Coronet* ridiculed sitters for defying the domestic ethos. "Only three girls in a group of 500 at the high school in Cheyenne, Wyoming, will take on household chores, while most organized bobby-soxers rule out even a bit of dusting."[131]

Perhaps men felt anxious about handing over control of their families to girls even for an evening because many returning veterans faced difficulties living up to the greater role in family life they were generally expected to play.[132] Wartime female autonomy, which had altered family roles and

diminished fathers' authority, had also accentuated male feelings of irrel-
evance.[133] Fatherhood conferred masculine status, but many men also felt
out of step with its newest formulations. Instead of providing discipline
and punishment, which were widely discouraged for their role in shaping
authoritarian personalities, postwar fathers were now expected to be sensitive and nurturing.[134] To their wives, many of whom read *Parents Magazine* and other periodicals that provided up-to-date advice, husbands'
methods of disciplined child rearing seemed outmoded.[135] Assessing the
debilitated position of dads in 1948, the anthropologist Geoffrey Gorer
observed, "In few societies is the role of father more vestigial than in the
United States."[136]

Advice givers eager to restore domestic order encouraged wives to be
submissive to their husbands and sympathetic to their needs. But teenage girls with a different conception of girlhood than adults (especially
men) broke curfew, socialized with disreputable friends, engaged in sex,
and generally gave their parents a "hard time." Some girls even disregarded
the power of the police who picked them up and charged them with status crimes, that is, offenses that are regarded as criminal only because of
the age of the offender.[137] In an effort to correct girls' behavior that adults
did not like, social guidance movies like *You and Your Family* (1946) encouraged daughters to collaborate with parents instead of quarreling with
them.[138] In that film, Mary was urged to develop a notion of girlhood that
parents could find acceptable. Instead of being defiant, she sought parental
permission to invite her boyfriend and other friends to the house where
they could play the radio, dance, and eat sandwiches.

But in popular movies of the period that reflected the anxious perceptions of adults, audacious girls unsympathetic to the worries of men often battled it out with hapless fathers.[139] In exaggerated representations of
postwar girlhood, teenagers typically disrespected their fathers' authority,
disregarded their place, and discounted their presence in the household.
In one newsreel depiction shown widely in 1945, a girl who monopo-
lized the telephone and took over the bathroom deflated and demoted her
dad.[140] In her survey of popular movies from the 1940s, American studies
scholar Ilana Nash found that "slangy, sarcastic, disobedient to authority,
aggressive, and determined" teenage girls steeped in their outwardly frivolous and self-indulgent youth culture continued to fluster fathers and ir-
ritate mature men, whose lives they disrupted in one way or another.[141]

Maddening teenage girls often befuddled fathers in the domestic comedies of the late 1940s.[142] The way in which babysitters stood for negative

conceptions of teenage girls is evident in the first motion picture about babysitting. In *Sitting Pretty* (1948), teenage girls rejecting requests to babysit aggravated Mr. King, whose panicked search for a last-minute sitter had been no more successful than his wife's weary efforts. But each girl he called put her own selfish pleasures above his priorities (dinner with the boss).[143] When one girl he called was not in, he slammed "the receiver down viciously," according to the screenplay by F. Hugh Herbert, a prolific writer and one of the architects of the teen girl stereotype. Through "clenched teeth" Mr. King asked another girl who also had turned him down if she could "go bowling some other night." After again slamming down the phone in frustration, Mr. King called yet another babysitter. But caring more about washing her hair than watching his kids, she would not babysit. In fact, she'd rather "drop dead."[144]

Finally, sixteen-year-old Ginger agreed, not because she liked babysitting but because she adored her boss. The double standard and early marriage were already reemerging as moral correctives to wartime sexual liberalism. But lingering male fantasies and fears about teenage girls' sexual agency found expression in the larger-than-life portrayal of Ginger. Projecting conflicts about what a girl could be onto Ginger made her into a silly sexual aggressor. She attempted to seduce Mr. King in the front seat of his car by audaciously waving her "pretty hands under his nose" and cooing.

> GINGER: I just did a new paint job on my nails. Like them, Mr. King?
> HARRY: They look fine.
> GINGER: I'm using a new perfume, too. It's called "Nuit d'Amour." That's French (romantic sigh)—means "Night of Love." (She practically spreads her palm under his nose) Like it?
> HARRY: (ribbing her) Oh, yes—keen. (Ginger snuggles up to him closer.)
> GINGER: (wistfully) Gosh, we're almost there. I wish you lived fifty miles away. . . ."[145]

Clearly aimed at eliciting laughter at her ludicrous seduction, the scene nevertheless spoke to underlying anxieties about the diminished authority of men, the ascendance of female youth, and what to do about it. The reorientation of gender roles and the reshaping of generational relations had left many men feeling vulnerable, especially to those on whom they depended if they wanted to advance their careers or enjoy their leisure.[146]

While satire is a "device that typically makes new ideas and social criticism seem less threatening and more palatable,"[147] the hostile humor found in postwar comedies also served to buttress male authority.

Visions of powerful females who threatened the authority of men abounded in the popular culture of the period. Especially in film noir, unsatisfied husbands succumbed to money-hungry women with immense sexual appetites.[148] Perceptions that teenage girls also traded care for cash—a vestige of the wartime V-Girl who had traded sex for stockings— contributed to a new description of babysitting in the popular culture as the "youngest" and "newest" profession.[149] The references related to more than the youthfulness of the work force, the prominence of the service occupation, and the title of a recent bobby-soxer movie. That prostitution was widely referred to as the "oldest" profession insinuated that babysitters commercialized intimate caring just as prostitutes did. It was a view of girlhood that troubled many an adult. "Sitter, Father Jailed," blazed the headline of the *San Francisco News* after a man left his wife and ten kids and ran off with sixteen-year-old Betty Joe Roberts, a "plump blonde sitter" described as an "accomplished siren despite her youth."[150]

Tapping undercurrents of anxiety about the autonomy of female adolescents in the face of male insecurity and social and sexual instability, Chicago's health commissioner warned parents to watch out for sitters who might carry syphilis and tuberculosis.[151] Nor was he alone in his warning. Others publicly imagined domineering teenage girls as destructive agents whose imperceptible assaults could devastate American men and their families. A doctor writing in *Good Housekeeping* issued similar cautions as the health commissioner. Be on the lookout, he warned, for babysitters "with a cough, cold, sore throat, skin eruption, or other obvious trouble."[152] As "protection against communicable diseases," a 1949 San Francisco ordinance was passed that required babysitters to be fingerprinted and to submit to a physical examination. Against the ordinance was the police chief, but only because he did not want to babysit the city's babysitters.[153]

Conclusion

Fleeing cities for the safety and security of the suburbs, young wives who spent their days cleaning, cooking, and caretaking had been eager to enjoy the fruit of their labor. But the heralded baby boom had been less cause for celebration than cause for consternation to many house-bound mothers who developed "cabin fever." In the years after the war experts had urged parents to enjoy their time out alone, but there simply were not enough sitters in suburbia to make that a reality. While preadolescent girls would no longer do as babysitters, their college-bound brothers looked good by comparison. It did not seem to matter that they were male. In fact, "responsible" boy sitters were even better than teenage girls, whose aggressive postwar push for social and sexual autonomy had made parent-employers, particularly males, uneasy. Shaped by a vestigial wartime culture that contributed to girls' ongoing redefinition of girlhood, teenagers became vocal critics of babysitting, the job that had become theirs whether they liked it or not. They protested the poor wages, the heaping on of housework, the lack of heat, and the overall threat to divest babysitting of its social dimensions. Girls launched unions, sometimes with the help of women (teachers and others) who supported their efforts and took pride in their accomplishments because they felt less conflicted about girls' new sense of girlhood.

But in the course of taking control over their own lives, teenage girls tapped a raw nerve. Male breadwinners charged with the duty to protect the family were finding it difficult to do so during the reconversion of the economy during the late 1940s. Female independence had become the object of men's anxieties about postwar social changes that threatened paternal authority. Feeling compelled to provide and protect a child-centered family, many young husbands on guard against babysitters felt increasingly threatened by teenage girls' autonomy, agency, and the authority they seemingly assumed over children, particularly poor Junior. These anxious fantasies about babysitters as demanding, adversarial workers who put their desired employment conditions on a par with parents' wishes reflected male fears and threatened masculine identity. Strapped by a shortage in sitters, men in particular felt squeezed between their need for a babysitter and their fear of her.

While disorderly teenage girls loomed large in the masculine imagination, babysitter unions in reality had been neither pervasive nor permanent. Moreover, they would not have been able to endure the conservative climate that would stifle union activities during the 1950s. The growing influence of domesticity—the ideology that proscribed female independence and prescribed feminine submission—would similarly have discouraged girls from organizing unions and others from joining them. Even *Calling All Girls*, the pioneering girls' magazine that had promoted girls' global awareness and career development during the war, soon changed its title to *Senior Prom*, signaling a significant shift in postwar girls' culture.[154]

Over time, male employers would be less likely to imagine teenage babysitters as belligerent bolsheviks and more likely to see them as irreverent "bobby-soxers." It would be a disconcerting perspective that their wives would also increasingly share as their sympathy for "bobby-soxer" babysitters began to ebb. As one man would soon observe, "The baby-sitter today provides a source of more indignant female conversation. . . ."[155] Flocking to the suburbs in even greater numbers, with large broods and high hopes, young parents in the 1950s would be distressed to find that just around the next block, there was an irrepressible babysitter who would rattle their nerves and shake the foundation of their suburban fantasy.

3

The Bobby-Soxer Babysitter

In an article entitled "Know Where You Stand with Your Sitter," *Better Homes and Gardens* magazine described young mothers out for the night, who often found themselves stealing "glances at the clock half-wishing they hadn't left home."[1] While many adults today look back longingly to the 1950s as a time when babysitters were both abundant and affable, that golden age of babysitters—and of girlhood—never existed, not even in the mind's eye of many postwar parent-employers. Rather than the militant, union-organizing babysitter, the figure that proved to be more noxiously persistent and pervasive was the more plentiful "bobby-soxer" babysitter who had first appeared as Ginger in the movie *Sitting Pretty* (1948).[2] Following her attempted seduction of Mr. King, Ginger hosted a party for friends at his home. Returning unexpectedly early, Mr. and Mrs. King found the "careless and irresponsible" teen whirling past them in the arms of a young man while other "jitterbugs" danced to the radio on full blast.[3]

This chapter examines the ways in which the figure of the bobby-soxer babysitter—the embodiment of postwar parents' expectations and anxieties about teenage girls—was shaped by constructions of gender and perceptions of girls' teen culture. While upwardly mobile middle-class employers hoped that teenage girls would practice domestic skills and develop maternal sensibilities according to the conservative postwar gender ideology, they harbored fears about reckless delinquents who messed up the household instead of maintaining it. During the 1950s the "bobby-soxer babysitter," who "raided the icebox and jitterbugged with the crowd, until Mommy and Daddy arrived after midnight to discover Junior sailing boats on the bathroom floor," dwelled in the imagination of middle-class adults anxious about the potential of teenage girls to disorder their living rooms and disrupt their lives.[4]

The "bobby-soxer babysitter" concealed another troubling reality: while the vast majority of teenage girls worked as babysitters, many felt as ambivalent about babysitting as did those before them. What differed among this generation of girls was not the nature of their grievances, nor decidedly different conceptions of girlhood, but their new forms of resistance. Unlike the previous generation of teenage girls that had produced manifestos, those in the 1950s devised an informal work culture that expressed their dissatisfactions by drawing upon the practices and principles of girls' culture. The second part of this chapter examines how teenage girls put to use the teen culture they shared with peers and not parents. Devising an innovative vocabulary, sitters expressed their dislike of the "supercharged" baby boomer "brats" they were hired to watch, the male "wadders" who ripped them off, and the stifling suburban "babyvilles" in which they lived.[5]

Gender and Generational Ideals: The Watchful Mother and Steady Sitter

In postwar America, young parents who had left cities for suburbs hoped to improve their standard of living and raise their social status. For many, upward mobility was made possible by the federal GI Bill, which enabled largely white veterans to receive low-interest mortgages on houses they could not otherwise have afforded. In addition to home ownership, the bill also provided for a federally funded college education program that enabled millions of veterans to get white-collar jobs in the rapidly expanding postwar economy. Not only did suburbanites construct homes, but they also built a way of life characterized by distinctive middle-class rhythms, patterns, and ideals learned from their neighbors and from idealized suburban families in the popular culture.[6]

While fathers were expected to be hard-working "breadwinners," mothers were prescribed to be "happy homemakers." For women, motherhood was to be a primary identity and home was the place over which they were to preside.[7] According to this newly constructed gender ideal, caring and cheerful mothers were to be emotionally responsive and psychologically engaged "seven days a week and 365 days in the year," explained the influential psychological theorist John Bowlby.[8] A staunch advocate of the mother/child bond, he maintained that the mothering of the nation's forty-six million babies born between 1944 and 1957 required "constant attention day and night."[9] Popularized psychological theories informed by Cold War perspectives had given shape to an ideology of domestic containment that prescribed mothers' crucial importance in child-centered child rearing. According to notions about good parenting during the Cold War, the "vigilant" mother sheltered her children from foreign ideas and foreigners.[10]

Yet beneath the glowing depictions of happy homemakers mothers felt anxious about the rigors of motherhood, the centrality of childhood, and the complexities of infant care. Fears that enemies might cause children harm led millions of couples to leave cities for the suburbs. Shortly after the war, popular magazines such as *Time, Newsweek,* and *Parents* had run sensationalized stories about sex crimes in major American cities. J. Edgar Hoover, director of the FBI, had fueled the national hysteria in 1947 with the publication of "How Safe Is Your Daughter?" *American Magazine* illustrated the article with an image of a giant dark hand grasping at girls fleeing on foot.[11] Reflecting shifting responses to new social realities, *Parents Magazine and Family Home Guide* also represented the suburban home as a place of possible danger. By providing parents with advice on how to achieve "peace of mind" while "out on the town," the premier child-rearing magazine may have aimed at allaying anxieties but actually stirred apprehensions.[12]

Articles such as "What a Baby Sitter Needs to Know" urged mothers to inform the babysitter about what her own children might be tempted to do in her absence. Tell the sitter if your three-year-old has a fascination with the gas stove. Tell the sitter where to find medical supplies, but make sure they are not within easy reach of your youngster. If your baby is in diapers, caution the sitter against putting pins within easy reach. Included in the advice about leaving emergency phone numbers for the police, fire department, doctor, and pharmacist was a new tone of urgency. Mothers were told not to forget to tell the sitter to sterilize the bottles and nipples so as to eliminate the unseen threat of insidious microbes that might also wipe out the family.[13]

While new disinfectants in the postwar housewives' arsenal and recent vaccines diminished mothers' worries about childhood diseases, just how were they to guard against sick sitters? Postwar parents increasingly worried not only about the personality problems that they might cause in their own children but also about the psychologically unbalanced babysitter they might hire. While just a few years back experts had focused on sitters' physical illnesses as a symptom of female power, in 1952 a judge warned parents about the dangers of mental diseases. After hearing a case against a disturbed babysitter, he cautioned mothers not to entrust their children "to just anyone."[14] While this babysitter was a 38-year-old married woman, parents were nevertheless urged to consider the psychological stability of other babysitters whose crimes had just begun to appear in newspapers. Though very few stories about criminal sitters had appeared before, within a year of the judge's prophetic warning, the *New York Times* reported that a seventeen-year-old, twice-married former stripper had taken off with the five-month-old baby boy she had been babysitting.[15] Even more frightening was the story about a sixteen-year-old babysitter who strangled an infant in its sleep and another about a "blond baby-sitter" charged with the murder of a three-year-old she tied to a crib and struck with a beer bottle.[16] The newspaper clippings that illustrated the sensationalistic magazine article—"The Baby Sitter, a New and Baffling American Problem"—described "unstable teenagers" and their heinous deeds. Photographs of teenaged babysitters reinforced the collage of bold headlines and magazine copy about those who had slain, strangled, or brutally beaten children in their care or who had splurged on the loot they stole from unsuspecting parent-employers.[17]

Fear-inspiring stories about the dangers that babysitters posed to American families appeared in a small number of new fictional works as well. Jackie, the working-class teenager in the detective novel *Baby Sitter* (1952), fell in love with her male employer, killed his child, and ended up in a psychiatric institution.[18] But the novel *Mischief* (1950), another story about a crazy sitter, reached a far wider audience when it was adapted to the screen as *Don't Bother to Knock* (1952). In the film version, Marilyn Monroe starred as Nell, a dangerously demented former mental patient who babysat for a little girl in a hotel where her uncle worked. Nell was joined in the hotel room by a man-on-the-make whom she believed was her lover who had not been killed in a plane accident after all. As Nell unraveled psychologically, she threatened the little girl in her care, hit her uncle for berating and belittling her, and eventually accused the man she imagined to be her lover of sexual molestation. While Nell's coverups led to further dissembling and greater danger for the little girl, justice prevailed when Nell got nabbed.

The movie, along with other sitter stories, kindled fears about the dangerous inclinations of teenage girls. Though there were not a lot of such stories published during the 1950s, sensational tales nevertheless led experts to advise that finding a "reliable" and "responsible" sitter would require careful selection, presitting interviews, and trial runs (such as having the sitter assist at a birthday party). *Cosmopolitan* urged mothers to ask for references from teachers and doctors. "Then check those references," the article strongly urged. "Her doctor may tell you that for reasons he cannot fully divulge, he feels that Doris wouldn't, er, be the best person you could get."[19] In an article published in the *San Francisco Examiner*, Dr. W. W. Baur, director of the Bureau of Health and Education for the American Medical Association, explained that because the "baby sitter can have a very real impact on the health of the children for whom she is asked to care and upon the happiness of the family, [the] choice of a babysitter should not be made casually or carelessly." Several years later he issued further warnings about the risk of babysitters who spread germs.[20] Whether it appeared as the first or final word of caution presented by experts, mothers were urged to thoroughly check references before they hired a sitter.[21]

In order to insure against disease and disaster, the "steady sitter" emerged as the postwar babysitter ideal. Drawing upon dominant notions of girlhood, the exemplary "steady sitter" pledged her exclusivity, reliability, and accessibility to one family, just as the ideal girl promised herself to one beau. The new dating ritual of "going steady" with one guy (as opposed to dating many during the previous decades) was also derivative of the postwar standard: it was based on middle-class notions of marriage and the security and safety it was meant to insure.[22] The construct of the "steady sitter" served to calm adults' anxious fears about the potential for disorder, disruption or, at worst, the disaster caused by teenage girls who hired themselves out and sometimes messed things up.

Imagining "Bobby-Soxer" Babysitters

"Few parents want a sitter from a social situation remote from their own," *Hygeia* magazine observed about suburban couples living in newly developed class-stratified communities.[23] The importance placed on being middle-class led parents to prefer to hire girls who shared their values and respected their routines. But just as adult suburbanites cast aside their working-class past in their movement upward into the middle class, teenage girls incorporated the music, fashions, dance, vernacular speech, values, attitudes (e.g., defiance, spontaneity), and other aspects of lower-class cultural practices into their teen culture.[24] These seemingly new-fangled characteristics of teenage girlhood provoked anxiety in adults, who expected babysitters to model femininity by nurturing children and reinforcing gender norms for girls and boys. While parents endeavored to raise their children according to the prevailing gender ideals that characterized the middle class, it did not strike them that girls steeped in teen culture necessarily shared their expectations.[25] Taking care of baby boomers required the kind of authority that parents believed teenage girls now possessed. But that girls might not know their own strength made parents worry that this new breed might be more than they bargained for. Instead of practicing thrift, girls indulged in excess; instead of respecting decorum, girls reveled in caprice. Indeed, it seemed as if girls were violating the beliefs, behaviors, and boundaries that adults held dear.

Parent-employers generally anxious about family and the future perceived babysitters through a distorted lens of preconceived notions about teenage girls. While scouting and summer camps promised to socialize children to be well adjusted and socialized, parents—even those who had themselves recently left adolescence for adulthood—saw antisocial teenage girls as a threat to the suburban sanctuary.[26] Tapping postwar parent-employers' fears about the potential dangers to family life was the omnipresence of the badly behaved babysitter. Adults might easily have concluded that the many offenses girls allegedly committed while babysitting were everyday events.

The behavior that disturbed adults the most occurred in the suburban home: the bedrock of the "American dream" for the upwardly mobile postwar generation. When girls disrupted the security of their suburban refuge—as with babysitters' indiscriminate use of their telephone—parent-employers grew understandably distressed. Though the Bell Telephone Company had recently begun to promote phone use by advertising in *Seventeen*, *American Girl*, and *Calling All Girls*, from the vantage point of parent-employers, girls who engaged in selfish "gab fests" hardly needed the encouragement.[27] Didn't sitters realize that parents phoning home might be alarmed by an unremitting busy signal? And didn't jabbering girls know that the telephone was not exactly free? Although a 1957 survey would show that only 16 percent of girls actually talked on the telephone, *Life* magazine reported that the indulgences of one sitter who cost her employer dearly represented the many.[28] "A Los Angeles mother lost her telephone for two years because she could not pay the long-distance bill run up by a sitter."[29] These stories reinforced employers' perceptions that teenage babysitters were self-indulgent, not selfless.

In addition to running up the phone bill, girls were also known to raid refrigerators. To adults who had suffered fifteen years of deprivation, girls' jaunty disregard of the value of food was hard to stomach.[30] As the new iconographic center of the American home purchased by millions, the "freezer" promoted by advertisers served as a fortification against the troubles of the world beyond the home.[31] A full refrigerator provided the assurance that nourishment would always be within easy reach, and so an emptied one left many adults feeling queasy.[32] Because food represented security, plenty, and freedom from want, it bothered adults that sitters consumed their "bobby-soxer staples," then cavalierly left "Coke bottles" on the living-room floor.[33] According to one irritated male employer, not only did fifteen-year-old Betty Ann consume an entire batch of cookies, but adding gall to gluttony, she also left a note suggesting that "[r]aisins would help these a lot" and "flavoring could be less subtle."[34]

While insatiable sitters were believed to devour the family's food supply, irreverent ones showed little respect for the other consumer goods that were important markers of middle-class success to adults.[35] In the continuing shift from prewar saving to postwar spending, middle-class adults with many unfulfilled material desires purchased entertainment systems along with other newly available household luxuries that symbolized "the good life." By purchasing radios, phonographs, television sets, other appliances, and furnishings, Americans drove up consumer spending by 60 percent during the 1950s.[36] While there is no way of quantifying the cultural meanings of materialism, commodities carried special significance to those in the process of replacing an ethos of self-denial with one of self-fulfillment.[37] Because the U.S. government also promoted the notion that consumerism symbolized the superiority of American democracy over Soviet communism, consumer goods were believed to strengthen families and reinforce parents' sense of themselves as providers.[38] For fathers, a household packed with goods was a material indication of manly success while for wives, household commodities rewarded domestic labors and justified part-time employment.[39] Consumerism was also a means by which adults attained their individuality, leisure, and upward social mobility.[40] Appreciating how "precious" father's "hi-fi" was to him, *Miss America*, a quarterly magazine for girls, advised babysitters to "[b]e sure you know how to use the phonograph correctly."[41]

To girls, their employers' possessions were not hard-won achievements symbolizing personal success but instead were useful for the reception and transmission of teen culture. In fact, since the 1920s, girls who had been singing, dancing, and discussing various musical styles with their friends had exasperated parents, teachers, and school administrators who had tried to contain access to popular music and to limit its excess. Music was a central aspect of girls' peer culture also objected to by the adults for whom girls worked.[42] Recall that when Ginger the babysitter blasted the radio in the movie *Sitting Pretty* (1948), her employers got upset that she had temporarily turned their home into a "jive hall."[43] She had invited over a bunch of friends, who rolled back the living room carpet in order to jitterbug.[44] On the front cover of *Baby Sitter* (1952), published several years after the movie, one teenage couple worked the record player, another slow danced, and a third pair smooched. In this "Shocking Story of Teen-agers in Search of Secret Thrills," the male narrator explained, "Some of these kids made a party out of their sitting jobs, gathering their friends and keeping the neigh-bors on edge with the blaring of the radio and their screaming laughter."[45]

Throwing parties had been a typical activity among teenage girls, ac-cording to a study conducted by *Seventeen* magazine.[46] "Many a fond parent has come home to find the cute little high school girl entertaining a group of boy friends," reported the *Boston Globe*.[47] One employer found his sitter sound asleep in the arms of her boyfriend, explained *The Saturday Evening Post*. After the two had spent an exhausting evening "cutting the rug," the baby's unheeded screams had failed to wake them from their slumber.[48] Along with other publications, *Business Week* reported that an ex-Marine and his wife returned home from an evening out to find their youngster teething on marbles and their teenage babysitter entertaining friends.[49] By 1953 adults declared teen parties to be an "American headache" despite the production of *What Makes a Good Party?* (1950).[50] That social guid-ance movie intended to teach teenage girls about how to plan a party that was decent, not dangerous.[51] But that movie and similar prescriptive works had not stopped girls from throwing parties without adult approval.[52]

Though teenage parties probably occurred more often in parent-em-ployers' heads than in their homes, they nevertheless believed that girls were living it up, not "settling down."[53] After all, Ginger had said as much in her generational declaration: "Golly, a person would go absolutely mad with nothin' to do but sit!"[54] A high school girl in Brookline, Massachu-setts, who also invited five of her friends over while babysitting, similarly explained, "It's too dull sitting all alone all evening."[55] Postwar parents who sought security and stability believed that by transforming the living room into a dance hall, bobby-soxer babysitters were trampling on middle-class standards and feminine ideals. In an effort to ameliorate teenage girls, even the makers of sanitary napkins encouraged female adolescents to exert greater control over their behavior and bodies. Beneath an illustration of a teenage party, a Kotex ad rhetorically asked, "What's smart strategy for 'baby-sitting'?" "Be a stand-in for his Mom?" or "Ask your gang over?"[56]

Whether girls invited boys over while babysitting or not, most teens were not nearly as wild as many adults at the time imagined them to be. Like teenagers before them, who also lacked access to legal abortion or birth control, those in the fifties constructed rules and regulations about "dating" (e.g., "going steady") that were more conventional than most adults realized.[57] Nevertheless, adults suspected teenage girls of de-fying sexual standards and threatening the code that restricted sexual passion to heterosexual marriage. Contributing to public anxiety about

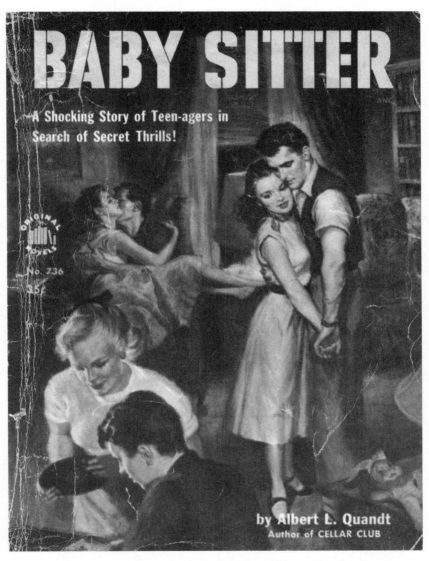

BABY SITTER

A Shocking Story of Teen-agers in Search of Secret Thrills!

ORIGINAL NOVELS

No. 236
35¢

by Albert L. Quandt
Author of CELLAR CLUB

Tapping Cold War anxieties about the safety of the nuclear family was the babysitter who allegedly threw raucous parties, used the telephone indiscriminately, ran raids on the refrigerator, and made liberal use of fathers' "precious hi-fi." Cover, *Baby Sitter*, by Albert L. Quandt.

female adolescent sexuality was the increasing sexualization of American popular and commercial culture, which not only influenced images of teenage girls but also affected how they presented themselves. Girls' exploratory performances of their sexual identities relied on the props of young womanhood. But to adults, all the bright red lipstick, nail polish, tight sweaters, high heels, and padded bras were presumptive evidence that teenage girls were having sex—and possibly while babysitting.

The "Billion-Dollar Night Out": Masculinity and Money

In its jaded assessment, *Newsweek* wryly described babysitting as "[o]ur billion-dollar night out."[58] From the perspective of hard-working white-collar fathers whose job it was to provide for the family in the midst of postwar inflationary anxieties, the problem posed by teenagers was also financial. Contributing to an impression that emerged during the late 1940s, teenage girls were understood to exploit a paternal obligation and commercialize a maternal virtue. That the average girl spent lots of "dough" on records, clothing, cosmetics, and other teen staples was proof to many adults that teenage girls were more avaricious than altruistic.[59] Critical of girls' economic motivation to babysit and contemptuous of their profligate habits of spending, some employers (including more wives) disparaged babysitters.

Take Diane, who was "small for her age, but surprisingly mature—at least where money was concerned. She loved the stuff. The merest hint of bonus pay, and Diane would break her date and appear at our door, urging us to depart early and stay late."[60] Diane's rankled employers imagined her "sitting on our sofa and ticking like a taxi meter." They thought it only fitting that, when the girl went off to college, she majored in accounting.[61] Yet Diane was a bargain compared to the three babysitters who posed for *Time* and *Newsweek* bedecked in recently purchased clothing and jewelry. Unlike most sitters, who earned their money, these three had stolen eighteen thousand dollars from a home safe in a Boston, Massachusetts, suburb while babysitting. Simply "ravenous for excitement" the trio then traveled to New York City, where they indulged in a "surrealistic shopping spree" before they were picked up by the police and photographed by reporters from national periodicals.[62] Other irresponsible sitters were also indulgent. In a cartoon that appeared in the *San Francisco News*, a little girl talking into the phone says, "Is it important enough to wake up the baby sitter, Dad? She's asleep and Tommy and I are making candy!"[63]

For beleaguered husbands, the cost of a babysitter was just another item that went into a "night on the town." One Seattle, Washington, businessman lamented, "It costs about $5 for a couple to attend a movie. Two 94-cent tickets with all the taxes, parking expense, cup of coffee or dish of ice cream and then the baby-sitter."[64] While house-bound wives, who were "sick and tired of being cooped up," looked forward to a night out, husbands who made the daily commute be-tween suburb and city yearned to put their feet up and relax at night. Trying to "keep up with the Joneses," many hard-working men who in-creasingly saw the suburbs as a gendered "battleground" were increas-ingly out of sync with their families. As a result, men's psychological expenditures got bundled into the financial costs that they figured in-cluded everything from their wives' visit to the beauty parlor to paying for the sitter's taxi ride home. While he'd rather be going to bed after a long day at the office and a night on the town than "walking a strange girl over to the other side of town and walking home again himself," the cost of a taxi jacked up the total even further.[65]

Tipping the balance in father's favor, *Look* magazine printed a satirical version of babysitter pay rates that mocked sitters' enumerations.

Since the United Auto Workers' stipend varies according to the cost of liv-ing, it is only reasonable that the basic rate for babysitting should vary in accordance with prevailing circumstances. A practical father-viewed pay-ment schedule, which takes these circumstances into account, follows:

Base rate with television	75 cents per hour
Base rate, without television	85 cents per hour
Late snack left out on kitchen table	65 cents per hour
Refrigerator privileges:	
(a) Partial selectivity	60 cents per hour
(b) Unrestricted selectivity	50 cents per hour
Dozing-off permitted	65 cents per hour
No dozing	85 cents per hour
Thermostat accessible	70 cents per hour
Thermostat inaccessible	80 cents per hour and up
Telephone privileges (local calls only)	50 cents per hour
Permission to bring date along	25 cents per hour
Date provided by employer	Sitting free
(Credit allowed on future jobs, depending on date)[66]	

While intending to be humorous, the payment parody revealed the prominence of the breadwinner's ethic as well as a hint of sexual prerogative. The scale expressed men's economic concerns and anxious misgivings about teenage girls perceived as more controlling than accommodating.

In 1954 *The Saturday Evening Post* devoted yet another one of its magazine covers to a babysitter allegedly at work.[67] Unlike previous ones, "Babysitter at Beach Stand" by the illustrator George Hughes portrayed an adolescent in an eye-catching fuchsia bathing suit, babysitting at a beach instead of in her customary place indoors. The unusual display of her bronze body was a sign of increasing male interest and unease about the expanding boundaries of girls' sexual autonomy that would burst at the seams over the following decades. (See chapter six.) In every other way, though, the brightly colored picture told the same familiar story about adult male disdain of self-absorbed teenage girls. This sitter, who stood for others, was getting greater pleasure from a bottle of soda than the little girl she was hired to watch. Although one hand on the handle of the baby buggy kept it within arm's reach, her eyes were momentarily shut as she sensuously sipped the soda. As she put her own pleasures before the baby's, the middle-aged male soda jerk, whose disdainful gaze viewers shared, was forced into the role of babysitter. With one arm akimbo and the other on a pan handle, he boiled the baby's bottle on the grill along with the row of broiled hot dogs that looked as succulent as the sitter's tanned limbs.

Bratting in Babyville: The Girl-Centered View

"For my girlfriends and I . . . baby sitting was probably the no. 1 job," explained Carolyn Passalqua.[68] State laws passed by well-intentioned progressives during the early 1900s had long forbidden the employment of girls under the age of eighteen in "street trades," where they had predominated during the 1800s. By the 1950s, that meant that in states like Wisconsin, newspaper delivering was for boys only.[69] Although allowances had become more widespread among eleven- to eighteen-year-old girls, a nation-wide study conducted by the Girl Scouts revealed that only about one-third of "older girls" received money from their parents.[70] As a result, in places like Iowa, three-quarters of the six hundred high school girls who participated in a 1951 survey worked as babysitters.[71] By 1957, *Life* magazine would report that 48 percent of America's 7.9 million teenage girls were babysitters.[72]

Babysitting sat at the center of the female adolescent experience, but to many girls in postwar America, the job hardly seemed worth it. That American teenage girls supposedly earned an estimated $670 million annually from babysitting must have sounded impressive to those who read the cover story about "The Profession of Babysitting" published in *Life* magazine in 1957.[73] But because most sitters only earned between thirty-five and fifty-five cents per hour (except for those who worked in a number of select cities like New York), most simply had to save if they wanted to shop.[74] Adults who saw girls as money hungry misunderstood sitters' economy of scale. For example, Liz Wilson saved the money she earned in order to shop for the things she wanted, as did other sitters who wanted "a spring suit, a special dress for the big dance, records, even a trip."[75] They had no choice but to buy desirables, like cashmere sweater sets, on lay-away.[76] Not only did teenage girls save, but they also spent with care. That was the case because the prices charged for girls' goods did not "fit the 'minding baby' salaries and allowances," one girl's mother explained in a sympathetic letter to *Seventeen*.[77]

Though many critics cast a wary eye on American girls for "wasting" their money on records, clothing, Cokes, candy, trinkets, and magazines, many in the business world had already realized that girls were savvy consumers.[78] They understood not only that girls knew what they wanted but also that the purchasing power of teenage girls was often based on sound decision making and financial planning.[79] *Seventeen* played an instrumental role in shaping an age- and gender-segmented consumer market that increased girls' consumer power and cultural clout.[80] Working closely with clothing and cosmetics manufacturers, the magazine shared vital information about adolescent desires, opinions, tastes, and habits.[81] These data then contributed to the availability of fads and fashions that circulated around high schools and contributed to the burgeoning of teen culture and the evolving notion of girlhood that valued autonomy and empowerment.[82]

While adults judged babysitters according to dominant gender ideals, it was girls' culture that framed female adolescents' attitudes about babysitting. The girl-centered teen culture of the era taught female adolescents to be more than just smart consumers in the marketplace.[83] Girls shared with each other the importance of labor market equality. When a somewhat older teenage Sylvia Plath wrote, "As a Baby-Sitter Sees It" for the *Christian Science Monitor* in 1951, she offered "a few bits of advice" about the disagreeable job that demanded diligence but paid in pennies.[84] After working six days a week as a "live-in babysitter" one summer for a well-to-do family in Massachusetts, the college sophomore urged babysitters to "make sure just what jobs you will be required to do in addition to caring for the children. In this way you won't be imposed upon by an employer who thinks you might just as well wash dishes after her dinner parties, and bake and iron for her as well as for the children."[85] In her more candid private correspondence to her mother over the summer, eighteen-year-old Sylvia more disparagingly described babysitting as "Slave labor."[86]

In her derisive quantitative assessment of babysitting as degraded labor, a fifteen-year-old babysitter from California shed further light on the everyday complaints of ordinary babysitters in *Calling All Girls*, one of the leading girls' magazines of the era.

Number of children to be taken care of	3
Ages of the little dears	3, 5, & 7
Time parents leave	8:00
Time first quarrel begins	8:01
Time children are supposed to go to bed	8:30
Time they actually go to bed	9:27
Time they go to sleep	11:49
Number of trips they make to the bathroom	35
Numbers of drinks of water	42
Numbers of times the light goes on and off in the bedroom	58
Time parents are supposed to return	11:30
Time they actually return	12:13
Minutes spent studying	12
Grade earned on test next day	D
Amount of money earned	$2.30
Amount of money received	$1.50
Amount of money expended:	
For bus fare to house	$.10
For cleaning dress Patty got her bubble gum on	$1.27
For aspirin	$.10
Total	$1.47
Net profit	$.03 [87]

A survey of sitters conducted around the same time revealed similar dissatisfactions. Such was especially the case when sitters were expected to undertake household tasks and also care for additional children at no extra pay.[88]

While adults at the time criticized girls for their "lack of interest in jobs that required commitment," they failed to acknowledge all the many little things that parent-employers themselves did and did not do that undermined the dedication of babysitters.[89] Sitters' complaints—covering nearly every aspect of their employment—began with the hasty retreat of their employers, which often set the stage for a sitting disaster. For example, after Mrs. Snow greeted Sylvia Plath during her first sitting job, showed her the living room, and gave her "a few hurried instructions," she "dashed out the door and was gone!" Sylvia was left to wonder, "Where, oh *where* were the children?" Neither Mrs. Snow nor her husband had even bothered to introduce the sitter to their three- and five-year-old sons.[90] Suggesting just how common this practice was, the National Safety Council manual for babysitters recommended that parents tell the children that they are leaving and introduce the sitter "BEFORE MRS. X LEAVES."[91] But as one girl with considerable babysitting experience explained at the time, "[a]ny sitter knows that it is common practice for parents to try to slip out of the house without letting the children know they are leaving. The explanation they make to the sitter is that they want to prevent a scene. (The scene comes when the children discover the deception and vent their outrage on the poor sitter!)" [92] For thirteen-year-old Helen Harbison of Princeton, New Jersey, the problem was not the rushed leave taking but the late home coming. She sarcastically suggested to those new to the field that they "[l]isten carefully to the parents but don't believe them if they tell you they will be home by eleven."[93]

In addition to inconsiderate employers, incorrigible children also aggravated babysitters. "The baby sitting business is a dangerous and often difficult way to earn money," continued Helen in a school essay published in *Bookshelf*, a YWCA publication.[94] She advised girls to "[n]ever accept a job baby sitting for a small boy until you have seen how tall and strong he is, how sharp his teeth are, and whether he wears glasses."[95] While delightful children surely made babysitting more of a pleasure than a pain, the challenges many girls faced managing unruly kids led Helen also to forewarn sitters to "[f]inish all your homework before reporting for duty. Never have the innocent thought that you will be able to study."[96] That was the case because instead of "sitting in a warm, comfortable living room listening to the radio, reading, and earning money at the same time while the small charges slumber[ed] peacefully, the children began slugging it out on the living-room floor," explained another sitter.[97] Just after this sitter pried apart the four boys and two dogs, she got a call from her employer asking whether things were "all right." "Oh, sure," she panted, "everything is under control."[98]

Though the National Safety Council publication entitled its pamphlet *You're in Charge*, in movies, comics, and cartoons of the period bratty boys undermined babysitters' authority.[99] In the Paramount Pictures cartoon *The Babysitter*, Little Lulu got a job taking care of a rambunctious little boy who knocked her out while resisting a nap.[100] In her unconscious state, Lulu dreamed that she had to chase the baby downtown to "The Stork Club," a society club for glamorous youth, where she eventually trapped and subdued the little rogue. The single coin she received at the end of her anxious escapade was meant to be comical. But to real girls there was nothing funny about being underpaid, overworked, and worked over. Thus, a decade later, Little Lulu came to the aid of another sitter, a young witch in a comic book. Despite her magical powers the baby boy commandeered her wand, shrunk her, and then ballooned into a giant. The inversion spoke to the anxiety that anyone would feel having to care for a big bad boy like that.[101]

While in 1953 the Institute of Life Insurance predicted that the rising population of teenagers would create "more rivalry" among the nation's babysitters, they had failed to factor girls' ambivalences into their actuarial tables.[102] Among girls, the term "babysitting" was not an accurate description of their social reality. While babysitting implied that it was easy enough to do while resting in a warm, comfortable chair, in reality, the term hid the hard work, just as a "labor of love" disguised rather than described motherhood. Knowing how to care for an infant according to prevailing methods minimally required that "the sitter knows how to pick up a baby, how to change him, where the diapers are, where the baby's bottle of sterile water is kept, how it should be warmed, how to cover the baby so there is no danger of suffocation. If a bottle of milk is to be given, she must know the procedure—the warming of the bottle, adjusting of nipple, how to get up bubbles of gas and so on."[103] Just how hard it could be was revealed on the front cover of a 1947 issue of *The Saturday Evening Post*, not at all typical of Norman Rockwell's other homey depictions of American family life. This one captured not only the anxious parental gaze but also the depths of sitter distress.[104] The colorful picture suggested that the young babysitter had expected to spend the evening doing her American history homework. But she never got a chance to crack open her textbook because the "big brutal boy" she was babysitting had been utterly inconsolable. The disheveled sitter had tried everything, but the baby's bottle was as useless as the babysitting manual.[105]

The poor reputation of bratty boys among neighborhood babysitters was the reason why Mrs. King, the mother of three in the movie *Sitting*

You're in Charge

. . . . . and in charge of a priceless possession when you act as a "Baby Sitter." The job is a big challenge, but fun, too, especially when you know the hows of keeping safe and happy these active youngsters who so eagerly explore the world about them.

Babysitters of "baby boomers" rarely felt as if they were as "in charge" as is this idealized sitter on the cover of the first manual for babysitters published in postwar America. The National Safety Council, *You're in Charge.* Reprinted courtesy of the National Safety Council.

This bedraggled babysitter, who appeared on the cover of *The Saturday Evening Post* in 1947, expressed the anxieties of postwar parents as well as the frustrations of babysitters. *The Saturday Evening Post*, 1947, cover. Printed by permission of the Norman Rockwell Family Agency. Copyright © 1947 Norman Rockwell Family Entities.

"PERSONALLY, I *LIKE* TO SIT WITH HIM. HIS FOLKS HAVE TO PAY DOUBLE IN ORDER TO GET ANYONE."

The girls in this cartoon exemplified the saucy and sassy babysitter parents imagined. Dennis the Menace personified the baby boomer "brat" about whom sitters frequently complained. *The Babysitter's Guide to Dennis the Menace.* 1954. Dennis the Menace © North America Syndicate.

Pretty (1948), had been turned down by "15 of the little darlings" she had called to babysit before her husband had taken over the task. No one wanted to babysit for her brood of bad boys. Nor did the independent and empowered teenage star of the sit-com *My Little Margie* want to babysit for the mischievous boy she referred to as the "little demon" and "young monster."[106] Yet, no one better represented a humorous critique of the undisciplined, impulsive, and unbounded baby boomer than Dennis the Menace, "The All-American Handful."[107] Even in *The Babysitter's Guide by*

Dennis the Menace (1954), the purported youthful author had the gall to provide teenage girls with advice on how to babysit.[108] That "aggravating, tyrannical, towheaded" boy personified in the extreme the middle-class suburban male baby boomer reared in a child-centered home.[109] In the manual's many cartoons, a mischievous, rambunctious, sneaky, tricky, playful, aggressive, condescending, and bossy Dennis intimidated babysitters. But in other cartoons, they were ready to clobber the miscreant. Some sitters simply walked off the job in exasperation. One proudly quipped that his parents "pay double in order to get anyone."

The phrase "sitting pretty," which frequently appeared in magazine articles, in babysitting manuals, and as titles of vocational films, more accurately reflected adults' conflicted attitudes about girls. While on the one hand the term encompassed the expectations that girlhood should consist of leisure, femininity, and domesticity, on the other, it reflected the adult assumption that girls in postwar America were privileged, pampered, entitled, and vain.[110] But from the vantage point of teenage girls in fiction and in fact, few actually spent their evenings enriched, in repose, or in control. The way sitters saw it, "The sittees between the ages of 3 and 10 usually see the sitter as a fascinating antagonist, gifted with more energy and less authority than parents, and fair game for harassing."[111] To seventeen-year-old Phyllis Church, babysitting was "not just a matter of sipping cokes and watching television while the children slumber. I once found myself with 14 supercharged children on my hands for a whole afternoon. (Several parents had pooled their children. I got a 15-cent bonus.)"[112] According to *The Saturday Evening Post*, most sitters did not mind the commotion. "A good brisk crisis makes them feel useful, important and necessary, and they rather enjoy it."[113] Not so for six hundred Iowa girls who worked as babysitters. The third most common explanation for why they turned down requests to babysit was that the children were "too ornery." Moreover, nearly half of eleventh and twelfth graders agreed with the survey statement, "When I have something else to do, I never baby sit."[114]

Girls' Culture and Work Culture

Rather than engaging their employers in dialogue, as had sitters in the 1940s, girls in the 1950s shared their dislikes with each other.[115] Their peer-based youth culture provided girls with opportunities to process employment experiences and prepare for future ones as babysitters. Common cultural experiences among teenage girls fostered a subculture not

shared with those outside their peer group.[116] Though channels of communication between girls other than through magazines remain largely
undocumented, it is clear that babysitters at midcentury shared customary values that enabled them to manage the limitations of their job, as
well as to make the most out of its possibilities.[117] Rather than organizing
unions, though, girls devised a variety of cultural practices that enabled
them to resist the constraints of their job, as well as adapt to them.[118]
Babysitters' tactical knowledge, derived from banks of generational skills,
enabled them to do as they pleased while staying under the radar of authority figures.[119]

Among the encrypted methods sitters devised to cope with employment challenges was their use of slang, the argot that had been developed
by generations of girls in order to circumvent authority and prohibitions.[120]
During the 1950s, sitters used slang with each other in order to refer to
employers who did not measure up to girls' ideal of a fair exchange. Using
terms with a shared system of meanings that excluded adults from understanding, babysitters could freely critique their employers. For instance, sitters disparaged those bosses who were "hour splitters," gypping girls out of
a fair wage by not rounding off their earnings to the next hour. Girls also applied the disdainful term "wadders" to describe male employers in particular who looked the other way as they "pressed a tight little wad of bills fur-
tively into their hands as if it were something nasty that shouldn't be seen
or talked about."[121] Girls did not like babysitting for adults they dubbed "the
Oaf," and "the Lord of the manor, his lady, Mrs. Fusspot, and Old Mr. I'll-
Sit-With-the-Sitter."[122] In retaliation against "tight-wad" employers who did
not leave snacks, sitters engaged in military-inspired "raids" on "fridges."[123]

"Bratting," the slang word girls contrived for babysitting itself, was
more than a form of employment: it was a blunt indictment of postwar
parents and the kinds of "permissive" child-rearing methods promoted by
their mentor, Dr. Spock. Because too many middle-class suburban parents
"caved in" instead of "following through," a generation of "brats" had been
born, explained a seventeen-year-old sitter who criticized parental incon-
sistency and hypocrisy in the magazine article "If I Were a Parent."[124] Instead of referring to themselves as "sitters," girls cynically called themselves
"bratters."[125] This term was used because undisciplined "brats" overran the
places girls caustically dubbed "babyville." In "Toddlerville" (Levittown,
Long Island), where toddlers outnumbered teenagers, there were sixty
playgrounds and "wading pools galore," recalled one sitter, as unhappy as
many with the communities that provided teens no place to "hang out."[126]

While youth in the fifties had more leisure time than previous generations, they also had less privacy in the suburban homes constructed with the needs of younger children in mind. Consequently, teenagers' recreation often took place outside of their homes and away from their families.[127] But because girls lacked the mobility available to boys, babysitting had the potential to provide hours of freedom away from their own family and the watchful eyes of other disapproving adults. If all went well and the brats were quiet, the babysitter could invite a friend to join her and the neighbor's home could become theirs for the night. There they could engage in the kind of imaginative, spontaneous, and unstructured recreation that was characteristic of girls' play.[128] Although sitters also knew that inviting girlfriends and boyfriends to join them while babysitting was frowned upon, some did it anyway. Most behaved themselves, as did Betty, a self-described "good girl," who accepted the conventional path laid out for females in the fifties. But some of her girlfriends challenged the paradox of postwar feminine ideals that prescribed teen matrimony and proscribed premarital sexuality. Not only would they invite their boyfriends over while babysitting, but "they even got into bed with them."[129] Far more typical were adolescent girls like Louise, who recalled, "A few times my boyfriend 'sat' with me. We watched the movie and necked."[130]

Conclusion

There was a lot that teenage girls in the fifties did not like about their "No. 1 job." Sitters' complaints began with their employers' exit but did not end with their return: some bosses did not even drive babysitters home.[131] In response to the problems girls routinely faced, they devised subcultural responses that made sense to them but not to adults. For ordinary girls with proto-feminist notions, their cultural practices enabled them to express dissent about employment practices they did not like. While adults perceived sitters as dangerous, in fact, work culture probably defused girls' subversion more than it ignited it. More likely than not, girls' griping about parent-employers siphoned off their rebellious impulses and stymied any real antisocial behavior.[132]

But that was not how adults imagined the bobby-soxer sitter who generated anxiety by undermining security. While trying to live the "American dream," parents encountered a nightmarish incubus—the female adolescent babysitter who flocked by night, undermining stability by disordering the suburban home.[133] Experts maintained that the babysitter was "a strong force for happiness and stability in family life today," whereas to parent-employers, bobby-soxer sitters were indeed a "strong force," but neither for "happiness" nor for "stability."[134] Though the *Boston Globe* optimistically reported that "Baby Sitters have given parents a new lease on life," many parents believed that "the supply of competent sitters is seldom equal to the demand."[135] What options were there for parent-employers frustrated with the bobby-soxers in their neighborhood?

4

Making Better Babysitters

In 1957, Jack Fletcher, a father and an engineer, climbed onto the roof of his suburban house in West Covina, California, in order to install a "closed circuit" camera. That device would at least enable his wife to watch on the TV their children playing outdoors while she ironed indoors.[1] What led to Jack's child-care innovation was a new reality—the scarcity of sitters—unforeseen by those riding the wave of suburban expansion. Many young couples like the Fletchers had not realized that what they had left behind in the move to the suburbs had been invaluable sources of child care. *Good Housekeeping* was among the many periodicals at the time that pointed out that for a great many—perhaps most—young couples there were no grandmothers and aunts who were regularly available to help out.[2] With active lives of their own, grandparents were increasingly declining requests to spend an evening with Junior and Jane.

In addition to grandparents, this chapter also examines other adults who posed problems for parents, such as the few household workers who frequented the postwar suburbs. "Maids" typically preferred to take care of the house rather than look after the kids. Mature women worked for recently established babysitter agencies, but parent-employers found them expensive and condescending. Parents also encountered more failure than success when trying to cooperate with each other as self-interested neighbors taking turns babysitting for little boomers. That was because neighborhood babysitting co-ops required a higher level of participation and a greater commitment than most adults were willing to make. The arithmetic of hours owed neighbors could get pretty complicated for parents in communities like Levittown, New York. And while magazines would portray co-op fathers and young males as superb sitters, not everyone was comfortable with male domesticity. Thus the cultural anthropologist Margaret Mead would observe that "[a] heavy responsibility falls on the two parents alone."[3]

Coming to the begrudging realization that adults could not be regularly relied upon to babysit, experts and educators set their sights on teenage

girls whose vocational education is also examined in this chapter. In order to make sitters more satisfactory, educators sought to channel teenage
girls' entitlement into professionalism. In an effort to purge the bobby-
soxer out of the babysitter, the subject of babysitting was inserted into
the curriculum of health and home economics courses from Connecticut
to California. Satisfied with the results of the new educational initiative,
Coronet magazine reported that no longer would fourteen-year-old June
"play dress-up in Madame's new outfit or eat the only jar of caviar in the
house."[4]

While educational experts sought to moderate girls' desire for autonomy
by elevating babysitting to the level of a professional "career," politicians
aimed to diminish babysitters' rights as workers. Along with attempts to
retrain girls vocationally, legislators' aimed to restrain babysitters legally. In
states like New York, politicians passed legislation that curtailed babysitters'
ability to seek legal penalties against "employers." By controlling the rights
of babysitters and containing their behavior as teenagers, politicians, educators, and others hoped to finally provide parents with girls who would not
abuse their authority and independence.

Not Such "Grand" Mothers

While generations of grandmothers had served as suitable stand-ins, extended family networks had been disrupted in the move from the city
to the suburbs.[5] In Orinda, California, the scarcity of grandparents and
"maiden aunts" posed a problem that few young suburbanites had considered in their flight from the extended family ties that many had found
both "stultifying and oppressive."[6] During the war a housing shortage had
forced six million married adults to share cramped quarters with their
parents and in-laws.[7] One typical Atlanta woman who lived with her in-
laws during the war objected to their interference with her child-rearing
methods.[8] The resulting family tensions and marital conflicts propelled
many young couples to escape to the suburbs, beyond the reach of parents
and relatives, as soon as they could. Sociologists and social workers urged
young parents to cut ties with the extended families that undermined nuclear "family togetherness."[9] Unfortunately, most couples and the experts
who advised them had failed to realize that nuclear family life had isolated
young parents from a network of caretakers who could have been helpful
on a Saturday night.

What contributed to the ensuing feelings of isolation of young suburbanites was that their own parents were not exactly sitting around waiting for the phone to ring.[10] "No longer are grandparents or maiden aunts in residence upstairs, or down the block, to be called on for child-care chores," reported the *New York Times*.[11] Peace and prosperity had enabled the retired to travel, socialize, and finally enjoy a leisurely life.[12] That many grandparents lived across the country instead of on the next block made babysitting for grandchildren increasingly impractical.[13] Similarly, unmarried aunts and uncles enjoyed life as "bachelors and career girls."[14] As one babysitting manual would explain, "Modern unmarried women of all ages are now leading such full lives, both professionally and socially, that they simply do not have the time to entertain their nieces and nephews, except on special occasions."[15]

Of course, there were some grandmothers around to help out, but those available did not always agree with their grown children's modern methods of child rearing.[16] This had been especially problematic for young parents who had moved in with their own parents. "No home is big enough to house two families, particularly two of different generations, with opposite theories on child training," editorialized a *March of Time* newsreel in 1948.[17] This advice was based on the theories and social prescriptions of psychologists and pediatricians who had done an about-face in the debate over effective child rearing since the interwar years.[18] For postwar mothers, the enormous popularity of Dr. Benjamin Spock's *Common Sense Book of Baby and Child Care* (1946), second in sales only to the Bible, had contributed to the erosion of faith in kin and community.[19] Consequently, "grandmother's 'know-how' [now] seemed as outdated as her hand sewing."

But to prewar mothers, young women seemed "bulwarked by their modern doctors' books."[20] On the rare occasion when my grandmother made the long trip to Smithtown, Long Island, from New York City where she lived, she criticized the less disciplined ways in which her three grandchildren were being raised. She had brought up her son and daughter on scheduled feedings, eliminations, and sleep, according to prewar behaviorist theories.[21] That parents like mine more freely chose between child-rearing styles had a lot to do with the fact that they had far less contact with and interference from their parents.[22] Moreover, because postwar parents had more children than the two previous generations combined, and spaced them closer together than had prewar couples, child-rearing experts like Dr. Spock urged parents to "dispense with the rigidities of traditional child rearing."[23] As *Good Housekeeping* aptly explained, "Today's mother has no time for clock watching and schedule keeping. . . . Babies today arrive in bunches and are raised like little birdies; when their mouths are open you feed them!"[24]

While many grandmothers experienced the joys of caring for grandchildren, others found babysitting rather nerve wracking.[25] "I was ready to fall apart," explained one grandmother after babysitting for her grandchildren.[26] Because suburban couples tended to have more children than their parents generation, grandparents sometimes found the larger broods taxing. Not only had the grandparent generation raised fewer children, but they had done so with more support from family, friends, neighbors, or a youthful "mother's helper." But increasingly feeling that they were forever "on call," some grandmothers now openly resented the expectation that they would always babysit. In a declaration of the rights of grandmothers published in a popular periodical in 1953, one grandmother asserted,

> Becoming a grandmother shouldn't require an active, self-respecting, attractive, and intelligent woman in her forties or fifties with a home, husband, and interests of her own to become a combination galley slave, scrub woman, and trained nurse, all rolled into one. She is entitled to a well-earned, peaceful existence now that her children have grown up and married.[27]

Baby-Sitting, Inc.: The Frustrations of Fictive Kin

Sometimes young couples tried to hire those who might at least assume some of the functions of family members. While my mother hired two older women to take care of my siblings and me, many newer communities lacked enough such inhabitants, let alone ones needing to or willing to babysit. Older women were as unlikely as other traditional caregivers to reside in newly developed suburban communities where economic, racial, and generational homogeneity reigned. For example, African Americans faced persistent housing discrimination in the racially exclusionary suburban market.[28] By 1960, not one of the eighty-two thousand residents in the quintessential suburb of Levittown was African American.[29] At seventy-five dollars per week, "live-in maids" had become not only uncommon but also "inadequate," according to child-rearing advisors.[30] "I'm quittin'—that's all. And right now!" said Mrs. Maypole, the "embittered-looking," "hatchet-faced" servant in the motion picture *Sitting Pretty* (1948). Having had enough of the three rambunctious baby boomers and their ox-sized dog, she left the family in the lurch when she departed in a huff.

Though Mrs. King had no one to babysit, her children were elated over the departure of the foul-tempered Mrs. Maypole. "Don't worry, Mom. She was a pain in the neck," said one son reassuringly.[31] But Mrs. King was fortunate, at least according to *America's Baby Book* (1951). Along with others, this parenting guide related some of the horrendous experiences mothers had faced when untrustworthy household servants had turned their worlds upside down. "Two mothers had come home to find their babies abandoned by irresponsible maids. One woman had twice employed housekeepers who turned out to be mentally ill."[32] Then there were those who regularly showed up later than expected or not at all.[33]

Desperate parents sometimes called a babysitter agency for help, even though most were located in cities.[34] In 1947, an ex-Marine lieutenant hired a "hundred or so A-1 carefully screened" mothers and grandmothers. Personal experience had led him to believe that teenage sitters "failed to take their responsibilities seriously."[35] By 1957, there were approximately 250 babysitting agencies in the United States; the largest, located in Los Angeles, employed eight hundred sitters who served the needs of twenty-five thousand families.[36] According to one contemporary, sitter agencies large and small "crassly commercialized" care, but what many businesses offered parents were the services of women who, at least on the surface, looked like they could be grandmothers.[37] "These outfits offer mainly female personnel of advanced middle age, charge the top rate of seventy-five cents an hour, and make a big thing of the maturity and dependability of their talent," reported *The Saturday Evening Post*.[38] Seventy percent of the women who worked for the Baby Sitter's Service were mothers; some were even grandmothers. "We believe the mature woman is best fitted to handle the emergencies that may arise in the home," explained the agency's owner.[39] The Willie Winkle Registered Sitter Service had a roster of sixty-five "responsible" and "experienced" women.[40] The fact that many of the women were mothers, widows, or grandmothers probably alleviated some concern about hiring nonkin to babysit.[41] So did the enchanting fairy-tale names of babysitter companies, such as Lull-A-Bye Sitters Registry, Peter Pan Nursemaid Service, Safety Pin Club, Rocking Horse Ranch, Story Book House, and Mother Hubbard.[42] The seventeen "leading specialists" who contributed to *Every Woman's Standard Guide to Home and Child Care* (1959) agreed that agency sitters could be used "with confidence."[43]

At the same time, child-rearing experts also advised parents to develop a special sensitivity to the "clues" that would aid in finding the best and ferreting out the worst sitters. Otherwise, most warned, you might get more than you bargained for! A New York City magistrate warned parents not to trust "just anyone" after a drunken babysitter was found guilty of beating a four-year-old boy and his nine-month-old brother. As parents became particularly sensitive to the psychological welfare of young children in the postwar years, they were urged to consider the "personality," "character," and "nature" of the women they hired.[44] Far and away the most important element was the "disposition" of the "maid, nurse, or foster mother," explained Dr. Spock.[45] Among other child-rearing experts, he recommended flexibility and spontaneity and warned against the dangers of discipline and rigidity.[46]

But what many parent-employers soon realized was that when judged by postwar standards, mature sitters were likely to be authoritarian and their methods antiquated. Some were also obsessive clock watchers. One mother panicked when she arrived home ten minutes late and found her five-year-old on the street with the house key in his pocket. Apparently the sitter "couldn't wait."[47] While other women tried to insinuate themselves into the bosom of the family, more tried to "maintain the household."[48] Then there were those who were judgmental. Babysitters in Los Angeles commonly complained about their employers' uncomfortable "modern" furniture and that there were no reading lamps.[49]

As one male parent-employer explained,

> My main objection to them is that air of having descended for the occasion, from moral and social realms so lofty that they are soiled by contact with the moral torpor of their clients and the squalor they live in. In paying one of them off one night, I got close enough so she could easily tell what kind of refreshments I'd had. "Well," she said huffily, "I hope you had a good time!" I had, as a matter of fact, until the contrast with her perfected virtue made it seem, in retrospect, like a further dribbling away of an already squandered life.[50]

In an essay in the *New Yorker*, the writer Peter DeVries similarly described how he and his wife were chastised by one sitter and criticized by another. "After looking around with short, critical glances, as though this were only one of a thousand tacky establishments she had been in," the older sitter mistakenly called him "Mr. Debris."[51]

Suburban "Sitretaries"

Over backyard fences and during coffee klatches, suburban mothers shared their predicaments about the "baby-sitter bugaboo."[52] The new domestic rituals of suburban women's lives provided them with opportunities to share perspectives, offer support, and explore alternatives while reinforcing family norms and cultivating community cohesion.[53] One suggestion current among suburban mothers was to create child-care organizations to provide relief from the unyielding domestic routines.[54] "Do-it-together, rather than do-it-yourself, is the answer of many young mothers," the *Ladies Home Journal* would report enthusiastically about women's attempts to arrive at a practical solution to a persistent problem.[55] "The age-old technique of 'you mind my baby and I'll mind yours sometime' needed only organization to become the sort of boon thousands of home-bound young parents dream of," reported the *New York Times* about the babysitter co-ops that sprang up in places like St. Paul, Minnesota.[56] Young mothers there formed one of many babysitter co-ops that emerged in suburban neighborhoods from coast to coast.[57]

Parent-run sitter "exchanges" or "co-operatives," largely staffed by mothers "like ourselves," succeeded in formalizing the "old-fashioned good-neighbor swap."[58] Typically, the officer or "sitretary" coordinated cooperation by bringing together a neighborhood mother who needed a sitter with one willing to babysit. In return, the sitter received a credit upon which she could draw when she needed a babysitter. Rather than keeping up with the Joneses, then, neighbors who shared child-care responsibilities cooperated with them. In Levittown, New York, neighbors formed a Jewish-Christian sitters' exchange service in keeping with the postwar trend that deemphasized sectarian differences and stressed common needs.[59]

For housewives and mothers seeking to push "horizons beyond the nursery walls," regular interactions with neighborhood women made suburban life less isolating.[60] "I particularly enjoy the companionship of the other mothers," said one mother.[61] "We've found our meetings most helpful," said another.[62] For another young parent, the co-op helped combat her anxieties about motherhood because the women provided assistance and support. "In the absence of our husbands, it has been a real help for each of us to have an interested and informed friend with whom to talk over anything that has been worrying us about our children."[63] Since most postwar suburban mothers raised their children without the steady assistance of kin, many sitter exchanges provided anxious young women with opportunities to learn from more experienced ones.[64]

Mothers were more likely to agree with their friends and neighbors than with their own parents on issues of child rearing. For example, members of the Sunrise Sitters shared common understandings with other suburbanites, because this generational cohort consisted of parents between twenty-five and thirty-five years of age. "Our lives are held closely together because most of us are within the same age bracket, in similar income groups, live in almost identical houses and have common problems," explained a resident in *Island Trees*, the Levittown community newspaper.[65] As a result, co-op members often forged strong bonds with one another. As one put it, "We're almost like a family. It's not like getting a sitter, it's more like asking a trusted relative who cares about you and your baby to help you out."[66]

For couples that wanted to "gad about," explained the *San Francisco News*, experienced mothers who were co-op members provided an importance sense of security.[67] As one mom explained, "[t]he best sitter in the world was another mother who could call on her own knowledge and experience should emergencies arise."[68] The notion that parents were essential to the healthy development of children meant that every parent made an ideal sitter.[69] As one resident exclaimed, "[r]eally, the only kind of sitter for a house full of children is another mother or father!"[70] By virtue of parenthood, adults could provide others like them with the sense of security while away from their children. "Just knowing our youngsters were in such dependable hands," another mother explained, provided much needed "peace of mind."[71]

Co-ops freed women from the seemingly never-ending homemaking routines; it was husbands who often cared for their own children while their wives went out to babysit for the neighbors.[72] The willingness of their husbands to do so enabled seven wives to form the nucleus of one co-op. Each conferred with her husband, and "[e]very one of them was for the idea and not a bit displeased at the prospect of 'sitting' with his own children when we were out sitting with others."[73] Wives were typically the principal co-op workers, but when husbands babysat for neighbors' children they were proclaimed to be "babysitters *par excellence*."[74] Unlike women, men allegedly "maintain better discipline" and have "less trouble on the job."[75] Though the new fatherhood ideal had reintegrated men back into home life after two decades, it had also reduced fathers' power and prerogatives. Babysitting, however, could provide men with opportunities to be manly. "Fathers [are] Preferred as Babysitters," explained the *Boston Globe* in 1956 in an article about an ex-Marine whose wartime experiences enabled him to act decisively in a way that "few adolescent baby sitters could command."[76] When men like him showed up with their favorite magazine tucked under their arm, explained one periodical, even the "wildest boys became meek as lambs."[77]

Despite all the initial optimistic assessments, however, taking care of someone else's children could strain a marriage. One mother decided that she could not join the sitters' exchange because "[m]y husband wouldn't want me going out and leaving him with the kids."[78] Despite new ideals about fatherly participation in family life, it seems that babysitting could also be a burden. The fact that fathers were providers before they were pals to their wives and children enabled them to skirt domestic commitments. In the competition for time, husbands' real jobs won out. As Robert Griswold makes clear in *Fatherhood in America* (1993), "Family togetherness and paternal engagement did not challenge the assumption that men's primary responsibility was bread winning while mothers' was child rearing; it simply enlarged the significance of fatherhood while leaving intact the patriarchal assumptions underlying a gender-based division of labor."[79] Despite the wished-for benefits, then, some wives ended up feeling more anxiety than enthusiasm about co-ops.[80]

The souring of the co-op promise was also due to the fact that differences emerged between couples and among neighbors. It seems that when co-ops were either too big or too small, problems arose. "It's been found," reported the *New York Times*, that "the plan won't work well with less than fifteen."[81] Yet "co-ops with more than 30 members tended to become unwieldy and friendly intimacy is lost."[82] When exchanges did work, friends were more likely to see less of each other because "we are rarely both at home at the same time."[83] There was also a problem of uneven utilization. "If you go out infrequently, your use of the pool is limited, yet it is embarrassing to be continually refusing requests from others."[84] Because "[b]eing called on too often kills your enthusiasm for the idea," one co-op member warned others to "[w]atch out for a group dominated by gay types who are off almost every week-end evening."[85] Though members in some co-ops were not permitted to "owe" more than a certain number of hours (and Friday and Saturday nights were counted at time and a half), there were some who somehow tended "to be perpetually in debt to the pool, and chronically unable to sit for you."[86]

Even though bylaws aimed to maintain "justice and insure domestic tranquility," and the co-op officer heard complaints and issued warnings, irreconcilable differences sometimes surfaced among neighbors.[87] Instead of cooperating, some ended up not speaking to each other. The resulting alienation, anger, and anxiety did not exactly foster community cohesion. "In our group, we did have a situation in which one mother and her rambunctious child proved to be very unpopular"; no one wanted to baby-sit for her "impossible kid."[88] "Eventually, it became clear that the co-op was not working for this mom, and she ended up withdrawing her membership."[89] Though good for the co-op, this did not exactly reinforce neighborly bonds. Had everyone expected to retire in the same community in which they raised their children they might have been more careful to maintain neighborly relations. But because of high mobility rates among young suburbanites, when they moved to "something better," neighbors who routinely pulled up their stakes also pulled out of the co-op.[90] In the opinion of one disgruntled husband, babysitting co-ops "don't work."[91]

The Bumbling Babysitter: Episodes of Ineptitude

Though fathers helped with the kids, the redefinition of fatherhood along a more egalitarian axis had generated more unease than enthusiasm. While magazines extolled the new ideal of Dad as in control but not controlling, in other cultural quarters fathers were often lampooned for their incompetence. In *Sitting Pretty* (1948), the father of three rambunctious boys was typical of other dads in domestic comedies, as ineffective as they were inept.[92] Whether fathers were depicted as absent or absent-minded, the portrayal of fathers expressed cultural concerns about the gap between the ideal of masculine authority achieved through involvement and the reality of paternal attenuation.[93] The anxieties produced by the difficult transition from patriarch to pal surfaced in stories in which grown men who tried to mind children were themselves too childish. For instance, the patrician-looking Vern Albright in the TV sit-com *My Little Margie* was more pathetic than powerful.

His teenage daughter, Margie, called the shots when she refused her father's plea to babysit for Sydney, the "little demon" grandson of a wealthy business client in the firm that employed Vern. Margie stood firm as her weak-willed father pleaded, "Please help me, don't leave me alone with him!" It was only when Vern momentarily asserted his paternal prerogative—threatening to cut Margie's allowance in half—that she gave in. But throughout the rest of the episode, Mr. Albright could live up neither to his position nor to his name. Instead of being intelligent and insightful, he was childish, gullible, incompetent, whiny, and meek. Though just a boy, Sydney easily manipulated Vern and ignored his instructions; an "Old Lady Robber" fleeced Vern; his landlord tried to evict him; a cop tried to arrest him; and his boss (who called Vern an "idiot" and a "coward") fired him. At the end of the episode, Margie shared the reward for capturing the Old Lady Robber with Sydney, who promised to use his influence with this grandmother to help Vern get his job back.[94]

Movies that featured grown men as babysitters also portrayed them as ineffectual father figures.[95] Although Mr. Belvedere was a far more competent babysitter than any teenage girl in "Sitting Pretty" (1948), he was still not the model father. While the boyish Three Stooges were their buffoonish selves in *Babysitter Jitters* (1951), Jerry Lewis was as inept as ever in *Rock-a-Bye Baby* (1952).[96] In *Jack and the Beanstalk* (1952) Lou Costello played an oversized prepubescent boy. In their arrested development, these emasculated men often had high-pitched, feminized voices, as was the case with Jerry Lewis in *Rock-a-Bye Baby* (1952). As a result, we believe him when he explains that he had joined the Camp Fire Girls in his youth and that he stopped a muscle-building course because he couldn't find any muscles to build. These fellows had even less control over other parts of their bodies. As stumbling nebbishes or uncoordinated nerds, none could make it in a man's world. While Jack lived with his widowed mother in a premodern European version of a postwar American suburb, he could only dream of defeating the fascist giant in the filmic parable of *Jack and the Bean Stalk*. Jerry Lewis also dreamed of saving Carla and yearned to be a "hero" like Sir Galahad. But because he was unable to control a firemen's hose, he caused disorder and destruction in the matriarchal suburban town of Midvale. Infused in these comic fantasies were fears that the emasculated American male had little in common with the "strong-minded man who pioneered the continent and built America's greatness," explained *Look* magazine in 1958. Postwar men paled in comparison to the barrel-chested cowboys in many classical Westerns on TV and in popular movies.

Because of the diminished development of these male babysitters, none was able to outwit Junior, the baby boomer who packed a punch across a wide range of media. Among the many examples was the child in *Jack and the Bean Stalk*, typically bratty, except that his mature psychological insights made him sound more like a child-rearing expert than a child. And, it was he who read the tale of *Jack and the Bean Stalk* to his illiterate male sitter, not the other way around. With his precocious intelligence and sophisticated pranksterism, Junior easily triumphed over pathetic Jack. Another defeated male sitter appeared in *Ma and Pa Kettle Go to Town* (1949), a movie in which the police had to rescue a bank robber posing as a babysitter from a mob of riotous children.

On TV the comedian Sid Caesar experienced similar frustrations to those of men in movies. In one comedy sketch, Caesar portrayed a neighbor who babysat for the young son of a couple whose teenage sitter had canceled just so that she could watch TV, of course. It was a decision this "good neighbor" would regret because although Sid Caesar was a large-sized man he was no match for "the champ," the little boy who would not "go down" (to sleep) so that Caesar could watch a prize fight.[97] Whether on TV or in the movies, men forced to cede their authority to children were comically indicted for their ineptitude.

This perspective about power even shaped news stories such as the one published in the *New York Times* about a mother who failed to return home and relieve the sitter. This sitter was a lightweight ex-fighter (a veteran of two hundred bouts) yet no match for a four-month-old infant. As the former boxer-turned-babysitter explained,

> I got maybe a hundred ten pounds the best of it in the weights, but that don't help me. . . . In my time I fight over 200 fights. I fight guys like Petey Herman and Tony Canzoneri and I do pretty good. But I can't figure out this kid's style. . . . I try to rock him and he give me that clinch. I try to out-fox him but he's way ahead of me. And boy, does he fight that bottle! He knows that ain't on the up-and-up. Even when I get him flat on his back what happens? He gets up. That's discouraging.[98]

At dawn, the New York City Police Department came to the rescue of the old-time pugilist.[99]

Skirt Clingers and Backyard Babysitters

If it was not the presence of effete men, then it was the absence of fathers that generated unease. Many social critics at the time worried that, with fathers at work all day, "suffocating mothers" could harm sons, if only by virtue of not being men. As insidious as overprotective mothers were to their son's autonomy, maturity, and manly identity, other mothers cloaked their domination with permissive child-rearing methods. Psychologists, sociologists, social critics, and others agreed that proper sex-role identification within the traditional nuclear family was critical to personal development. But, "[b]ecause boys were brought up almost exclusively by women, it was feared that they would identify with their mothers' behavior and fail to develop a firm sense of their masculinity."[100] "Mama's boys" could even become "psycho," the title of the 1960 Alfred Hitchcock film that would speak to the intensity of contemporary fears about the overly mother-identified male.[101]

Unlike inept fathers and inadequate girls, boy sitters were once again promoted as effective role models for suburban sons. Perhaps adults hoped that teenage boys would turn away from the dangers of music, movies, comic books, and other aspects of youth culture believed to cause juvenile delinquency.[102] Parents praised boy babysitters for being "extremely capable."[103] Wholly unlike girls, "business-minded" boy sitters were widely described as "professional," "interesting," "intelligent," and "refined."[104] "We had an Eagle Scout for a babysitter, and, naturally, he came prepared," exclaimed one enthusiastic mother.[105] Popular magazines portrayed sitters like him as active, considerate, responsible, reliable, sensible, and serious. One enchanted mother reported that the boy she hired arrived for work "combed and scrubbed, with an algebra book under one arm and a most engaging boyish smile."[106]

Elsewhere in the popular culture boy sitters continued to play leading roles. On the heels of Henry Aldrich and his many male helpers, Archie Andrews—the quintessential caricature of the teenage boy—babysat in a radio episode that included the cast of characters also featured in the enormously popular Archie comic books.[107] As other forms of technology eclipsed the radio, however, boy sitters suffered no such obsolescence. On the 45 rpm record *Donald Duck, Baby Sitter* (1950), the male Disney character serenaded young audiences as he confidently quacked,

> Donald Duck is a baby sitter,
> He rocks all the babies—
> And when they are fed,
> He tucks them in bed—
> Oh, he's a good baby sitter.
> His name is Donald Duck,
> He's a baby sitter duck—
> When the babies cry
> He sings, "Rockabye."—
> All boys and girls love Donald Duck.[108]

Donald Duck shared the babysitting field with other male animals such as a large pachyderm who in *The Big Elephant* (1949) left the circus in order to live in a town, run errands, and babysit for his human neighbors.[109] And mother was able to do her housework only because a male cat kept baby company in *T-Bone the Babysitter* (1950).[110]

In addition to writers who cast boys as caring animals, were experts who emphasized boy sitters' "gentle determination." Fathers' "strong" arms were also believed to provide children with the "best qualities of masculinity—tenderness, protection, and strength."[111] Yet fearing the association between androgyny and homosexuality, experts reassured parent-employers that boy sitters were "entirely masculine" and definitely "non-sissy!"[112] Boy sitters were even promoted in *Army Wife* (1954), the authorized handbook published for the spouses of army personnel.

> Baby-sitting is a rewarding job opportunity for boys as well as girls. More and more high-school boys–and college fellows, including football players and basketball stars–are becoming baby-sitters. It is no job for a sissy: if you think so, try to dig up that old movie, "Sitting Pretty," in which Clifton Webb starred as a baby-sitter! This is a job that requires ingenuity, intelligence, and the ability to think clearly and act decisively. If baby-sitting is good training for future mothers, it also has some valuable experience to offer future fathers.[113]

No male sitter served as a better symbol of masculinity than the beefy football player of the quintessential male sport. According to the Columbia University coach who established a sitter agency for his players, "The spirit that makes a good football player makes a good baby-sitter."[114] According to one young mother who relied on the Princeton undergraduates she hired through the Tiger Tot sitter service, sometimes four of them "would turn up, for the price of one, in order to have a bridge game. I loved the idea of four strapping young men watching over my baby daughter. Diapers were changed with efficiency and aplomb."[115] Other manly babysitters included Bill Cowperthwait, a 21-year-old architecture student who did his homework while babysitting in his Chicago workroom for one dollar per hour. Eighteen-year-old Roger De Weese, a babysitter in West Los Angeles, was able to pay for his own car and its upkeep. Both were included in a *Life* magazine cover story about babysitting that reported that 23 percent of the 7.9 million American teenage boys worked as babysitters. In 1957 they collectively earned an estimated $319 million.[116]

In spite of the fact that other magazine articles claimed that males of all ages felt "confused about what they should and should not do to fulfill their masculine roles," child-care experts maintained that hiring a male sitter would develop rather than diminish a boy's gender identity.[117] The masculine training ground where male bonding flourished was the outdoors: the zone where fathers could also cook barbecued meals without neighbors raising an eyebrow.[118] It was there that playing sports was believed to foster masculine identification between father and son.[119] Critically important to the development of sons' masculine identities, according to Dr. Spock and other child-rearing experts, were friendly, fun, caring, and emotionally engaged fathers. The problem was that during weekdays most dads were far from home. Nearly half of all fathers worked nearly fifty hours a week, not including the time they spent commuting between city and suburb.[120] Thus, in father's absence, boy sitters could pry loose the "skirt-clinger," and by playing "rough-and-tumble" games outdoors, instill the manly hardiness experts anxiously promoted.[121] While female sitters were to occupy interior spaces where domesticity reigned, male sitters and boys, beyond the cloying reach of domesticity, could have a "real man-to-man affair."[122]

While grown men and teenage girls struggled to achieve control over the rambunctious, little boys seemingly starved for male attention, were like putty in the hands of male sitters. "Many a fifteen-year-old can wind young Master Four-to-Seven [years old] around his little finger," reported *Parent Magazine and Better Homemaking* in one romanticized report.[123] One eight-year-old boy was even said to have pleaded with his parents to go out just so that his sitter, whom he talked about in "a worshipful tone," could babysit. When the sitter finally arrived, little Billy "glowed with pleasure."[124] The feelings between teenage boys and toddlers were also represented as reciprocal, even when the older boy was not the babysitter. In "Baby Sittin' Boogie," a rock 'n' roll hit that would sell more than a million copies, the teenage boyfriend of the babysitter perceived the baby as a buddy who "isn't too young to really feel the beat / He rocks back and forth in his little seat / He claps both his hands and he taps his feet / And he sings: 'Doo, doo, da, da, da, da.'"[125]

Just before he turned twelve years old in 1950, Bruce Osburn began babysitting for his nephews and nieces in Hamlet, North Carolina, where he learned how to "squirt milk from a bottle's nipple onto my arm to see if it was at the right temperature before I poked it into his mouth."[126] Yet other boys found the job to be more than they had bargained for.

One of the undergraduate founders of the Tiger Tot babysitting service at Princeton recalled that "it was hard work and not overly lucrative at thirty-five cents an hour, particularly when the clients would pool kids at one house so that we ended up with five or six kids to watch, feed, change diapers, etc., on the same assignment."[127] Along with girl sitters, boys occasionally felt unsettled by wild children. According to seventeen-year-old Jack Turner, "I sit with one nine-year-old kid who is supposed to go to bed at 8 o'clock and it takes till 10 to get him out of my way so I can study." Jack also found it irritating when the boy shot darts at him while pretending to be an "Indian."[128] While Jack controlled his anger, other boy sitters unleashed theirs. After striking an infant in his care "because it cried," an eighteen-year-old youth was arrested and charged with homicide when the baby died of a ruptured liver.[129] In Des Moines, Iowa, a fourteen-year-old boy confessed to shooting an eight-year-old boy because the child wanted to "play guns" instead of "go to sleep."[130]

During a period in which gender ideals were polarized and hypermasculinity authorized, boy babysitters were not demonized the way girls were. Nor were they normalized. Because taking care of children could be infinitely more challenging than mowing front lawns, not enough boys wanted to babysit, and certainly not as a "steady sitter." While none made a strong case for why only boys should serve as the nation's babysitters, experts and educators already had begun to transform "swooning, giggling bobby-soxers" into America's "future women."[131]

"Sitologists": Training and Containing Teenage Girls

In 1947 the Berkshire Hill School for Girls in Great Barrington, Massachusetts, established a babysitting course. "Parents hailed this attempt to bring order out of chaos as a boon to harried mothers," commented the *Boston Globe*.[132] What made mothers in Massachusetts anxious and what led the mayor of West Orange, New Jersey, to request that babysitting basics be taught to girls in his jurisdiction had been a "wave of mishaps."[133] Among the news stories about incompetent babysitters that sent shivers down the spines of parents was one that appeared in the *San Francisco Call-Bulletin*. Having forgotten something at home, one mother had returned unexpectedly to find the sitter putting her baby in the gas oven. "A lot of the girls do that with small babies," allegedly explained a sitter to the reporter covering the story. "The gas makes them sleep and then they don't cry." And while some girls stuck the babies into the oven, others held them face downward over the open stovetop jet.[134]

Whether this was, in fact, an actual practice among babysitters or an urban legend in the making (the reporter had no idea whether the practice was widespread or not), training courses that aimed to make girls into "satisfactory sitters" would soon flourish.[135] At the Finch Junior College in New York City, psychologist and guidance counselor Gladys Romanoff sought to correct misinformation in order to check "mishaps." Her students were some of the many who learned how to care for children at the babysitting demonstration center Romanoff established with the support of the Quaker Emergency Service and the New York City Health Department. "So great was the interest aroused that organizations from New Britain, Connecticut, to Seattle, Washington, have gone to work on planning for sitter training," enthusiastically reported the *Women's Home Companion*.[136] By 1957, *Life* magazine would report that "more than half of the nation's junior high schools would give instruction in baby-sitting."[137]

In order to attract girls, shape their behavior, and qualify them for demands as sitters now and mothers later, students in South Gate, California, spent ten weeks studying babysitting in a course offered at their high school.[138] After a survey of eighth graders revealed that three-quarters were babysitters, the director of homemaking for Monrovia City Schools in California transformed the child-care unit of the curriculum into a training center for babysitters.[139] In Greenfield, Massachusetts, a fire safety inspector certified teens enrolled in a babysitting course offered at the fire department.[140] The success of the course led to its duplication in towns all over New England.[141]

Schools and centers, institutions and organizations that joined together to establish schools for sitters developed a national curriculum.[142] Together the Board of Education, the New Jersey State Safety Council, the National Safety Council, the Greater New York Safety Council, and the Child Study Association issued a pamphlet that provided girls with babysitting instruction.[143] In places like Minnesota, the Duluth Women's Institute, the Chamber of Commerce, and the Parent-Teacher Association produced and distributed five thousand copies of their babysitter manual through the Mrs. George Welles Duluth Babysitters Council.[144] In an effort to get materials into the hands of girls in 1952, twenty thousand copies of a babysitting guide were sent to PTAs, women's organizations, home economics teachers, and other organizations throughout New Jersey.[145] More than two million girls and women received another free pamphlet, *Handy Guide for Parents and Babysitters.*[146]

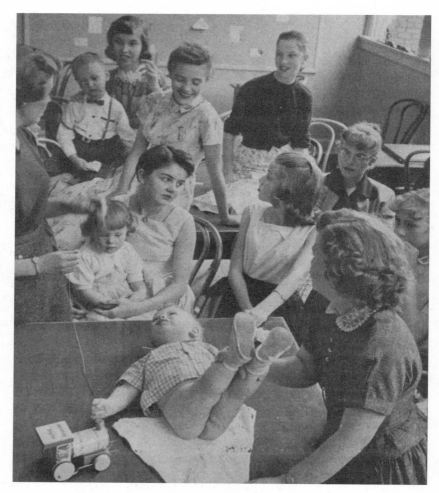

By mediating girls' feelings of ambivalence about babysitting, training courses aimed to provide parent-employers with professionalized "sitologists." "The Profession of Sitting," *Life*, July 29, 1957.

The way the YWCA saw it, "To meet the needs of every family," it was up to communities to provide girls with sound training in babysitting.[147] In San Jose, California, for example, students viewed *The Babysitter*, an educational film shown to those enrolled in the Baby Sitters' Program sponsored by the City Health Department, City Recreation Department, and City Library.[148] The Girl Scouts also provided lessons on babysitting

The perception that "bobby-soxer babysitters" like this one were indulging in all the pleasures of postwar teenage girls' culture they brought to the neighbor's house led to the emergence of "schools for sitters." Virginia Richards, "This Baby-Sitting Business," *Coronet*, April 1949, 101.

through articles in *The American Girl*, the official organ of the Girl Scout organization.[149] The National Safety Council prepared a "planning guide" that provided "an outline for gathering facts on the situation in a particular community, advice on public relations, copies of a playlet, sample radio scripts, suggested women's club programs, and outlines for a community course for 'parents-by-the-hour.'"[150]

Furthermore, educators sought to provide competent caretakers for the nation's baby boomers by harnessing teenage girls' autonomy to "professional" accountability. Whether in advice columns, manuals, films, or vocational courses, babysitting was elevated from the ranks of industry to the status of a white-collar career.[151] In the *Baby-sitters' Handbook* (1952), a chapter on "Management and Labor" and another on "The Wages of Sitting" had represented the babysitter as a "worker"; elsewhere the handbook foreshadowed adults' reinvention of the babysitter as a "professional."[152] "Many a high school girl feels mighty important being a sitter; to her it is a career," explained the author of "Sitters Are Career Girls," published in *Hygeia* magazine.[153] The "certificates" that graduates received not only certified babysitters' expertise but also conferred a middle-class

Seen as both commanding and caring, boys like thirteen-year-old Murdoch
Finlayson, seen here practicing bottle feeding in a "Graduate Course in Baby-
sitting," were widely touted as better babysitters than teenage girls.
Life, April 12, 1954, 54.

professional identity.[154] "With baby-sitting becoming such a science, we'll
have to be calling the girls 'Sitologists,' instead of just plain 'Sitters,'" explained the *Boston Globe*.[155]

Still, parents' persistent impression that "girls are not as serious about
baby-sitting as they might be" led them to prefer "boys to mind their children." That led the Visiting Nurse Association in Needham, Massachusetts, to establish a "graduate course" for boys chronicled in *Life* magazine.
Though their numbers were far fewer and the motivation to train them
was different, boys also listened to lectures and observed demonstrations

on topics such as how to powder and diaper, feed, and burp a real baby.[156] The portable "pocket-sized certificates" graduates received enabled boy sitters to present their credentials to potential employers with confidence.[157]

For the professional training and taming of teenage girls, however, magazines, manuals, and other resources provided "rules of conduct" on the "very special art of babysitting" in accessible "pictorial guides."[158] These didactic pieces often included illustrative photographs with informative captions, such as, "Before sitting down for a rest the sitter tidies the living room" and "The sitter tells the parents she'll be happy to sit for them again."[159] Grooming undisciplined girls to be "professional" and not proletarian, civic organizations, health departments, and numerous other associations devised "babysitter codes."[160] In Providence, Rhode Island, a statewide committee of representatives of the Rhode Island Congress of Parents and Teachers, the YWCA, the Girl Scouts, the Camp Fire Girls, and the Bristol Police Department developed a code of their own.[161] Aiming to transform bobby-soxers into babysitters who would share the same values as their middle-class employers, babysitting codes—such as this acrostic poem—defined the conduct that promoted self-control.

> **B**e prompt in arriving for your job.
> **A**lertness will prevent unnecessary accidents.
> **B**aby-sitting is your "career" for the time being.
> **Y**our reputation will be based on the impression you make.
> **S**upplies for children may be needed, so know their location.
> **I**nformation which you may need in an emergency should be in writing.
> **T**emptation to raid the ice box should be conquered unless you have an invitation.
> **T**elephone conversations should be limited.
> **E**ntertaining friends while baby-sitting may be unwise.
> **R**espect and protect the rights and property of your employer.
> **S**afety and welfare of the children depend on you.
> **C**hild care is a responsibility, so know the home routine.
> **O**btain information regarding the time your employer expects to return.
> **D**ividends in attractiveness result from care in grooming.
> **E**very child needs understanding and security.[162]

While the code's acronym facilitated the recall of information, professionalization itself required specialized training in the development of skills and sensibilities, or what one babysitting instructor referred to as

"the proper attitude."[163] Using codes to elevate behavior to a higher standard, disciplined teenage girls were told not to treat an employer's home
as "hers for the night to do as she wished" but instead as her "place of
business."[164] Along with other codes, babysitter manuals emphasized the
importance of respectability, proficiency, punctuality, competence, reliability, responsibility, deference, and dependability.[165] The YWCA publication *Babysitting* (1956-57) taught girls that "maturity, calmness, and good
judgment are indispensable."[166] Vocational films similarly provided examples of exemplary behavior by capable, responsible, and reliable babysitters. In *The Babysitter* (1949), a film produced in collaboration with the
Finch Junior College, Mary was alert, responsible, organized, and efficient.
After successfully putting the children to sleep and telling a friend that she
couldn't "tie up" the telephone "without permission," Mary settled down
to do her history homework like a good girl.[167]

Short stories in magazines also aimed to reinforce lessons learned elsewhere. In the "Babysitter's Boy Friend," a story first published in *Teen-Age
Tales* and subsequently reprinted in *National Parent-Teacher* magazine,
Nancy Preston was caught in a serious dilemma. Having double-booked,
she promised both Mrs. Cullen that she would babysit and Ricky Holden,
the senior she adored, a date. Coming to the realization that "[s]he [just]
could not let Mrs. Cullen down now," Nancy dutifully honored her commitment to her employer.[168] However they did it, educators, social workers, and guidance counselors everywhere urged female adolescent babysitters to conceive of themselves as "career girls."

Yet the picture of the clean-cut babysitter sporting saddle shoes, pedal
pusher pants, and a pixie haircut featured on the cover of *The Saturday
Evening Post* in 1958 suggested that adults remained unconvinced about
the extent to which adolescent girls had accepted gendered and generational norms. This sitter rang in the New Year with a glass of milk toasting
a couple of merry partygoers pictured on the black and white TV who
could just as easily have been her employers. The neat arrangement of an
opened book, an uneaten slice of chocolate cake, an apple, and a clump of
grapes on a small round coffee table by her side suggested a sense of order,
balance, and control. And yet in a darkened room off to the side lay an
evidently sleepless toddler. While this babysitter was an obvious improvement over untrained ones, the toys that lay strewn at the base of the crib
suggested that all was not right. The sights of this babysitter were still not
where they should have been. Instead of devoting herself to the baby in
the next room she sat transfixed by the televised partiers. In so doing this

babysitter, who stood for other adolescent girls at the end of the fifties, transported herself beyond the confines of the home into a realm where pleasure abounded.[169]

The "Baby Sitter Bill": Employers' Rights and Wrongs

Despite adults' efforts to professionalize babysitting, by the end of the 1950s, one self-confident thirteen-year-old claimed that "[t]he baby sitting business is a dangerous and difficult way to earn money, and for those just beginning, I am writing some advice based on my own experience. I hope that, with the help of my suggestions, some spirited girls will avoid many bruises, broken bones, and law suits."[170] Either missing or dismissing the point of the babysitter's article published in the YWCA's *Bookshelf*, an editor's note suggested that the advice might provide a "light interlude" to a course on babysitter training. While the YWCA had failed to take the sitter seriously, it probably should have because, as *Good Housekeeping* explained to parent-employers, "If you employ a baby sitter you may expose yourself to liabilities."[171] While that warning had appeared earlier in the 50s, parents toward the end of the decade had new reason to worry about the self-confidence nurtured by girls' culture and fostered by vocational experts.

As "war babies" coming of age swelled the teen population, the babysitter became the heart of such hits as "I'd Like to Sit with the Baby Sitter" (1954); "Baby Sitters" (1957); "Diana" (1957); "Baby Sitter Boogie" (1958); "Baby Sitter Rock" (1958), "Baby Sittin'" (1959), "Baby Sittin' All the Time" (1959), and "Sitter's Rock" (1960).[172] Teenagers celebrated the babysitter in love songs and also in lawsuits. "Does your insurance cover your babysitter?" asked *Parents Magazine*, because "your babysitter can sue you," the headline in another national periodical seemed to answer.[173] "Does it pain you to pay $1 an hour, or more, for a babysitter? Friend, that's nothing," explained a reporter for *Coronet*, who summarized recent court rulings.[174] Among potential employers, a rising number of court cases initiated by sitters began to make babysitting look even more costly than the usual "night out."[175] One teenage girl who had slipped on a loose rug and broken her hip had won a judgment against a Kansas family. They were ordered to pay her five hundred dollars. A New Jersey court awarded $275 to another sitter who had fallen down a flight of steps. In Los Angeles, two sitters filed claims in a single week for injuries caused by rambunctious youngsters.[176] The wave of lawsuits was not limited to teenage sitters. In California, a 55-year-old woman had won the right to sue after a five-year-old boy knocked her down and broke her wrists. As *Parents Magazine* explained,

> Baby sitters rarely came a second time to the D'Angelo home in Los Angeles, California. Five-year-old Sal made a game of ramming into them—head down, full-tilt. One uninitiated sitter, spending her first night with Sal, hit the floor and came up with two broken wrists. The state court awarded the woman damages. Since Sal's parents knew of his playful tendencies they should have warned the woman. Because they failed to do so they were guilty of negligence.[177]

In New Jersey, where babysitters were legally considered "employees," parent-employers were supposed to pay their sitters' workman's compensation.[178] Those employers who were not fully protected for injuries to sitters "faced double-indemnity penalties."[179] That was the case because as illegal employers, parents were held accountable under both workman's compensation requirements and the penal provisions of the education law.[180] Moreover, under older child labor laws that had been designed to protect children from nighttime employment, babysitting was illegal, though no section of the labor law had specifically covered "babysitting."[181] A dozen states had laws that required separate work permits for each employer, and also placed limits on hours of work per school day, but these were routinely ignored. In fact, no one had even applied for an employment certificate in New York between 1953 and 1958.[182] "Probably not since the days of prohibition has any law been so widely and blithely ignored as that governing the employment of part-time guardians of the young."[183] What that meant, explained *Good Housekeeping*, was that "[t]hree nights a week fifteen-year-old Betty Brown leaves homes to go out and break the law."[184]

Earlier in the decade, the California state attorney had ruled that child labor laws did not apply to babysitters. In Alaska, "an indignant lobby of parents and sitters induced the legislature to write this specific exception into the law."[185] In 1958 Frances K. Marlatt, a Republication assemblywoman from Mount Vernon, New York, introduced a bill in the New York legislature. Its purpose "was to relieve parents of the legal liabilities that they incurred when they engaged sitters."[186] The bill aimed to eliminate the "legal complications and complexities" and "protect the sitter and all concerned" by defining the legal status of babysitters and delineating the legal role of employers.[187] The bill would have licensed babysitters who, without the working papers required under child labor laws, had been working illegally. Marlatt's bill was backed by both the Education and Labor Departments, which would have awarded badges and permits "to those qualifying as sitters."[188] To qualify, sitters would have had to undergo periodic physicals "which would weed out emotionally disturbed youngsters and give the Labor Department real control of setting standards of employment to be met by the employer."[189]

While parent-employers were interested in asserting legal control over babysitters, they did not want to do so at the expense of their own independence. As a result, other Republican legislators who maintained that the bill "would justify invasion of the home by state officials" led the opposition to the proposal.[190] Within the context of anticommunist fears about state control and intervention, assemblywoman Janet Hill Gordon charged that the bill would open Americans' homes to inspection by a small army of Labor and Education Department officials, and all at the taxpayers' expense. Tapping into anxieties about the primacy of parents, assemblyman Lawrence R. Rulison (a Syracuse Republican) objected to a provision that took the authority to establish standards for babysitters out of the hands of employers and placed them into those of state Labor and Education Department officials. "My wife is perfectly capable of setting her own standards," explained the legislator and a father of nine.[191] Facing overwhelming defeat, the proposal was withdrawn and redrafted by "Mrs. Gordon who agreed to help Miss Marlatt draw a bill that might achieve her objective without resort to licensing and without making homes where sitters were employed subject to state inspection."[192]

The revised bill that sailed through both houses without debate or dissenting vote "legalized" babysitting in New York. It did so by exempting sitters (fourteen-years-old and older) from the state's child labor laws that required work permits from the State Labor Department. By exempting babysitters from work permit requirements, the law freed parents from assuming the statutory liabilities of employers.[193] As a result, none would be obligated to pay workman's compensation. The New York State law signed by Governor Harriman in 1958 declared that "babysitting shall not be considered employment as such; thus no parent hiring a sitter will become an employer and subject to an employer's legal obligations."[194]

Conclusion

Whether it was because of the shortage of teenage girls willing to babysit or because they believed they were short on skills, frustrated parent-employers turned to other adults to babysit. But no one, not even many grandparents, were keen to do so. Nor were many all that "good" at it, according to young couples whose child-rearing expectations had been shaped by Dr. Spock's more lenient methods. Despite the many problems posed by having grandparents, neighbors, housekeepers, and other adults babysit, none became the object of anxiety in the ways that teenage girls did. Clearly, the gap between generations of adults paled in comparison to the gulf between grownups and girls, which would only get wider over the next decades.[195] Thus, experts and educators focused their efforts on the training of teenage girls to be competent, yet compliant, "professionals." Experts appealed to girls' desire for autonomy, yet sought to control it by transforming sassy sitters into subservient ones. Consequently, the *Journal of the National Education Association* optimistically commented that "[it] may be the era will produce . . . a generation so thoroughly grounded in family-life experience and ideals that the American family will be strengthened."[196]

Despite educators' efforts to contain babysitters vocationally and legislators' attempts to curtail them legally, many girls remained unsatisfactory and unsatisfied sitters. Efforts to indoctrinate girls to be more accepting and less demanding did not halt the spread of a teen culture that had nurtured sitters' sensitivity to gender and generational equality.[197] In a cartoon that appeared in the *San Francisco News* in 1958, a newly confident sitter explained to a mother of two obviously rambunctious children, "Normally I charge 50c an hour—but it's time-and-a-half when I'm outnumbered!"[198] As a harbinger of things to come, some girls questioned babysitters' restrictions and employers' rights. Shouldn't they have to "meet certain qualifications, too?" sniped a sitter.[199] Perhaps she had read *The Baby Sitter's Guide by Dennis the Menace* (1951), which satirized babysitter-training programs. Dennis offered sitters such sage advice as, "You should always find out what time a kid is supposed to go to bed. This doesn't mean much, because he won't go to bed until he gets sleepy, but it will make you look businesslike."[200]

While girls felt self-assured, they were also nervous about things that went "bump in the night."[201] In 1957 *Life* reported that "[m]any a young baby sitter, alone in a strange house, has wished she had a sitter herself."[202]

While watching a "late, late murder movie" one night while babysitting in 1960, one sitter thought she heard footsteps creaking down the stairs. "Rigid with terror, she grasped a fire poker, and turned on her assailant." It was then that the sitter came face to face with an "old, old woman in a bathrobe who politely asked to her lower the TV."[203] The sitter naturally wondered why her employers had not bothered to tell her that someone else was in the house. While there was nothing new about her irritation, the trepidation foreshadowed terror. During the following two decades, it would not be elderly women who would terrify teenage girls into behaving better. Getting girls to be more dependable and less independent would require the assistance of those with more cultural clout as well as the willingness to coerce sitters who did not "check the children."

5

Boisterous Babysitters

The litany of complaints about irresponsible "bobby-soxers" disappeared from popular periodicals during the early 1960s. However, uncertainties about teenage girls remained. In fact, girls' growing rejection of such traditional ideals as domesticity, virtue, and submission and their pursuit of new pleasures—sex, drugs, and freedom—heightened adults' old anxieties. Fears about girls found expression in new stories about bad babysitters who appeared in new cultural forms—from humorous movies, toys, and TV sit-coms to fear-inspiring vocational films and urban legends. In one story that gripped the popular imagination, a teenage girl took LSD with her boyfriend while babysitting for an infant.[1] Although now recognized as an urban legend, back then the story expressed girls' rejection of conventional feminine expectations and their acceptance of expanding possibilities set into motion by the counterculture, second-wave feminism, and the sexual revolution. The urban legend about the misdeeds of a stoned babysitter expressed adults' escalating anxieties about which path the teenage girl would take to womanhood: the conventional course they wanted her to follow, or the illicit one they feared she desired.

This chapter examines the ways in which the disorderly babysitter who appeared everywhere in American culture during the 1960s simultaneously stimulated girlhood rebellion but also stifled it. On the one hand, the babysitter provided girls with models of teens who routinely defied gender customs. On the other hand, the babysitter characters created by adults anxious about the acceleration of adolescent independence served to caution girls against straying too far from fundamental ideals. Some narratives provided examples of feminine self-control while others threatened the noncompliant with retribution. During the 1960s, board games as well as bogeymen would command girls to be compliant, dependent, and domestic, as well as caution those exploring their independence to watch their step and limit their horizons. Or else.

Bitching Babysitters

"Since spending money seems to be a constant need of teen-agers, this new occupation [of babysitting] has become a thriving business," observed one contemporary about the millions of baby boomer babysitters.[2] In 1960, six million girls swarmed into the billion-dollar babysitting industry needing money in order to buy records, clothing, books, jewelry, and other goods marketed to preadolescents and teenagers. Though many teenage girls turned to babysitting to supplement their allowance, earning somewhere between fifty cents and one dollar did not always seem worth the effort.[3] When one sitter tried to put her young charge to bed, he ran

> inside his bedroom closet, closing the door, and screaming "No" for about 10 minutes. I would like to think that as an Official Babysitter, I used some of the knowledge gained from my vast 200 minutes of childcare education to coax him out of the closet, but I suspect he just ran out of oxygen in there. He came out and fell asleep so quickly that I hovered for a few minutes to make sure he was still breathing.[4]

When my sister came of age during the 1960s, she occasionally turned down requests to babysit kids who gave her a hard time. My sister-in-law, who also joined the millions of girls who worked as babysitters,[5] recalled that the "totally wild and out of control [children] never listened and kept testing me."[6] Stories in the popular culture reflected similar sentiments. In "The Baby Sitters," a short story published in *Redbook: The Magazine for Young Adults*, Charlotte liked the fifty cents she got when she babysat but found the six-year-old girl to be a "miserable creature."[7]

That increasingly "uppity" girls were turning down requests to babysit was an all too familiar event among mothers frustrated by the futility of endless telephoning. So common was the occurrence that it even provided material for Phyllis Diller, a highly successful stand-up comic whose routines about housewives' daily lives drew upon her own experiences as a mother of five. "Don't feel you should invariably go by child guidance experts, as it isn't always possible to follow their advice. One said, 'Always have a baby sitter who is acquainted with your children.' If they were acquainted with my children, they wouldn't sit."[8]

For many girls babysitting was no laughing matter, not when children were occasionally obstinate and parents often inconsiderate. One sitter recalled that while her parent-employer put on her coat she said hurriedly, "You've already met Michael don't worry he'll be fine once he gets to know you the number of where we'll be in case of an emergency is on the fridge help yourself to whatever snacks you'd like we won't be back too late Michael be a good boy we're running late see you later bye."[9] For fifteen-year-old Bonnie of Rye, New York, "[i]t's the limit when they don't tell you where the thermostat is and how it works, especially when it's a clock one, that goes off at 10. Some houses get so cold you have to put your coat on and roll up in blankets to keep from freezing."[10] While the technology might have changed, clearly the problems associated with babysitting had not. In Great Neck, New York, another girl spoke for generations of sitters when she complained, "They tell you they'll be home by 11:30 and they drift in at 2:30."[11] But, "[t]he worst is when they expect you to be day-worker and scrubwoman while you 'sit,'" explained another sitter. "One woman once left me a big can of wax and written instructions for waxing her kitchen floor by hand. I never went back there again."[12] When Nancy was twelve, she began working as a babysitter for fifty cents an hour at a home where she had to "clean up" after her employers, who entertained friends before they went out.[13] "Excessive housework is a fairly frequent complaint," commented the *New York Times*.[14]

"From the girls' standpoint" there was still a "baby-sitting problem," explained a Girl Scout official. Some of the major issues babysitters faced had not been addressed in the Girl Scout curriculum for those earning a "Child Care" badge.[15] Scout leaders weren't alone in their observations about the persistence of labor problems. The results of a joint survey conducted by the YWCA and Child Labor Committee and sent to 250 "Y" leaders nationwide revealed "major problems" for sitters who still had to "cope with abuses."[16]

HOURS: Indefinite, too long and too late.

WAGES: Low, no payment, and unfair wages.

TRANSPORTATION: No transportation to homes after baby sitting.

PLACEMENT: Lack of knowledge on the part of the employee and the employer. Legal and moral points involved here. How to be sure a sitter is reliable and qualified.

EXTRA DUTIES: Sitters are involved in household tasks for which they had not contracted and the care of animals some of which are unfriendly.

PROTEST—Excessive housework and insufficient briefing head the list of sitters' complaints.

Although babysitters neither picketed homes nor protested the poor working
conditions, teenage girls influenced by the social movements and counterculture
of the sixties nevertheless roused the anxieties of parent-employers.
"Protest," *New York Times Magazine*, May 22, 1960, 38.

Having yet to devise a category to describe a rising problem, the YWCA
added, "Alone in isolated areas, intoxication of parents on return home
from parties."[17]

In 1960, the year that seventy thousand students staged "sit-ins" to
protest segregation, seventeen-year-old Carol Aspinwall created a "code
of conduct" for parent-employers.[18] In Westport, Connecticut, seventy junior high school girls who were enrolled in a babysitting course offered
by the Young Woman's League endorsed Carol's "code."[19] In her youthful workers' version of the Magna Charta, reported the *New York Times*,
Carol "laid down the law" in "a sort of fair employment practices act."[20]
Nevertheless, babysitters such as the sixteen-year old who wrote a letter
printed in the *Boston Globe* continued to feel taken advantage of by the
"chiselers" who employed them. Other "underpaid baby-sitters of America" wrote in to offer their support and suggestions.[21] One explained that
"in some communities baby sitters have formed 'unions,' and they have
agreed among themselves not to work unless customers agree to pay according to the above rates."[22]

A former babysitter, now a mother of four, expressed her "contempt for
people who will cheat youngsters."[23] Yet to comedian Alan King this new

generation of teenage girls truculently asserting their rights were a cross between wastrel wives and professional contractors. In his book *Anybody Who Owns His Own Home Deserves It* (1962), he explained that "[g]etting a baby sitter is not as easy as you think. They're all organized. You don't hire a baby sitter today, you put in a sealed bid, and then you have to negotiate." When asked if she would like to babysit, "She comes right back with, 'What do you have to offer?'"[24]

Anxious Tales about Bad Girls

There were other signs of incipient unrest among girls growing increasingly critical. According to *Look* magazine, "youth everywhere is exploding into action."[25] The influence of the counterculture, the sexual revolution, the civil rights movement, and feminism were leading many girls to mount challenges. Asserting greater control over their lives by challenging traditional sources of authority, girls increasingly contributed to the ongoing transformation of girlhood.[26] In school and at home, ever more rebellious girls talked up and talked back. In their everyday lives, girls who questioned authority and defied customs brazenly hiked up hemlines, donned bell bottoms, grew their hair long, blasted rock music, and took drugs. Rejecting hierarchy and conformity and embracing egalitarianism and individuality, this new generation of girls would energetically "bitch" about fundamental institutions and structures, like school, parents, the government, patriarchy, and babysitting.

Adults' alarm about teenagers who drank alcohol, took drugs, and had sex found broad expression in popular books, newspaper articles, and magazine exposés.[27] "Little girls are too sexy too soon," declared *The Saturday Evening Post*, one of many periodicals that condemned girls' sexual precocity and forecast its perilous impact.[28] *Look* asked readers why "teen-agers from 'good' homes steal, take dope and shock their parents with their sexual delinquency."[29] That teens were choosing to take a different path than the one adults had laid out for them particularly distressed those who looked to girls as the next generation of American mothers, as well as those who looked for girls to babysit. The specific concerns of parent-employers could be found in stories about bad babysitters.

"Now all the sitters do is SIT!" observed a 27-year-old mother (and former sitter) who wrote a letter to columnist Abigail Van Buren.

The kids can pull the place apart and the sitter doesn't lift a finger to straighten it up. And sitters can eat you out of house and home. But what gets me is they won't bother to carry their own empty bottles, glasses, and dishes into the kitchen, let alone wash them. They just leave everything right in the room where they had their refreshments. I think I'd faint if one ever cleaned up after herself.[30]

While some girls appeared to care little about domestic order, others allegedly turned their backs on feminine virtue. Speaking volumes about adults' perceptions of teenage girls, *Today's Health* published this faux note written by a parent-employer.

Dear Judy:
    Before arriving to baby-sit, you had two telephone calls.
    Betty's coming over at eight with the latest album by the Electric Hand.
    Johnny said he's bringing over one of his cool friends who will really turn you on.
                                    Mrs. Wilson
PS: We're coming home early tonight. [31]

Adults' anxieties about other aspects of girls' rejection of traditional gender ideals also found expression in supposedly "true" stories. Among one of the urban legends was this one about a babysitter who chose delirium over domesticity.

One night a teen-aged girl hurried to babysit a neighbor's child. She is visited by her boyfriend who has some LSD, [and] they both take some. A number of hours pass and then the mother calls home to check on the children. She got a very incoherent girl on the phone, one that in no way resembled the girl whom she left with her children. The girl says something about a turkey in the oven which [sic] the woman cannot understand because there was no turkey at the house. She then became very alarmed and rushed home to find that the girl in her drug induced stupor had mistaken the infant for a turkey and cooked it in the oven.[32]

By cooking the infant, the babysitter in this hair-raising story had distorted gender norms. Doing so, she was more like the evil witch than the victimized innocent, the latter being the more typical and submissive position of girls in cautionary folk tales. To some parents who heard the story from neighbors, it probably served as a news bulletin warning them to be on the lookout for bad babysitters. But to girls in the process of exploring their autonomy, the babysitter's rebellious rejection of feminine ideals could be read as (1) an acknowledgement of the challenges girls posed to dominant beliefs; (2) a critique of girls' subversion of feminine and maternal standards; and (3) a warning to girls about the dangers of drugs and desire.

Another cautionary tale that emerged during this period featured a sitter whose behavior also had multiple meanings: resistance to traditional expectations; an absence of good judgment, domestic skills, and "maternal instincts."

A young couple decided that they deserved a vacation. They called a babysitter that regularly babysits for their young, eighteen month old baby. The couple were waiting for their babysitter to arrive, but the departure time of their plane was fastly approaching. Waiting right up to the last minute, they decided to tie the baby in the high chair, thinking that the babysitter was going to arrive in a short time. Three days later, they came back from their vacation and found the baby dead. The babysitter never showed up and the baby ate its fingers and eventually died of dehydration.[33]

The narrative element of binding the infant and leaving it to its own fate however, also served to remind parents of the need to delay their own gratification for the children's sake. Perhaps these parent-employers had similarly neglected to read the revised edition of the U.S. Children's Bureau's publication *Infant Care* (1963). Like other child-rearing works at the time, the pamphlet reflected the expert opinion of physicians and mental health professionals who had begun to issue warnings about only hiring "someone who can be trusted."[34] Hire only the "well balanced," child-care expert Dr. I. Newton Kugelmass had recently cautioned in *Complete Child Care in Body and Mind* (1959).[35] Employ only the "reliable," the director of the FBI had similarly urged parent-employers.[36] Had these parent-employers been up to date, they would have known that this no-show sitter did not exactly fit the revised criteria for "trusted" babysitters. Unlike the magical Mary Poppins who came to personify the ideal nanny following the popularity of the blockbuster movie in 1964, this mythological babysitter was a ninny.

Commercialized Girls' Culture: Accommodating Resistance

The expansion of the highly profitable girl market led to the production of other popular movies and new cultural products—toys, TV shows, and the like—that adroitly reflected social changes at the same time that they reinforced traditional ideals.[37] Cultural goods of varying sorts served to both capitalize on and contain girls' desires for greater freedom. As a figure with whom girls identified, the babysitter now embodied old and tempered new definitions of girlhood.

Nothing better reflected gendered and generational changes at the same time that it reinforced traditional ideals about girls than did the Barbie doll.[38] Though she had made her debut back in 1959, Barbie had not started "sitting" until 1963, when Mattel provided her with a pink and white striped "Baby Sitter" apron. (Not one of the millions of girls working as babysitters ever wore one of those.) Barbie's babysitting outfit also came with domestic accessories (a white telephone and list of important telephone numbers), maternal accouterments (a baby doll, bassinette, blanket, etc.), and books. Titles such as *How to Lose Weight* reinforced a feminine ideal, but others, such as *How to Get a Raise*, spoke to the empowerment of employment, a feminist issue that came to the fore with the passage of the Equal Pay Act of 1963. While for Barbie employment and consumption were associated with liberation, Ken served as a potent reminder about the importance of marriage to future happiness. The actual Barbie could not stand on her own two feet, but the doll that was always "on the go" straddled the mounting tensions between residual femininity and emergent freedom. Like Barbie, real American girls were encouraged to compete in school and to pursue careers and causes, all the while keeping an eye out for Mr. Right.[39]

Along with Mattel, the Ideal Toy Company also assumed the role of guiding girls toward young womanhood. The goal of the *Baby Sitter* board game they manufactured was to complete "chores" and earn money without triggering the mechanism that would wake Stanley, the bald pink plastic creature with a gaping red mouth, "asleep" in a purple bed at the center of the game board. Playing cards that directed girls to "Play a record" or "Turn off the radio" taught the skills of quiet stealth that appealed to girls as well as the methods of self-monitoring sanctioned by adults. If, by chance, poor Stanley's slumber was disturbed, he "yelled" (squeaked, really), and players were forced to forfeit the money they had already earned for completing chores.

While the board game spoke to girls' desire to make money and have fun, the game also tried to get girls who were in the process of finding their voices to quiet down.[40] That was not going to be easy because girls were at the center of a vast, flourishing cultural rebellion.[41] Girl groups and boy bands had already ignited the romantic urges, sexual desires, and shrewd independence of girls who were energetically dancing to the songs they knew by heart.[42] During the Beatles' American tour in 1964, youthful female fans had shattered eardrums, broken wooden barricades, and breached social barriers that gave way to rapid and profound changes in the beliefs and behaviors of American girls.

Aiming to entertain and educate this vast audience coming of age were teen-oriented TV shows. These playfully instructed girls about the risks of independence and light-heartedly admonished them for straying off course. The *Patty Duke Show* was the first of a number of successful girl-centered TV shows that explored changing definitions of adolescent femininity, as well as the apprehensions those transformations were generating.[43] The episode in which Patty tried to launch a babysitter service functioned like other weekly installments of the sit-com except that her agency was expressed in visions of entrepreneurial success. And like Patty's other hare-brained schemes, this venture was motivated by a traditional feminine goal: to earn enough money to buy a dress that would reawaken her boyfriend's affections. But unable to hire girls in the neighborhood to take part in her babysitting service, Patty ended up having to take the job herself, convincing her cousin, Cathy, and her boyfriend, Richard, to assist.

While this episode validated the potential agency of teenage girls, it also diminished it. Though the teens outnumbered the tots, they were no match for the notorious boy brat. What was different about this prankster was his claim to be the "Killer of 2nd Avenue." This was an early, eerie reference to a newcomer to babysitter lore whose character sprang forth as urban crime rose. The insinuation into girls' culture of the all-too-human maniac (as opposed to the hideous monster), who used psychological horror rather than annoying pranks to disrupt everyday life, prefigured Michael, the babysitter murderer in *Halloween* (see chapter 6). Michael would soon remind girls, as Richard did at the conclusion of this *Patty Duke Show* episode, that girls were helpless without heroes.[44] (This was a message Patty's mother would reiterate.) By moderating teenage girls' quest for autonomy, the show repeatedly reminded energetic teens about the ultimate necessity of containment. Patty herself reinforced the message that girls should not exceed the limitations of their independence and should gratefully acknowledge the security of dependence.[45] As a babysitter, her acceptance of established gender ideals aimed to contain the disruptive energy of irrepressible teens.

Similar to previous eras when teenage girls were perceived as threats to the social order, their correction occurred alongside the approbation of boys. Sounding like expert advice from the past, a 1965 babysitting manual explained, "You can understand why mothers and fathers feel safe in having 'a man around the house.'"[46] The advice that teenaged Henry Reed received from his aunt sounded a lot like the handbook published around the same time. "Some women I know prefer boys" to babysit, she explained to her fifteen-year-old nephew in *Henry Reed's Baby-Sitting Service* (1966).[47] Yearning for "something that takes some initiative and judgment," Henry took his aunt's advice, figuring that babysitting would serve as useful training for his future as a man. Realizing that babysitting had a lot of "advantages over other occupations," the self-described "dependable, resourceful, competent young man" launched his career as an entrepreneur of a "well-organized [baby-sitter] business."[48] Henry was successful at cornering the babysitting market in Grover's Corner, New Jersey, because this "very serious and dignified" boy was guided by a business ethos and fueled by a massive ego.[49] Thus, it only took a summer for the adolescent entrepreneur to come to the conclusion that "[t]he Henry Reed Baby-Sitting Service is probably the best-known organization of its kind in New Jersey and maybe even in the east."[50] Unlike poor Patty Duke, Henry won the Business of the Month award at the county fair for best exemplifying "the ideals of American enterprise and community service."[51]

While Henry Reed's character was actually based on the babysitting experiences of the author's daughter, the ongoing perception of girls as disruptive continued to find expression in other domains. A rise in phone use, especially among preadolescent and teenage girls, had resulted from the changing nature of the telephone—a function of AT&T's aggressive marketing of colored phones, in a variety of cute designs, multiple extensions, and for a reduced price.[52] Restraining girls from "gabbing" became the job of experts of all kinds, for whom babysitting provided an opportunity to reach girls and teach them about phone pathology and how to cure it. A mid-1960s vocational film, *Kids' Stuff* (1964), was one of several that made use of the babysitter in order to convey preferred standards. In that movie, the sitter yammered on about her "groovy date" while cooking dinner for a little girl forced to eat by herself while the sitter, still tethered to the telephone, sprawled across the kitchen counter. "If you are serious

PICTURES BY ROBERT McCLOSKEY

While girls were widely depicted as both irrepressible and irresponsible babysitters in the popular culture, boys like the eponymous Henry Reed were praised for their diligence and dependability. *Henry Reed's Baby-Sitting Service* by Keith Robertson, 1966. Illustrations by Robert McClosky. Reprinted with permission from Penguin Group (USA) Inc.

about earning a few dollars, shape up!" demanded the Carnation Foods Co., albeit an unlikely source of expertise on babysitting. The pamphlet *Tips for Teens* (1967) sought to amend the bad behavior of girls who set off to sit with "a long list of telephone numbers" they used for "a four-hour gab session."[53]

Other major American corporations joined forces with social service organizations in order to take part in "[a] national campaign to alert the public to the dangers of hiring unprepared and irresponsible baby sitters." While Pepsi Cola and Union Carbide approached the Girl Scouts about producing a babysitting movie, it was AT&T that worked with the American Academy of Pediatrics, the National PTA, and the National Safety Council to produce *The Baby Sitter* (c. 1965).[54] In that vocational film, in which a sitter's uninvited friend tied up the line, the mother grew upset when she tried to phone home. Then, because of the girls' combined carelessness, the baby boy got hurt. Though just an infant, his mini-masculinity nevertheless afforded him the authority to opine, "Some babysitter she'll make!"[55]

The Babysitter and the Maniac: Commanding Compliance

While some babysitter stories urged girls to behave, others exhorted them to do so or else face their own peril. Warning independent girls that they faced sexual dangers was the point of *Girls Beware* (1961), a short educational film based on allegedly "true" stories about girls with uniformly poor judgment. One narrative focused on Judy, who advertised her services as a babysitter at the local supermarket in her suburban California neighborhood. Just hours after posting her ad, Judy got an offer to babysit from a man who claimed that the family's regular sitter was unavailable. The week after Judy left to babysit, her frantic mother was informed that her daughter's murdered body had been found on a "lonely desert road." Judy had put trust in someone who turned out to be "mentally sick," explained the policewoman who delivered the bad news and narrated the film, aimed at presumably impressionable girls.

Judy's was not the only cautionary tale. The instructional movie produced by the Inglewood, California, Police Department and the Unified School District provided other tragedies. One girl got pregnant and another was gang raped though neither was babysitting at the time. But unlike these girls, who failed to protect their virtue while exploring their independence, Barbara the babysitter experienced no such "heartache and disaster." When a strange man knocked on the door where she was babysitting, the level-headed babysitter did not open the door to danger.[56] While Barbara lived to tell her tale, Mary Henson did not, according to the newspaper headline "Search for Missing Girl Baby Sitter." This is not an "unusual" headline, but it is an "unnecessary" one, explained the male voiceover in *The ABC's of Baby Sitting* (c. 1965), an instructional film produced with the cooperation of the Los Angeles County Medical Women's Auxiliary, the Glendale, California, Police and Fire Departments, and the Youth Bureau of the Chicago Police Department.[57] Like *Girls Beware*, this film also delivered a stern warning to girls: watch yourself or pay the price.

Fears about what dangers awaited teenage girls in the process of expelling old values and embracing new ones found expression in other allegedly "true" stories. The most compelling and enduring was the one about a girl who watched TV instead of "checking the children." Ella Stefan recalled hearing this version.

> There was this girl babysitting in a two-story house in New York and she received a phone call from a man laughing and he tells her she better go check the children. She doesn't believe him and she goes back to watch TV. She receives a second call and the man with a deeper voice is laughing and tells her she better check the children up stairs. And then she gets scared and calls the police and the police tell her if it happens again that they're going to trace the next call. So the third time, he called and he was really laughing and she got more scared. The police call her back and tell her to leave the house right away without going upstairs or anything. The police come over and told her the call was coming from upstairs and the man had been calling after he killed each child.[58]

Now known among folklorists as "The Baby Sitter and the Man Upstairs," this urban legend, which continues to be the basis of many slasher films and much horror fiction, first appeared sometime during the early 1960s. Like other babysitter narratives, it served to both reflect and retard changing notions of girlhood. Unlike the numerous "trickster tales" used to teach the powerless how to use their wits to evade the powerful, the babysitter and the maniac tale fits more squarely within another didactic tradition.[59] Like bogeymen in other cultures, the one in this story threatened retribution to those who did not do as they were told. Though phrased as a rhetorical question, "Have you checked the children?" was a directive that commanded compliance in females who had grown more cocky. To hammer home his point in one particularly gory version, the maniac attached a note to the baby's mangled body that read, "I told you to check the baby!"[60]

The horror fantasy revealed the ways in which the rapidly shifting sexual terrain had set off girls' anxieties. By the late 1960s, being a girl already meant "negotiating many different messages about what it meant to be female."[61] The maniac who preyed upon fears about the high cost of freedom attempted to help girls take the right road through this confusing sexual landscape. Unable to achieve the sitter's acceptance of the traditional gender system, the maniac's extreme coercion served as a warning to girls that the individual pursuit of desire was detrimental to the safety of domesticity. In this urban legend, as in the horror movies that would follow in the 1970s (see chapter 6), the babysitter served as the "final girl," the surviving one with whom female adolescents should identify.[62]

This urban legend, along with others, also expressed anxieties about women as well as women's anxieties about the contradictions of postwar gender norms. Many women seeking self-fulfillment had begun to choose childlessness over "togetherness." They played a critical role in the plummeting of birth rates that had put an end to the baby boom by 1964.[63] The delaying of marriage and parenthood that gave rise to the new "singles culture" exposed the conflicted choices many women faced between family and freedom. While many women delayed the start of family life as they pursued careers, others chose to combine motherhood with paid employment. In 1960, one in five mothers with children under six years of age, and 39 percent of those with children between six and seventeen, had become wage earners.[64] By the end of the decade, half of all women with children under five worked for wages.[65] The flood of women into the work force was the consequence of consumer desire, personal satisfaction, and the influence of new feminist ideals. While many wives worked to supplement husbands' incomes, others became the sole supporters of their families as the divorce rate began to surge.

Regardless of their motivation to work, wage-earning mothers often faced problems both practical and psychological. Whether laboring in feminized jobs or entering male bastions, working women were challenged by the growing problem of child care.[66] In 1963 the national Commission on the Status of Women identified the inadequacies of child care nationwide.[67] The way *Today's Health* saw it, because "so many mothers with small children are employed outside the home," mothers needed help "now more than ever before."[68] For those who wanted a teenager to babysit, there were often too few who were willing, despite their abundance in the population. As one mother explained, "It would be good for all of us if I could just get away from the kids and the kitchen one day a week, but . . . who would take care of my children?"[69]

Despite changing conditions for women, the notion persisted that mothers should put their children's needs before their own.[70] Experts like Dr. Benjamin Spock had been advising women to consider the serious consequences of employment for their children. In 1963, he had suggested that "[t]he mother of a young child should not go to work until she has really made up her mind, after full consultation with a social worker in a family agency if possible, that it is the best course for herself and her child."[71] For working mothers who wanted to go out on the weekends, their young children's protests could easily generate guilt. "Don't go! Don't go!" a three-year-old cried to his mother, while the babysitter grabbed his arm and leg and dragged him back into the house. It would be yet "another fun-filled, guilt-ridden evening away from the children" for this young mother.[72] While articles in *Good Housekeeping* and other popular magazines explained how women could find a "reliable substitute," the allegedly "true" stories about irresponsible sitters raised questions about whether there was such thing as a "stand-in for mother."[73]

As wives left home for work, the breadwinner ethos to which fathers had been bound—and that had bound them to the home—also had begun to unravel.[74] "Nothing posed a greater challenge to the ideology of male bread-winning and traditional male prerogatives than the transformation of the household economy," explains Robert Griswold in *Fatherhood in America* (1993).[75] That American mothers were leaving home, entering the workplace, and ending marriages intensified male feelings of inadequacy, alienation, anxiety, and anger.[76] The complex contradictions of masculinity during this period of profound gender transformation found expression in the legendary maniac who stood for dissatisfied husbands, authoritarian fathers, and exasperated employers. The legacies of such masculine ideals as responsibility, commitment, and self-discipline had left many "perpetually irritable" husbands feeling constrained by unreachable expectations and unreasonable demands.[77] Unable to realize the postwar ideal of domestic masculinity that combined providing with parenting, many frustrated fathers had been becoming increasingly joyless, compulsive, and consumed by concerns about family finances (including how much to pay the babysitter). As one-quarter to one-third of all marriages consummated in the 1950s ended in divorce by the late 1960s, 6.8 million men would spend even less of their time with their children.[78]

Despite the new trend toward joint custody as the divorce rate soared, declining paternal authority and increasing detachment accelerated the crisis of masculinity begun decades earlier.[79] Female breadwinners and freedom seekers who challenged "patriarchy" further undermined the role of husbands. Though the maniac instructed the babysitter to "check the children," in the end, it was the father who had "checked out."[80] Giving new meaning to the husbandly directive to "get a sitter," the absence of a protective patriarch provoked intense fears of a family left vulnerable. This double-edged fantasy of a father run amok was a flight from commitment and a fight for containment. It was also a paradoxical reaffirmation of traditional manhood. Longing for a way to express manliness, some men also found self-affirmation in pornography that featured babysitters (see chapter 7).[81]

In some versions of the urban legend, a female telephone operator offered help. Yet all the disembodied maternal voice could do was to inform the babysitter that the maniac's calls were coming from inside the house.[82] As women left the home to work, it would be the babysitter and the maniac who negotiated the gendered geography of the home.[83] With no wife to contain his impulses and with his masculinity challenged by far-reaching social transformations, despair was unleashed by desire. In the legend's many versions, the maniac's "heavy breathing" conflated raging hostility with sexual dominance.[84] No longer a protector, mutated dad was a sexual predator.[85] This sexual threat was made even more explicit in especially lurid variations of the legend in which the maniac sometimes used "dirty language" and at other times made obscene sounds.[86] In still other accounts, the animal under the couch who licked the sitter's hand provided her with comfort until, to her horror, she discovered the maniac's blood-scrawled message, "Humans can lick too."[87]

Dangerous Dads

In the early 1960s, *Better Homes and Gardens* published an allegedly true story about fourteen-year-old Teresa, who had accepted a job babysitting for her new neighbors, the Kents.[88] Within the first hour of babysitting, Teresa had misgivings; the two boys, ages six and two, had made the atmosphere so "tense." Then suddenly, "wild screams of pain and terror cut through the silence of the house." In the living room, Teresa found the baby on the rug "dripping blood from a large cut in his forehead." Nearby, his older brother stood stunned. Recalling her mother's calm disposition in the face of crises and the skills she had learned in the Girl Scouts, Teresa nursed the boy's wound. Then she called home. Her dad arrived in due course, declared the crisis over, and departed in short order. Later on that night when Teresa called home once again, she felt thoroughly reassured by her father's "voice, calm, smooth but very masculine, very deep, a part of his whole position in the family, for he was always the rock, the last word."[89] A strong father and a nurturing mother—the ideal nuclear family—had provided Teresa with the skills she had needed to be a good babysitter and the sensibilities she would need to be a devoted mother.

Despite the happy-ever-after ending of the *Better Homes and Gardens* story, its near-horror twist hinted at other anxiety-provoking changes. Stories like this one, and the babysitter/maniac legend, expressed fears about the dangers of disintegration increasingly visible in American cities that were rapidly becoming places of decline and decay. For example, in Philadelphia, a man escorting a thirteen-year-old babysitter back home was murdered and the babysitter stabbed twenty-five times with an ice pick.[90] Despite the rising tide of migration out of cities, suburban communities seemed to increasingly suffer from "social problems." That was partly due to the miles and miles of government-supported highways that had not only fueled suburban development but had also linked suburbs to cities. While it might have made for a more convenient commute, the famed "megalopolis" did not exactly create tranquility. Though more Americans lived in the suburbs by the early 1970s, suburbia had already begun to feel like an uncertain refuge to inhabitants, who increasingly feared the "strangers" in their midst. A growing fear that the subdivision might be harboring the heinous contributed to apprehensions about those who might live next door, but who were not necessarily neighborly. Together with a continued longing for connection, there was a growing fear of choosing the wrong sort.

"Special Pointers for Girl Sitters," a section in one babysitting manual, published in 1965, urged young girls to take precautions.[91] One handbook suggested that "[w]henever you have a late sitting job, the parent—usually the father—should see you back to your home."[92] Good advice, except when the employer pounced instead of protected! This was a relatively new issue when it was addressed in *When Teenagers Take Care of Children* (1965). "Some men forget—or almost forget—that sitters are sitters. They try to treat them like girl friends instead of baby sitters. You'll probably never run into such a man, but it pays to be on your guard."[93] As we shall see in the next chapter, some men, both stimulated and scared by teenage girls' new sexual agency, would go much further in order to frighten babysitters into behaving.

Conclusion

Despite obvious differences among many stories about babysitters, their similarities shed light on the complex construction and criticism of girlhood in the 1960s. Representations of rowdy sitters had issued warnings about risks that lay on the path to womanhood and the consequences of straying off course. Spunky sitters, found frequently in situation comedies, provided girls with tales of momentary pleasure along with cautious counsel. Their message was similar to that delivered by scared sitters in vocational movies and urban legends. Sitters' defiance of prevailing customs in popular and folk narratives reflected changing social realities but also reified fears about the dangers of the new principles, practices, and pleasures of girls' culture. Babysitters in the movies and on TV inspired girls to be independent, while metaphorical maniacs exacerbated girls' anxieties. Real girls would think twice about leaving home to babysit after hearing the story about the lunatic, although the tale failed to prevent girls from doing more of what they pleased during the 1970s.[94] As a result, when it came to taming teenage girls, there was more work to be done, and more men to do it.

6

Vixens and Victims
Porn and Horror

"In an era where morals are undergoing a major upset, when actions which used to be kept under wraps are brought out into the open, 'The Babysitter' is daring and current as next week's news," read the publicity material for the hot new movie *The Babysitter* (1969).[1] The sexually provocative film about a liaison between a babysitter and her middle-aged boss featured Candy, who represented the "sexually active girl"—at least as adult males in the 1960s imagined her. Exaggerated fantasies about female adolescent sexuality in movies like this expressed new erotic possibilities for American men excited by the sexual freedom of teenage girls. In numerous books and movies with similar titles and themes, sexy sitters signified a version of teenage girlhood seemingly desirable to men and girls alike. In reality, pornographic fantasies about girls like Candy gave men a leg up on controlling girls whose values were even now at odds with their own. Despite the fact that girls continued to be relatively uninterested in babysitting—especially when a male employer made advances—they were forced into fantasies in which they simply could not wait to babysit for Mr. ——! Also projected onto babysitters in men's improbable fantasies were fears that their dreams might come true. Babysitters like Candy were cock teases and catalysts able to destroy men's marriages and diminish male authority.[2] "Don't let her in your house unless you want real trouble," expounded the titillating movie trailer that warned men to steer clear of temptresses like Candy or face certain ruin. She is a "devil and angel combined."

As girls influenced by the spread of feminism staked their claims during the 1970s, however, the former object of desire became the target of punishing discipline. Not only raspy-throated lunatics—ghoulish stand-ins for the powerless husband, weak father, and incapable employer—but also ineffective experts rebuked babysitters for behaving badly. Lewd stories about sexy sitters turned painfully nightmarish in slasher movies in which horrific figures come forward to tame the temptress in new cultural forms. Along with educators, experts, entertainers, and other adults who had sought to reconcile the conflict between a vision of girlhood that was feminine and one that was feminist, a gallery of maniacs pressured teenage girls to stop their nontraditional sexual, social, and economic activities. Using aggressive containment strategies, including intimidation, submission, and victimization, maniacs communicated adults' expectations to girls exercising their independence.

While teenage girls shaped by feminism and youth culture still would not behave, boy babysitters—idealized as always as adolescents *par excellence*—functioned in a parallel field free from horror and hormones.

The Sexy Sitter Playing the Field

Back in 1957, *Life* magazine had reported that sitters sometimes faced the problem of an "amorous father or older brother."[3] So did sitters in the early 1960s complain that "husbands" who had "a little too much to drink" made them feel ill at ease.[4] Sometimes men went further than just making suggestive comments. A 32-year-old father of three who pleaded "no contest" to a statutory rape charge spent one year in the Marin County jail, according to the *San Francisco Examiner*.[5] A few years later that newspaper would report that babysitters had grown fed up with male employers who uttered such worn-out lines as, "Hi, kid, are you the baby sitter? Say, you're a knockout. Maybe I'll have my wife take the children out and stay home and let you sit me."[6]

Though most girls felt uneasy about overly "friendly" male employers, a new trend in pornographic books, magazines, and movies depicted teenage sitters as sirens.[7] Stimulating the fantasies of men were fictionalized babysitters with suggestive names like Kitty and Candy. The appearance of the hypersexual teenage babysitter in pornographic works had been due to the steady liberalization of sexual norms reshaping values and behaviors. Changing standards of sexual morality influenced the publication of bestsellers like *Sex and the Single Girl* (1962) that advocated promiscuity and lesser known paperbacks such as Vin Field's *The Baby-Sitter* (1964), a soft porn work that inaugurated the new public portrayal of babysitters as sex pots.[8] The spicy cover of this novel featured a well-endowed teenager who was even more carnal than her contemporary, the Barbie doll. Charna's breasts spilled out from her halter top, and her short shorts could barely contain her labia.

THE BABY-SITTER

She was jailbait . . .
a teenage man-trap
with a talent for
trouble and a
weakness for
married men
twice her age!!

by VIN FIELDS

FIRST PRINTING ANYWHERE

Mounting excitement and anxiety about the emergence of the "sexually active girl" influenced by the sexual revolution, youth culture, and feminism led to the appearance of the sexy sitter in soft porn fiction and movies in the 1960s. Cover of *The Baby-Sitter* by Vin Fields.

Charna's oozing sexuality stimulated men but also scared them. While men objectified girls' naked bodies, they also felt threatened by female sexual agency that was undermining the male sexual prerogative. The text on the back cover of the novel explains why sexy sitters like seventeen-year-old Charna inspired desire and elicited dread in her employer.[9]

> She came into his life as a baby-sitter but it wasn't long before she became something much more important, something much more dangerous. Beneath the schoolgirl exterior, she was more of a woman than any he'd ever known, a creature of pleasure with the morals of an alley-cat and the claws of a tigress. She was like a terrible drug, a special kind of madness. There wasn't a thing she didn't know, a thing she wouldn't do . . . either for him or to him!! HE KNEW SHE'D DESTROY HIM AND YET SHE WAS TOO STRONG A TEMPTATION FOR HIM TO RESIST. . . .[10]

Since the recent publication of Vladimir Nabokov's *Lolita* (1956), eroticized teenage girls had become an object of desire for men increasingly anxious about manhood.[11] As we have seen, the expansion of white-collar employment in the postwar era had left many men feeling as powerless and inadequate at work as at home. In response, men badly in need of an ego boost in fiction were paired with teenage babysitters like Charna. One such fellow was Cliff Morton, the 35-year-old Madison Avenue advertising executive in *The Baby-Sitter*, who, like other "organization men," felt emasculated by his monotonous job.[12] But that was not Cliff's only problem. He also felt burdened as a breadwinner and husband unhappily married to Kay, "frigid as a frozen hunk of meat" and a "powerful bitch."[13]

Unlike his unresponsive wife, and distinct from what men knew "real" babysitters were like, Charna was Cliff's irresistible "symbol of youthful femininity," a teenage girl who was sexually powerful as well as properly submissive.[14] In this male sexual fantasy that made uninterested sitters into irrepressible sirens, Charna would purr with platitudes ("I've never felt this way before"), moan mellifluously ("I never thought it could be like this . . . never"), and offer up such tributes to virility as, "I'm really a woman now . . . and you made me one."[15] Yet what might have appeared as female agency was really Charna's sexual objectification by Cliff and his perverted client, a "dirty old man" who would also bed her in this male fantasy of sexual liberation. Although such stories contributed to a growing acceptance of sexual fantasies about sitters, bedding them violated a taboo that was still entrenched. In order to instruct male readers not to do as Cliff did, the book concluded with the affair put to an abrupt end by Charna's uncle and his policemen buddies (signifying moral authority), who beat Cliff to a pulp.

Another babysitter story published around the same time made it clear that middle-class men were not the only ones with babysitters on their minds. The babysitter/boss fantasy also spoke of working-class yearnings. Published the same year as *The Baby-Sitter*, "The Promiscuous Babysitter" appeared in *Men*, a magazine for working-class males. The magazine, packed with advertisements for vocational training in meat cutting, auto mechanics, locksmithing, and upholstering, was aimed at men seeking new lines of work. For men seeking to improve their sexual fantasies, the sitter story focused on Joe Hadley, a draftsman at the Wechsler Tool and Dye Co., who was dissatisfied with his job, distressed by his aging body, and displeased with his wife. She had "made a bargain not to fight on-coming middle-age." That compromise did not strike Joe as "premature deadness" until he met nineteen-year-old Kitty, a blonde "teetering uncertainly between a girl and a woman."[16] "From the first moment he saw her, Joe Hadley knew this yellow-haired, morning-fresh girl who'd come to take care of his children was different from the other sitters. And he knew too that some night, irresistibly, he would go to her and seek out exactly what that difference was. . . ."[17] That difference was that unlike your everyday sitter, Kitty desired Joe "from the very start" and willingly acceded to him so that she would have this moment to "remember forever and ever."[18]

Though Kitty was shaped by the changing sexual practices of girls during the 1960s, she was not the subject of her own sexual imagination. Instead, Kitty's character was shaped according to the needs of men like Joe. In one pornographic scene after another, Kitty was cast as the desirably undemanding object of Joe's fantasies. Joe watched Kitty in his bedroom, where, in front of a "Victorian" mirror, she stood admiring herself in her bra and panties and his wife's fur stole. "I wanted to see what it would be like to be Mrs. Joe Hadley, to be in her bedroom, to try on her clothes," Kitty explained to Joe later that night. Then, too distraught to go to work, Joe drove to a lake where, as luck would have it, he got another chance to watch Kitty as she pranced around in a skimpy two-piece bathing suit. Then, while babysitting again, Kitty stripped off her clothes to Joe's visual satisfaction.

In "The Babysitter" (1964), Robert Coover's high-brow story about another man dissatisfied with married life, the sexy sitter also became the object of desire and control.[19] Along with everyone else in the story, she too entertained thoughts about sex. While the little boy in her care had his own fantasies, and two teenagers were unable to control theirs, it was the husband who recklessly attempted raping the sitter. In this story, the hazard that female adolescent sexuality posed to males was so intense that it blurred the line between reality and fantasy and fractured the narrative sequence.

It would take thirty years for Coover's babysitter to reach movie theaters and then very quickly go to the home video market. Until then, fantasies that expressed male ambivalence about teenage girls' erotic nature continued to find expression in the popular culture during the mid-1960s. "Lois Lane, Super Baby-Sitter" was the same male fantasy although this one was in a comic book intended for children, not a paperback for men. *Superman's Girlfriend Lois Lane* was tailored for boys surging with powerful prepubescent desires. Yet it also expressed men's curiosity and fear about sexual change, female control, and how to cope with young women. Male desire for female attention was projected onto Lois Lane and Lana Lang, her competitor in the field of love. The young women had been motivated to babysit, not to make money but to marry Superbaby, who they believed was really Superman. They knew that he had been working on a "youth restoring experiment." (It seems that even Superman was worried about advancing middle age!) What the young women did not know, however, was that this Superbaby was from a parallel universe where bigamy was legal. The comic book fantasy ended with Superbaby growing up to marry both Lana and Lois, parallel doubles who inhabited the expanding universe of men's dreams.[20]

Nor were Lois and Lana there alone. In addition to a second printing of Vin Field's *The Baby-Sitter* another sleazy paperback, *The Baby Sitter* (1968) was published, about yet another seductive sitter and her excited employer.[21] Those books appeared the same year that *Photoplay* magazine broke the story about "Paul Newman's Love Affair with the Babysitter." As it turned out, readers learned that Newman was not cheating on his wife at the time. But, ten years earlier, Newman had left his first wife for the babysitter, Joanne Woodward, who had since become his life partner.[22] While the news story was a decade old, what was new were the rapidly changing sexual activities that accelerated a new sexual ethic, one that no longer privileged marital relationships.[23] That adults and adolescents were increasingly exploring their own sexual independence opened up new avenues for the male imagination by the end of the 1960s.

Candy was "Great with kids, [and] even better with Daddy," explained the sensational trailer for the sexploitation movie *The Babysitter* (1969), about the relationship between a free-spirited teenage girl and her mid-dle-aged employer.[24] The movie reflected changing sexual standards that it also reinforced for "older voyeurs and maybe for professional married men who think about a new lease on life," surmised the *San Francisco Examiner*.[25] Promoting the film and the fantasy among men, Crown-In-ternational Pictures sent theater managers a variety of risqué publicity materials. In addition to the "teaser trailer," other provocative promotions included sexy business cards, advertisements, posters, lobby cards, and ra-dio spots. Further reifying the fantasy, the movie company also suggested that "[w]hen running teaser ads have a cashier or girl with a sexy voice read the following copy into a recording machine:

> Hi! I'm Candy the Babysitter. I'm very enthusiastic about my work and charge practically nothing. Don't ask for reference's [sic] though—I haven't been able to get any—In fact, some people won't let me back into their homes—but I'm great with kids—and even better with daddyies [sic]. I'm available most every night and some afternoons. If you want to see me in action drop by —— theatre. [26]

Candy, the blonde-haired, blue-eyed babysitter, represented for male day-dreaming the uninhibited world of adolescent girls' sexual and social freedom. At the suburban Southern California home where she babysat, Candy got "high" with a bunch of guys she invited over and danced topless to psyche-delic rock music. Candy loved the vitality and passion of rock music because, as she would later explain, it was "like sex."[27] Candy and her counterculture friends, who challenged mainstream canons of respectability, symbolized a commitment to self-gratification, self-expression, and self-liberation, sexual and otherwise.[28] As the epitome of the freewheeling, "sexually active" teenage girl of her generation, Candy would unambiguously explain to her employer later on that night how she wanted "to have fun, feel things, be free."[29]

Candy rejected the restrictive double standard that in reality continued to limit the sexual practices of many girls. She seduced her intimacy-starved, middle-aged employer, George Maxwell, a prominent lawyer and an as-sistant district attorney—an obvious symbol of the "system." But George had been growing weary of the sexual repression and social conformity that characterized his generation, and like other husbands who let their hair grow long, he yearned to "do his own thing." (So did his lesbian teenage daughter and his heroin-addicted wife.) The skyrocketing divorce rate signaled that men like him, dissatisfied with middle-class life and marriage to a "carping

PROMOTION

TEASER TRAILER
A 60 sec. teaser trailer on "THE BABYSITTER" is available from your Crown International distributor. Use at least 2 weeks in advance of play date and cross plug wherever possible.

MUSIC TIE-UP
Contact your local tower record distributor for tie-up on Candy's Theme from "THE BABYSITTER" sound track,

RADIO CAMPAIGN
Buy spots on the "rock" stations. Your local Crown International distributor has 10 30 and 60 second E.T.s available.

TELEVISION CAMPAIGN
Crown International has available an exciting set of TV spot announcements. These include one 60-second, and one 20-second spot. Start your TV schedule in advance with a teaser-type campaign; use shorter spots and building as you approach opening day. Available at your local Crown International exchange or homeoffice.

SPECIAL TEASER CAMPAIGN

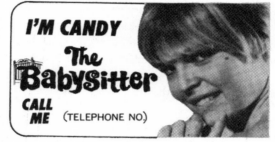

I'M CANDY
The Babysitter
CALL ME (TELEPHONE NO.)

T-1

NEED A Babysitter
CALL ME AT...
(TELEPHONE NO.)

T-2

When running teaser ads have cashier or girl with sexy voice read the following copy into a recording machine:

Hi! I'm Candy the Babysitter. I'm very enthusiastic about my work and charge practically nothing. Don't ask for reference's though — I haven't been able to get any — In fact, some people won't let me back into their homes — but I'm great with kids — and even better with daddyies.

I'm available most every night and some afternoons. If you want to see me in action drop by_____ theatre.

bitch," were willing to take new risks.[30] Along with others, this husband hungered for the sexual freedom and self-gratification that Candy offered.

The way adult men portrayed babysitters like Candy reflected their feelings about teenage girls whose cultural practices thrilled and threatened. Candy's sexual liberation pointed toward the excitement of new possibilities for men and the endangerment of marital fidelity and patriarchal privilege. After a fun-filled dalliance with Candy, George chose to revive his "true" manliness by resurrecting his marriage and securing his position. Unpunished for her premarital erotic assertions, Candy would continue to seek fulfillment through personal liberation. She was unlikely to follow a conventional path and become a wife or mother anytime in the near future.[31] Candy would nonchalantly move on to the next guy, the next job. What remained at the end of the movie, then, were the continuing dangers posed by an independent girlhood free from social strictures.[32]

"Beware all Daddy's. Those Babysitters are Back to Back. And They're Twice the Trouble Together!" declared an ad for a double feature in the *San Francisco Examiner*.[33] In addition to *The Babysitter* (1969), *Weekend with the Babysitter* (1970) revolved around another babysitter named Candy, only this one was a brunette instead of a blonde. "She is every man's first love but she's trouble," explained the promotional trailer. In another attempt to reach men older than the typical teenage audience, the film was also promoted as "[a] motion picture that hits home. Maybe your home."[34] Despite the differences in hair color, this Candy was just as sexually promiscuous, emotionally detached, and potentially threatening as her namesake. Wearing a mini-skirt and go-go boots, Candy rode a motorcycle to the suburban home where she babysat. This biker babysitter, like other sexualized girls pictured on motorcycles in soft porn and advertisements of the period, sat coolly astride the pleasures and perils of a girlhood infused with a new sexual ethos, youth culture values, and women's liberation ideals.[35]

Active Girls and Movie Maniacs

The trickle-down influence of feminism and other social movements had led many teenage girls to actively question accepted definitions and assumptions, challenge sources of authority, explore new alternatives to

Sexually suggestive advertisements aimed to woo audiences to view the soft-porn movie *The Babysitter* (1969), both stimulated desire and fueled suspicions about teenage girls.

traditional gender roles, and seek new ways to define themselves as young "women."[36] In the context of these changes, babysitting seemed like an increasingly unacceptable way of making money even in the face of the gloomy economic market in the 1970s.[37] Girls found objectionable the criticism of female employers expressed in such "familiar lines" as, "When I baby-sat at your age, Linda, I charged only 50 cents for an entire evening" and "Of course, it is none of my business since I'm not your mother, Linda, but if I were, I certainly wouldn't let a daughter of mine go out at night wearing a dress that short."[38]

The impact of increasing numbers of girls not wanting to babysit was felt by mothers such as feminist writer and mother Alix Kates Shulman. She sometimes spent a good hour making one phone call after another in her quest to find a sitter so that she could get out of the house.[39] The most common problem reported in all the letters sent in by readers of *McCall's* dealt with finding a sitter in the suburbs.[40] The refrain many mothers routinely uttered to others, according to *Who Cares for the Baby: Choices for Child Care* (1978), was, "If I can find a sitter."[41]

Girls' pursuit of empowerment and autonomy continued to shape their outlook about the job that was still closely identified with teenage girls. As hospitals and community centers that offered training courses pursued their efforts to reach potential babysitters, girls' critiques of babysitting reflected the influence of feminist and countercultural ideals.[42] One contributor to *Seventeen* magazine wrote, "Baby-Sitting Isn't Bliss!" in which the young author shared her disaffected realization.[43] "Baby-sitting was no fun! In fact, it was *hard work*, frequently boring, often painful, definitely confining and the pay was barely enough to keep me in pantyhose."[44] Another sitter went one step further in "Baby-sitter Blues." "Sooner or later you [too] will be faced with that 'superduper' baby-sitting job. It will shatter your nerves, destroy your peace of mind—and you'll be wondering why you ever thought that taking care of kids could be fun!"[45]

Though girls' attitudes about themselves had been evolving for decades, it was during the 1970s that the supervision and surveillance of girls by their parents rapidly gave way to changing beliefs about girls' rights to their own bodies. In a host of decisions that "had important consequences for the autonomy, as well as the anatomy, of America's female adolescents," explains historian Joan Jacobs Brumberg, the Supreme Court responded to changing practices by establishing new principles.[46] Over just a few years the Court sanctioned teenage girls' new sexual identity in decisions that validated girls' reproductive independence.[47] *Ordway v. Hargraves* (1971) protected pregnant girls from being expelled from public school. Congress made birth control services available to teenage girls. In *Eisenstadt v. Baird* (1972) unmarried girls were granted the right to birth control without parental permission. Then in 1973, *Roe v. Wade* legalized abortion.

During the 1970s, 75 percent of teenage girls became sexually active by age seventeen. Teenage girls increasingly acquainted with feminist ideas about freedom and self-fulfillment found validation for their behavior in a spate of new books.[48] In such feminist works as *Our Bodies, Our Selves* (1970) and *Fear of Flying* (1973), teenage girls and young women were able to explore their sexual selves.[49] Among other works, Marlo Thomas's *Free to Be You and Me* (1974) promoted an ethos of autonomy and individuality free from gendered expectations. Novels published for young adults also emphasized the importance of girls' control over their maturing bodies and their sexual choices.[50]

These themes also reverberated in popular music—especially songs written by men—that reveled in the sexual activities of babysitters. "I was much too late to be the first to make you a woman / But you were the one who made my mother's son a man," went the chorus of Harry Chapin's "Babysitter" (1975) song.[51] In the vanguard of punk rock were the Ramones, whose "Babysitter" (1977) described a girl who insisted that "it's alright" for her boyfriend to join her while babysitting.[52]

Female adolescents' independence, which had begun to generate ever greater anxiety during the 1970s, found further expression in soft porn movies. In *Jail Bait Babysitter* (1977) seventeen-year-old Vicki March had mixed feelings about sex.[53] While her friends called her "jailbait," they also belittled her for being a prude. Though she snuck her horny boyfriend into the house where she babysat and hung around with hoodlums, she would prove herself to be a good girl in the end. But in the meantime, she got mixed up with a prostitute who introduced her to Jerry, a middle-aged man without hair and self-esteem. Vicki tried to build up his confidence with ego-boosting observations like, "You're in better shape than most guys my age" and "You have something they'll never have. Wisdom."[54] But despite her best efforts, she could not summon the passion that would thaw her ice-cold legs that felt like "steel beams" to him. The effort that he was forced to put into "making it" with this underage virgin induced a heart attack that ultimately landed him in the hospital after quick-thinking Vicki called his physician. As Jerry was being taken away in the ambulance (diagnosis: "too excited"), the doctor spoke for the "establishment" when he said to Vicki, with her boyfriend now by her side, "It would be better for all of us if you hung out with kids your own age."[55] Though she was merely a figure in a male fantasy about the thrilling and threatening possibilities of female sexuality, it was the teenage girl who was ordered to change her ways.

Already conservatives had begun to mobilize against girls' freedom.[56] In response to feminist ideals, "pro-life" advocates became staunch defenders of conservative social values that buttressed the traditional family structure in which fathers were heads of households and mothers were help-mates. Whether identified as "Middle Americans," the "Silent Majority," or the "Moral Majority," those opposed to the era's changing social values assailed access to birth control, abortion rights, and the independence of teenage girls.[57] Moreover, as these forces began to attack sex education, so would movie maniacs assault girls for their agency and autonomy. Although legislation had contributed to a loosening of sexual mores, horror movies would serve to check desire by showing girls the punishment that awaited their transgressions.

The dark characters who issued warnings about the perils of liberation in the sixties also populated sitter stories in the seventies.[58] The novel *Are You in the House Alone?* (1976), produced as a made-for-television movie in 1978, traced the everyday life of a high school senior, Gail, who appeared battered and bloody in the lurid opening scene. Because Gail refused to identify the rapist, the movie plot focused on an array of possible suspects. Had it been Gail's current boyfriend or a former one still angry at her for not sleeping with him? Had it been her seductive middle-aged teacher for whom Gail had babysat? The fact that this could happen to a girl like Gail was, it was implied, because her family was torn apart by the profound social changes of the era, especially the gendered ones that had left Gail vulnerable to violence. "As Parents' Influence Fades—Who's Raising the Children?" asked *U.S. News & World Report* in 1975.[59] Not Gail's mother, who had grown deeply dissatisfied with her marriage and her full-time role as household drudge. She joined the majority of American mothers with school-age children who now held jobs outside the home.[60] Shaped by liberal feminist notions about individual achievement, she had shrilly justified her decision to go back to work with the declaration that "[i]t's necessary for me!" Concerned that Gail would make the same "mistake" and marry as a teenager, she encouraged her daughter to "[s]ee the world . . . make choices . . . have it all!"

Father's opposition to his wife's wage earning was offset by the loss of his job, not all that unusual during the economic dislocation of the era. To make matters worse, his wife decided that now it was up to the women of the family to protect him and his wounded pride. Unable to find another job, he drowned his sorrows in drink and denial. He resembled other American men during the inflationary 1970s. "Reluctant to give up the privileges that traditionally accompanied being a man in American society," explains Sophia Hoffert in *The History of Gender in America* (2003), "they dug in their heels and resisted the demand that they help with the childcare and housework . . . they retreated to their bars and clubs in order to avoid having to face the changing demands that were being made on them."[61] Yet even before this dad lost his job, he failed as a father who didn't prevent the loss of his daughter's virginity (a fact that made it more difficult to prosecute the rapist). Poor Gail. Not only was her dad emasculated; her mother was inaccessible and uncaring. "[You] asked for it!" she screamed at Gail unsympathetically.[62] In fact, Gail was not a virgin. Having slept with her boyfriend, she believed that sex between those "in love" was acceptable.

While Gail reflected a more conservative viewpoint than that held by other girls, her attitude nevertheless provoked those who opposed the growing sexual agency of female adolescents represented in other movies. Though Amanda was still a virgin, she looked as if she wasn't one. In *Fright* (1971), she went babysitting dressed in go-go boots and a tight-fitting dress hemmed just below the chain-link belt that could do little to protect her chastity.[63] (Clearly, she had not read the chapter about forestalling problems by dressing appropriately, published in *The Franklin Watts Concise Guide to Baby-Sitting* [1972]).[64] Because the babbling psychotic husband imagined her to be his rejecting ex-wife (a woman damned for her youthful desire), Amanda would take the blame for all "sexually active" females. In a one-two punch, Amanda would be raped by the homicidal maniac, then sexually exploited by the camera's relentless breasts-in-brassiere shots.

As the "final girl," the one left standing after all her friends had fallen, Laurie in *Halloween* was spared (rewarded, really) because she was "pure at heart."[65] Laurie was romantic, lonely, and maternal, while changing sexual ideals had shaped her girlfriends' beliefs and behaviors.[66] All Lynda and Annie talked about was sex. Though a woman wrote their dialogue, the girls' sex talk made them sound a lot like guys in a locker room. Thus, Annie's sexual bravado and bitchiness got her hacked to death, while Lynda, who had orgasmic sex with her boyfriend while babysitting, died a similarly violent death at the hands of Michael. He was the monster who had begun his killing spree at age six when he had mercilessly slashed his nude sister with a butcher knife for making love with her boyfriend while babysitting.

Deadly Markers: Liberation and Containment

By 1974, a growing number of American fathers had custody of their children, reported *Newsweek* in an article about the challenges they faced as wives pursued careers and sought divorces. Feeling caught between the demands of his job and his children, "I became bitchy, resentful, unkempt, and shrill," explained a 34-year-old father of two.[67] Bewildered—even enraged—by the ascendance of feminist ideals, many men did "everything they could" to resist change.[68] According to one gender historian, "They subjected their female co-workers to varying degrees of harassment. . . . Some even beat their wives and children out of sheer frustration of not being able to stem the tide of changing expectations."[69] Men fought to preserve their prerogative and to assert their dominance at home, at work, in sports, and in the cultural imagination. One media scholar theorized that "the horror film plays out the rage of a paternity denied the economic and political benefits of patriarchal power."[70]

A handful of horror films featured male monsters just as sinister and sexual as the legendary maniac. They served as mutant surrogates for the emasculated husband and father tormented by their diminished role in family life. The faceless movie maniac, in the many horror movies that included babysitters, knew no bounds. Madmen's favorite victims would be those who threatened the traditional social order: teenage girls who followed their mother's footsteps right out of the front door. In one movie after another, young income-earning females, unconstrained by family, empowered by feminism, liberated by the sexual revolution, and self-gratified by youth culture would get what they deserved.[71]

Over the course of the 1970s, the maniac's hold on the imagination grew stronger as men's grip on patriarchal power loosened. At the beginning of the decade the bloody power struggle over definitions of gender led a psychiatric hospital escapee searching for his rejecting wife in *Fright* (1971) to terrorize the teenage girl babysitting for his three-year-old son.[72] In retaliation for all women who now put their selfish desires before family obligations, this maniac cut the phone lines, raped the sitter, and murdered her boyfriend. By the end of the decade, *Halloween* (1978) featured Michael, the deranged man with a murderous passion for sitters. (The film's financial backer had initially wanted the movie entitled "The Babysitter Murders.")[73] Another teenage babysitter fell prey to Malcolm, a crazed ex-husband who escaped from an insane asylum in *Trick or Treats* (1982). Malcolm turned his lust for vengeance against his rejecting wife on the sitter who already had been forced to put up with his son, a monstrous practical joker who could have taught Dennis the Menace a thing or two.

Meanwhile, a maniac had terrorized a babysitter in *When a Stranger Calls* (1979), the box-office smash hit closely based on the babysitter/maniac legend.[74] When Carol Kane, the young actress who starred as the babysitter, first read the script, she was so frightened that she had to spend the night at a friend's house. "I didn't want to be alone," she explained.[75] Nor would other timorous teens after seeing the film, in which the sitter was tormented by a caller who commanded her to "check the children." (According to one woman, that movie "terrified all of us babysitters back then!"[76]) In addition to murderous men, what made this movie and the others so frightening was the encoding of anxieties, ambivalences, suspicions, hostilities, and feelings of alienation in everyday objects. Seemingly ordinary things became weapons in back-and-forth reappropriations between generations in conflict over issues of gender: the suburban house and the telephone became tools of liberation and mechanisms of containment.

For instance, the ordinary yet omnipresent suburban ranch or split level became the standard site for modern horror just as the gabled Victorian house had been the scene of many Gothic tales.[77] Though its open floor plan lacked mystery, it now haunted the imagination. Emptied of nurturing mothers and protective fathers who spent less time at home and more time at the office, the suburban home ceased to be imagined as a haven. Rising divorce rates, one-parent families, working mothers, and geographical mobility were all factors that created a crisis and exacted a "high toll on emotions of both parents and children—bringing to many families a widening 'generation gap' of mutual hostility, suspicion, or simply noncommunication," explained *U.S. News & World Report* in 1975.[78] Expressing the intense anxieties of those caught up in the sweeping gender and generational shifts of the 1970s, the figure of the babysitter drew attention to the family cut off from itself.

The typical American dream house turned nightmarish as new notions of gender brought about transformations that benefited some family members but unsettled others. As adults and adolescents redefined relationships, roles, and identities, in modern horror movies the house came to reflect the irrepressible impulses of those trying to break free from limitations.[79] In babysitter movies in particular, being able to escape the house that fostered a sense of entrapment released teenage girls from confining gender expectations. Yet the tortuous struggle they endured in the process revealed the tenacity of traditional notions. Menaced by the maniac who annihilated the social order, the teenage girl who had merely disturbed it would be left to yearn for the protection of patriarchy and the comforts of domesticity.

Babysitter horror movies that featured maniacs expressed particular apprehensions about the changing nature of fatherhood, especially as crimes committed by ordinary suburban dads appeared to rise. Far less notorious than other crimes covered by the mass media was the story reported in the *New York Times* in 1977, about an employer who caught his babysitter drinking beer with boys and raped the sixteen-year-old in front of his six-year-old daughter.[80] That same year, several girls were raped by a robber while babysitting in suburban New Jersey. And a thirteen-year-old girl who went to babysit never returned to her home outside of Minneapolis, Minnesota.[81] A growing fear of neighbors in suburban communities assumed to be safe retreats led *American Home* magazine to advise members of new-style babysitter cooperatives not to recommend new members "cavalierly."[82] Though girls were unlikely readers of *The National Locksmith*, an article in it urged babysitters to take every precaution, suggesting that "[a]fter the parents leave, check and lock all the doors, leaving the key in the lock; you might want to get out in a hurry."[83]

In the event that something did go wrong, there was always the telephone. In "Birds on the Wire: Troping Teenage Girlhood through Telephony in Mid-Twentieth Century U.S. Media Culture," media scholar Mary Celeste Kearney argued that in the history of girls, the telephone functioned as a "signifier of girlhood . . . simultaneously representing girls' liberation from the domestic sphere while also suggesting a method for their containment within it."[84] Kearney argues that between the 1940s and early 1960s "a notable shift in the construction of this trope occurred . . . moving from girls talking to their girlfriends about a variety of individuals and social activities while being supervised by their fathers, to girls talking solely about their boyfriends and romantic experiences without parental supervision. . . ."[85] While this study is useful for understanding the role of the telephone as an object that both constituted and contained female adolescents in postwar America, it unfortunately ends just as girlhood was on the brink of critical transformation and containment strategies were shifting to more sinister forms. In fact, by the time *Bye Bye Birdie* (1963) was shown in movie theaters, far more aggressive narratives that utilized the symbolically significant telephone already had begun to circulate. While fathers had ceased to monitor their daughters' telephone calls (widespread since the mid-1940s), it was horrific villains in urban legends and vocational movies who threatened girls they called on the telephone. And as growing numbers of pleasure-seeking, anti-authoritarian girls continued to mount challenges to traditional standards of girlhood, more maniacs attempted to contain girls by silencing them.

What accounts for the many popular-culture images of men who victimized girls with telephones? Representations of teenage girls on the threshold of independence and the telephone as a synecdochic object characterizing female adolescence suggest soaring cultural anxieties. Reading the meanings encoded in images and embedded in objects, reveals that the telephone functioned as a technological tool and as an ideological instrument. The telephone communicated dominant as well as dissonant notions by constituting, critiquing, cautioning, controlling, and contesting girlhood.

While the telephone was a sitter's tool of the trade, it also functioned as the maniac's weapon of war. In the hands of the murderous anti-hero, the handset became a phallic tool used to intimidate and victimize girls. Babysitters' inappropriate, indiscriminate, and indulgent use of the telephone would lead them to be cut off and cut up. Spliced telephone lines as well as dangling phones became standard tropes of the ongoing struggle over girlhood. In *Wanted: Babysitter* (1975) a thug cut the telephone lines after he threatened and verbally abused the babysitter. In the hands of more violent men in horror movies, telephones also became instruments of torture. Michael strangled Lynda with a telephone cord in *Halloween* (1978). Lynda was already cut off from her friend because Michael had cut the phone lines.

Menacing telephone calls placed by creepy men also served to remind girls that retribution was inevitable. The creep who stalked Gail called to ask, "Are you in the house alone?" and to tell her that he was "getting closer." One year later, Jill Johnson was similarly informed in *When a Stranger Calls* (1979). In that film, the director made "the most of that fearsome modern weapon, the telephone," observed film critic Janet Maslin.[86] Babysitter narratives further punished girls by placing the audience in the uncomfortable role of an accomplice to an obsessive, sadistic voyeur.

Based on the influential urban legend that had emerged during the 1960s, the maniac who appeared in seventies slasher films such as *When a Stranger Calls* punished girls who explored their autonomy. *When a Stranger Calls*, movie still.

For girl viewers, the convergence of familiar narrative conventions—dark theaters and cinematic devices—forced them to see themselves through the eyes of deranged men and to feel the sitter's terror. A girl could identify with the fear of impending catastrophe because she had failed to do as she was told. Sharing the maniac's leering gaze and symbolic inversion of the telephone, which either facilitated or frustrated communication, any parent-employer could also have identified with this revenge fantasy in the days before "call waiting."

Boy Babysitter "House Guards"

While irresponsible girls were irresistible magnets for maniacs who sought to contain them, boy sitters continued to be seen as exemplary child-care providers even though they comprised less than 5 percent of students enrolled in babysitter courses.[87] Since the 1930s, boys had served as gendered and generational counterpoints to teenage girls and adult men. Despite public discourses about male juvenile delinquency in all its forms, boy sitters never became threats to the gendered order and generational hierarchy. Instead, they functioned as a cultural ideal, a magical anodyne, capable of bridging the problems associated with gender and youth. That is apparent in the publication of the children's book *George the Babysitter* (1977). Though influenced by the counterculture and changing gender roles, the long-haired, bell-bottomed babysitter maintained his manliness. While George looked more feminine than the single working mother mannishly dressed in a pants suit and cowboy boots, George was just as responsible as legions of boys who babysat during previous periods.[88] George cooked and cleaned each day for the kids in his care, yet he remained every inch a man. At the end of a long day, George liked to sit and read a football magazine—an unmistakable marker of masculinity. Unlike their fathers, teenage boys managed what their elders could not: domestic safety within the masculine domain.

Babysitter training films also promoted the idea that boy babysitters were tried and true. Following George's lead, boy babysitters dwelled in a horror-free domain they maintained with masculine authority. The vocational film *Understanding Babysitting* (1980) explained why nothing ever went wrong when a boy was in charge. Learning how to be "businesslike," the boy in this training film took "all the guess work out" of babysitting. In *Planning Babysitting* (1980), another boy spotted potential hazards just "like a detective." In the followup film *Handling Emergencies* (1980), a boy explained, "I'm not quite old enough for what I really want to do which is to be a professional firefighter. In a lot of ways, being a babysitter is like being a firefighter: responsibility and training."[89]

Conclusion

As teenage girls steadily removed themselves from the field of babysitting, the babysitter became the object of multiple cultural anxieties. Concerns about profound social transformations led conservative political movements to halt the contraction of fathers' place in the family and economy, and the expansion of mothers' roles outside the home. Trepidation about paternal absence, maternal neglect, and youthful female rebellion also found expression in myths and movies.[90] Stories that blamed the babysitter for being sexy and sassy served to bind anxieties about the tensions between girls' feminist ideals and antifeminist goals. In retaliation for the purposeful redefinition of girlhood and womanhood and the attenuation of manhood, male maniacs stalked those destroying the domestic ideal that girls contested and sitters represented. At the end of babysitter narratives, girls were left longing for the safety of domesticity and the protection of patriarchy.

Two female adolescents appeared in the movie *Wanted: Babysitter* (1975). One a victim, the other almost a villain, together they signaled what lay just ahead for girls: victimized babysitters would become scarce and villainous ones abundant. In Oregon a pediatrician, police captain, PTA official, school nurse, and director of public safety devised a "sitter test" aimed at screening out problem sitters like the mental hospital escapee who had recently beaten a twenty-month-old baby.[91] In Southwest Missouri, a babysitter legend circulated among girls and their families who sought an explanation for a mysterious natural phenomenon: a light "that seemed to come at you then disappear." According to neighbors, a girl who had been babysitting the four children of a local banker in their "nice country home" "went crazy" one night and murdered three of "her charges." Though the surviving child escaped into the woods, the babysitter who shined her flashlight on the horizon had been in a murderous pursuit ever since. While some argued that the light was nothing more than swamp gas, the story unsettled children as well as adults living in Neosho, Missouri.[92] What light this legendary babysitter shed was not on a natural phenomenon, however: on the cultural horizon in the 1980s lay a population of spoiled, self-centered, and "spooky" teenage girls.

7

Sisterhoods of Sitters

In 1979 the *Kansas City Times* reported that "[o]ne of the most indispensable persons in the world—and one around whom your social life revolves to some extent—is the sitter."[1] Just a few years later, the newspaper would cover the case of a babysitter serial killer. During the 1980s, many teenage girls in movies turned into monsters as dangerous as the maniacs who had been stalking babysitters for decades. The transformation of sitters from victim to victimizer—from powerless to powerful—led deranged teens to turn the tables on their attackers and direct their fury against parent-employers. In popular movies examined in this chapter, a revised version of the teenage babysitter who was hired to keep the place clean made a mess in living rooms and lives. Hired to be the cop, she became the criminal. Hired to ensure safety, she threatened security. Hired to mother, she murdered children. I argue that this raw depiction of sitters as killers was due to the ever increasing self-sufficiency of teenage girls: Imagining the sitter as a feminist Frankenstein enabled adults to express their displeasure with girls who now preferred a job at a mall to caring for kids.[2]

Yet, the vilification of teenagers occurred in tandem with the valorization of preadolescents. This chapter demonstrates that the good-natured preadolescent girl—as opposed to her bad-tempered older sister—served adults as the most promising candidate for the feminization of girlhood. After a forty-year hiatus, the preadolescent girl was reconceptualized as less vulnerable and more valuable in self-help literature and girls' fiction, sources on which this chapter also draws. Manuals and magazines from *Women's World* to *Weekly Reader* promoted the "Super Sitter," the miniature version of the "Superwoman." Updated handbooks and training courses emerged to develop girls' skills, buttress their confidence, stimulate their interest, and empower them as babysitters. In order to make babysitting appeal to young girls whose aspirations had been fueled by feminism, children's fiction reframed babysitting as a "business." The best-selling Baby-sitter's Club book series promoted the notion that "determination, ambition, individual achievement, competence, and hard work [like babysitting] would enable girls to realize their dreams."[3] At the same time that babysitting literature promoted empowerment, it also aimed to attenuate young girls' autonomy, as horror movies, handbooks, course curricula, and babysitter fiction had for decades. The Super Sitter who appeared during the last two decades of the twentieth century served to neutralize feminist notions by glorifying babysitting. Walking a tightrope between female empowerment and accommodation, the preadolescent, presexual Super Sitter made American girlhood more endearing than dangerous.

A Serial Sitter

In 1982, the *Kansas City Star* was one of a number of newspapers that covered the case of the notorious babysitter serial killer, Christine Falling.[4] It all began when a two-year-old girl died while in the care of the eighteen-year-old junior-high-school dropout. No one in the poor Florida community where she resided blamed the babysitter.[5] Although no autopsy was performed, the cause of death was declared to have been encephalitis. When a four-year-old boy died next while also in the care of Christine Falling, local authorities believed that he had died of myocarditis. Several days later, the dead boy's cousin died suddenly while his parents attended their nephew's funeral. Guess who was babysitting at the time? Baby number four who also died suddenly was Christine Falling's eight-month-old step-niece. Authorities suggested the baby had a fatal reaction to vaccinations she had just received the day before at a local clinic. Again, no autopsies were performed because the local officials who had investigated the deaths believed that all the children had suffered from health problems caused by poverty.[6] While investigators declared Christine to be a "victim of circumstance," how about the three other children who became seriously ill while under her care? "I tell you," Christine pondered, "sometimes I wonder if I don't have some kind of spell over me when I get around young 'uns."[7] After a fifth child was found dead in the ramshackle trailer the babysitter shared with her boyfriend, even Christine had to admit that it was an "awful weird coincidence."[8] Then, in her confession to a forensic psychiatrist, Christine was purported to have explained that "[t]he way I done it, I seen it done on [a] TV show."[9]

Feminist Frankensteins

There was certainly no shortage of out-of-control babysitters on TV during the 1980s,[10] as well as proto-maternal monsters who went off the deep end in movies.[11] Ambivalence and anxiety about the challenges that girls and women posed to the traditional social order were projected onto this new breed of fictionalized sitters who stood as perverse personifications of feminist ideals. Such was the case because not everyone was enthusiastic about women's new social standing, political achievements, and economic status. Not when nearly half of all mothers with preschool children held jobs by 1980 and the divorce rate continued to skyrocket.[12] Reflecting the unease of those who conceived of feminism as a hostile force, teenage girls were cast as mommy/maniacs whose rejection of gender conventions was expressed in mayhem.[13] Madness had long appeared as a metaphor in American literature of the threat posed by female rebels. Yet far more like evil step-mothers than fairy tale daughters, murderous babysitters wielded power that was social, sexual, economic.[14]

Along with other psychotic monsters in postmodern horror films, Joanna violently disrupted everyday life as she effortlessly took over the daily life of a family in *The Babysitter* (1980 TVM). She was able to do so because she seemed like a competent homemaker, especially compared to the alcoholic mother, Mrs. Liz Benedict, who employed her. Like other drug-addicted hysterical moms in movies of the period, Liz was "driven batty by subordination, repression, drudgery, and neglect."[15] "I'm a rotten mother," Liz confided to Joanna. She was also not much of a wife, observed her husband. Occasionally drunk and often depressed, Liz was oblivious to the ways in which her sitter aggressively competed for her husband's attention, as had sexy sitters over the past two decades. Joanna stole ("borrowed") one of Liz's negligees. Though Liz's husband, Dr. Jeff Benedict, resisted Joanna's seduction for much of the movie, the lovely and licentious eighteen-year-old sitter was an irresistible male fantasy, the kind that had been circulating since the 1960s. The fantasy of the sitter unconstrained by cultural codes also exemplified the dangers of female sexual agency (see chapter 6). Drawing upon a misogynistic literary tradition that held women accountable for sexual transgressions, the sexually aggressive babysitter in this film went berserk.[16] Emptied of affection and full of aggression, the knife-wielding babysitter took deadly aim at the father and his family.

Though unhinged by her murderous passion, the teenage vixen was made to act out adults' anxieties. The dynamic had been pervasive for decades. The intensity of changing gender roles, sexual mores, and family life during the seventies and eighties, however, fueled nightmarish fantasies about empowered girls and emasculated men. Identifying babysitters as deviant served to contain the ubiquitous threat they represented. Asserting his authority, Dr. Benedict, as head of household, restored law and order in *The Baby Sitter*. While his masculinity had been bolstered by Joanna's rampant attraction, it was now solidified by the babysitter's unqualified submission. Joanna's arrest symbolized the necessity of restraining female sexuality, reestablishing sanity, restoring familial stability, and repressing the teenage girl.

Psychotic babysitters and baby killers entered the family living room in the many made-for-television movies of the 1980s. Diane Franklin was another emotionally unbalanced teen in *Summer Girl* (1983 TV), a thriller about a family disrupted by a ruthless babysitter who plotted to seduce the husband. And in *The Sitter* (1991 TV), delusional and sadistic, Nell was unable to distinguish fantasy from reality. With her flowing golden locks, frilly apron, ballroom gown, and yearning for Prince Charming (she memorized romantic movie dialogue), Nell seemed like a modern-day Cinderella. The only problem was that, while she appeared innocent (she donned the uniform of an English nanny when she babysat), Nell was certifiably insane.

This early 1990s version of Nell stood in sharp contrast to the more vulnerable young woman played by Marilyn Monroe in *Don't Bother to Knock* (1952), discussed in chapter 3. This late-twentieth-century Nell and other movie sitters who were products of broken homes and dysfunctional families reflected broader concerns about family instability. Nell was illegitimate and abandoned in *The Sitter* (1991), while in *The Babysitter* (1980), Joanna's parents had died and she lived with numerous foster "families." Unable to alter her past, Joanna tried to "change the things to come," according to the lyrics of a song to which she slow danced at a make-out party she threw, while babysitting, of course. While feminist criminologists would shortly examine girls' pathways to crime from a more sympathetic perspective, the media drew upon the "Liberation Hypothesis" that correlated the high rate of female offenses to women's changing status. "It is Women's Liberation come to kill us," one publication would report about the rising rates of female offenders.[17]

The only one not drawn into Joanna's machinations was a neighbor, a retired doctor—true professional expertise in patrician form—who discovered another family mass murdered by Joanna. Although child abuse as a social problem had been "discovered" in the 1870s, "rediscovered" in the 1960s, and legislatively addressed in the 1970s, it was during the early 1980s that babysitters were added to the list of potential perpetrators.[18] Reflecting cultural anxieties about the impact of gender and generational changes on families and individuals, one psychiatric study concluded that "[t]roubled childhoods where fathers are unavailable and mothers are demanding allies during the critical Oedipal phase of development can lead adolescents—with the opportunity that unrestricted baby sitting provides—to become sexual abusers."[19] Another team of psychiatrists found that between one-third and one-half of the babysitters surveyed had hit the children in their care.[20] Within a climate attuned to the problem of child abuse, family disintegration, and female autonomy, teenage babysitters represented the dangers of girlhood toward the end of the twentieth century.[21]

More Bidders Than Sitters

While not every babysitter who appeared in movies from the 1980s was a raving lunatic, even babysitters in comedies routinely broke laws, rules, codes, and customs. Such was the case in *Adventures in Babysitting* (1987), a comedy about a teenage girl who takes the kids from the safety of the suburbs into the wilds of Chicago where they encounter hijackers and gang members. In *The World According to Garp* (1982), the babysitter had sex with her male employer. (In the book upon which it was based, there are many such babysitters.) In *Mystic Pizza* (1988), a film that examined the nuances of girlhood in the 1980s, all three teenage characters engaged in sexual transgressions. It was Kat, serious and spotless, who had sex with the man who employed her to babysit.

While babysitters were plentiful in popular movies, there were actually few to be found in American neighborhoods.[22] After the "baby boom" and "baby bust" (from 1961 to the mid-1970s), a "baby boomlet" in the 1980s pushed birth rates back up again.[23] The shifting demographics meant that there were only one million potential teenage babysitters nationwide, not enough to care for the four million new babies.[24] "We don't even go out. It's too frustrating to even look," Richard Uelow, a father and Justice Department attorney told the *Washington Post* in 1984.[25] One harried mother who brought her wailing infant along to a romantic restaurant explained to a disapproving waiter, "We couldn't get a sitter."[26]

The reasons why female adolescent babysitters were becoming a "rare commodity" can only partly be explained by demographics, however.[27] While most newspapers and magazines focused on age ratios, the *Boston Globe* explained that increasing rates of homework and more after-school activities led fewer teens to babysit.[28] "Today's teens spend even less time at home than you probably did," *Business Week* explained to adults of the baby boom generation.[29] Eager and able teenage girls with growing opportunities were expanding their horizons. "The kids of baby-sitting age are very socially active, and I have the feeling that most don't need the money," said a Washington, D.C., parent.[30]

Yet even the more active lifestyle of female adolescents did not fully explain the sitter scarcity. Sounding a lot like previous generations, babysitters in one study revealed that taking care of children was often not a "positive experience."[31] In *Seventeen* magazine an exasperated sitter explained that what she objected to was the job's low pay and status.

> When I came home from a hard day's baby-sitting one winter night last year, I was discouraged and disappointed. I'd arrived on the job at 11 AM and made lunch for the two children. . . . When the parents finally came home, I got a thanks and a ten-dollar bill—for eleven hours of hard work! Back in my own house, I thought I could forget about what I considered unfair wages. But then came the crowning blow. My parents had paid the boy down the block three dollars to shovel snow off our front walk—a task that takes fifteen minutes.[32]

Clearly inspired by feminist ideals, this sitter called upon others to "demand equal wages."[33]

Honoring Babysitting's Male Heroes

That teenage girls were either scarce or scary led male sitters to reenter babysitting's fertile field. New manuals such as *Oh Boy, Babies!* (1980) that documented the training of boy sitters sought to stimulate boys' interest in child care.[34] Stories about babysitter heroism also could be found on network television shows. *Charles in Charge*, a sit-com that aired on CBS from 1984 to 1985 and then again from 1987 to 1990, focused on a nineteen-year-old male college student who worked as a live-in babysitter. Unlike the murderous female adolescents who threatened the security of American families, Charles was "in charge," not out of control. "I want Charles in charge of me," was the chorus of the sit-com's theme song as seen through the eyes of the family's young son.[35] That show's second run overlapped with ABC's *Mr. Belvedere*, a somewhat updated version of the male babysitter who starred in *Sitting Pretty* (1948). While there had been several attempts to make Mr. Belvedere the focus of television shows during the 1950s and 1960s, it was not until 1985 that changing social conditions finally created the right fit. Because the mother was a law student and then a lawyer no longer able to be a full-time mother, the typical suburban nuclear family relied on Mr. Belvedere to rescue them with his wit and wisdom.

Shaping the Preadolescent "Super Sitter"

Some parents turned to boys to babysit but more looked to preadolescent girls. When *Newsday* conducted an informal poll in 1987, they found that most of the sixth graders in their daily sample of Long Islanders started sitting at age eleven.[36] Similarly in places like St. Louis, Missouri, Molly started babysitting at eleven and Jennie, Ruby, and Danica when they were nine or ten years old.[37] "I babysit a lot so I know a lot," eleven-year-old Lisa Bilodeau of Roxbury, Massachusetts, explained to a reporter for the *Boston Globe*.[38]

"The age has really come down a lot," observed one instructor who had been teaching babysitters since the 1970s.[39] In 1973, a Census Bureau survey had revealed that almost half of all babysitters were under the age of sixteen and an additional third between the ages of sixteen and nineteen.[40] By the end of the 1970s, the majority of girls who enrolled in a babysitting course offered at New England Memorial Hospital were only between the ages of ten and thirteen.[41] In Illinois, mothers hired eleven- and twelve-year-olds to babysit on weekends, on holidays, and during summer vacations.[42] Several years hence the *Boston Globe* would report that what parents liked about young girls was that they were "often especially fond of babies and toddlers, and they're too young to have busy social lives or other jobs."[43] Not yet interested in either drugs or sex, the younger sitter seemed more selfless than self-absorbed, more wholesome than whorish, more boyish than boy crazy.

Yet the young age of babysitters also made parent-employers uneasy. While some believed that "[t]he kids are more grown up at 11 years old now," others wondered about preteens' level of responsibility.[44] "In the old days, everyone had big families and children knew how to care for younger children because they were able to watch their mothers taking care of their siblings."[45] Lower birth rates along with rising divorce rates had contributed to the shrinking size of the American family (which, in the 1950s, averaged three to four children). The demographic dip that brought about the "baby bust" decreased the supply of teenage sitters and deprived children of siblings on whom they could practice their child-care skills. Worried about whether children had enough experience, many parents were left with the nagging question, "Is it really worth the evening out?"[46]

In an attempt to address the problem and assuage the anxieties of mothers shaped by the "new momism" ethos that was elevating standards of motherhood beyond the reach of most women, experts in the 1980s promoted a new sitter ideal. By drawing upon the rhetoric of empowerment, experts everywhere authorized the notion of the preadolescent "Super Sitter," who followed on the heels of the "Superwoman," a concept that became a standard for women's personal perfection and social satisfaction.[47] Yet unlike real working mothers stressed out by the persistent problem of child care, "Super Sitters" were true superheroes.[48] Highlighting the new importance of preadolescent girls, a *Kansas City Star* headline pronounced, "Super Sitters to the Rescue!"[49] By the mid-1980s, 54 percent of mothers with children under the age of six, and 70 percent of women with children between ages six and seventeen worked outside the home.[50] "These days, with so many mothers in the work force, the demand for sitters is even higher," explained *Baby-Sitting Safe and Sound* (1990).[51] This manual was among many that aimed to help girls prepare for their new social role. For just $24.95, girls could order the *Super Sitters* training kit and video or purchase the handbook, *How to Be a Super Sitter* (1991).[52]

In the new babysitting materials that aimed to provide information, generate enthusiasm, and forge an identity, girls were encouraged to conceive of themselves as miniature "businesswomen" for whom the "business" of babysitting would be an entrepreneurial (ad)venture.[53] It was a message not only designed to reach girls in middle school but also directed at those still in elementary school. Winifred, a plucky prepubescent in one children's story from the mid-1980s, represented this emergent cadre of sitters. She was an effective and empowered entrepreneur. Winifred advised her younger brother to "go find a job." "Then you'll be rich like me," she gloated while licking a double-dip ice cream cone, probably purchased with her babysitting earnings.[54] By all accounts, Winifred was a very successful businesswoman who operated the sitter service she launched from

Fears about teenage girls and a shortage of them during the 1980s led to
the widespread promotion of preadolescent "Super Sitters" who became
the focus of experts, educators, and fiction writers. Illustration from *Jerome
the Babysitter* by Eileen Christelow. Copyright © 1985 by Eileen Christelow.
Reprinted with permission of Clarion Books, an imprint of Houghton
Mifflin Harcourt Publishing Company. All rights reserved.

a home office, complete with a table, telephone, and wall calendar. The
mounted graph charted her business success.

Numerous self-help videos, magazines, and handbooks inundated the
inexperienced girl with information and an identity.[55] Along with other
manuals, *Things to Know about Babysitting* (1985) and *The Complete
Babysitter's Handbook* (1980) prepared girls for a "career" in babysitting.[56]
So did popular girls' magazines. *Teen* urged girls to "upgrade on-the-job
performance" and prepare "pre-sitting strategies."[57] *Seventeen* suggested
that sitters devise "start-up strategies" and provided quizzes designed to
make a girl into "a baby-sitting whiz."[58] The Pleasant Company (producers
of the American Girl Dolls) soon would publish the *Babysitter's Business
Kit* (1999), which would include such "Super Sitter Stuff" as the Client

Address Book. The business cards in the kit were deemed "tools" essential to "help you run the best business on the block."[59] Its children's-book-like illustrations made it clear that this kit was marketed to the elementary school crowd. Overall, the illustrations of babysitters in handbooks now depicted preadolescent and not teenage girls.[60]

In a departure from vocational films that had characterized girls as culpable (see chapter 5), new ones now cast young girls as capable. In *Understanding Babysitting* (1980), one girl suggested that a "confident business-like attitude" would lead to a "successful part-time business."[61] Reflecting the broader support for working women in *Working Girl* (1988), a movie about plucky women in corporate America, *Planning Babysitting* (1980) promoted a similar message to girls. Building up preadolescent girls' confidence was a strategy used in other movies and manuals. *How to Be a Super Sitter* (1991) taught girls how "[t]o build up confidence in yourself—confidence you'll carry with you for the rest of your life."[62]

Experts aimed to instill confidence as well as impart a body of knowledge. Courses taught babysitting basics to elementary and middle-school students in cities and towns across the country. In Roxbury, Massachusetts, fourth and fifth graders studied babysitting essentials, a six-week course designed by the 4-H Club.[63] So did local hospitals in Jamaica Plain, Framingham, Medford, and Faulkner.[64] *Career World* urged young girls to take one of the many new babysitting courses that developed girls' competence and also earned parents' trust.[65] Dr. Patricia Keener, chief pediatrician at an Indianapolis hospital, launched Safe Sitter Inc., a not-for-profit national program that provided the kind of babysitting classes *Career World* had in mind. "To enhance the lives of young adolescents by providing them with the opportunity to acquire competencies in rescue skills, basic first aid, and safe child care" was the mission of Safe Sitters.[66] Middle schoolers (sixth through eighth graders) could attend one of the many Safe Sitter courses run by volunteer parents, nurses, or other adult graduates of the workshops, offered at local hospitals, schools, YWCAs, and community centers. Based on the belief that on-the-job training was inadequate, the two-day course taught preadolescents (ages eleven to thirteen) about child development, first aid, safety skills (for sittees and sitters), and, of course, "business practices."[67] Numerous other organizations and institutions such as the American Red Cross also established babysitting training courses for preadolescents. Building on the model of its parent organization, the Kansas City chapter offered an eight-hour course on the basics of first aid and routine child care.

Consequently, by 1990, there were more than five thousand preadolescent Safe Sitters who had been trained in 216 locations in thirty-nine
states.[68] The courses that built girls' confidence had also alleviated parents'
anxieties. The mother of a ten-year-old girl in Utica, New York, believed
that her daughter showed "more confidence" after learning "the common
rules of safety." She now felt more comfortable leaving the ten-year-old
with her preschool-age siblings.[69] One parent-employer claimed that her
Safe Sitter graduate had made her think about "what's essential for the security and safety of my children."[70] Another observed that preadolescent
sitters with training were "often more prepared than adult caregivers."[71]
According to one fourteen-year-old girl, "[p]eople want sitters who know
what to do in an emergency, so I get a lot more jobs."[72]

Building a girl's skills and sense of self were laudable goals that served
to benefit everyone, parent-employers, babysitters, and the children in
their care. Babysitter training also served the needs of a society desperate for a reliable corps of caretakers. Yet the liberal feminist ideology that
went into the making of the pint-sized businessgirl exploited rather than
accepted girls' quest for autonomy. The Super Sitter business ethos had
aimed to attract girls who might otherwise have balked at babysitting.
Appealing to their desire for greater authority and independence, the Super Sitter ideal had made girls sit up, take notice—and babysit. It was a
cultural strategy that had been used by previous generations of adults to
corral the largest number of American girls in order to satisfy the need
for babysitters. Training programs, handbooks, and vocational films all
served to shape the skills, sensibilities, and social identities of girls in ways
that kept them in a home. And, eager to make money and unable to get
a "real" job, preadolescents existed as a captive audience. Moreover, the
inclusive indoctrination that addressed their yearning for autonomy and
artfully steered it toward domestic ends could be found elsewhere in girls'
lives.

"The Baby-sitters Club" and Sitter Empowerment

In addition to handbooks and training courses other significant cultural
resources contributed to the transformation of preadolescent girls into
socially useful Super Sitters. To generate excitement about babysitting
among girls not yet old enough to earn a certificate, *U.S. Kids, A Weekly
Reader Magazine* published "Becoming a Safe Sitter." In pictures and in
print, the late 1990s article informed elementary school students about

the Super Sitter ideal.[73] But chances were that girls already were familiar with this notion of girlhood. Along with self-help literature, the Super Sitter already had been inscribed into volumes of girls' fiction.[74] While fictionalized babysitters had appeared sporadically in children's books and young adult fiction before, they took center stage after 1980—just as the pressing need for babysitters emerged.

By far, the best known fictionalized babysitters of them all were those in the Baby-sitter's Club book series (BSC).[75] The BSC series of books, which a Scholastic editor had recruited children's book editor Ann M. Martin to write, directly drew upon a long tradition of book series that dated back to the early decades of the twentieth century. They featured champions who were every bit as competent, courageous, and careerist as the Super Sitter handbook heroine.[76] As the first BSC books rolled off the press, a book reviewer noted that Martin combined "the prolific practicality of Edward Stratemeyer (who created and packaged the Nancy Drew books under the name of Carolyn Keene), the more personal, hands-on vision of writers like Alcott and Montgomery, and her own 1990's egalitarianism."[77] She would also draw on the Horatio Alger series, which created a code of behavior for boys that promoted the work ethic, material success, and business culture.[78] Alger's books appeared one hundred years before the BSC; Martin's series would adapt these quintessential late Victorian boyhood values to late-twentieth-century girlhood goals.

Martin claimed that most books at the time provided nine- and ten-year-old girls with only a meager supply of "positive" images. That was not strictly true. A handful of writers had already begun to elevate the sitter's status. Young adult fiction writers drew upon late 1970s sex role theory, which emphasized the importance of positive images in shaping desirable behaviors and values. Consequently, a handful of heroines had already experienced thrilling adventures as heroic babysitters before the BSC even appeared in bookstores.[79] For instance, *Katie's Baby-Sitting Job* (1985) chronicled the coming of age of an ambitious and eager seventh-grade babysitter suspected of stealing jewelry. Fearing the end of her fledgling career, this "Super Sleuth" unraveled the mystery, cleared her name, and earned the badge of "Super Detective."[80] In *Baby-Sitting Is a Dangerous Job* (1985), the red-headed, thirteen-year-old heroine—independent, intelligent, observant, and outspoken—solved problems instead of causing them.[81] And not only did thirteen-year-old Laurel in *Baby-Snatcher* (1984) confront her employer for kidnapping his daughter from his estranged wife; she also snatched the youngster away from him.[82] What empowered all of these heroines was their new role as babysitters.

Because heroines got to sneak off to places that were ordinarily off limits to girls, girl characters, and babysitters, readers were able to enter alternative domains where they could exercise meaningful power. Twelve-year-old Stevie in *How Can I Be a Detective If I Have to Baby-Sit?* (1993) posed as a babysitter in order to solve a crime involving an international smuggling ring.[83] By reimagining herself as a sleuth while babysitting for her younger brother, the ten-year-old protagonist of *Angel in Charge* (1985) felt just "like a detective."[84] Also influenced by the theory that "positive images" could transform beliefs and behavior, Martin would soon contribute to the depiction of girls as sleuths who pursued thieves, burglars, and forgers in action-driven books. By privileging the mysterious over the mundane in The Baby-sitters Club Mysteries and Super Mysteries, Martin enabled her female characters to solve "spooky" mysteries and confront supernatural foes, like ghosts and vampires that haunted houses, bookstores, and libraries in the upper-middle-class suburban town of Stoneybrook, Connecticut, where BSC stories took place.[85]

The pioneering book that launched the fabulously successful BSC series was *Kristy's Great Idea* (1986). In that book, Kristy didn't solve a puzzling mystery but instead fixed a widespread social problem: finding a babysitter. After watching her mother "make one call after another, trying to find an available sitter," Kristy realized that mothers like hers could be best served if they could "make just one phone call—and reach a whole bunch of sitters."[86] Kristy's brainstorm—to create an employment service—was one that transformed a handful of seventh-grade girls into babysitters. In the hundreds of books that followed *Kristy's Great Idea* (1986), girls endowed with just as much authority and agency as handbook Super Sitters were empowered as babysitters. These socially responsible middle schoolers who earned high self-esteem as babysitters could then overcome problems instead of being undone by them. "I'm through being scared," declared Kristy, shrugging off her worries about strange phone calls that she believed were related to a recent spate of jewelry burglaries. "I'm a babysitter."[87]

While babysitting is typically a solitary endeavor, the BSC girls, who inspired and supported each other, mirrored the importance of all-female communities to the development of their identities. The girls did not need grownups, which was good because, in a reflection of the changes wrought by divorce and female employment, there were not many adults around. As a result, BSC girls felt empowered by their friendships, which bridged the differences among them. The seven members of the multicultural BSC forged friendships that overcame their individual forms of feminist expression. Kristy was more of a tomboy and future CEO; Claudia, an artist; and Mallory, a writer-in-the-making. In the years before Girl Power, the BSC was a model "sisterhood" that celebrated girl bonding and fueled girls' "confidence, assertiveness, and self respect."[88] In *Kristy and the Snobs* (1988), BSC friends helped Kristy deal with a pack of stuck-up neighborhood girls. As a demonstration of the "relational" feminist theory formulated by Carol Gilligan and others during the 1980s, the empowering friendships between the BSC girls demonstrated how their "selves" developed "in relation" to others.[89]

In fan mail sent to the author, girl readers claimed that these books were "about me."[90] "I really wanted them to be [about me] so I would try to be more like the BSC when I was babysitting," explained Lisieux.[91] What encouraged readers' identification was the character-driven nature of the books, as well as their girl-centered perspective.[92] Martin validated girls' subjectivity by giving characters the voices of preadolescent females. The books also featured allegedly handwritten diaries, an aspect of girls' culture that probably resonated with female readers/writers. Furthermore, in the "Notebook Pages" included at the end of every BSC book, girls were encouraged to define themselves. One embryonic feminist wrote that the BSC member she liked most was Kristy, because "I'm not girlish." And the name of the club she would start? "Girls Only Club!"[93]

Deeply absorbed female fans have been long criticized by adults who set cultural standards. Yet as Henry Jenkins has argued, "there is something empowering about what fans do with those texts in the process of assimilating them to the particulars of their lives."[94] It would appear that the articulation of thoughts and the expression of feelings by empowered BSC characters enabled real girls to assert themselves.[95] When one irritated father asked his daughter, "Why don't you read something else?" she flashed him an "annoyed look" and declared, "Because I don't want to. I'm reading these books because I like them."[96] While Scholastic maintained that "[t]he books make girls feel good about just being themselves," fictionalized babysitters probably did more than that: they also sanctioned girls' use of their marginal status in new and meaningful ways.[97] Girls who wrote fan letters to Martin (at the rate of fourteen thousand letters per year) occasionally appealed to her to intervene with parents on their behalf.[98] One girl wrote, "Dear Ann: I absolutely love your books. . . . My mom won't let me baby-sit. At first she said I could. But she said no after awhile. Please write to my mom and dad—my mom so I can baby-sit, my dad so I can get a private phone."[99]

"A New Attitude": Marketing Empowerment

Girls also asserted their authority in the marketplace, where the first thirty thousand copies of Kristy's Great Idea (1986) quickly sold out. By the sixth title, girls like Nicole proclaimed themselves "rabid fans" of the enormously popular series. By 1991, forty-one million BSC books had been sold.[100] The books were catapulted to the top of children's best-seller lists.[101] After she read the fifth BSC book, Nicole began to phone her local bookstore every day to see if the next one had come in yet. "I mean, I couldn't wait," she said. "Who could?"[102] Not Kathy. "I sit glued to the books," she explained about the titles that were pumped out on a monthly basis.[103] By the late 1990s, with BSC titles in excess of two hundred and millions of books in print and translated into many foreign languages, the series had clearly become a spectacular success with girls.[104]

Enthralled fans bought the BSC fantasy in part because of Scholastic's marketing of a new girlhood ideal based on a particular brand of female egalitarianism. Although the series predated the cultural phenomenon known as Girl Power, Scholastic seized upon and commercialized this popular form of feminism, along with everyone else who used it to promote goods and gadgets. In Scholastic's anniversary editions of the BSC, the publishing company incorporated the Third Wave feminist position that power was gained through girls' new economic role in the consumer market. Aiming to reach "a whole new generation of readers" with their marketing slogan, "A New Decade, A New Look, A New Attitude," Scholastic reinforced the popular notion that girls' empowerment could be achieved through pleasure, style, fashion, and attitude.[105]

In order to get girls to consume the empowerment notion that Scholastic commodified, the publisher added additional series that built on the original 131-title BSC series: the BSC Super Specials, BSC Mysteries and BSC Super Mysteries, and Portrait Collections.[106] They also developed a handful of spin-off series, including BSC Friends Forever and BSC Friends Forever Super Specials, among others. Aiming to reach an even younger audience of girls—the "little sisters of BSC fans"—Scholastic also launched the Baby-sitters Little Sister series. The 76-book series focused on one empowered little girl, Karen, who had stood out from the background as Kristy's stepsister in the original series and leaped into her own spotlight.[107] The Baby-sitters Little Sister Specials spin-off series included an additional eight titles.

Some of Scholastic's more significant merchandising tie-ins designed to perpetuate girls' eagerness about both books and babysitting included a computer game (the Baby-Sitter's Club Friendship Kit), clothing, pads and bags, audio and video tapes, dolls, a board game, and a TV series.[108] "We hope if they watch on television, some will begin to buy books," explained a company spokesperson.[109] Always on the lookout for more markets, Scholastic repackaged the BSC book covers to tie in with the release of the movie *The Baby-sitter's Club* (1995). Scholastic then published a new edition of *The Baby-sitter's Club* that promoted the series and the movie on the book's cover.[110] "We knew that there was a whole new group of BSC readers out there, and wanted them to feel that these books were for them—not just passed down from older sisters and cousins," explained Scholastic.[111]

Ironically, as girls bought BSC titles, they also undermined Scholastic's profits by sharing books with each other. "I traded books a lot, instead of buying our own copies," explained one avid reader. "There were so many people involved in my trading of BSC books because I had all my friends and my older sister's friends."[112] Like other girl readers of mass-market fiction, BSC devotees constituted themselves as a reading community engaged in an especially social form of cultural exchange.[113] As one mother explained, "Last summer my daughter, Teal, made a new friend named Alice. They spent hours together, talking and playing softball and card games. What they really had in common, however, was their devotion to The Baby-Sitters Club series of books. They read, swapped, and discussed the books endlessly."[114] By sharing the texts produced by the "official culture" with each other, fans helped to create a community of readers that made their own meanings out of what they read.[115] BSC titles brought together girls who, like the protagonists in the books, formed clubs and communities to act and think collectively.[116]

Clubs modeled on the BSC provided girls with the opportunity to feel that they belonged to a more inclusive sisterhood of sitters, although only for a short while.[117] As one girl explained,

My sister and I tried the club idea, but it didn't make it. I don't think we even had three meetings. When we talk about it now, my sister and I agree that it was because we were 11 and 13 and we didn't really have time to schedule meetings with other girls at times that would work for everyone because we all had several extra-curricular activities—dance, karate, sports, choir, Girl Scouts, music lessons, etc.[118]

Perhaps unaware that younger girls' lives were changing along the same lines as busy teenagers', Scholastic published a Baby-Sitters Club kit ($1.95), a how-to book for those eager to launch a club. It included a pad for "important phone numbers," a club oath to "hereby promise to combine our talents and become the best baby-sitters we can" (to be signed by each member), advertising brochures, and a newsletter with "sensational tips for super sitters."[119]

Whether they started clubs or joined the official one, girls could meet the inspiring author at one of the many book tours that took place in cities and suburbs in every state of the union. Coinciding with Martin's book tours were Scholastic's "grassroots publicity campaigns," which included "extensive promotional kits with posters, buttons and other materials" designed to generate interest and enthusiasm about the BSC and babysitting.[120] For girls who missed the hoopla, there was always more hype.[121] On web sites, in books, and elsewhere, Ann M. Martin, who turned out a new book every few weeks, was presented as the paragon of female empowerment with a Girl Power formula: competence plus hard work equaled success.[122] Along with her characters, Martin also popularized the "girls can do anything if they try hard" notion found far and wide in the consumer culture aimed at girl shoppers.[123] On Scholastic's web site, the author explained that "[w]hen you're making up a story, you're in charge."[124]

A Code of Behavior: Accommodating Acquiescence

"Aren't these the kind of role models we want for our daughters?" asked the author of "Why Girls Can't Get Enough of The Baby-Sitters Club," an article published in *Parents Magazine*.[125] That depends, for in the imaginary town of Stoneybrook, Connecticut, female empowerment coexisted tensely with feminine accommodation.[126] As one critic pointed out, "As a feminist sleuth, Nancy Drew was active, smart, fast-driving and as independent as Frank and Joe Hardy or any other young male hero. Although sometimes rescued by a boy, she inspired generations of future feminists. Depending on point of view, Martin's books both advance and retreat from that early feminism."[127] In truth, one can find similar contradictory messages in earlier series books published for girls.[128] Even "[t]he Nancy

Drew series serves two masters at once, [by] relying on conservative ideologies of race, class, and even gender while simultaneously promoting a
somewhat progressive version of girls' agency," explains American Studies scholar Ilana Nash.[129] As literary scholar Nancy Tillman Romalov has
similarly argued, "[a]nyone who has read these books quickly discovers
that the girls' adventure series is a genre often at odds with itself, replete
with contradictory impulses and convoluted narrative strategies, meant, it
seems, to reconcile greater freedom and fitness for girls with their continued subordination to a patriarchal, genteel order."[130] Because babysitter
books similarly offset the discourse of empowerment with one of appease-
ment, critics wondered whether "books about girls who live to baby-sit
encourage or confine female expectations."[131]

Although the boundaries of real girls' lives had been expanding in
new directions for decades, the reiteration and repackaging of traditional
themes that were commodified in books and movies reinforced conventional gender norms.[132] Babysitter books "put girls on the mommy track
very early," explained a *New York Times Magazine* critic.[133] Responding
to both liberal feminist ideals and the backlash feminism generated, the
BSC fantasy empowered preadolescent girls to delight in domesticity. The
books reinforced conventional femininity for girls in other ways as well.
Though girls became eager readers, their intellectual development was not
really challenged by the cute but simple plots. BSC books addressed difficult social issues (e.g., divorce, death) but solved complicated problems
with easy remedies that failed to foster girls' intellectual development.

In all the many babysitting books published during the 1980s and 1990s,
the challenge that the characters faced while babysitting was to successfully
pilot the passage from carefree girlhood to responsible young womanhood.
It required shedding undesirable characteristics and developing more socially acceptable ones. Babysitting provided the context for success in the
coming-of-age formula. Laurel's real task in *Baby-Snatcher* (1984), a book
that predated the BSC, was to prove to her family and to herself that she was
not the careless, immature, and "impractical dreamer" they believed her to
be. It was through her caretaking role that Laurel recreated herself and re-
shaped her identity. Similarly, though her mother believed her to be careless
and irresponsible, thirteen-year-old Karen in *Tough-Luck Karen* (1982) was
also transformed into a responsible babysitter.[134]

"At a time when the battle for political and financial equality is not yet
won, feminists find the popularity of baby sitters as role models disheart-
ening," explained one critic.[135] That was because Girl Power had made

feminism seem no longer useful to young women and girls.[136] The cultural
ethos of Girl Power that the series drew upon was a rather tame version of
the more radical Third Wave feminist ideology that had emphasized girls'
"doubly marginalized" status as youth and as females. But pretty much
everywhere in BSC stories, gender, race, class, and age inequalities were
no longer obstacles to girls. Though the series was launched before Girl
Power became a mass-culture phenomenon, the BSC nevertheless foreshadowed the ethos. It would also disseminate Girl Power ideals as the
series juggernaut spread into the next century. In so doing, the BSC normalized the postfeminist, upper-middle-class, suburban, and largely white
Super Sitter as the dominant girlhood ideal.

The culturally constructed Super Sitter appropriated feminist ideologies but neutralized empowerment so that girls would not become too
powerful.[137] Although the new ideal of girlhood sanctioned autonomy, it
did so by first revealing, then resolving, girls' ambivalences about babysitting. Such was the case in *How Can I Be a Detective If I Have to Baby-sit?*
(1993), in which the heroine, an independent girl, simply hated babysitting. As she explained, "When they had a baby-sitting course at school, everyone in my whole class signed up except me. I'd rather deliver papers, I'd
rather mow lawns, I'd rather feed hunks of raw meat to starving tigers."[138]
While the story seemingly espoused emancipation for girls, a more restrictive ideology ultimately reaffirmed the heroine's realization that she really
did enjoy babysitting after all.

As a Super Sitter herself, BSC author Ann M. Martin also reaffirmed
traditional constructions of gender in her earnest effort to help girls retain
their self-esteem as they came of age. According to Martin's authorized
biography, "[s]he was not a good baby-sitter—she was a fantastic one."[139]
Though she appeared to be a lot like the empowered girls she wrote about
and inspired girls readers to be, Martin was also portrayed as disarmingly
girlish: her hobbies were "reading, sewing, needlework—especially making clothes for children."[140] She lived with a cat named Mouse and another
(a male) named Rosie. She was also a faithful friend who liked girls (she
went to a woman's college) and loved children (though never had any of
her own).[141] Presented on a first-name basis to her readers, "Ann" was like
a supportive sister, a caring confidante, and a reliable ally. But as a per-
petual girl herself, Ann Martin embodied the Super Sitter ideal that both
empowered girls and encapsulated them. That order always was restored
at the end of each story contained the dangerous potential of autonomous
girls.[142]

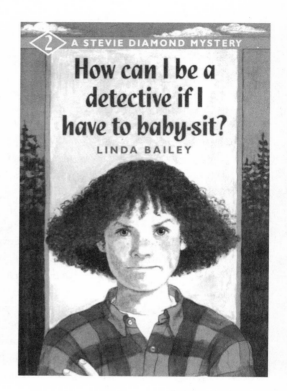

Along with babysitter training courses, handbooks and girls' fiction contributed to the development of a work force of capable rather than culpable babysitters. Cover from *How Can I Be a Detective If I Have to Baby-sit?* by Linda Bailey. Used by permission of Kids Can Press Ltd., Toronto. Cover illustration © 1993 Pat Cupples.

Conclusion

In opposition to the teenaged babysitter—scary in popular movies and scarce in American communities—the business-minded "Super Sitter" in popular fiction, babysitting manuals, and course curricula sanctified a version of preadolescent girlhood satisfying to adults. Regardless of the liberal feminist ideology that underpinned babysitter materials, the Super Sitter was empowered but not powerful. Despite the promise of eventual independence, girls were provided with an illusory, highly bounded sense of agency. In the end, the Super Sitter ideal contained girls' aspirations and controlled their behavior. Unlike the unmanageable teenage monster that threatened marital fidelity and family stability in popular and made-for-TV movies, the well-balanced preadolescent "Super Sitter" reconciled anxieties about the dangers of female autonomy with the desirability of feminine accommodation. The preadolescent Super Sitter created by adults was the perfect solution to the problem of unchecked girlhood independence and authority: she resolved for parents their own internal struggle between the self-confidence they liked in girls and the sauciness they did not care for.

The enormous number of training programs and handbooks that mushroomed throughout the eighties and nineties had similarly fostered girls' empowerment along with their accommodation. By 1997, there were over eight hundred Safe Sitter teaching sites in cities, towns, and rural areas in all fifty states.[143] Reflecting ambiguities about female autonomy, these courses trained girls to feel good about themselves, especially as future mothers. "Better Sitters Today, Better Parents Tomorrow" read the motto of Safe Sitter, Inc.[144] It was a message not lost on Shawna, a training program graduate who explained that "I'll never leave my baby with just anybody. [When I have a child] I'll leave her with a Safe Sitter!"[145]

For grownups, Super Sitters had provided a safe solution to a persistent child-care problem: their youthfulness meant they still liked to play, and, because they hadn't reached puberty, they did not pose a sexual threat. They were not yet interested in boys, drugs, and alcohol, and were more likely to be available and trained. Moreover, they were willing to take a lower wage and were more tractable than teenaged sitters. The Super Sitter ideal appealed to parents who hired girls, the communities girls served, and the commodity culture that consumed girls' hard-earned babysitting wages.

While adults questioned the realism of the BSC books, girls like ten-year-old Leila explained that they "describe life as it really is for girls of that age."[146] Erin even got "ideas on what to do with the kids" from reading the BSC books. "Those books were my favorite when I was younger, and they probably made me look forward to being able to babysit."[147] While Ann M. Martin was credited with having given "commercial legitimacy . . . to the voices of young girls," had the BSC books captured the way girls really felt about babysitting? While Lisieux had been a big fan of the book series, when it came to babysitting she felt "wholly inadequate compared to the BSC [girls]. I was really shocked to see that most children could behave badly."[148] Just what other girls at the end of the twentieth century had to say about babysitting is the focus of the next chapter.[149]

8

Coming of Wage at the End of the Century

> Sure, baby-sitting is great. The sense of accomplishment. The money. The fun of being with young children and helping to mold and shape them. The money. The independence, the responsibility—and, of course, the money. But tell the truth. . . . Don't you get just a little bit tired, a little bit bored, a little bit annoyed about some of the not-so-great parts about being a baby-sitter? Well, join the club! The Bad Baby-Sitters Club!

So began *The Bad Baby-Sitters Handbook* (1991), a slim and sardonic volume aimed at girls who had had enough of the Baby-sitter's Club book series—and of babysitting. It was sentiments like these that led one girl to write author Ann M. Martin to suggest "[k]illing off all the [BSC] girls."[1]

Both factual and fictional materials had been disseminating the notion that babysitting promoted girls' self-esteem, autonomy, and empowerment. "Taking care of other people's children, planning your own schedule and making money helps you gain responsibility, self-confidence and a sense of accomplishment," *Teen* magazine had explained in 1980.[2] While babysitting continued to be popularly presented as an identity-forming opportunity for girls in end-of-the-century advice literature and fiction, it was hard for real babysitters, who are the focus of this chapter, to feel as enthusiastic about babysitting as the experts did. Ironically, the "Super Sitter" ideal, which had combined Second Wave feminist criticism with Girl Power optimism, had contributed to rising numbers of girls who felt discontented with the job exalted by experts. Caught between conflicting gender expectations and employment realities, babysitters reacted negatively to the last-minute calls and cancellations, low wages, bounced checks, and late returns. Yet what left sitters feeling especially uneasy was working in the intimate, unchecked domain of neighbors' homes, where employers sometimes drank and occasionally engaged in sexually inappropriate behavior. Working all alone in unfamiliar houses, girls often felt

frightened that "creeps" would victimize them, as they did other babysitters in horror movies and horror fiction series aimed at girl readers (see
chapter 9).

The children of their employers sometimes stirred fears and stimulated
frustrations as well. Though generations of sitters had been following the
advice published in "survival guides" that suggested ways to cope with the
"brat," many girls found that it was sometimes nearly impossible to turn
a "devilish little demon into a perfect angel."[3] Sitters continued to be fair
game for mischief makers (especially boys), who "acted out" troublesome
feelings they had difficulty articulating. The way the sitter interpreted kids'
play and pranks—especially as things got out of hand—was critical to the
ways in which she negotiated their needs, her employers', and her own.

Expectations, Identity, and the Employer: "More often than not, I should have been paid more."[4]

The *Washington Post* headline "Sit Snit" was meant to describe employers' exasperation with babysitters. Yet the caption could just as easily have
characterized the grievances of underpaid babysitters.[5] What had motivated
girls to babysit throughout the twentieth century had been the desire to earn
money in return for taking care of agreeable children.[6] All too often, the reality did not meet their expectations. "[For] this one job I had to babysit 3
kids for 5 hours and I only got $20.00," complained sixteen-year-old Gin-
ger.[7] "My beef is that when I baby sit I never get paid enough money. I think
I should get paid more for looking after kids," explained Julie.[8] While most
employers who paid sitters the "going rate" understood it to be a neutral index of economic value, it was typically more fluid than "fair." Before moving
to New York City, where she earned a very comfortable ten dollars per hour,
Katie made between two and three dollars babysitting in a small Pennsylvania town. "No one should make that little for any sort of work," she argued.[9]
Like others before them, girls continued to feel that they deserved more
money for babysitting "brats." "I mean, $1.50 is pretty low."[10]

The feminist notion of comparable worth—paying the same wage for
similarly valued jobs—informed girls' perceptions of the field of babysitting.
Cindy was not alone in her observation that "I have always thought that it is
odd to pay a boy $10.00 to shovel your walk for an hour and a girl a dollar
an hour to watch your most precious creation."[11] One sitter whose perspective was also shaped by Girl Power ideals explained that "[b]oys mowing
lawns make so much more $—I think it's more important to pay the people

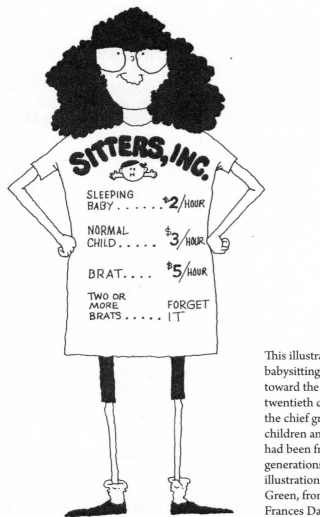

SITTERS, INC.

SLEEPING
BABY $2/HOUR

NORMAL
CHILD $3/HOUR

BRAT $5/HOUR

TWO OR
MORE   FORGET
BRATS . . . . . IT

This illustration from a babysitting manual published toward the end of the twentieth century identified the chief grievances—difficult children and low wages—that had been frustrating sitters for generations. "Sitters, Inc.," illustration by Anne Canevari Green, from *Babysitting*, by Frances Dayee (1990).

who take care of your kids."[12] After all, every handbook acknowledged that babysitting required a high level of proficiency in communication and diplomatic skills in addition to imagination and patience. As a veteran sitter who had taken care of kids since she was nine aptly wrote, "B-sitters are taking care of kids, not lawns."[13] It was not only that boys were still paid more for jobs that required fewer skills; girls also considered it unfair that the same work was valued differently when boys did it. James was paid more than the girls who babysat for the very same families in Sedalia, Missouri. When local girls found out about the gender-based wage scale in their neighborhood, they felt resentful. So did Helen when she found out that a guy she knew was paid at "rates almost twice what she was paid."[14]

Despite girls' insights into the economic inequalities of babysitting, many felt caught in a gendered paradox. Sitters who feared that they would come across as money hungry rather than maternal were unlikely to assert themselves. Erin worried that if she mentioned money her employers might think that her motivation to babysit was purely financial.[15] Associating child nurture with female self-sacrifice and daughterly duty reinforced the expectation that babysitting would be a "labor of love." When asked why she started babysitting, Jessie's answer was a most emphatic "Money!!" Jessie's transformation of the exclamation marks into a smiling face indicated how joyful money made her feel. The friendly expression also neutralized her money-making motive by toning down its emphasis. In fact, despite Jessie's enthusiasm about earning, she did not "want to be rude" and "ask for more."[16] The traditional gender ideals that continued to shape girlhood made negotiating for wages "especially difficult" for girls.[17] In a "Dear Beth" letter published in the Boston Globe in 1983, a fifteen-year-old "Protesting Worker" sought advice about her mere fifty cents an hour wage. "What do I say?"[18] Nor was she alone in her quandary. Cindy "just took whatever the parents offered."[19] "Whatever you think is right," Mary told her employers.[20] A study conducted in 1999 revealed that slightly more than half of the babysitters surveyed still left wage rate decisions up to their employers.[21] Only "[i]f the parents ask what I charge, [do] I tell them," said Alley.[22]

When it came to negotiating raises, enduring notions about femininity continued to disadvantage girls.[23] Not wanting to appear shrewd, many girls behaved submissively instead. According to sixteen-year-old Margaret, "If I wanted more money I kept quiet because I thought it would be inconsiderate."[24] Debbie was given a raise, "but I never asked," she hastened to add.[25] But not all sitters were as accepting as these. When a father asked whether the going rate had changed, Madeline told him that it had increased by one dollar. "I felt I deserved [that] for putting up with his young boys' ridiculous behavior," she explained.[26] Helene felt proud of herself when she finally got up the nerve to ask for a raise. But the next time she babysat, she was disappointed to find that she had been paid less than the rate she had negotiated.[27]

Socialized to seek approval, many girls also felt timid about discussing forms of payment with their employers.[28] According to Megan, "The parents will take out their checkbook and ask if I'd like a check or cash. They already started writing the check, so why did they even ask? It's stupid. 'So I guess I'll take the check.'"[29] While most girls preferred cash, checks were preferable to being paid in goods. Even though one eleven-year-old was "so ripped" when her employer paid her a dime and gave her a wristwatch for three hours of work, she still "didn't know what to say" and so said nothing.[30] Even parents who paid in goods were unlikely to know how much that bothered babysitters who wanted dollars.[31] After Heather's employers claimed that they had no cash on hand and would pay her the next day, they never did. "I was afraid to call them. What would I say?"[32] Appearing to be more accepting than angry was not unusual among sitters who worried about how they might be perceived. Fourteen-year-old Beth "never brought it up" after her employers "forgot" to pay her because "I don't know, I felt stupid."[33]

Sitters responded similarly to the widespread problem of employers who never returned home "on time." "Some call, some don't," explained Amelia about the problem that had persisted for three-quarters of a century.[34] Although girls felt irritated, they frequently said nothing. When one sitter's employers finally arrived back home, "they apologized for being so late—it was past two o'clock—and explained that after the party a couple had invited them over to their house for coffee. I smiled and said it was all right but that I had been a little worried. All the while I was thinking, 'You should have called and told me.'"[35] However annoyed most girls might have felt, the persistence of gender and generational codes made them more likely to be compliant than to complain when employers "ran late."[36] If a Pittsburgh girl had known beforehand that her employers were going to be that late, she told the police, "I wouldn't have taken the job." When the parents failed to return at the end of the night, reported the New York Times, the fourteen-year-old sitter skipped school for several days to care for the four children. She also organized a round-the-clock network of friends to help dress, feed, and care for them until the parents finally arrived back home.[37]

When parent-employers disrupted babysitters' own schedules, girls got annoyed. Still, they did not show it.[38] When Kathleen's employers "lost track of time," she felt "mad" because she had to "totally cancel" her plans.[39] When employers cancelled at the last minute or did not even bother to call, many sitters felt "put-out."[40] Although she never told them so, Honora felt that her employers "seemed to be treating me like, because I'm 11 years old, that my life didn't matter."[41] Jennifer's employers "just kind of blew it off like it didn't matter."[42] Fifteen-year-old Meagan suggested that employers who "banked their night on babysitting" should reimburse sitters for lost time.[43] Some occasionally did, but when employers pressured girls to "sit" at a moment's notice, girls often felt "guilty for not wanting to come over."[44] "[I] hate it when they call . . . and you already have plans," explained fourteen-year-old Amelia.[45] But Lisieux "never felt too guilty about it. I would always recommend someone else, but only because they were in a bind. I never cancelled plans so I could babysit."[46]

Sitters also paid the price when parent-employers did not provide them with important information. In 1997, Safe Sitter, Inc. reported that "more than half the parents who leave their children with babysitters under 16 don't leave emergency telephone numbers."[47] While many employers left cell phone and/or pager numbers, and printed checklists and time schedules, one sitter recalled,

> one time, one of my friends and I were babysitting together and the kids are afraid of the dark. There was this bad storm and all the lights went out in the middle of watching TV and stuff. . . . I brought out some candles and when the parents got home an hour later, the father said, "Oh, the fuses have been going on and off. I forgot to tell you." It would have been nice to know that ahead of time.[48]

That was just how Caitlin felt after she received a frightening phone call while babysitting. When she told her employers about it, they informed her that the calls had been going on all week long. Even the police were investigating the problem, but no one had bothered to tell the sitter.[49] Once, when Megan was babysitting, a man became enraged when he discovered that the security chain prevented him from opening the front door. "He had a really thick accent of some sort and it was really hard to understand what he was yelling. All I could tell at that point was that I was scared out of my wits." When she called her employer, Megan found out that the man was the woman's brother-in-law, who occasionally dropped by to make house repairs.[50] In situations like these, most girls were more likely to enact acquiescence than express irritation.[51] Of course there were also those, like Lisieux, who insisted that "[i]f a parent hadn't pointed out the list of emergency phone numbers, I would ask them for it until they gave it to me, even if they were on their way out the door and had to come back inside to do it."[52]

Fears and Fantasies

Babysitters often had positive experiences with caring parents of cooperative children. Many employers who read articles such as "Caring for Your
Child-Care Person" probably followed the advice published in *Working
Woman* and other magazines that recommended treating babysitters like
professionals. "Make your sitters feel they're more than just employees,"
recommended *Working Mother* in an article about establishing the "good
working relationship" that was key to keeping a sitter.[53] Molly found
that one mother she worked for was "very supportive" and felt that she
"trusted my judgment."[54] Amy felt great after her employer, a mother of
eight, agreed that she should be paid more.[55] Nor did all girls always mind
the last-minute cancellations—just as long as they were not "put out." For
Katie, it was "good to have a day off."[56] For Julian it was "a last minute opportunity to go out with friends."[57]

That the very next employer might come home drunk, however, stirred
sitters' doubts about whether babysitting was even "worth it."[58] That was
how Julian felt after she had babysat for one couple who went bar hopping.
When they finally arrived home, the lipstick-smeared couple, who looked
"messy" and smelled "stinky," left Julian feeling "uneasy."[59] Beth worked for
a couple who did a better job of dividing their recreations and responsibilities: one was the designated driver, the other the delegated drinker.[60]
But because sitters often relied on their employers to drive them home at
the end of the night, drunk ones placed babysitters in a bind. Alyssa found
herself in an "awkward situation" with drunk employers who insisted on
driving her home even though "they could barely walk in the door."[61] After an evening out, Chris's inebriated employer drove her home—while
the sitter "held her breath, held the door handle and prayed I'd get home
safely."[62] Lauren recalled that when she let her drunk employer drive her
home, "I swear, I almost died."[63] Because June's employers were too drunk
to drive her home, she got a lift from their "sober" friends.[64]

Sometimes girls faced sexual dangers from the men who employed
them. Karen recalled that when she was a babysitter fathers would try to
kiss her on the ride home.[65] While that did not trouble Karen, Cassidy
found the drive home "uncomfortable" because she found the husband "a
little creepy."[66] "Dads who take advantage of babysitters made me hesitant
about some," explained Margaret.[67] Girls often avoided being alone with
their employers, especially those whose behavior they had difficulty inter-
preting. "I wasn't sure if the husband was flirting with me or not," Michelle

Though the cause of the sitter's unease is ambiguous, the painting alludes to illicit aspects that occur in the imagination and in the homes where babysitters are
sometimes sexually harassed by male employers. Bo Bartlett's "The Babysitter"
(1999), Hunter Museum of American Art. Reprinted by permission of the artist.

explained.[68] What did it mean, Amelia wondered, when one "father once
talked about he and his wife's personal problems and personal lives?" "[I]
pretended to listen and left quickly when he dropped me off."[69]

Working in the private domain and objectified in male fantasies, babysitters were especially vulnerable to sexual harassment—even assault—by
male employers who caused sitters both psychological stress and physical harm. The *Atlanta Journal-Constitution* reported that a "respected civil
and business leader" forced his eighteen-year-old sitter to engage in "aggravated sodomy"—in the same bed with his three-year-old daughter.[70]
Though Sherri never experienced anything that bad, once when she was
babysitting, her drunken employer stripped down to his underwear. Sherri
continued to babysit for this family, until the husband tried to touch her.
While Sherri told his wife, sitters who fear retaliation were often reluctant to report incidents of harassment or assault.[71] Because babysitters

and employers shared social connections (whether as neighbors, friends, or family), girls were often reluctant to say anything. Moreover, fears of unsettling social networks caused girls to hesitate before taking action. Naomi said nothing to her parents about the employer who "hit on" her, because his wife was a colleague of her mother's.[72] Girls also knew that their accusations could have had personal costs. In 1997, a biology teacher and football coach hired two sixteen-year-old girls to babysit. At his home, he offered them good grades for sexual favors, a quid pro quo that led to his arrest for molestation.[73] When the coach was found guilty the girls felt that justice had been served until the football players he coached began to harass them in retaliation.[74] As they had in the 1980s edition, the authors of *The New Complete Babysitter's Handbook* (1995) suggested that sitters who found themselves in that situation should speak up and get out.[75]

An "Overactive Imagination": The Ramifications of Representations

"I was once uneasy about driving home with a father," recalled sixteen-year-old Abigail. "I had just read about an incident that happen[ed] to one girl. I acted naturally and nothing happen[ed]. It was all in my head."[76] Whether it was or not, girls often doubted themselves and blamed their suspicions on an "overactive imagination." The *Washington Post Magazine* reported that "in her 14 years, Leslie Ruley has seen enough horror shows to know that Saturday night can be cruel to baby-sitters."[77] Once when one girl was babysitting, a man called and told her that he was watching her from across the street. "I freaked so bad," explained yet another girl after she thought she saw a man dressed in black outside the sliding glass door.[78]

Stories about victimized babysitters in newspapers, novels, movies, and myths provoked thoughts about "creeps" and primed girls to experience an intergenerational fearfulness, especially while babysitting alone.[79] Feminist scholars have argued that although representations typically exaggerate social realities, cultural images and stories nevertheless have an impact on how females experience reality. As Leslie climbed the stairs of the house in Bethesda where she babysat for $1.50 during the early 1980s, she listened for thumps and creaks, all the while remembering movies in which "the babysitter walked upstairs to find the kids were gone or had been eaten by ants or something."[80] "I always got nervous late at night after the kids were asleep," explained Debbie. "The house would make weird noises . . . and it would make me really scared."[81] Alone in an unfamiliar house, girls were likely to associate dissonant noises—heavy footsteps, creaking doors, dripping faucets, caterwauling cats, noisy pipes, and shrill telephone rings—with the voyeuristic men who stalked babysitters in the many horror stories that became staples of popular culture generally, and a part of late-twentieth-century girls' culture in particular (see chapter 9).

Horror stories provided the groundwork for other scary scenarios, especially when a girl was babysitting alone in a strange house on a dark night. Such could also be the case when friends placed prank calls asking, "Have you checked the children?"[82] For decades, girls passed along the babysitter/maniac legend at slumber parties and sleep-away camps, engaging in a ritual of sharing scary stories that enabled them to confront their fears amidst friends. Storytelling can bolster a sense of safety through control over what appears to be a nightmarish predicament. Like an anxiety dream, the babysitter/maniac story combines real-world frustrations of being trapped in an unsatisfactory job with unbounded fears of threat from fathers or father figures.

Some girls might have identified with the more rebellious side of the maniac they saw forging alternative roles for girls. Film theorist Isabel Cristina Pinedo has argued that horror films produce for "female spectators a pleasurable encounter with violence and danger." [83] Yet other girls frightened by horror curtailed their mobility and dampened their aspirations. After watching a high school play based on the babysitter/maniac legend, one teen decided to never babysit again.[84] One girl was so scared after hearing a horror story when she was eight that she could not bring herself to babysit until she was nearly thirteen.[85] While fright forced some to delay employment, others remained anxiously vigilant while babysitting. One girl's babysitting experiences were framed by a degree of dread after she heard the babysitter/maniac story. Although she kept on babysitting, she never once fell asleep before her employers came home.[86] Even girls who understood the legend to be fiction, not fact, became "more conscientious, if more nervous, sitters."[87] When one thirteen-year-old girl heard the babysitter/maniac legend from her older sister, she became so "frightened of baby sitting in general" that she relinquished all her jobs to her sister. Only later did she realize that that had been her sister's intention.[88]

"If someone pranks me, I blow my whistle into the phone," explained Tammy, a girl who did not opt out of babysitting because of the horror stories she had heard.[89] Other sitters also found creative ways to overcome anxieties and combat would-be assailants.[90] One girl talked on the phone more than usual, both to ease the stress and to prevent any strangers from calling.[91] Nor was she alone in her imaginative reappropriation of the sitter's most important tool of the trade: "This person started saying weird stuff so I blasted the radio into the phone. I'll bet it killed his ears."[92]

Angels and Devils: Babysitter Hell and Horror

In addition to the "creeps" girls feared might endanger them, babysitters sometimes felt harassed by the children in their care. The more children there were, the more sitters felt outnumbered, overwhelmed, and over-powered, explained the author of "A Baby-Sitter's Guide to Survival."[93] That was the experience of Allicia, who found "[b]abysitting more than 3 kids at a time" stressful "because it's hard to get them to do anything."[94] The author of "My Adventures as a Quint Sitter" explained that multiple births could multiply problems.[95] When children had friends over, that further increased the chances for "all hell to break loose."[96] "One time I was babysitting for these four kids that were all cousins. The oldest one continuously picked on the youngest one until he would start to cry," recalled Mary.[97]

Babysitters felt especially anxious when fights broke out between children. "When boys fight I hate that. You can't make them stop," Ginger explained.[98] Jane hated it when there were "big kids picking on smaller kids, or small kids antagonizing older kids."[99] That was just the situation that Debbie found herself in. "After the parents left one kid started to bawl and the other one started teasing him, which made the first cry harder. I was really stressed trying to get them to stop."[100] While sitters frequently mentioned teasing as a major source of friction, so were fights for control of the TV, VCR, and game systems.[101] Although experts pointed out that fights between siblings were natural and that they would work it out, this was not always the case. "Major blow-outs" between siblings led Julian not to babysit for one family. "I don't think the parents realized how disturbing their knock-out fights were, even if I told them it was too much for me to handle."[102] One researcher found that when siblings fought each other, sitters were more likely to "lose it."[103]

Family pets also contributed to sitters' worries and woes. The first few times Amelia babysat for one family, "the dog chased me and the kids around the house and tried to bite me."[104] Caring for pets while babysitting was okay with Britta except "when there are a set of rules like the dog isn't supposed to be in a certain room and I let it in there by accident, [and] the kids all start yelling at me. I hate that. That's when I mind taking care of the pet."[105] And, "Sometimes you have to babysit the dog more than the children," explained Jill.[106] Once while she was babysitting, a dog had a seizure.[107] That Mary had to walk a potty-training puppy every half-hour "definitely added to the stress."[108] Another sitter recalled that once while she was babysitting, a boy "locked the family dog in his bedroom to avoid walking him but the howling hound made a mess."[109] Ginger explained that although babysitters are not paid extra to care for pets, they should be because "[i]t's just another thing I have to watch."[110]

Babysitters also felt stressed by ordinary occurrences that become uncontrollable. Such was especially the case when children started to cry and could not stop.[111] Although Mary was pretty sure that the children in her care were crying because their parents had just left, having to think "of ways to get their minds off of their parents" amidst the pandemonium added to the stress she felt.[112] Not being able to quickly determine why kids cried distressed sitters. "Fifteen-year-old Margaret did "everything" she could but "it wouldn't stop."[113] As one girl explained, "It's one thing to learn about a crying baby in class but another to hold one and have to make it stop."[114] Deciphering the reasons why children cry is sometimes a formidable task even for parents who know them well. But even when sitters could figure out the cause of tears, trying to stop the flow was another matter. What upset Katie was when "the child wouldn't stop crying no matter what I did to try to ease them."[115]

Putting children to bed—and keeping them there—was another routine many sitters dreaded.[116] "Can we stay up longer?" "We don't need much sleep," and "We slept last night" were the kinds of "pleas and protests" experts advised sitters to flatly reject. One adviser to babysitters explained,

> Going to bed often means having to be alone in a dark room. And it's natural for many children to be afraid of the dark. Going to bed means having to be away from grownups. A small child can feel lonely or unprotected without his parents or a sitter in the room with him. . . . Another reason why nighttime can be scary is because sleep sometimes brings bad dreams to the child.[117]

Yet children who felt vulnerable about going to sleep could make bedtime into a battleground with their caretakers.[118] According to fifteen-year-old Dawn, "The kids never want to go to bed and when they're finally there, they find some way to sneak out of the room."[119] These skirmishes were often attempts to negotiate disconcerting thoughts and feelings children typically expressed behaviorally rather than verbally. The ultimate provocation—"You're not my Mom!"—was the one that all sitters were loath to hear. "Mommy lets us do it" and "My Mom said I didn't have to" were clichéd refrains children used to test the boundaries of babysitters' authority.[120]

Many children's books published during the last decades of the twentieth century became populated with scamps whose behavior was often atrocious. However adorable the juvenile alligators in *Jerome the Babysitter* (1995) and other wild animals elsewhere were, all served as common metaphors for the abominable. *Never Babysit the Hippopotamuses!* (1993) suggested that children could be as hard to manage as a herd of pachyderms.[121] While "Hide-and-go-Seek" was a popular children's pastime in fiction, experts warned babysitters to discourage children from playing the game.[122] Though children might work through their feelings toward their parents' absence by hiding, the game provides opportunities to express conflicted feelings, serves as a form of protest, and leads to power struggles. It also allows children to express hostility by frustrating the babysitter who does not know the house and is unlikely to probe its crevices. Many a sitter was scared by a loud "BOO!" and it was she, not the children, who felt the tension of the situation, just as the child intended. Holding fear and anxiety is just one of the services sitters provide.

Whether represented as wild animals or just incorrigible kids, fictionalized sittees were frequent practical jokers. Yet real children's pranks often left babysitters feeling frustrated, angry, and scared. Once when Corinne was babysitting, she felt "paranoid" after someone kept calling and hanging up the telephone. After the sixth time, she found little Bobby downstairs making calls from a separate phone line.[123] Other children took advantage of ready-made opportunities to scare sitters. While Laura was babysitting, a fuse blew in the house. When the entire house was in darkness, one of the kids said, "There's a big, hairy man standing behind me and he won't let me go." When Laura screamed, the kids dropped to the floor laughing hysterically. "I just wanted to psych you out," said one amidst peals of laughter.[124]

When games got out of hand and some children got too physical, many sitters felt violated.[125] "The boy I baby sit now is very physical," explained Katie. The four-year-old boy pulled her hair, punched her breasts, and pinched her.[126] According to one girl's calculations, "Boys —> boobs OUCH."[127] "Some boys used to say rude remarks about my body," recalled Ginger.[128] Another sitter explained that "I was babysitting three kids one time and they kept leaning over the back of the couch trying to look down my shirt. They even tried to open my shirt a little to get a better look." While this sitter told them "to find something else to do," such experiences sometimes left girls feeling violated.[129]

In a study of 358 college students, researchers found that babysitters believed that taking care of girls was easier than babysitting boys.[130] Babysitters of both sexes perceived boys to be "more aggressive and less easily controlled."[131] Another study similarly revealed that babysitting for boys could be especially hazardous to sitters. Six-year-old Danny kicked, hit, and pinched Margaret.

> He then ran to the kitchen and opened the knife drawer and took one out. The knife wasn't just one of those rounded, butter knives, but the big, shiny cutting knives that always reflect the light in horror movies. I told him to put the knife away, but no luck. Then his sister came in, pulled out a knife and told him that she wasn't going to put hers away until he put his away. I guess she was trying to help, but she certainly didn't. I couldn't stand it anymore. I burst into tears. They finally put their knives away. . . .[132]

Another boy "went bonkers" while Nancy was babysitting. "He threw glass bottles at me and swung one of those wooden toy rifles at my head a few times but missed. He was completely out of control."[133] Only minutes after their parents left, two kids "changed into gremlins so devious they made the Spielberg kind look like Care Bears," explained Gini Sikes in the *Seventeen* magazine article "Baby-sitting the Brat." "It was Attack the Babysitter," recalled the seventeen-year-old from Old Greenwich, Connecticut. "They jumped on my back, pulled my hair, punched and kicked me."[134] When she was thirteen years old, Tammy spent six unforgettable hours babysitting for "four miniature little Damiens" (referring to the satanic boy in the 1970s horror movie *The Omen*).

> The oldest one thought it would be fun to hurl kitchen knives at my head while the younger ones decided to take advantage of that moment and snatched up another knife and went charging out the door. He decided to use his weapon to try and force the neighborhood kid to eat an elephant plant. . . . I was half wishing some crazed lunatic would call the house so at least I would have a legitimate excuse to flee the house screaming like a banshee.[135]

Some sitters did summon the bogeyman to do their bidding. While it was a story that set many girls' nerves on edge—and was obviously used to good effect by kids themselves—some girls told little ones the babysitter/maniac story in order to regain control over their small charges and over themselves. It was one way they could vent anger, exact vengeance, capture attention, and obtain compliance, at least temporarily. One boy first heard the urban legend from a babysitter who was taking care of him and his siblings. Years later he wondered whether the babysitter told them the story "in order to shut us up!"[136] One college student at the University of California–Berkeley theorized that "[s]ince all the children die, the story reflects some hostility babysitters have towards their wards."[137] Another suggested that

> [s]ince babysitting is a "practice" for future mothering, the legend gets its power from fears and possibly resentment towards taking care of kids. Young girls often are limited to babysitting jobs, and I know from experience that those kids can be brats. . . . Why doesn't she check on the kids [in the legend]? Probably because she doesn't mind that they're being killed.[138]

But when the bogeyman was found to be bogus by the children, some sitters resorted to threats. "No snack unless you take a bath," was one Beth used.[139] Containment and isolation was Mariane's method when she threatened to send the kids to their rooms "if they could not behave."[140] When Jayme and her cousin pretended to call the kids' parents, their threat "worked like a charm" and the kids "went right to bed."[141] Megan pretended "to use the phone, you know, actually dial some numbers, and then say, 'Hello, Mr. So-and-So. They're right here. They're just fine. Do you want me to get them on the phone to tell you how wonderful they're being?' The kids quiet down immediately."[142]

Though babysitters in children's fiction successfully transformed "little devils" into "little angels," real sitters were likely to feel frustrated when their methods failed.[143] Sitters experienced anxious moments when they were not sure whether they could gain the upper hand or would end up using it. Julian was just eleven when a slightly younger girl smacked her "really hard across the face." Though Julian pushed her, she regained her self control.[144] Once when Amelia was babysitting,

> It was getting dark and I told the girl to come in, but she said "no." Next thing I knew, she was two houses down on her bike and she was not

supposed to be riding her bike. I went after her and finally caught up to her. She started pinching me and biting me. I was like, "Stop it! That hurts!" but she pinched me again. I told her I was going to start pinching back. She said, "Oh no you won't!" I told her that I was going to tell her mother, and she finally gave in and went back to the house with me.[145]

When things looked especially bleak, babysitters occasionally turned to their own mothers for "help or advice."[146] When a man called and said "someone was choking," Jean did not call the operator as did the sitter in some versions of the babysitter/maniac urban legend but called her mother instead. When six-year-old Danny brandished a knife, Margaret called her mother in a panic. When Danny saw Margaret's mother walking toward the house, "the fuse in his energy blew. He stopped everything and desperately searched for a hiding place but was unsuccessful."[147]

But in mothers' absence, many sitters protected themselves by sending the children to their rooms.[148] That was how one-third of the adolescents in a 1980 study punished the children in their care. Yet, "[e]ven the best-intentioned sitter can't always tame a wild child," explained *Seventeen* magazine sympathetically.[149] "I know I yelled at the two year old a lot when she wouldn't stop screaming for three hours after her parents left," recalled one girl.[150] Her response was not unusual. Researchers found that nearly half the college students in their study had gotten angry at a child.[151] Researcher Leslie Margolin concluded that incidents routine to babysitting that typically generated sitters' irritation included energetic play by over-active children; refusals to eat, sleep, and obey; requests for quiet, and spilling liquids or soiling clothes, furniture, floors, and even the sitter. For some sitters, desperation increased as each attempt to eliminate undesirable behavior was met with failure.[152] When sitters judged children's behavior to be purposefully rude and disrespectful, frustration sometimes gave way to fury.[153] As Jean ominously forewarned, "It's no good if the kids boss the boss."[154]

What eroded the confidence and undermined the judgment of babysitters were the very ordinary occurrences inherent to caretaking. "Crying babies makes me think that I've done something wrong," admitted Elyse about the children whose cries she could not quiet.[155] Lisieux similarly wondered, "What am I doing wrong?"[156] Cindy felt that when the children cried and cried she was "not doing a good enough job."[157] Integrating distressing emotions and disturbing thoughts in high-stress situations might be more than one could expect of anyone, especially younger sitters still in the process of negotiating their own psycho-social developmental issues. In fact, Margolin found that there was a correlation between sitters' immaturity, insecurity, and inclination toward violence.[158] "The intensity of negative emotion derives not simply from 'frustration' in an abstract sense, but from baby-sitters' feeling of personal threat. . . . The motive is self-preservation."[159]

Even when conditions deteriorated to the point where a child-care nuisance evolved into a child-abuse nightmare, sitters who responded angrily, aggressively, and inappropriately were not necessarily the brutal batterers adults feared them to be. Instead, their extreme reactions should be understood within the context of a complex labor system in which parents played an important role as "employers." While sitters were expected to be responsible, provocative children and insensitive employers left many feeling frustrated, even furious. "One sitter attributed the violent outburst in part to the fact that the child's parents paid her less than she deserved and made her work longer hours. Another complained that the child was dropped off on short notice."[160] "Four sitters claimed that they had warned the parents that they were having difficulty managing their children, yet the parents made no changes in the care-giving arrangements."[161]

In one of Margolin's studies, he found that social workers in Iowa paid more attention to describing child "abuse" than to the babysitter's "intentions, feelings, and interpretations of what happened."[162] One social worker's description of the bruises inflicted by a babysitter were so graphic that they were "no longer simply bruises but were now defined as out of the ordinary, strange, and grotesque." The larger significance of this fact, argued Margolin, was that "[b]y removing the bruises from everyday experience, the stage was set for redefining the babysitter who supposedly did this to the child. In this manner, a person whose social status had been taken for granted could now be seen as potentially suspicious, foreign, and malevolent.[163]

Framing the Sitter

Girls often walked tightropes as babysitters. They wondered what their employers would think if the children were still up when they got home. What most girls feared was that their employers would think they weren't "in charge."[164] Because many girls, especially younger ones, often identified with the children themselves, they did not want to get "in trouble" with the parents. That identification led sitters to ponder whether "to squeal or not to squeal," as one explained.[165] Experts advised sitters that "[w]hen telling the parents, you need not feel embarrassed or like a tattletale. Explain the situation and how you handled it."[166] But, "No sitter wants to present the parents with a laundry list of a child's wrongdoing," explained the author of "Baby-Sitting the Brat."[167] Debbie tried to explain the difficulties she had encountered but they got "really mad even though I did all I could."[168] Many employers were sympathetic to sitters' struggles, but "a lot of parents [also] believe that their children were perfect angels & couldn't do wrong."[169] Moreover, employers often relied on their kids to report on the babysitter. "She ate everything in the refrigerator . . . watched TV and made us go to bed," was what four-year-old Angela told her mother about the teenage girl who babysat for her and her brother.[170] Because parent-employers were likely to suspect them of wrongdoing—even without the slightest provocation—sitters feared that the kids would get them in trouble.[171]

One father who arrived home earlier than expected was "thoroughly surprised" when he found the sitter cradling his infant son back to sleep. "We're so lucky," he thought to himself. "[T]he average babysitter would have had her feet up on the table and been talking to her boyfriend on the phone." Had the sitter not "proven how much she cares about our kids" this father "almost certainly would have suspected her of neglecting her babysitting duties on subsequent occasions."[172] What led this devoted father to suspect the sitter without cause was exposure to a lifetime supply of bad babysitters.[173] While all the various babysitter narratives served as a reprimand to unruly girls—whose bad behavior signified adolescents' rejection of culturally defined middle-class notions of femininity—they also perpetuated unjust distrust. Just by virtue of being female and a babysitter, she became a reprehensible character in an unflattering and unfair cultural script.

The ways in which teenage babysitters were framed was especially obvious in *The Beast and the Babysitter* (1989), one of many cultural indictments of female adolescents. In this children's book, Veronica was not an especially kind or clever babysitter, a job for which she was clearly not suited.[174] She would rather read than wash dishes or play with the children she was hired to watch. When little Lewis informed her that his baby sister had awoken, Veronica angrily snapped her book shut and uttered the expletive, "Oh fudge!"[175] She continued impatiently, "If you expect me to take you to the playground this afternoon, you'll have to keep [your sister] Maggie happy in her crib until I clean up these dishes." While Lewis took over the task of minding his sister, for the rest of the story Veronica remained on the periphery—just where she wanted to be. It was a point made even clearer by the book's illustrations, which never included more than a portion of the babysitter's body.

Conclusion

Bad working conditions constructed by unrestrained employers and exacerbated by unmanageable kids were enough to challenge even an easygoing babysitter. Even so, the average babysitter at the end of the twentieth century was more likely to be bothered than to batter.[176] As Marianne explained, most girls like her felt positively about the kids, "when they behave."[177] When kids did not, babysitters were less likely to express aggression toward children and more likely to act acquiescent with parent-employers. At the end of the sitting stint, most fell back on the rhetorical explanation that "everything went OK." For girls, it was a gendered performance that drew upon a wellspring of traditional behaviors and beliefs that shaped their identity as babysitters and as girls. Babysitters' acquiescence made them appear like model babysitters doing what girls were raised to do.[178] By the end of the century, though, many sitters had had their fill of the field that had kept them at odds with themselves.

9

Quitter Sitters
The Fall of Babysitting

In 1989, *Parents Magazine* published "How We Survived Our First Night Out," about a yuppie couple who hired Jennifer, a gum-chewing sixteen-year-old babysitter, to watch their five-month-old while they dined at a bistro. But before she arrived, the mother ("remembering her own baby-sitting days") had spent hours sweeping the house clean of liquor bottles, prescription pills, and other possible enticements. Meanwhile, the fretful father—representing a new model of the devoted dad—had diligently compiled a lengthy emergency phone list he posted on the refrigerator with six teddy bear magnets. Despite their elaborate preparations and precautions, their dinner out was not worry-free. The anxious couple were certain that the sitter's negligence had led to catastrophe: either their daughter had fallen down the basement stairs or she had been poisoned with toilet bowl cleaner. They raced home only to find the babysitter watching a video and their daughter, Annie, sound asleep. While tidying up after the sitter left, however, the mother found a tiny white pill next to her daughter's infant seat. "She's drugged Annie," she cried out in horror! "I read about a baby-sitter who did that," responded her alarmed husband. After examining the "pill," they realized it was just a Tic-Tac and, moreover, that their overactive imaginations had led them to mistrust Jennifer.[1]

After nearly a century of sustained efforts aimed at taming the teenage girl, adults' anxieties about hiring one to babysit would continue. Following the release of *The Hand That Rocks the Cradle* (1992), the suburban horror story about a demented, murderous, and seductive nanny, one periodical warned, "[t]he hired hand that rocks the cradle may belong to an unstable, even dangerous, baby-sitter."[2] Reifying long-held suspicions about babysitters were new arrivals on the movie screen unsettling parents in many of the same old ways. Wild exaggerations of female adolescent empowerment and entrapment in popular and pornographic movies continued to stir the fears of adults. By the end of the century there was a marked expansion of well-known modes of containment—training pro-grams and handbooks—as well as new methods of control—babysitter dolls and babysitting horror fiction.

Despite endeavors aimed at getting girls to conform, many at the end of the century turned their backs on babysitting. Though a fifteen-year population decline had come to an end during the 1990s, the swell-ing adolescent population had not alleviated the labor scarcity that had been hobbling babysitting since its halting emergence.[3] Young girls con-tinued to pursue academics, athletics, and other sources of employment that left few with either the time or desire to babysit. "Many teens have other priorities than watching the kids," reported the *Atlanta Journal and Constitution* in 2000. Suggesting that girls' preferences for "real" jobs were not only a recent development but an unusual decision and un-natural choice, the newspaper assumed that "[a] few years back, lots of teenagers were happy to spend their weekends baby-sitting to earn a few bucks."[4] Not exactly. Girls had been deserting babysitting for more desir-able jobs for a very long time. Rather than enumerating the everyday problems of ordinary babysitters, however, girls grew bolder and their complaints broader as the century came to an end. Among those having their say about the under-remunerated and undervalued job of babysit-ting were female musicians who used media to challenge oppressive gen-dered prescriptions. Still vying with grownups over notions of girlhood at the dawn of the new millennium, girls and young women transformed the legendary sitter into a brassy figure who stood for the downfall of babysitting.

The Cyber Sitter: Extending Babysitting, Furthering Anxieties

In 1995 a headline published in the *New York Times* read, "Teen-Age Baby Sitter Unaided Fends Off Would-Be Kidnapper."[5] Covering the same story with a different title, "My Babysitter, My Hero," *Redbook* magazine also made sitter heroism newsworthy in the age of Girl Power.[6] Despite the newly celebrated authority of the female adolescent, the theme of teen-age irresponsibility persisted. One mother reflected the sentiments of the more typical anxiety-laden parent: "The teens aren't what they used to be. They're more experienced at life now. I'm always afraid they're either go-ing to be on the phone and my children will be doing whatever, or unex-pected company will come over."[7] Girls dying their hair green, donning belly shirts, and sporting body tattoos reinforced adults' uncertainties.

Stories that highlighted girls' recklessness—and what to do about it—showed no signs of abating. An article entitled "Are Your Kids Safe?" told the same old tale about a mother who came home to find the front door unlocked, the sitter fast asleep in front of the TV, and her five-year-old in the backyard where he was constructing his own playhouse—with a real saw![8] Mothers could take the usual precautions or they could use the latest technology. The headline "Nannycams Check Out Caretakers" in the *Rocky Mountain News* was followed by information about a product sold by Babywatch, Inc. It enabled "[w]orried parents to use hidden cameras to see baby sitters' behavior."[9] In order to catch bad babysitters, other businesses also provided parents with undetectable, in-home surveillance technologies. Nanny Watch, Inc. sold the Nannycam, a video camera that attached to a VCR. "Nationally, it has been found that over 70 percent of all parents that covertly monitor their care provider immediately find due cause to fire their provider after viewing their first video tape," claimed the company on its web site.[10] NannyCheckonline.com promoted their "state-of-the-art covert surveillance equipment" with a website video that reenacted the familiar fantasy of the notorious teenage sitter. Too preoccupied with television and snacks, she did not notice the baby falling to the floor.[11]

The cyber sitter was not all that different from the gadflies who had been similarly criticized by generations of experts. Underlying their common complaints about babysitters had been an ongoing critique of female adolescents and the principles and practices of their subculture which imperiled families, marriages, children—even girlhood itself. Ever since the first observation that high school girls flirted with men on street corners instead of caring for little ones, adults had found fault with the nation's babysitters. The essentializing of teenage girls as sexual transgressors recurred over the issue of cosmetics and clothing during the 1930s, problems with public decency during the 1940s, the antics of bobby-soxer babysitters in the 1950s, the sexual escapades of "liberated" sitters in the 1960s and 1970s, as well as purported acts of murderous sexuality in the 1980s. By the 1990s, the claims to sexual expression by a new generation of female adolescents, influenced by Third Wave feminism, focused adults' fears on the erotic exploits of babysitters.

Predictably, babysitters in the popular culture headed down that well-trodden path of destruction. In *The Babysitter's Seduction* (1996), the intellectually confident, sexually secure, athletically built, and level-headed eighteen-year-old girl of the 1990s appeared to revise previous depictions of babysitters. Yet the shift of portrayals was more apparent than real. Though this sitter, like others of her generation, had been shaped by Third Wave feminist ideals that promoted female sexual agency and targeted male violence, her own sexuality ultimately generated devastation and death. By outsmarting her rapacious male employer and surviving his brutal assaults, this Girl Power heroine had been expected to appeal to girl viewers who themselves now wielded vast financial resources.[12] In reality, she provided girls with a false sense of subjectivity and security and adults with a mistaken impression of who girls were and what they wanted.

There were other serious, smart, and selfless teenage girls who also posed dangers to marital bonds and family life, as did Ann, the live-in babysitter in *Baby Monitor: Sound of Fear* (1998). Though the selfish woman who employed her was more interested in running the family's diamond business than in her own household, Ann's irresistible appeal to her male employer destroyed the marriage and endangered the kids. The threat of other enticing adolescents found expression in *Gross Indecency* (1993) and—of greater cultural importance—*The Baby Sitter* (1995), the blockbuster movie based on Robert Coover's short story previously discussed in chapter 6. As she had thirty years earlier, the babysitter again caused utter devastation by fueling obsessive fantasies and arousing intense rivalries in men and boys. The continuity of fears about the destructive potential of the female adolescent—and especially about her unchecked sexuality—would continue to inform representations of babysitters.

Tracked to the home video market with unusual alacrity, *The Baby Sitter* (1995) sat at the intersection between popular culture and pornography. These cultural forms shared common ground in regard to the portrayals of the teenage girl suspected of having ulterior motives for babysitting. According to Mr. Peepers Amateur Home Videos, "mock babysitting" had long been a "favorite activity" in "sinful suburbia."[13] Such was the perspective as porn spread to cyberspace where sites like www.yourbackyard.com featured an "everyday girl next door." The sexual conquests of the "very naughty babysitter" on this site included fathers, uncles, mailmen, and paperboys.[14] Babysitters in mainstream movies were typically contained within the house; babysitters in pornography often represented the transformation of the suburban house into an erogenous zone. *Back Door Babysitter*, the title of a number of different videos, was also a pun on the metaphoric representation of women's bodies and the indiscretion of anal sex.[15]

Babysitters doing desire in mainstream movies had much in common with those in porn readily and discreetly available over the internet by the late 1990s. In typically bare-boned pornographic plots, sitters were imagined as only somewhat more unreliable, irresponsible, indiscriminate, and insatiable than those in conventional narratives.[16] These hard-core videos were just a bit more extreme than the mainstream babysitter fantasy that had been circulating for decades. Naughty girls often invited guys over after the parents leave for the night. Making explicit the sexual underpinnings of the sitter stereotype, all the "hot" babysitters in *The Babysitter 15* (2003) "love to get into trouble."[17] In that adult video, "Mr. Holmes is shocked to find his babysitter, Haley, passed out on the floor, naked with her butt up in the air. It's obvious she has been drinking and threw a party in his house. Wait until he tells her mother about this. But Haley has ways of keeping the secret between them."[18] In *The Babysitter 17* (2003)—as in all others from *The Babysitter 02* (2000) to *The Babysitter 25* (2006)—promiscuous babysitters were so insatiable that they needed multiple partners, and numerous penises to penetrate all orifices, at once, and often in tandem.[19] In *Babysitter 02* (2000) the babysitter "gets both holes stuffed at once! Channel finds herself being double penetrated, her backdoor boffed and blasted with loads of six men!!"[20]

However desirable the fantasy of sexy sitters might have been to men, underlying fears about the insatiability of teenage girls required that their young bodies be contained and controlled. Representations of babysitters as sluts sought to define and denigrate female adolescents. "There's no excuse for being a filthy teenaged slut and these girls aren't looking for one!" explained the website that sold *My Favorite Babysitters 17* (2008).[21] These babysitter stories made it clear that the struggle over the nature of girlhood was an unresolved conflict within men who yearned for the rewards but feared the costs of female independence and empowerment.

What accounted for the spread of the sexual fantasy, as well as for the fact that a growing number of male employers were in reality having sex with babysitters was the appeal as well as the apprehension of men about changing notions of girlhood, womanhood, and manhood. Though the sexual fantasy had never been acknowledged or analyzed in the past, *Men's Health* magazine attempted to explain why it was becoming more of a reality in American households during the 1990s.

It isn't that they are *actually* sexually attracted to their children's caretakers, but that nannies (and sitters) fill a void left by the modern mother's absence. Dad is a busy, exhausted, over scheduled zombie, and so's Mom, but that's precisely why the household is so vulnerable. Once upon a time they could at least unite emotionally over the joys and sorrows of child-rearing; for a two-career couple, that most primal of bonds has been disturbed. Now, the father who wants to talk about Jake's temper tantrums will seek out—the nanny. She's the woman who's raising his kids. Forget lust: On some level, she's bound to be the recipient of his feelings of gratitude and protectiveness. It's similar to the man who falls in love with his secretary. . . .[22]

Absolving men for their tabooed indiscretions, the analysis blamed American mothers influenced by feminism.

What the interpretation failed to account for was the rising number of cases of rape and sexual abuse. The *Boston Globe, Atlanta Journal and Constitution, Plain Dealer, Chicago-Sun Times,* New York *Daily News, Seattle Times, St. Louis Post-Dispatch, Milwaukee Journal Sentinel,* and *San Diego Union-Tribune* all ran frightening stories about men arrested, charged, and jailed for the sexual abuse of babysitters.[23] As an assertion of power rather than the pursuit of a marriage partner, the rising sexual violence against babysitters by male employers constituted the most egregious form of the control and containment of girls at the end of the twentieth century.

Masculinity: The Dangers of Male Sitters

A softer solution to the problem of bad girls could be found in children's culture at the end of the century. Drawing upon a superior reputation for babysitting know-how that stretched back to the 1930s, valiant young males appeared in *Dinobabies* (1994), *The Baby-Sitters and the Boy-Sitters* video (1993), and in many children's books such as *Arthur Babysits* (1992) and *Never Babysit the Hippopotamuses!* (1993). In many children's stories like these, male babysitters were often animals at the top of the food chain, as was the Rottweiler in the Carl the Dog (1987–2002) picture books. Instead of using brute force to control children, though, those like the alligator in *Jerome the Babysitter* (1995) used their intelligence to prove themselves as babysitters and as young males.[24] Rather than diminishing sex-role stereotyping by working as babysitters, however, boy sitters ended up bolstering unfavorable assumptions about girls.

In contrast to girls, male characters continued to reinforce the perspective that boys were dependable. In a Tom and Jerry cartoon from the 1990s, for instance, Jeannie courted danger by talking on the telephone instead of taking care of the little boy she was hired to babysit.[25] So absorbed in her conversation about the upcoming prom was she that Jeannie failed to notice the baby crawling out the window and onto the roof. Ceasing their game of "cat and mouse" in order to protect the baby from harm, Tom and Jerry tried to contain the baby and capture Jeannie's attention. Because Tom was tossed out of the house for interrupting Jeannie's phone call, he was ultimately able to rescue the baby—and save the day. To further underscore Jeannie's deficits, the cartoon ended with her duplicitous acceptance of payment for the poor services rendered and her "[s]ee you same time next week" commitment.

A study published in the *Juvenile Justice Bulletin* (a publication of the U.S. Department of Justice's Office of Juvenile Justice and Delinquency Prevention) in 2001 reported that, in reality, "[b]abysitters are responsible for a relatively small portion of the reported criminal offenses against children." The study was based on a sample of 1,427 victimizations committed by paid babysitters (both adolescents and adults who were not family members) against juveniles in seventeen states from 1995 to 1998. The results, drawn from the FBI's National Incident-Based Reporting System were admittedly not national in scope. The researchers nevertheless concluded that babysitters only accounted for 0.5 percent of offenders who committed crimes against juveniles (under age seventeen) and 4.2 percent of those who committed crimes against young children (under age six). Additionally, only 0.5 percent involved kidnapping and 0.6 percent involved homicide. The study's authors concluded that "[g]iven the large number of children exposed to babysitters, this is a relatively small percentage."

Among babysitters who committed crimes against children, however, far more were male than female. Despite their portrayal in the popular culture then, boys did not make better babysitters. In fact, among male babysitters, teenage boys were more likely to commit a sex crime against girls in their care than were female adolescents. In his extensive research Leslie Margolin found that the strongest correlate of child abuse is the gender of the caregiver. That included nonfamiliar adolescent males as well as mothers' boyfriends, grandfathers, and uncles.[26] "[T]he gender of the caregiver is the strongest risk factor for sexual abuse, regardless of the type of child care examined. Although males perform only a small fraction of child care, they are responsible for the vast majority of child sexual assaults."[27] Widely depicted as heroes in American culture throughout the century, the male babysitter posed the greatest danger to children. In fact, it was the extremes of masculinity—consistently represented as boy babysitters' most valuable asset—that made the male babysitter a greater risk. According to the *Juvenile Justice Bulletin* report,

> Overall, among babysitters, male offenders outnumbered female offenders (63 to 37 percent) in police reports. However, this percentage masks the true disproportion in the risk of male offending, in that most children are exposed to more female than male babysitters, both in terms of numbers and the amount of time spent in their care. No reliable information is available about the overall gender ratio of babysitters, but one teen survey found that females were twice as likely as males to have had babysitting experience (Kourany, Martin, and LaBarbera, 1980). Among adult babysitters, the ratio is considerably higher (U.S. Bureau of the Census, 2001). Therefore, the true risk of a male babysitter offending is likely much greater than the two-to-one ratio of male to female offenders found in the data.

Margolin similarly found that male babysitters in Iowa were more than five times as likely to assault, abuse, molest, or murder a child while babysitting.[28]

Ultimately, it was family members who posed a greater danger to children than their babysitters. Family members accounted for 21.4 percent of those who committed crimes against all juveniles and slightly more than half of those who committed crimes against young children (those under six years of age).[29] Thus, despite the persistent archetype of the bad babysitter firmly fixed in American culture and the popular imagination, female adolescent babysitters were *least* likely to hurt the children they were hired to help.

Containing and Correcting the Babysitter and Girls' Culture

Whatever the findings of researchers, cultural producers sought to domesticate girls not boys. The many new babysitter dolls that appeared in the toy market at the end of the century were representations of girls for girl consumers. There had been few babysitter dolls either before or immediately after Barbie. It was not until the rise of the preadolescent Super Sitter in the 1980s that Barbie's younger sister, Skipper, had launched her sitting career. So had Ginny, though she had not been a babysitter originally. These dolls traded Barbie's ludicrous striped apron for blue jeans, yet the dolls' other accouterments (e.g., a baby, bottle, phone, notebooks, etc.) had changed little from Barbie's babysitting days. Joining these veterans were newcomers such as Kristy, a doll based on the tomboyish girl in the Baby-sitter's Club book series. The eighteen-inch, fully-jointed vinyl doll sported a pale blue denim shirt, a baseball tee, black shorts, white vinyl sneakers, and red socks. Other similarly represented babysitters were also available as paper dolls. When read as cultural texts, such dolls reveal that, while they reflected girls' more active lives, they privileged caretaking over money making. So did the electronic Pixel Chix Babysitter, an interactive game made for "tweens" created by Mattel that tamed "everyone's favorite sassy girl" by giving her a "job taking care of the neighbor's baby."

> The better job she does, the more money and privileges she earns. But [because] it's not so easy with four rooms in the house, help Pixel navigate with the turn of a knob. This job will keep Pixel on her toes! Is the baby hungry or is it time to play hide and seek? Pixel will have to decide. To help her, the lights and sounds of the baby monitor will let Pixel know when the baby needs something in another room.[30]

Pixel provided girls with yet another opportunity to ground their identity in "playing house." So did Babysitter Mania, in which a computer-generated girl who has just completed her babysitter training races against the clock as she cleans the dishes, dusts the furniture, and cares for the kids.

> You finally passed your babysitting course and are ready to help your school raise money. To achieve your goal, you'll have to work through some of the craziest houses. Babysitting Mania starts you off slow but soon you will have to face a barrage of kids, Birthday parties and huge houses to get in order all before bedtime! Get the kids to bed and the house clean before the parents come home. Are you the Ultimate Babysitter?[31]

For older girls, dolls gave way to novels, such as the Baby-sitter's Club book series still popular among girls around the turn of the twenty-first century. And for still older girls there were horror novellas that featured babysitters.[32] Whether in the material culture or the print culture, the training of babysitters played a critical role in the socialization of girls. Moreover, as girls continued to embrace emancipation, ambition, autonomy, and individualism, they were provided with a steady supply of cautionary tales about the risks of freedom and power.[33] In Kate Daniel's *Baby-Sitter's Nightmare* (1992) the character Alice was punished for her drive and determination.[34] That was nothing compared to the fate of other babysitters confronted by the maniac who returned at the end of the century to remind girls about the dangers that dwelled within them and that lay ahead. In *Baby-Sitter's Nightmare Part II* (1994),

> When someone starts making prank phone calls to baby-sitters, Karin isn't scared. Even when Karin is attacked on the way home from a baby-sitting job, she thinks it's all a joke. But then Karin's best friend is killed while baby-sitting. Now no one's laughing. . . . Now everyone's dying. But Karin isn't scared. She thinks she knows how to win the killer's game. But she doesn't know what she's up against. This killer hates baby-sitters—a baby-sitter let the killer's sister die. Now all baby-sitters are going to pay.[35]

This was not the maniac's first appearance in girls' series fiction. He had already stalked sitters in R. L. Stine's *Point Horror*, a four-volume book series published between 1989 and 1995, about a girl with rich fantasies and poor judgment. In the first volume, *The Babysitter* (1989), Jenny babysat in a rundown house on the edge of town, "surrounded by nothing but dark woods."[36] She took the job even though "some creep in a ski mask was breaking into homes and beating up babysitters and she received menacing phone calls asking, 'Are you all alone in that big house? Well, don't worry. Company's coming.'"[37] She never suspected her extremely "nervous" employer, Mr. Hagen, though there were numerous clues that he was emotionally unstable. She even let him drive her home after she found a shoebox stuffed with dozens of newspaper clippings about recent attacks on babysitters. By *Baby Sitter IV* (1995), Jenny so identified with her vicious employer that she began to place menacing phone calls to another babysitter. Then Jenny kidnapped a baby she threatened to kill. Along with other cautionary tales, this book featured a moral maniac with a good excuse for his bad behavior. "I had a baby. A little girl. She was only two. But the baby-sitter wasn't quick enough. The baby-sitter wasn't smart enough. The baby-sitter wasn't GOOD ENOUGH!"[38] This proscriptive

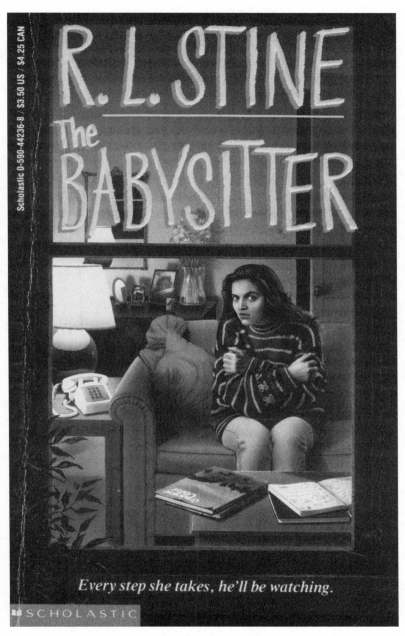

On the book cover:

R.L. STINE
The
BABYSITTER

Scholastic 0-590-44236-8 / $3.50 US / $4.25 CAN

Every step she takes, he'll be watching.

SCHOLASTIC

Transgressive teenagers got what they deserved from voyeuristic maniacs in discursive horror series that sought to frighten girls into submission. From *The Babysitter* by R. L. Stine. Cover illustration copyright © 1989 by Scholastic, Inc. Reprinted by permission.

tale—like other controlling babysitter narratives—revealed the inherent badness in seemingly good girls like Jenny.

Along with the text, each of the colorful book covers in Stine's series transformed readers into voyeurs of themselves as girls, sexual beings, and babysitters. As the object of the maniac's sexually threatening gaze on the cover of *The Babysitter* (1989), Jenny covered her breasts and pressed her knees together. And for good reason, too, because "[e]very step she takes, he'll be watching," read the tag line. This misogynistic monster was listening, too, for the telephone also functioned as a sexual threat in preteen fiction. On the four covers of the *Baby-Sitter's Nightmares*, yet another horror series with a babysitting theme, a different-colored phone dangled from its cord.[39] Even when girls used cordless or cell phones, they remained psychologically tethered to their tormentors, who exhorted them to conform to an adult-approved standard of girlhood. Yet faced with sitters who perpetuated the changes among girls that had been mounting throughout the twentieth century, the maniac became even more sadistic in new millennium horror movies such as *When a Stranger Calls* (2006), *When a Killer Calls* (2006), and *Babysitter Wanted* (2008).

The Rise of the Tween and the Fall of Babysitting

While babysitters were as abundant as ever in the culture, they had become even scarcer in communities. In 1994, there had been "38.6 million under age nine, 17.6 million teenagers 15-19," reported *USA Today*.[40] When the adolescent population finally began to expand during the late 1990s, it ended the fifteen-year drought of teenagers, but not of babysitters. What explained the continued imbalance between babies and babysitters? "Teens don't seem to babysit any more," observed one mother who, like others, could not easily find one to watch her kids.[41] Either girls are "too busy" or "not interested," explained another woman.[42] Other explanations for why girls turned down offers to babysit could be found on the internet. After surveying babysitters in the San Francisco Bay Area in 1997, *YO!* (*Youth Outlook*), a literary journal of youth life in the Bay Area, published its findings. *YO!* also printed a "Baby-Sitter's Bill of Rights," in which the West Coast sitters declared their right not to be accused of stealing ("unless there's major proof").[43]

Other sitter-centered perspectives could be found in daily newspapers. In a letter to Ann Landers published in newspapers everywhere, one teen wrote "to protest the way teen-agers are put down."

Everywhere you look, they are portrayed as disobedient, untrustworthy, violent and hateful. No generation of teen-agers has ever been 100 percent honest, pure and good. While there are rotten apples in every barrel, the majority of teen-agers are decent people. We are the baby-sitters who diligently watch your children. We are the store clerks who help you when you need assistance. . . . If people would take the time to get to know us, they might find we remind them of a lot of themselves when they were our age.[44]

In a letter written to Abigail Van Buren (aka "Dear Abby"), a fourteen-year-old self-proclaimed "responsible babysitter" enumerated the labor practices of inconsiderate employers. Reappropriating the proscriptions that adults had handed out to generations of babysitters in handbooks, advice articles, and training curricula, this youthful expert made it plain that the problems associated with babysitting were not due to irresponsible, reckless, self-indulgent, impertinent, disruptive, disorderly, home-wrecking babysitters. Instead, she offered parent-employers the following advice:

1. Write down all phone numbers, bedtimes, medications, allergies, etc. It's easier for me should there be an emergency, and I also don't have to argue with the kids over their bedtime.

2. Tell me if anyone will be stopping by. I have locked out two cable companies and a telephone repair crew because I wasn't about to let them in if the parent hadn't informed me they were coming.

3. Inform me of the rules of the household. I don't want to let the kids get away with something they aren't allowed to do, or punish them for something that is in their normal routine.

4. Be home on time. I can understand getting stuck in traffic, but if it happens every time, I'll turn you down the next time you call.

5. Pay me on time. I'll baby sit for free if necessary, but if we had arranged for payment, I would appreciate it on time. That is my paycheck.

6. Please remember that when you leave your children with any babysitter, you are entrusting the sitter with your most precious possessions. Help them a little in keeping the kids safe.[45]

Sounding more like an adult than an adolescent she declared, "I'm sick and tired of some of the parents I sit for who show such a lack of responsibility."[46] "Dear Responsible Babysitter," responded Abigail Van Buren sympathetically to the mature Michigan teen. "Your letter . . . intelligently summarizes the problems that face many teens who are trying to earn extra money from baby-sitting."[47]

Yet in articles published in popular women's magazines some mothers urged others to "find the way to a sitter's heart." Offer food, give gifts, compliment hair styles, round out the payment to the nearest hour, and come home on time.[48] While it is not clear whether employers followed the advice dispensed in magazines, it is certain that girls' complaints about the inappropriate and impulsive employers they encountered while babysitting did not cease. And like those before them, frustrated and disgruntled sitters stood up and walked out, on bad parent-employers. "I never sat for them again," explained Sherry after her employer stripped down to his underwear for the second time.[49] And when the kids Jane babysat for behaved like "brats," neither did she "babysit for them again."[50] After her hellish experience with the little Damiens, Tara vowed to "never, never again babysit."[51]

Adults had not been entirely wrong about girls' culture—it had fostered female agency. The rise of girls' expectations and the growth in opportunities had been a long-term social shift that had first emerged during the 1920s, expanded during World War II, and flourished as service sector jobs during the 1980s created innumerable employment opportunities for teenage girls. "The teenager is really in the driver seat because there are so many options for them," explained the vice-president of Teenage Research Unlimited, a marketing research firm based in Chicago in 2000.[52] That the unemployment rate remained generally favorable enabled girls to get part-time work in retail stores and fast food restaurants typically located in suburban malls that sprang up all over the country. In the 1990s, 42 percent of all sixteen- and seventeen-year-old girls already worked on the other side of the counter in places that had been traditional hangouts for teens.[53] Thus, if a [babysitting] job did not pay "$5 an hour they're not interested," a school counselor explained about Illinois teenagers.[54]

Yet what went into the decision to babysit was usually more than just the wage. Even when a babysitting job paid at a higher rate than that earned from working in fast-food restaurants, clothing stores, and other retail establishments, girls preferred the low-skilled work, short work shifts, regular hours, better pay, employee discounts, and greater opportunities for status and sociability. Even though one high school senior earned less per hour working at a retail store than babysitting, she preferred dealing with customers to managing children.[55] "Baby-sitting takes more patience," she explained. A study conducted in 2000 revealed that by their senior year, teenage girls in Washington were more likely to work at jobs other than babysitting: "None of the most common occupations held by girls involve childcare."[56]

However, employment opportunities alone do not fully explain why fewer girls were willing to babysit. "Teenagers are deciding to work less," explained Gerald Celente, director of Trends Research Institute in Rhinebeck, New York. "They feel like they're working very hard in school, and they have full calendars these days."[57] In fact, after-school activities—such as sports practice, debate, and music lessons—left girls with less time to babysit. In 1995, "37 percent of Ohio public high school girls participated in sports programs, compared to 29 percent in 1980," reported the Ohio High School Athletic Association.[58] In Annandale, Virginia, basketball practice kept fifteen-year-old Sarah Krebs from babysitting most weekday evenings, according to U.S. News & World Report in 1998.[59] Parents' greater acceptance of their adolescent daughters' personal autonomy also led girls to socialize more often during the week and especially on weekends. "I think a lot of people would rather go to a party than go to someone's house to baby-sit" on weekend nights, explained one high school senior about her friends who worked weekdays at the local mall.[60]

What further contributed to the decline of babysitters in the nation was the trickling down of social trends from teenagers to tweens. "If you wait until they're 13 or 14, by that time, they're too interested in other things—boys and dance—and they don't want to baby-sit anymore," a mother told the Cincinnati Enquirer.[61] Parents realized that they had "to get them early, while they're still in middle school or even grade school, and before they are busy every night of the week with extracurricular activities designed to get them out of high school and into one of those prestigious universities that don't necessarily count 'babysitting' as a life-enriching experience."[62] That was why one mother who lived in the suburbs of Annapolis, Maryland, relied on an eleven-year-old to babysit for her two babies.[63] Preadolescents had just recently entered the job market, but it was clear that even they could not commit to babysit.[64] By the end of the century, the Washington Post would report that for parents these were "desperate times."[65] And indeed they were for one couple who drove forty-five miles to pick up their thirteen-year-old niece even though the club they attended was just down the road from their home.[66]

The shortage of babysitters had led the American Red Cross and other organizations to reach out to younger ones. Those as young as eleven were now permitted to enroll in babysitter training courses offered everywhere at community centers and schools from coast to coast.[67] It seemed essential to get girls on the right track early, especially following the involuntary manslaughter conviction of nineteen-year-old British au pair, Louise Woodward, in 1997. The death of the baby boy in her care provided fresh evidence in the century-long case against female adolescent babysitters. As a result, by 2005 the American Red Cross estimated that the organization had trained 150,000 babysitters annually.[68] So did Safe Sitters Inc., the national nonprofit organization founded by the pediatrician Dr. Patricia Keener. By 2006, Safe Sitters, Inc. offered training courses in all fifty states and Great Britain.[69] Other courses elsewhere were offered by community hospitals and other organizations.

The "Crummy Job" of Babysitting: Reappropriating the Babysitter

Occasionally over the course of the twentieth century, girls had shared their thoughts and feelings about babysitting with journalists, researchers, and experts. Yet it was not until the end of the century that they began to express themselves in their own cultural productions. Now some girls reappropriated the figure of the babysitter and transformed her into a symbol of defiance and liberation. Drawing on girls' youth culture—its music, performance, books, and visual entertainment—young women created fictionalized babysitters who articulated girls' escalating resistance to mainstream feminine ideals. While adults had long deployed the iconic sitter, girls and young women gave the babysitter new meanings that defied traditional ideals and oppressive representations.[70] The new representations of babysitters that challenged nearly a century of adults' damaging portrayals were informed by feminist ideals of the Third Wave, which focused attention on the double oppression that girls faced because of their gender and age.[71]

Exploring themes of gender and adolescence in her folk songs was Dar Williams, an American singer-songwriter. Seen through the adoring eyes of a little girl, the teenage girl in the song "The Babysitter's Here" (1995) was reconstructed as a positive force. "She's the best one that we've ever had / She sits on her hair, and she's tall as my dad / And she tie-dyed my shirt, and she pierced her own ear / And it's peace, man, cool, yeah, the babysitter's here." The song's other lyrics narrated a story about the sitter's relationship to her boyfriend and her own future. It also reinforced girl bonding as well as the diffusion of this subcultural value from one generation of girls (sitters) to another (sittees). "Do me a favor, don't go with a guy who would make you choose," the sitter says to her admiring young charge at the end of the song about the boyfriend who is forcing her to make a choice between college and marriage.[72]

In the new millennium other young women and adolescent girls had begun to reinvent girlhood and girls' culture more vigorously.[73] Heavily influenced by punks' "Do It Yourself" ethic (which emphasized the importance of self-reliance and self-expression), the radical Riot Grrrl movement focused new attention on the victimization, abuse, and exploitation of girls in a patriarchal and misogynistic culture. Deliberately repudiating the oppressive ideals of female adolescent beauty in the commercial culture, Riot Grrrls pioneered antifeminine fashions that embodied their feminist politics. Their avant-garde hair styles, thrift store clothing, Doc Marten boots, tattoos, piercings, and epithets written on their bodies would soon reshape the collective identity of ordinary American girls as the influence of the Riot Grrrls spread from the cultural backwaters to the mainstream.[74]

Among a number of all-female bands who pioneered this countercultural movement were the Lunachicks, who audibly, visually, and linguistically reconfigured girlhood with their confrontational music and rebellious style. Their song "Babysitters on Acid" (1990) aggressively reappropriated the "Wasted and Basted" urban legend that had been circulating among girls since the 1960s. At one level, the retelling of the familiar narrative in song seemed to reinforce dominant perceptions of girls as harmful. Yet the Lunachicks' raw musical style, their hard-hitting performance, and the song's biting lyrics sought to liberate girls from gender constraints. It also aimed to free sitters from the "crummy job" of babysitting. The song's chorus—"babysitters on acid / babysitters on acid / babysitters on acid / babysitters on acid / every town in the usa!"—reclaimed the babysitter as an American symbol and site of female adolescent subversion.[75]

Reaching a broader audience with her outrageous song "Bad Babysitter" (Concetta Music, 2002), was Princess Superstar (aka Concetta Kirschner), whose persona paid homage to the history of girls' culture in the twentieth century. She had been heavily influenced by the Riot Grrrls, who had also reappropriated female sexuality; they creatively derided the derogatory language (e.g., "bitch") used to demean and degrade women and girls by writing it on their own bodies and clothing.[76] Princess Superstar was also "the hip-hop Debbie Harry, the white Lil' Kim, the blonde Pink, the female Eminem . . . but prefers the ironic moniker the 'black Shirley Temple,'" observed *Time* magazine.[77] Informed by these influences, Princess Super Star constructed an intentionally grotesque exaggeration of the stereotyped sitter. Drawing upon all the many recursive artifacts and activities that had come to define the sitter, this bad girl shattered the dominant ideal of feminine submission to maternity, domesticity, and purity. This very bad babysitter did everything that every parent-employer had ever feared—and more: she rifled through their drawers, stole their jewelry, came on to her male employer, took their prescription pills, sadistically taunted the boy in her care, masturbated (with a cucumber that would be eaten by the family), and had oral sex with her boyfriend. Acknowledging the legendary problems of babysitting such as washing stacks of dishes and the low pay, she offered girls coming of age the assurance that "[o]ne day you'll know how nice it is to get laid while you' gettin paid."[78] More direct than the sarcasm of the chorus—"I'm a bad babysitter, got my boyfriend in your shower, Woo! I'm makin 6 bucks an hour"—was the ultimate declaration that "babysitting sucks."

Girl Power had commercialized, feminized, neutralized, and marginalized Riot Grrrls' radical critique and subculture, yet it had also aided in the dispersal of an expanded conception of girlhood among ordinary American girls.[79] Though many adults found the clothing fashions, musical taste, and forms of self-expression of twenty-first-century girls' culture objectionable, a tamer version of female adolescent transgression found expression in a celebratory song by Rebecca Frezza (a woman who had turned to writing and singing children's songs after she became a mother). Like Dar Williams's song, Frezza's "Babysitter" (2003) was written from the perspective of a girl who looked forward to the arrival of the babysitter she thought was "pretty cool." Not only did the sitter drive "a screaming red car" and wear polka dot pants and pink high-top sneakers; she also had "glitter in her hair" and "earrings everywhere." She also liked to sing and dance and let the children do whatever they wanted. Consequently, they cleaned up and settled down just to insure that she would be back to babysit the following weekend.[80]

Influencing a new generation of female youth had been the overall shift away from social justice issues to a focus on consumption and style. Other cultural influences were the "females-can-do anything" feminist position and the "Do It Yourself" punk ethos. Girls who put to creative use their subcultural practices made its forms of fashion, language, and behavior their own.[81] Some girls turned to video as an accessible form of cultural expression. By 2007, YouTube provided girls with an audience for their satiric stories about the babysitter and the legendary maniac. One homemade video, "Who Killed the Babysitter," reappropriated the legend by substituting male violence with female supremacy. While talking on the telephone, the long-haired blonde babysitter was attacked by a female maniac in this counter-fantasy about transgression, usurpation, and the termination of controlling narratives. While at one level the fantasy perpetuated female powerlessness, the killer's triumphant declaration that "[t]he bitch is back" asserted girls' commitment to female power.[82] Informed by female youth culture, especially the "angry girl" genre of movies from the 1990s, these amateur video artists expressed their dislike and discontent with babysitting—the job that had long symbolized gender inequality, not opportunity.[83]

By the summer of 2007, a report on the CBS *Early Show* made it clear that the scarcity of even preadolescent babysitters had become a reality in the new millennium.[84] While *Parents Magazine* had been publishing advice articles since the dawning days of babysitting, its senior editor admitted that the field looked barren. While babysitting had long served as "a reliable source of cash for teenagers, now younger girls have more school commitments and more opportunities for entertainment."[85] In fact, instead of babysitting, doing their homework, playing sports, or flipping hamburgers for a minimum wage, other girls were spending their time producing babysitter parodies. With girlfriends at home (yet beyond the gaze of controlling adults), they resisted the oppressive expectations that defined them in other video narratives of their own making. In their satires, contemporary American girls contributed to a long-standing tradition of girls' culture that creatively eschewed submission and sought self-confidence. "The 'Real' Babysitters Club," a dark parody on YouTube of a Baby-sitter's Club movie, contrasted the syrupy commercialized version of girlhood depicted in the bouncy BSC theme song against their own cheeky critique. We see a group of plucky girls in mock pigtails, shorts, and sneakers, kick, punch, push, and smother the dolls they are babysitting.[86] This artistic expression of defiance lampooned mass-produced girls' culture and reinserted genuine feelings into more authentic forms of play. Significantly altering the portrait of the babysitter, these mock babysitters subverted the framework used to construct adolescent femininity and control teenage girls.

Girlhood and the Embattled Business of Babysitting

Yet in *The Babysitters* (2008), the very latest popular movie on this topic,

> High school senior Shirley works as a babysitter to save money for college. She has a serious crush on Michael, father of two of her regular charges.

One night, Michael and Shirley share a forbidden kiss, and he gives her a nice bonus on top of her regular babysitting fee. After Michael's married buddies find out and want in on the babysitter action, Shirley becomes a high-school madam, arranging dates between her girlfriends and the upstanding family men of their neighborhood with her trusty black book. An innocent flirtation soon spirals into an affair that causes everyone involved to lose more than they bargained for.[87]

The poster that advertises *The Babysitters* (2008) depicts the shapely naked torso of a slender teenage girl in low-rise jeans. She is tugging her white t-shirt over her ample breasts. Combining sexual innuendo with an empowerment ethos, the tag line reads, "These girls mean business." What girls' creative productions and adults' mainstream ones reveal is that the conflict and competition over girlhood long waged between girls and grownups will continue to be played out in the field of babysitting and in the battleground of the imagination.

Notes

Introduction

1. H. Smith, "Good Babysitter."
2. Tsao, "Pied Piper."
3. Dow, "Finding—and Keeping," 28–30.
4. Abigail Van Buren, Dear Abby, "What's That about Underpaid Sitters," 24 December 1969, *San Francisco Chronicle*, 27, C3939, box 42, The Peter Tamony Collection, Western Historical Manuscripts Collection, Columbia, MO.
5. Kourany, Gwinn, and Martin, "Adolescent Babysitting," 939–45.
6. *Literary Digest*, "Juvenile Jazz," 31–34; and Groves and Groves, *Wholesome Childhood*, 9.
7. *Business Week*, "New Field for Insurance," 88. Right after the war, "An important women's air race was almost ruined because four of the pilots were stood up by their sitters," carped *The Saturday Evening Post*. Ellison, "Baby Sitting's Big Business," 37. Grace Deschamps, "Ex-Marine Lieutenant 'Boss of Baby Sitters': Tending Junior Becomes Big Business," 16 October 1947, *San Francisco News*, 19, C3939, box 42, The Peter Tamony Collection, Western Historical Manuscripts Collection, Columbia, MO.
8. Fitzpatrick, "Choose a Good Sitter."
9. Palladino, *Teenagers*, 50. For a more nuanced view see Mintz, *Huck's Raft*, 237, 240.
10. For further discussion, see DeLuzio, *Female Adolescence*, 1–8.
11. See Nash, *American Sweethearts*.
12. LeFavre, *Mother's Help*, 166.
13. Adams, *Nursery-Maids*.
14. Tooker, *All about the Baby*, 53.
15. Barrie, *Peter Pan*, 19.
16. M. West, *Infant Care*, 26.
17. For further discussion, see Peiss, *Cheap Amusements*; Odem, *Delinquent Daughters*; and Alexander, "Girl Problem."
18. On motherhood see Douglas and Michaels, *Mommy Myth*; and Warner, *Perfect Madness*.
19. Devlin, "Female Juvenile Delinquency," 83–106.

20. On postwar family life see May, *Homeward Bound*; and Coontz, *Way We Never Were*.

21. Mead, "Family Life Is Changing," 679.

22. "It may be the era will produce, instead, a generation so thoroughly grounded in family-life experience and ideals that the American family will be strengthened." N. Thompson, "Baby-Sitting Is Growing Up," 565.

23. Inness, *Delinquents and Debutantes*, 5.

24. Schrum, *Some Wore Bobby Socks*.

25. Breines, *Young, White, and Miserable*, chaps. 3, 4.

26. J. Gilbert, *Cycle of Outrage*, 15.

27. Kenny, *Daughters of Suburbia*, 8; and Helford, *Fantasy Girls*, 8.

28. Casper, "Who's Minding Our Preschoolers?" 1–89.

29. As one African American mother explained, "I never intended for my children to have to work for any body in the capacity that I worked. Never. And I never allowed my children to do any babysitting or anything of the sort." Thornton-Dill, "'Put My Children Through,'" 192.

30. *Boston Globe*, "42 Girls, 3 Boys"; and Sheldon, "Trap and Train," 42–43, 68.

31. Moore, *Baby Sitter's Guide*, 135.

32. Steve Grant, director, *Operation Babysitter*, 1985.

33. Seymour Kneitel, director, *Little LuLu: The Baby Sitter*, Famous Studios, 1947.

34. Holt, *Good Housekeeping Book*, 70.

35. Douglas and Michaels, *Mommy Myth*.

36. Lavitt, *Knopf Collector's Guide*, 278.

37. Hudson, "Femininity and Adolescence," 40. On girl culture and popular culture, see Driscoll, *Girls*.

38. McRobbie and Garber, "Girls and Subcultures," 16; and Palladino, *Teenagers*, 50.

39. Ellison, "Baby Sitting's Big Business," 36.

40. Frank, "Baby Sitter's Job," 32.

41. Barclay, "Community Interest in Baby Sitters," 34.

42. Block, "Code for Sitters," 38.

43. Kourany, Gwinn, and Martin, "Adolescent Babysitting," 939.

44. Leslie Margolin has published extensively on child abuse and babysitters. See "Child Abuse by Baby-Sitters"; "Abuse by Adolescent Caregivers."

45. In his study of slightly more than two thousand high school students in the Puget Sound region of Washington State, sociologist John Robert Warren recently found that not even girls "typically count babysitting as a job." Warren, "Labor Market Stratification," 9, 15.

46. On girls' history and culture see Hunter, *Young Ladies Became Girls*; Nash, *American Sweethearts*; Inness, *Delinquents and Debutantes*, 5; Scheiner, *Signifying Female Adolescence*; Devlin, *Relative Intimacy*; Kearney, *Girls Make Media*;

McRobbie, *Feminism and Youth Culture*; Brumberg, *Body Project*; Douglas, *Where the Girls Are*; Breines, *Young, White, and Miserable*; Alexander, *"Girl Problem"*; Odem, *Delinquent Daughters*; Schrum, *Some Wore Bobby Socks*; Mazzarella and Pecora, *Growing Up Girls*; and Harris, *All about the Girl*.

Chapter 1

1. Groves and Groves, *Wholesome Childhood*, 9.
2. On the shift from Victorian to modern notions of child rearing, see Stearns, *Anxious Parents*, 1–16.
3. On the rise of youth culture in the 1920s, see Schrum, *Some Wore Bobby Sox*; Fass, *Damned and the Beautiful*; B. Bailey, *Front Porch*; and Odem, *Delinquent Daughters*.
4. Quoted in Weiner, *Working Girl*, 104.
5. See D. Brown, *Setting a Course*.
6. On the history of housework see Cowan, *More Work for Mothers*; Strasser, *Never Done*; Matthews, *"Just a Housewife"*; and Deutsch, *From Ballots to Breadlines*, 59–61.
7. Mintz, *Huck's Raft*, 191.
8. Forman-Brunell, *Made to Play House*, 135–60.
9. Groves and Groves, *Wholesome Childhood*, 9; and D. Brown, *Setting a Course*, 108.
10. Groves and Groves, *Wholesome Childhood*, 24.
11. Katzman, *Seven Days a Week*, 245.
12. Jackson, "Baby Boom," 252.
13. Hunter, *Young Ladies Became Girls*, 15, 33, 43. See also Kett, *Rites of Passage*.
14. Gilmore, "Forging Interracial Links," 288.
15. See Zelizer, *Pricing the Priceless Child*.
16. Groves and Groves, *Wholesome Childhood*, 9–10.
17. Lynd and Lynd, *Middletown*, 142; and Palladino, *Teenagers*, 36.
18. Lynd and Lynd, *Middletown*, 142. See also Jacobson, "Allowance," 34–38; Jacobson, *Raising Consumers*, 80.
19. Jacobson, "Allowance," 35; and Schrum, *Some Wore Bobby Socks*, 30.
20. Mintz, *Huck's Raft*, 225–26.
21. Scheiner, *Signifying Female Adolescence*, 29.
22. Tim Lussier, "Ella Cinders," Silents Are Golden, http://www.silentsaregolden.com/featurefolder/ecellacindersfeature1.html (accessed July 7, 2008).
23. Beeman, "Brief Study," 900; and Mintz, *Huck's Raft*, 215.
24. Beeman, "Brief Study," 900.
25. Freedman, *History of the Family*, 11; Hubert, *Raising America*, 296; D'Emilio and Freedman, *Intimate Matters*, 256; and Alexander, *"Girl Problem,"* chap. 1.
26. Schrum, *Some Wore Bobby Sox*, chap. 1.

27. D'Emilio and Freedman, *Intimate Matters*, 173. On girls' and high school culture, see Schrum, *Some Wore Bobby Sox*.

28. Hall, *Adolescence*; and Mintz, *Huck's Raft*, 187–88, 216.

29. Mintz, *Huck's Raft*, 215–16; Alexander, *"Girl Problem,"* 23; D'Emilio and Freedman, "Sexual Revolution," 170; Schrum, *Some Wore Bobby Sox*, 12–13; Fass, *Damned and the Beautiful*, 211; Scheiner, *Signifying Female Adolescence*, 25; Beeman, "Brief Study," 900; Odem, "Female Sexuality," 279; and Odem, "Teenage Girls," 50–60.

30. Mintz, *Huck's Raft*, 215–16, 226; D'Emilio and Freedman, *Intimate Matters*, 256; and Alexander, *"Girl Problem,"* 23.

31. Groves and Groves, *Wholesome Childhood*, 9; and Fass, *Damned and the Beautiful*, 13–52.

32. Groves and Groves, *Wholesome Childhood*, 9–10.

33. Stearns, *Anxious Parents*, 1–16.

34. Groves and Groves, *Wholesome Childhood*, 9.

35. B. Bailey, *Front Porch*, 78–80; Fass, *Damned and the Beautiful*, ch. 6; D'Emilio and Freedman, "Sexual Revolution," 172; and Mintz, *Huck's Raft*, 229.

36. Walker, *American City*, 230.

37. Ilene Fairbanks, Personal Communication, March 2004; Steffens, "Mother's Helper," 56; Mintz and Kellogg, *Domestic Revolutions*, 153; and May, *Pushing the Limits*, 46.

38. Ilene Fairbanks, Personal Communication, March 2004.

39. Steffens, "Mother's Helper," 56.

40. Palladino, *Teenagers*, 35; Mintz, *Huck's Raft*, 239; and Schrum, *Some Wore Bobby Sox*, 33.

41. Schrum, *Some Wore Bobby Sox*, 15, 35.

42. Palladino, *Teenagers*, chap. 3; and Mintz, *Huck's Raft*, 237.

43. Schrum, "Bobby Socks," 48.

44. Schrum, *Some Wore Bobby Sox*, 88–89.

45. Steffens, "Mother's Helper," 57.

46. Schrum, *Some Wore Bobby Sox*, 25, 39, 89, 124, 172.

47. Mintz, *Huck's Raft*, 219, 234–35; and Grant, *Raising Baby*, 161.

48. Palladino, *Teenagers*, 4.

49. Kearney, "Recycling Judy and Corliss," 265–95; and Steffens, "Mother's Helper," 57.

50. Mintz and Kellog, *Domestic Revolutions*, 139.

51. Lynd and Lynd, *Middletown*, 170–71 cited in Scheiner, *Signifying Female Adolescence*, 61.

52. Mintz, *Huck's Raft*, 251; and Nash, *American Sweethearts*, 29–70.

53. Schrum, *Some Wore Bobby Sox*, 98, 110; and Daufmann, "From Ragtime to Swing," 29–32.

54. Mintz, *Huck's Raft*, 237; and Palladino, *Teenagers*, 37.

55. M. Thompson, "Boys as Mothers-Helpers," 53.

56. Ibid., 24.

57. Ibid., 24.

58. Robert Benchley, "The Vanishing Father" (1934), quoted in Hoffert, *Gender in America*, 336–37.

59. Palladino, *Teenagers*, 37; and Grant, *Raising Baby*, 165.

60. M. Thompson, "Boys as Mothers-Helpers," 54.

61. Schrum, *Some Wore Bobby Sox*, 39; and Hoffert, *Gender in America*, 324.

62. Steffens, "Mother's Helper," 57.

63. Ibid. On slang, see Devlin, *Relative Intimacy*, 91–92.

64. Scheiner, *Signifying Female Adolescence*, 60.

65. Palladino, *Teenagers*, 21; and Nash, *American Sweetheart*, 97–98.

66. Palladino, *Teenagers*, 38.

67. Steffens, "Mother's Helper," 56.

68. Ibid.; and Lindenmeyer, *Greatest Generation Grows Up*, 4.

69. Mintz, *Huck's Raft*, 236.

70. DuBois and Dumenil, *Through Women's Eyes*, 500. On women and the Great Depression see Scharf, *Work and to Wed*.

71. Steffens, "Mother's Helper," 56.

72. Grear, "American Custom," 102.

73. Ruth Lowenstein, personal correspondence, May 2000.

74. Mintz, *Huck's Raft*, 256, 260.

75. *Life*, "Teen-Age Girls," 96.

76. "Teen-Age Girls"; Grear, "American Custom," 102; Campbell, *Women at Work*, 208; and Hartmann, *Home Front*, 170.

77. Social Security Online, "Social Security Handbook." Many high school students between the ages of fourteen and seventeen worked on a part–time basis as scores of schools enacted "school-and-work programs," which shortened the school day. Merrit and Gray, "Child Labor Trends," 594. Palladino, *Teenagers*, 66.

78. May, *Pushing the Limits*, 46; and Fass, "Creating New Identities," 97.

79. Lake, "Trouble," 45; "Child Labor," *Monthly Labor Review*, 759; Mintz and Kellogg, *Domestic Revolutions*, 167; and Hinant, "Paging Miss Bobby Sox," 83.

80. Mintz, *Huck's Raft*, 259; Balcomb, "College Days without Men," 40; and Bridges, Interview.

81. Hinant, "Paging Miss Bobby Sox," 83.

82. Merritt and Hendricks, "Trends of Child Labor," 764.

83. Ibid., 772–73. In *Relative Intimacy* (92), Rachel Devlin cites a 243-percent increase.

84. Merritt and Hendricks, "Trends of Child Labor," 772–73.

85. Ibid.; *Monthly Labor Review*, "Child Labor," 774–75; and Kirk, "American Children," 270.

86. Woloch, *Women*, 321; May, *Homeward Bound*, 59; Mintz and Kellogg, *Domestic Revolutions*, 161; Tuttle, *Daddy's Gone to War*, 75; H. Wright, "Children of Wage-Earning Mothers," 21; Mackenzie, "Grandmothers Are Needed Again," 33; and Griswold, *Fatherhood in America*, 179.

87. Quoted in Tuttle, Jr., *Daddy's Gone to War*, 77.

88. Quoted in Woloch, *Women*, 324.

89. Mintz, *Huck's Raft*, 261.

90. May, *Pushing the Limits*, 28.

91. McElravy, "Grandma Is Drafted," 11–12.

92. Opdycke, *Routledge Historical Atlas*, 102; Winkler, *Homefront U.S.A.*, 56.

93. May, *Pushing the Limits*, 27.

94. Tuttle, *Daddy's Gone to War*, 77–78.

95. Brendall, Interview. Jones, *Labor of Love*, 225. But the war had also disrupted traditional child-care patterns upon which black mothers had also relied. See Jones, *Labor of Love*, 254–55.

96. Mintz, *Huck's Raft*, 261.

97. On latch-key children, see Tuttle, *Daddy's Gone to War*, 69–90; "Training High School Students," Government Printing Office, 2; Daly, "Sitting Pretty," 156; Norton et al., *People and a Nation*, 818.

98. Young, "Baby Sitters Service," 15.

99. Merritt and Hendricks, "Trends of Child Labor," 760, 773–74.

100. Schrum, *Some Wore Bobby Sox*, 232.

101. Wrenn and Harley, "Time on Their Hands," 361.

102. Mintz and Kellogg, *Domestic Revolutions*, 167.

103. *Life*, "Teen-Age Girls," 91; Mintz, *Huck's Raft*, 266; and Palladino, *Teenagers*, 53; Schrum, *Some Wore Bobby Sox*, 137, 161.

104. Mintz and Kellogg, *Domestic Revolutions*, chap. 8; Mintz, *Huck's Raft*, 258.

105. Schrum, *Some Wore Bobby Sox*, 35. Schrum argues that the term (in various forms) was in use since the late nineteenth century. Moreover, that unlike the term "adolescent," "teen" and "teenager" were more frequently used for girls. Also see Devlin, *Relative Intimacy*, 91.

106. Mintz and Kellogg, *Domestic Revolutions*, 167. On unsuccessful terms invented by manufacturers, see Schrum, "'Teena Means Business,'" 137; and Palladino, *Teenagers*, chap. 4.

107. Schrum, *Some Wore Bobby Sox*, 54–55.

108. Palladino, *Teenagers*, 7; and *New York Times Magazine*, "What Is a Bobby Sock?" 23.

109. Palladino, *Teenagers*, 54; *Life*, "Life Goes to Slumber Party," 72–75; *Life*, "Teen–Age Girls," 91–99; *Life*, "Sub-Deb Clubs," 87–93; and *Life*, "High–School Fads," 65–69.

110. "Teen-Age Girls."

111. Palladino, *Teenagers*, 51–52, 64. Figure cited in *Life*, "Teen-Age Girls," 91.

112. Schrum, *Some Wore Bobby Sox*, 25, 45; and Kelly, "Riddle of the Zoot," 139–40.

113. Musselman, "Teen Trouble," 8; and *Newsweek*, "Combating the Victory Girl," 88, 91. See Hegarty, *Victory Girls*.

114. Palladino, *Teenagers*, 74.

115. Ibid., 75.

116. Musselman, "Teen Trouble," 6.

117. Cox, "Homemakers in the Making," 152; and Mintz, *Huck's Raft*, 260.

118. Parenting quoted in May, *Homeward Bound*, 74. Also cited in Kearney, "Recycling Judy and Corliss," 265–95.

119. *Newsweek*, "Combating the Victory Girl," 88.

120. "Youth in Crisis," *March of Time*, vol. 10, no. 3; and Palladino, *Teenagers*, 83.

121. Lake, "Trouble," 43.

122. Quote from Woloch, *Women*, 324. Also see Mintz, *Huck's Raft*, 260; Palladino, *Teenagers*, 74, 82.

123. *Ladies Home Journal*, "'We're Telling You,'" 20–21. Studies conducted by the army and at universities found that "the percentage of [sexually] active teenagers did not shift significantly" during the war. Palladino, *Teenagers*, 76.

124. Gould and Gould, "Baby-Sitters," 6; and Grant, *Raising Baby*, 182.

125. Daly, "Sitting Pretty," 156.

126. *Education for Victory*, "Higher Educational Institutions," 25–26; S. Smith, "So Many Children," 224; and Gould and Gould, "Baby-Sitters," 6.

127. *Recreation*, "Some Wartime Programs for Girls," 23.

128. Cited in Palladino, *Teenagers*, 73.

129. Lake, "Trouble," 46.

130. *Recreation*, "Some Wartime Programs for Girls," 23.

131. Daly, "Sitting Pretty," 156.

132. Gould and Gould, "Baby-Sitters," 6.

133. K. Pollock, "Helping the Mother-Aides," 31.

134. Fillman, "Dolores Learns," 10.

135. Ibid.

136. Gould and Gould, "Baby-Sitters," 6.

137. Palladino, *Teenagers*, 72.

138. Quoted in Mintz, *Huck's Raft*, 258.

139. Pollock, "Helping the Mother-Aides," 31.

140. Quoted in Palladino, *Teenagers*, 72.

141. Pollock, "Helping the Mother–Aides," 31.

142. Musselman, "Teen Trouble," 8.

143. Steffens, "Mother's Helper," 57.

Chapter 2

1. "Teen-Age Girls."

2. Figure cited in Devlin, *Relative Intimacy*, 98.

3. Grear, "American Custom," 102.

4. Ellison, "Baby Sitting's Big Business," 36.

5. Ibid., 37.

6. Ibid., 36–37.

7. May, *Homeward Bound*; and McLeer, "Practical Perfection," 83.

8. *McCall's*, "Live the Life of McCall's," 27–35.

9. Coontz, *Way We Never Were*, 77; Mintz and Kellogg, *Domestic Revolutions*, 183; and K. Jackson, "Baby Boom," 245–46. On postwar suburbia also see Clark, *American Family Home*, chaps. 7, 8; Jackson, *Crabgrass Frontier*; Cohen, *Consumer's Republic*; and Wright, *Building the Dream*.

10. Jackson, "The Baby Boom and the Age of the Subdivision," 244.

11. Meyerowitz, "Beyond the Feminine Mystique," 229–62.

12. Spock, *Baby and Child Care*, 114–15; and Evans, *Born for Liberty*, 238.

13. Vaneck, "Time Spent in Housework," 195; and Hickey, "More Free Time," 30.

14. Leavitt, *Catharine Beecher*, 174.

15. Moscrip, "Time Off for Mother," 42.

16. Ibid.; Meyerowitz, "Beyond the Feminine Mystique," 242; and J. Gordon, "Come Over at 7," 51.

17. Helen Lawrenson, "The Great Baby-Sitter Problem," *Today's Woman*, July 1946, 170, C3939, The Peter Tamony Collection, Western Historical Manuscripts Collection, Columbia, MO.

18. N. Weiss, "Mother," 283–303; and *New York Times*, "'Infant Care,'"46.

19. New York Herald Tribune Home Institute, *America's Housekeeping Book*, 53.

20. DuBois and Dumenil, *Through Women's Eyes*, 558; and Griswold, *Fatherhood in America*, 186.

21. May, *Homeward Bound*, 86.

22. Breines, *Young, White, and Miserable*, 38.

23. Spock et al., *Every Woman's Standard Guide*, 58.

24. U.S. Children's Bureau, *Infant Care*, 39.

25. Ogren, "Nightlife," 1713; and Miller and Novak, *Fifties*, 147.

26. Casey, "We Saved Our Marriage," 100.

27. May, *Homeward Bound*, 27.

28. D'Emilio and Freedman, *Intimate Matters*, 172; Coontz, *Way We Never Were*, 27; *Life*, "Profession of Babysitting," 79; and Greer and Gibbs, *Your Home and You*, 271, 276.

29. May, *Homeward Bound*, 165.

30. *Woman's Home Companion,* "Sitter's Rights," 150; and Norton et al., *People and a Nation,* 531.

31. Middle-classness is based on those with incomes between three and ten thousand dollars. E. West, *Growing Up,* 174; Coontz, *Way We Never Were,* 24.

32. *The San Francisco Call-Bulletin,* "Club to Popularize," 17.

33. Jane Sudekum, "Peninsula Women Get Organized to Beat the Baby-Sitter 'Bugaboo.'" *The San Francisco News,* 31 August 1950, 30, C3939, box 42, The Peter Tamony Collection, Western Historical Manuscripts Collection, Columbia, MO.

34. Helen Lawrenson, "The Great Baby-Sitter Problem," *Today's Woman,* July 1946, 170, C3939, The Peter Tamony Collection, Western Historical Manuscripts Collection, Columbia, MO.

35. Richards, "This Baby-Sitting Business," 102.

36. *Kiplinger Magazine,* "Baby-Sitting Co-Ops," 13.

37. DuBois and Dumenil, *Through Women's Eyes,* 556.

38. Kourany, Martin, and LaBarbara, "Adolescent Babysitting," 940.

39. Norton et al., *People and a Nation,* 930.

40. J. Gordon, "Come Over at 7," 50.

41. Church, "If I Were a Parent," 36; and Jackson, "Baby Boom," 247–48.

42. Church, "If I Were a Parent," 36. Eventually, Levittown would grow to 82,000 residents living in 17,400 single-family homes. K. Jackson, "Baby Boom," 248.

43. "Report."

44. Cited in Richards, "This Baby-Sitting Business," 102.

45. Ibid., 101.

46. Ibid., 102.

47. *Princeton Alumni Weekly,* "Photographs."

48. Ibid.; and *New York Times,* "No Men Are Wanted," 19.

49. *New Yorker,* "Ideal," 20; and *New York Times,* "Babysitter by the Ton," 25.

50. *Life,* "Community Sitter," 148, 151–52.

51. "Captain of Industry," advertisement for Electric Light and Power Companies, *Life,* May 10, 1947, 4.

52. "Babysitting," *The Aldrich Family.*

53. In an episode of *Our Miss Brooks,* a radio program that starred Eve Arden, fourteen-year-old Eddie skipped school for a week in order to babysit.

54. Cited in Stanton, "Baby Sitters United," 150.

55. Kenyon, "Baby Sitter," 129.

56. Robert L. Heilbroner, "The Baby Sitter: A New and Baffling American Problem," *Cosmopolitan,* April 1952, C3939, box 42, The Peter Tamony Collection, Western Historical Manuscripts Collection, Columbia, MO.

57. Buell, "Little Itch Babysits."

58. E. West, *Growing Up,* 217.

59. Holt, *Good Housekeeping Book*, 70.

60. Keane, "Who Is Baby Sitting?"

61. *New York Times*, "Santa Claus Sitters for Hire," 50.

62. Girl Scouts of America, *Girl Scout Handbook*. See *New York Times*, "Scouts to Aid Voting," 50; *New York Times*, "Baby Sitters to Spur Voting," 18; *New York Times*, "Baby Sitters to Aid Voters," 31; and *New York Times*, "N.Y. Young Women's Republican Club."

63. *New York Times*, "Greenbush Summer Theatre," 12; *New York Times*, "No Discord," 31; *New York Times*, "Barn," 12.

64. "A Chicago newspaper recently hinted that hospital nurses might accept sitting jobs in their off hours. For two days switch-boards in the main hospitals were so jammed that people with broken ulnas and hardening arteries couldn't get through to their doctors. Authorities angrily called the deal off, and the paper had to apologize." Ellison, "Baby Sitting's Big Business," 36.

65. *New York Times*, "Baby Sitters at Dental Clinic," 19.

66. "Baby Checking Service," *The San Francisco Examiner*, 27 May 1956, 26, The Peter Tamony Collection, Western Historical Manuscripts Collection, Columbia, MO.

67. *Life*, "Profession of Babysitting," 81.

68. Hickey, "More Free Time," 29.

69. Dunlop, "Baby Sitter Co-Op," 40.

70. Rossio, "No Trapped Housewives Here," 6.

71. Dunlop, "Baby Sitter Co-Op," 40.

72. *Saturday Evening Post*, "The New Baby Sitter," cover.

73. Robert Ruark, "Baby Sitters," *The San Francisco News*, 4 September 1946, 11, C3939, box 42, The Peter Tamony Collection, Western Historical Manuscripts Collection, Columbia, MO.

74. Block, "Code for Sitters," 38.

75. Ellison, "Baby Sitting's Big Business," 92.

76. Devlin, *Relative Intimacy*, 93, 98.

77. Lindenmeyer, *Greatest Generation Grows Up*, 240.

78. Sally Wilcox, personal correspondence, April 2004.

79. Daly, "Sitting Pretty," 156.

80. Sylvia Plath, "From the Memoirs of a Babysitter," 2 December 1946 (written for an English class), Plath MSSII, box 8, folder 12:e–h, Lilly Library Manuscript Collections, Indiana University, Bloomington.

81. Ibid.

82. Ibid.

83. Devlin, *Relative Intimacy*, 93; and Social Security Online, "Social Security Handbook."

84. J. Gordon, "Come Over at 7," 50–51; and Stanton, "Baby Sitters United," 150.

85. *Boston Globe,* "Some Baby Sitters."

86. J. Gordon, "Come Over at 7," 51.

87. Stanton, "Baby Sitters United," 150.

88. Ibid.

89. *New York Times,* "Rules for Baby Sitters," 15.

90. Mintz, *Huck's Raft,* 258. Several years earlier the *New York Times* published a "Teen-Age Bill of Rights" that had aimed to codify at least some of the liberties adolescents had gained during the war. Nash, *American Sweethearts,* 144.

91. Elsewhere "[d]uring the late 1940s, a number of books invoking the term ["rights"] appeared, enumerating children's needs, such as a right to an education, a right to play, and a right to be loved and cared for." Mintz, *Huck's Raft,* 330.

92. Ibid., 320; and Woloch, *Women,* 332–33. See also Ellison, "Baby Sitting's Big Business," 36; *New York Times,* "Baby Sitters Set Up Working Conditions Code," 15; and Marcin, "Part-Time Parents," 104.

93. Neisser, "Standards for Baby-Sitters."

94. Mintz and Kellogg, *Domestic Revolutions,* 166; and Fass, *Damned and the Beautiful,* 123–26.

95. Stanton, "Baby Sitters United," 150.

96. Ibid.

97. *New York Times,* "Rules for Baby Sitters," 15.

98. Ibid.

99. Stanton, "Baby Sitters United," 150.

100. *Woman's Home Companion,* "Sitter's Rights," 152.

101. *New York Times,* "Rules for Baby Sitters," 15.

102. Tuttle, *Daddy's Gone to War,* 149.

103. *New York Times,* "Baby Sitters Win Pact," 28.

104. Ellison, "Baby Sitting's Big Business," 37. The quotation is the reporter's paraphrasing.

105. Palladino, *Teenagers,* 93.

106. J. Gordon, "Come Over at 7," 50.

107. Stanton, "Baby Sitters United," 150.

108. Richards, "This Baby-Sitting Business," 101–2.

109. With the cooperation of a local high school and women's club, a Girl Scout leader organized a course that led to the development of a "Club Agreement." *New York Times,* "Baby Sitters Win Pact," 28. See also Richards, "This Baby-Sitting Business," 102–3.

110. *Boston Globe,* "Some Baby Sitters."

111. May, *Pushing the Limits,* 68.

112. N. Thompson, "Baby-Sitting Is Growing Up," 565.

113. *Boston Globe,* "Some Baby Sitters."

114. Richards, "This Baby-Sitting Business," 102–3.

115. *Woman's Home Companion,* "Sitter's Rights," 150.

116. Ibid.

117. Richards, "This Baby-Sitting Business," 102–3.

118. Stanton, "Baby Sitters United," 150.

119. Ibid., 151.

120. *Woman's Home Companion*, "Sitter's Rights," 151.

121. Ellison, "Baby Sitting's Big Business," 37.

122. Gross, "Baby Sitters I Have Known," 5; *Good Housekeeping*, "Entertaining a Baby-Sitter," 172–73; and Kelder, "Know Where You Stand," 258.

123. Ibid.

124. Ellison, "Baby Sitting's Big Business," 37.

125. Robert Ruark, "Baby Sitters," *The San Francisco News*, 4 September 1946, 11, C3939, box 42, The Peter Tamony Collection, Western Historical Manuscripts Collection, Columbia, MO.

126. As quoted by Wini Breines in *Young, White, and Miserable*, 8. May, *Pushing the Limits*, 56. On postwar manhood see Graebner, *Age of Doubt*.

127. Breines, *Young, White, and Miserable*, 33. On the fears of postwar men see Pleck, *Myth of Masculinity*; Filene, *Him/Her/Self*; and J. Gilbert, *Men in the Middle*.

128. The sitter was so "impressed by the glamour of her employer's life" that she ran away from home and engaged in prostitution until she was picked up by the police. See "'Gay Life' of City's Night Ends for Two Girls of 14," *The San Francisco News*, 11 March 1946, 1, C3939, box 42, The Peter Tamony Collection, Western Historical Manuscripts Collection, Columbia, MO.

129. George Foster, "Too Much Baby Sitting," *The San Francisco Examiner*, 12 June 1949, 19, The Peter Tamony Collection, Western Historical Manuscripts Collection, Columbia, MO.

130. Gross, "Baby Sitters I Have Known," 5.

131. Richards, "This Baby-Sitting Business," 102.

132. See Graebner, *Age of Doubt*.

133. Mintz, *Huck's Raft*, 235; and May, *Homeward Bound*, 88.

134. May, *Homeward Bound*, 146.

135. Griswold, *Fatherhood in America*, 180.

136. Gorer, *American People*, 54, quoted by Rachel Devlin in *Relative Intimacy*, 9.

137. Devlin, *Relative Intimacy*, 53.

138. George Blake, director, *You and Your Family*, 1946.

139. On the relationship between dads and daughters in postwar popular culture see Nash, *American Sweethearts*; and Devlin, *Relative Intimacy*.

140. "Teen-Age Girls."

141. Nash, *American Sweethearts*, 124.

142. Ibid., 166–67.

143. Ibid., 151.

144. Daly, "Sitting Pretty," 14–15, 17.

145. Ibid., 19.

146. Mintz, "Parenting," 651–54; May, *Homeward Bound*, 65–66; Graebner, *Age of Doubt*, 15; and Hatch, "Fille Fatale," 165–66.

147. Kerber, "Republican Mother," 120.

148. May, *Homeward Bound*, 92–98; Graebner, *Age of Doubt*, chap. 1; and Douglas, *Where the Girls Are*, 48.

149. See *Life*, "Profession of Babysitting," 81.

150. *San Francisco News*, "Sitter, Father Jailed," 1.

151. Cited in Ellison, "Baby Sitting's Big Business," 36.

152. Kenyon, "Baby Sitter," 131.

153. *The San Francisco Examiner*, "Police Chief Mitchell Balks at Job of Checking Baby Sitters," 20 January 1949, 31, C3939, box 42, The Peter Tamony Collection, Western Historical Manuscripts Collection, Columbia, MO.

154. Nash, *American Sweethearts*, 171.

155. Robert Ruark, "Baby Sitters," *The San Francisco News*, 4 September 1946, 11, C3939, box 42, The Peter Tamony Collection, Western Historical Manuscripts Collection, Columbia, MO.

Chapter 3

1. Kelder, "Know Whether You Stand," 259.

2. The movie *Sitting Pretty* was based on the novel *Belvedere*, by Gwen Davenport (1947).

3. Daly, "Sitting Pretty," 156; and *Sitting Pretty*, final script, 26.

4. N. Thompson, "Baby-Sitting Is Growing Up," 565; and E. Kahn, "Profiles Phenomenon: II," 35–48.

5. Church, "If I Were a Parent," 37.

6. May, *Homeward Bound*, 23.

7. West, *Growing Up*, 174. See B. Bailey, *Front Porch*, 43.

8. Bowlby quoted in Daly, *Inventing Motherhood*, 101. Also see Kaledin, *Mothers and More*.

9. *Life*, "Profession of Babysitting," 81.

10. Coontz, *Way We Never Were*, 192. On the postwar nuclear family see May, *Homeward Bound*.

11. Hoover, "How Safe Is Your Daughter?" 32–33.

12. Safety and peace of mind appeared in B. Brown, "What a Babysitter Needs to Know"; Pinson, "Pictorial Guide," 38–40; and *Coronet*, "Hiring That Baby Sitter," 18.

13. Brown, "What a Babysitter Needs to Know;" and Freeman, "Safety Is No Accident," 150.

14. *New York Times*, "Parents of Babies Warned," 2. See also "The Baby Sitter," *Alfred Hitchcock Presents*, May 6, 1956.

15. *New York Times*, "Baby Sitter Is Jailed," 25; *New York Times*, "Sitter Seized," 19; and *New York Times*, "Kidnapping Charge Filed," 85.

16. *New York Times*, "Baby-sitter Held in Slaying."

17. Robert L. Heilbroner, "The Baby Sitter: A New and Baffling American Problem," *Cosmopolitan*, April 1952, 34–37, 123–24, C3939, box 42, The Peter Tamony Collection, Western Historical Manuscripts Collection, Columbia, MO.

18. Quandt, *Baby Sitter*.

19. Robert L. Heilbroner, "The Baby Sitter: A New and Baffling American Problem," *Cosmopolitan*, April 1952, 34–37, 123–24, C3939, box 42, The Peter Tamony Collection, Western Historical Manuscripts Collection, Columbia, MO.

20. W. W. Baur, "New Profession—Baby Sitting," *The San Francisco Examiner*, 29 December 1953, 18, The Peter Tamony Collection, Western Historical Manuscripts Collection, Columbia, MO; W. W. Baur, "Baby Sitter Needs Skill," *The San Francisco Examiner*, 20 December 1957, sec. II, p. 2, The Peter Tamony Collection, Western Historical Manuscripts Collection, Columbia, MO; and "The Baby Sitter" (editorial), *San Francisco Progress*, 24–25 July, 1957, 14, The Peter Tamony Collection, Western Historical Manuscripts Collection, Columbia, MO.

21. Brown, "Babysitter Needs to Know."

22. On going steady see B. Bailey, *Front Porch*, chap. 2.

23. Bell, "Sitters Are Career Girls," 761.

24. Breines, *Young, White, and Miserable*, chap. 4.

25. Mintz, *Huck's Raft*, 295.

26. Ibid., 282.

27. Kearney, "Birds on the Wire," 581; Barclay, "Two Problems," 40; and *Life*, "Profession of Babysitting," 86. According to Mary Kay Lenihan, who was a babysitter in 1956, "when everyone was in bed I talked on the phone a lot." Mary Kay Lenihan, Personal Communication, November 2001.

28. *Life*, "Profession of Babysitting," 81.

29. Ibid.

30. Gould, "TV Transforming," 1.

31. Leavitt, *Catharine Beecher*, 189–91; Devlin, "Female Juvenile Delinquency," 84; and Palladino, *Teenagers*, 107.

32. Leavitt, *Catharine Beecher*, 190–91; and E. West, *Growing Up*, 186–87.

33. May, *Homeward Bound*, 166; Brumberg, "Emergence of Slenderness," 366; *Boston Globe*, "School Teaches Babysitting"; Schrum, *Some Wore Bobby Sox*, 72; Schrum, "Bobby Socks," 301–2; and Rodgers, "We Love Our Babysitters," 40. For more information, see Block, "Code for Sitters," 38.

34. Gross, "Sitters I Have Known," 5.

35. Richards, "This Baby-Sitting Business," 102.

36. May, *Homeward Bound*, 165.

37. D'Emilio and Freedman, *Intimate Matters*, 172; McLeer, "Practical Perfection," 88; and May, *Homeward Bound*, 165.

38. May, *Homeward Bound*, 12, 18.

39. Ibid., 164.

40. May, "Visions of Family Life in Postwar America," in Jabour, *Major Problems*, 385.

41. *Miss America: Quarterly Magazine for Girls*, "Baby-Sitting Is Big Business," 51.

42. See Johnstone and Katz, "Youth and Popular Music," 563–68; Schrum, *Some Wore Bobby Sox*, 107; and Illick, *American Childhoods*, 121.

43. *Sitting Pretty*, Walter Lang, director, 1948.

44. Written by F. Hugh Gilbert, who is also the author of *Meet Corliss Archer*, one of the premiere girl texts of the period. Kearney, "Recycling Judy and Corliss," 1.

45. Quandt, *Baby Sitter*, 12.

46. "Life with Teena," quoted in Devlin, *Relative Intimacy*, 97–98.

47. *Boston Globe*, "School Teaches Babysitting."

48. Ellison, "Baby Sitting's Big Business," 37.

49. *Business Week*, "New Field for Insurance," 88.

50. Nichols, "Teen-Age Parties," 49.

51. *What Makes a Good Party?*; and Nichols, "Teen-Age Parties," 49.

52. As a result, "Mothers air it over the bridge table, fathers compare sleepless hours at lunch, organized groups meet, newspapers editorialize," and employers complained about teen parties in their homes. Nichols, "Teen-Age Parties," 49.

53. Ibid.

54. *Sitting Pretty*. Quotation from the movie is similar though not exactly the same as the one in the script (27).

55. *Boston Globe*, "Some Baby Sitters Now."

56. On postwar advertising, see Brumberg, *Body Project*, 48.

57. On the history of dating practices in the 1950s see B. Bailey, *Front Porch*.

58. *Newsweek*, "Our Billion-Dollar Night Out," 87–88.

59. Schaller, Scharff, and Schulzinger, *Coming of Age*, 331; and B. Brown, "What a Babysitter Needs to Know"; Mintz, *Huck's Raft*, 308; and *Life*, "New, $10-Billion Power," 78–85.

60. Rodgers, "We Love Our Babysitters," 40.

61. Ibid., 40, 42.

62. *Time*, "Little Women," 24; *Newsweek*, "Three Smart Girls," 38; and Schrum, "Teena Means Business,'" 141.

63. Galbraith, "Side Glances," cartoon, *The San Francisco News*, 9 December 1957, 7, C3939, box 42, The Peter Tamony Collection, Western Historical Manuscripts Collection, Columbia, MO.

64. Gould, "TV Transforming," 36

65. *Boston Globe*, "Some Baby Sitters."

66. Stinnett, "Baby-Sitting Rates," 132.

67. *Saturday Evening Post*, "Babysitter at Beach Stand," cover.

68. Passalaqua, "1950s History: Information, Notes."

69. E. West, *Growing Up*, 334.

70. "Adolescent Girls," 84.

71. Kohlmann, "Teen-Age Interest in Children," 23.

72. *Life*, "Profession of Babysitting," 81.

73. Ibid.

74. *Good Housekeeping*, "1956 Price List," 53.

75. Stanton, "Baby Sitters United," 151.

76. Jean Sid, Personal Communication, June 2004.

77. *Seventeen*, Letters to Editor, November 1944; and Palladino, *Teenagers*, 277.

78. "Teen-Age Girls."

79. On *Seventeen's* youth market research, see Schrum, *Some Wore Bobby Sox*; and Palladino, *Teenagers*, chap. 7.

80. *Life*, "Teen-Age Girls," 91; and Schrum, "'Teena Means Business,'" 135.

81. Jacobson, "Consumer Culture," 156; and Palladino, *Teenagers*, 103.

82. Palladino, *Teenagers*, 106.

83. On postwar female youth culture see Douglas, *Where the Girls Are*, chaps. 2, 3; and Mintz, *Huck's Raft*, chap. 15.

84. Plath, "As a Baby-Sitter Sees It," 19, 21.

85. Ibid., 19.

86. Sylvia Plath to mother, 6 July 1951, Plath MSS. II, box 2, letter 136, Lilly Library Manuscript Collections, Indiana University, Bloomington.

87. Barnes, "Statistics on Babysitting," 30.

88. Newsletter survey cited in Barclay, "Two Problems," 40.

89. Mintz, *Huck's Raft*, 284; and Ellison, "Baby Sitting's Big Business," 94.

90. Sylvia Plath, "From the Memoirs of a Babysitter," 2 December 1946 (Written for an English class), Plath MSSII, box 8, folder 12: e–h, Lilly Library Manuscript Collections, Indiana University, Bloomington.

91. National Safety Council, *You're in Charge*; and Marke, "Does Child Know," n.p.

92. Church, "If I Were a Parent," 91.

93. Harbison, "This Baby Sitting Business," 4.

94. Ibid.

95. Ibid.

96. Ibid.; Church, "If I Were a Parent," 36. Harmon and Ketcham, *Babysitter's Guide*; and Jenkins, "Dennis the Menace," 123.

97. Block, "Code for Sitters," 38.

98. Ibid.

99. Kasey, "City Health Department," 1,052. See also National Safety Council, *You're in Charge*, 1946 and 1948.

100. Seymour Kneitel, director, *Little LuLu: The Baby Sitter*, 1947.

101. It was not until the two girls joined forces and the young witch placed a spell on the baby that made him slumber that order was restored. Buell, "Little Itch Babysits."

102. *New York Times*, "More Rivalry," 25.

103. Daly, "Sitting Pretty," 156.

104. Rockwell had passed up a neighbor's "dainty girl" for the large baby boy who was as "good-natured as a kitten full of milk . . . [and] wouldn't even frown." Instead, "the babysitter sat, the baby sat, [and] Rockwell sat" until the baby dropped his cookie and let out a yell. Rockwell quickly snapped the photo and then painted the picture. See *Saturday Evening Post*, Cover, *Babysitter*, November 8, 1947, 3.

105. *Saturday Evening Post*, Cover, *Babysitter*, November 8, 1947. It is interesting to note that Rockwell painted another picture, also entitled *The Babysitter* (1947), that featured the same sitter only two hours earlier. Unlike the better-known version, the baby is asleep in the crib while the studious sitter is sitting nearby doing her homework. That picture of sitter skill was not featured on the cover of *The Saturday Evening Post*. See Rockwell, *Norman Rockwell's America*, 18.

106. "Margie Baby Sits," *My Little Margie: Collection 2*, DVD, directed by Hal Yates (CBS, February 17, 1954; USA: VCI Entertainment, December 19, 2000).

107. Jenkins, "Dennis the Menace," 121. Term used by Richard Hofstadter and mentioned in Don Romesberg's entry on baby boomers in Fass, *Encyclopedia of Children and Childhood*, 75.

108. Harmon and Ketcham, *Babysitter's Guide*.

109. Ibid., introduction; and Jenkins, "Dennis the Menace," 120.

110. Daly, "Sitting Pretty," 156. "Sitting Pretty" was also the title of a publication published by the Indiana State Department of Public Health. Kasey, "City Health Department," 1051.

111. Block, "Code for Sitters," 99; Berg, "Does Your Insurance," 98.

112. Church, "If I Were a Parent," 37.

113. Ellison, "Baby Sitting's Big Business," 94.

114. Kohlmann, "Teen-Age Interest in Children," 25.

115. Illick, *American Childhoods*, 121.

116. Mintz, *Huck's Raft*, 282.

117. Benson, *Counter Cultures*, 228.

118. Ibid.

119. Austin and Willard, *Generations of Youth*, 5.

120. *Wikipedia*, s.v. "Slang."

121. Ellison, "Baby Sitting's Big Business," 94.

122. Ibid.

123. Louisa Bergson, Personal Communication, June 2000.

124. Church, "If I Were a Parent," 36; West, *Growing Up*, 180; and Church, "If I Were a Parent," 91.

125. Church, "If I Were a Parent," 37; and *Life*, "Profession of Babysitting," 85.

126. Church, "If I Were a Parent," 36. Sociologist Herbert Gans observed at the time "that as suburban youngsters grew into their adolescent years, they became more unhappy with their families and with the communities, complaining bitterly about the lack of transportation and the lack of a place to 'hang out.'" Quoted in Strickland and Ambrose, "The Baby Boom, Prosperity, and the Changing Worlds of Children, 1945–1963," in Hawes and Hiner, eds., *American Childhood: A Research Guide and Historical Handbook*, 565.

127. Mintz and Kellogg, *Domestic Revolutions*, 167.

128. On gender differences in play, see Mintz, *Huck's Raft*, 284.

129. Betty Tom, Personal Communication, October 2005.

130. Louisa Bergson, Personal Communication, June 2000.

131. Newsletter survey cited in Barclay, "Two Problems," 40.

132. See Brettell and Sargent, *Gender in Cross-Cultural Perspective*.

133. Block, "Code for Sitters," 38.

134. Lowndes, *A Manual for Babysitters*, 7; and Schrum, *Some Wore Bobby Sox*, 191–200.

135. Marke, "Does Child Know," n.p.; Spock, et al., *Every Woman's Standard Guide*, 458–59.

Chapter 4

1. *Life*, "Profession of Babysitting," 81.

2. Kenyon, "Baby Sitter," 129; Libien, "Try a Baby-Sitting Co-Op," 32; Mintz and Kellogg, *Domestic Revolutions*, 185; and Southard, "Early Marriages," 5.

3. Mead, "Family Life Is Changing," 679.

4. Richards, "This Baby-Sitting Business," 101; and N. Thompson, "Baby-Sitting Is Growing Up," 565.

5. *Life*, "Profession of Babysitting," 85.

6. Mintz and Kellogg, *Domestic Revolutions*, 185; Hickey, "More Free Time," 29; and Coontz, *Way We Never Were*, 26

7. Jackson, "Baby Boom," 245.

8. *Time*, "They Think."

9. Richards, "This Baby-Sitting Business," 102.

10. West, *Growing Up*, 177.

11. Barclay, "Business of Baby-Sitting," 28.

12. Saunders, *Franklin Watts Concise Guide*, 2.

13. Ellison, "Baby Sitting's Big Business," 37; and Saunders, *Franklin Watts Concise Guide*, 2. "Not only did relatives live in a different house; they likely

lived in another town or state, perhaps on the other side of the country. Visiting grandma and grandpa became a special occasion, indeed." West, *Growing Up*, 182.

14. Mead, "Family Life Is Changing," 679.

15. Saunders, *Franklin Watts Concise Guide*, 2.

16. *Good Housekeeping*, Letters to the Editor, 28.

17. Quoted in Coontz, *Way We Never Were*, 26.

18. Ball, "Mother: The Pushover," 137.

19. May, *Homeward Bound*, 26; and Mintz and Kellogg, *Domestic Revolutions*, 187.

20. Ball, "Mother: The Pushover," 137.

21. Watson, *Behavior*; and Watson, *Psychological Care*.

22. Breines, *Young, White, and Miserable*, 61.

23. Mintz and Kellogg, *Domestic Revolutions*, 187.

24. *Good Housekeeping*, Letters to the Editor, 28.

25. See, for example, White, "Foremothers," 17–45.

26. McElravy, "Grandma Is Drafted," 11–12.

27. Ball, "Mother: The Pushover," 134.

28. Mintz and Kellogg, *Domestic Revolutions*, 13; and Matusky, "Solved Our Sitter Problem," 60.

29. Jackson, *Crabgrass Frontier*, 241.

30. *Life*, "Profession of Babysitting," 81.

31. Walter Lang, director, *Sitting Pretty*, 1987, script, p. 8.

32. Montgomery and Suydam, *America's Baby Book*, 176.

33. Ibid.

34. Julian, *Miss Pickett's Secret*, 2, 9.

35. Deschamps, "'Boss of Baby Sitters,'" 19.

36. *Life*, "Profession of Babysitting," 81.

37. Ellison, "Baby Sitting's Big Business," 92.

38. Ibid.

39. Young, "Baby Sitters Service," 15. One hundred women in Chicago worked for Baby-Sitters, Inc. Marcin, "Part-Time Parents," 104.

40. Marcin, "Part-Time Parents,"103. Between 1946 and 1949, the Kansas City Baby Sitter's Service received thirteen thousand calls from parents in need of the eighty women who supplemented their income working for the service. In 1949, Kansas Citians were charged fifty cents/hour for a minimum of four hours, plus carfare; babysitters were charged between fifteen and fifty cents to the service for each babysitting job. Young, "Baby Sitters Service," 15. Whatever it cost her, the wife of a midwestern railroad conductor liked babysitting because it was "so profitable." Young, "Baby Sitters Service," 16.

41. Jetty, "Babysitter Impresario," 86; and Marcin, "Part-Time Parents," 104–5.

42. *Life*, "Profession of Babysitting," 81.

43. *New York Times*, "Parents of Babies Warned," 12; and Spock et al., *Every Woman's Standard Guide*, 458.

44. F. Benton, *Etiquette*, 369; and Spock, *Baby and Child Care*, 488.

45. Spock, *Baby and Child Care*, 488.

46. Mintz, *Huck's Raft*, 279.

47. Applebaum, "She Trains Baby Sitters," 53.

48. "One installed herself as a sort of unofficial godmother." DeVries, "They Also Sit," 98–99.

49. *Life*, "Profession of Babysitting," 81.

50. Ellison, "Baby Sitting's Big Business," 92.

51. DeVries, "They Also Sit," 99.

52. Jane Sudekum, "Peninsula Women Get Organized to Beat the Baby-Sitter 'Bugaboo.'" *The San Francisco News*, 31 August 1950, 30, The Peter Tamony Collection, C3939, box 42. Western Historical Manuscripts Collection, Columbia, MO.

53. Chafe, *Road to Equality*, 37.

54. May, *Homeward Bound*, 25.

55. *Ladies Home Journal*, "More Free Time," 29.

56. Hickey, "More Free Time," 29.

57. Hickey, "More Free Time," 29–30; and Barclay, "Child Care 'Co-Ops,'" 40. For example, see *New York Times*, "Baby Sitters' Clinic Aids Church," 11; *New York Times*, "Baby Sitters Now Help Parents," 12; *New York Times*, "Veterans to Test Exchange 'Sitting,'" 25; and *Good Housekeeping*, "Sunday Baby-Sitting," 115.

58. Hickey, "More Free Time," 30; Dunlop, "How to Set Up a Baby Sitter Co-Op," 40; Matusky, "Solved Our Sitter Problem," 60; May, *Homeward Bound*, 25; and *Good Housekeeping*, "How to Be Absolutely Sure," 133.

59. See, for example, *New York Times*, "Baby Sitters' Clinic Aids Church," 11; *New York Times*, "Baby Sitters Now Help Parents," 12; *New York Times*, "Veterans to Test Exchange 'Sitting,'" 25; and *Good Housekeeping*, "Sunday Baby-Sitting," 115.

60. Rossio, "No Trapped Housewives Here," 13.

61. Libien, "Try a Baby-Sitting Co-Op," 58.

62. Ibid.

63. Moscrip, "Time Off for Mother," 174.

64. Mintz and Kellogg, *Domestic Revolutions*, 190.

65. Quoted in Jackson, "Baby Boom," 248.

66. Postelle, "Sitters Money Can't Buy," 57.

67. Jane Sudekum, "Peninsula Women Get Organized to Beat the Baby-Sitter 'Bugaboo.'" *The San Francisco News*, 31 August 1950, 30, The Peter Tamony Collection, C3939, box 42. Western Historical Manuscripts Collection, Columbia, MO.

68. Heller, "Why Not Organize a Sitters' Exchange?" 53.

69. Ibid.; and Illick, *American Childhoods*, 112.

70. Heller, "Why Not Organize a Sitters' Exchange?" 52.

71. Ibid., 125; and Postelle, "Sitters Money Can't Buy," 56–57.

72. Postelle, "Sitters Money Can't Buy," 56.

73. Heller, "Why Not Organize a Sitters' Exchange?" 123.

74. Dunlop, "Baby Sitter 'Co-Op,'" 40.

75. Ibid.

76. *Boston Globe*, "Fathers Preferred as Babysitters"; and Whitbread, "Baby-sitting Fathers," 7–8, 10.

77. Dunlop, "Baby Sitter 'Co-Op,'" 39–40.

78. Ibid., 40.

79. Griswold, *Fatherhood in America*, 186–87.

80. Douvan, "Age of Narcissism," 588.

81. Barclay, "Child Care Co-Ops," 40.

82. Dunlop, "Baby Sitter 'Co-Op,'" 40.

83. Moscrip, "Time Off for Mother," 174.

84. *Kiplinger Magazine*, "Baby-Sitting Co-Ops," 13.

85. Heller, "Why Not Organize a Sitters' Exchange?" 123.

86. Ibid.

87. *Life*, "Baby-Sitting with By-laws," 69.

88. Hickey, "More Free Time," 30.

89. Morton, "Starting a Baby-Sitting Co-Op," 72.

90. May, *Homeward Bound*, 26.

91. Rossio, "No Trapped Housewives Here," 6.

92. *The Case of the Babysitter* (Screen Guild Productions, 1947) was a forty-minute mystery movie about a man (Tom Neal) hired to babysit by a couple of thieves. A story of a bumbling babysitting grandfather can be found in Detzer, "My Day with Susan," 5–6.

93. Jenkins, "Dennis the Menace," 121.

94. Toward the end of the decade, babysitter episodes appeared on *Bachelor Father, Make Room for Daddy, The Rifleman, Alfred Hitchcock Presents, Ford Television Theatre, Lassie,* and *Beulah*.

95. Nash, *American Sweethearts*, 173.

96. *Babysitter Jitters*.

97. Caesar, "So I'm a Baby Sitter?" 52.

98. *New York Times*, "Veteran of 200 Bouts," 1; and *New York Times*, "Champs Mother Found," 27.

99. *New York Times*, "Champs Mother Found," 27.

100. Mintz and Kellogg, *Domestic Revolutions*, 189–90.

101. Bloch, *Psycho*; and Alfred Hitchcock, director, *Psycho*, 1960.

102. On postwar youth see J. Gilbert, *Cycle of Outrage*.

103. *Boston Globe*, "School Teaches Babysitting."

104. *Life*, "Graduate Course," 107; N. Thompson, "Baby-Sitting Is Growing Up," 566; Kugelmass, *Complete Child Care*, 202; Rodgers, "We Love Our Babysitters," 40; *Columbia Alumni News*, "Lou's Littles," 17; and *Seventeen Magazine*, "Baby Sitting: Your First Big Job," 52.

105. Rodgers, "We Love Our Babysitters," 40.

106. M. Thompson, "Boys as Mothers-Helpers," 24.

107. "Babysitting for Money for a Tuxedo," *Archie Andrews* radio program, NBC, May 29, 1951.

108. Walt Disney's *Donald Duck Baby Sitter* (New York: Simon & Schuster, 1950) 45 rpm, Golden Record.

109. Jackson and Jackson, *Big Elephant*.

110. Newberry, *T-Bone the Babysitter*.

111. From *Parents' Magazine*, quoted in Hoffert, *History of Gender in America*, 327.

112. Thompson, "Boys as Mothers-Helpers," 24

113. First appeared in the 1954 edition and is found in the chapter entitled "Army Juniors—And Teenagers Too!" Shea, *Army Wife*, 231.

114. *New Yorker*, "Ideal," 21.

115. *Princeton Alumni Weekly*, "Photographs."

116. *Life*, "Profession of Babysitting," 81.

117. B. Bailey, *Front Porch*, 103; and Mintz and Kellogg, *Domestic Revolutions*, 189.

118. Jenkins, "Dennis the Menace," 131.

119. Mintz and Kellogg, *Domestic Revolutions*, 190.

120. Devlin, *Relative Intimacy*, 10.

121. Mintz, *Huck's Raft*, 282; Barclay, "Boy-Sitter," 48; and Church, "If I Were a Parent," 92.

122. Barclay, "Boy-Sitter," 48; and West, *Growing Up*, 190.

123. LeShan, "How to Choose a Babysitter," 52

124. Thompson, "Boys as Mothers-Helpers," 24.

125. J. Parker, *Baby Sittin' Boogie*.

126. I Remember Hamlet, http://www.irememberhamlet.com/baby.html (site now discontinued).

127. *Princeton Alumni Weekly*, "Photographs."

128. *Boston Globe*, "Some Baby Sitters."

129. See *New York Times*, "Held in Child's Death," 54.

130. See *New York Times*, "Babysitter, 14, Held in Killing," 67.

131. Thompson, "Baby-Sitting Is Growing Up," 565.

132. *Boston Globe*, "School Teaches Baby Sitting."

133. *New York Times*, "30 Girls Complete," 32; and Applebaum, "She Trains Baby Sitters," 53.

134. Jack S. McDowell, "Memo from Mac," *San Francisco Call-Bulletin*, 14 January 1947, p. B, The Peter Tamony Collection, Western Historical Manuscripts Collection, Columbia, MO.

135. Ritter, "School for Sitters," 25; and Brooks, "School for Sitters," 38–40.

136. Applebaum, "She Trains Baby Sitters," 52–53.

137. *Life*, "Profession of Babysitting," 80.

138. Thompson, "Baby-Sitting Is Growing Up," 566.

139. Toms, "How We Teach," 46–47.

140. *Boston Globe*, "303 Girls."

141. Ibid.

142. Ritter, "School for Sitters," 50; McIntosh, "Baby Sitting," 10–11, 36.

143. *New York Times*, "Baby-Sitting Guide Mailed," 38; *New York Times*, "Folder and Film Strip," 32; *New York Times*, "Safety Council Urges Talks," 30; and YWCA, *Babysitters*, 64.

144. *Parents' Magazine and Family Home Guide*, "Training for Baby Sitters," 134.

145. *New York Times*, "Baby-Sitting Guide Mailed," 38.

146. *Life*, "Profession of Babysitting," 81.

147. Southard, *Babysitters: Training Manual for Sitters*, 5.

148. Kasey, "City Health Department," 1,051.

149. Romanoff, "Big-Sister Role," 22–23; and Bowman, "All Set for Sitting," 13, 38–39.

150. Barclay, "Community Interest in Baby Sitters," 34.

151. *Boston Globe*, "42 Girls."

152. Flander, *Baby-sitters' Handbook*, chap 3.

153. Bell, "Sitters Are Career Girls," 761.

154. *Boston Globe*, "303 Girls"; and *Boston Globe*, "42 Girls."

155. Ibid., "42 Girls."

156. *Life*, "Graduate Course," 107–8; Marcin, "Part-Time Parents," 104; and *Boston Globe*, "42 Girls."

157. *Life*, "Graduate Course," 107–8.

158. Pinson, "Pictorial Guide," 38–40.

159. Ibid.

160. The code, included in a course at the Somerset high school in Pennsylvania, was also used in similar courses at other schools. "Baby-Sitters Code," 539.

161. *New York Times*, "Baby Sitters' Code Proposed," 78.

162. "Baby-Sitters Code," *Journal of the National Education Association*, 539.

163. Moore, *Baby Sitter's Guide*, preface; Greer and Gibbs, *Your Home and You*, 271; and *Boston Globe*, "42 Girls."

164. *Today's Health*, "Fine Art," 28.

165. "Baby-Sitters Code," *Journal of the National Education Association*, 539.

166. YWCA, *Babysitters*, 14.

167. Lewis Baer, director, *The Babysitter*, 1949.

168. Emery, "Baby Sitter's Boy Friend," 23, 37.

169. *Saturday Evening Post*, "New Year's Babysitter," cover.

170. Harbison, "This Baby Sitting Business," 4.

171. Frey, "Your Baby Sitter," 51.

172. Hal (Lone Pine), "I'd Like to Sit"; Riley, "Baby Sittin'"; Gunn, "Baby Sitter Boogie"; James, "Baby Sitter Rock"; Lee, "Baby Sittin'"; Hicks, "Baby Sittin' All the Time"; and Ireland, "Sitter's Rock."

173. Berg, "Does Your Insurance," 52; and Bernard, "Your Baby Sitter," 96.

174. Bernard, "Your Baby Sitter," 96.

175. Riley, "Baby Sittin'"; LeGarde Twins, "Baby Sitter"; Ward, Baby Sitter"; Gunn, "Baby Sitter Boogie"; James, "Baby Sitter Rock"; Lee, "Baby Sittin'"; Hicks, "Baby Sittin' All the Time"; and Clifford, "Baby Sittin' Boogie."

176. Bernard, "Your Baby Sitter," 97.

177. Berg, "Does Your Insurance," 96–98; and *New York Times*, "Boy, 4, Liable," 8.

178. Frey, "Your Baby Sitter," 204; and *New York Times*, "New Baby-Sitter Bill," 35.

179. *New York Times*, "Measure to License," 25.

180. Barclay, "State Exempts Sitters," 34; Barclay, "Law Widely Ignored."

181. *New York Times*, "Legal Guide Urged," 21.

182. Ibid., "Measure to License," 25.

183. Barclay, "State Exempts Sitters," 34.

184. Frey, "Your Baby Sitter," 51.

185. Ibid., 202.

186. *New York Times*, "Measure to License," 25.

187. Barclay, "Proposing a B.S.,," 49.

188. *New York Times*, "Measure to License," 25.

189. YWCA, National Board, Consultation on Desirable Standards of Employment for School-Age Baby-Sitters (minutes), 22 October 1958, 1–2, Sophia Smith Collection, Smith College, Northampton, MA.

190. *New York Times*, "New Baby-Sitter Bill," 35.

191. Barclay, "Proposing a B.S.," 49. Also, see New *York Times*, "New Baby-Sitter Bill," 35.

192. *New York Times*, "Measure to License," 25–26; Barclay, "State Exempts Sitters," 34.

193. Ibid.

194. Ibid.; and *New York Times*, "New Baby-Sitter Bill," 35.

195. Richards, "This Baby-Sitting Business," 104.

196. Thompson, "Baby-Sitting Is Growing Up," 565–66.

197. Mintz, *Huck's Raft*, 285. Teenage girls had already begun to express their dread of ending up like drudges, according to Wini Breines in *Young, White, and Miserable*, 78.

198. Tizzy cartoon, *San Francisco News*, 8 May 1958, 15, quoted in Robert Ruark, "Baby Sitters," *San Francisco News*, 4 September 1946, 11, C3939, box 42, The Peter Tamony Collection, Western Historical Manuscripts Collection, Columbia, MO.

199. As cited by S. Pollock, "Do You Rate," 44. See also *New York Times*, "Legal Guide Urged," 21.

200. Harmon and Ketcham, *Baby Sitter's Guide*.

201. *Life*, "Profession of Babysitting," 81.

202. Ibid.

203. Block, "Code for Sitters," 38.

Chapter 5

1. Rossio, "No Trapped Housewives Here," 6.

2. Block, "Code for Sitters," 38.

3. Sheldon, "How to Trap and Train," 68.

4. S. Kahn, "Sitting Bull," 57.

5. Figures cited in Greer and Gibbs, *Your Home and You*, 276; and Block, "Code for Sitters," 38.

6. Colette Brunell, Personal Communication, December 1999.

7. As for thirteen-year-old Flossie, she likes to babysit, but only because she loves to read books. Delston, "Baby Sitters," 86–87, 207–8, 210. Nor was Charlotte alone in her admittedly harsh conclusions. Thirteen-year-old Gwen Austin of Independence, Missouri, did not like that the kids did not "mind" her. Olwine, "Baby-Sitter Clinic."

8. Diller, *Housekeeping Hints*, 72. For practical recommendations on better communication between babysitters and bosses, see Daniel R. Campbell, "Code for Baby Sitters," 54, 80.

9. S. Kahn, "Sitting Bull," 57.

10. Block, "Code for Sitters," 98.

11. Block, "Code for Sitters," 38.

12. Ibid.

13. Nancy Hana, Personal Communication, October 1998; and *Life*, "Profession of Babysitting," 79, 86.

14. Ibid.

15. Gwen Elsemore to Mary Weeks, memorandum, 23 October 1958, file Program—Health and Safety—Activities-Babysitting, Girl Scout Archives, New York, NY; and YWCA National Board, Consultation on Desirable Standards of Employment for School-Age Baby-Sitters, Minutes, 22 October 1958, 1, Sophia Smith Collection, Smith College, Northampton, MA.

16. YWCA, National Board, Consultation on Desirable Standards of Employment for School-Age Baby-Sitters, Minutes, 22 October 1958, 1–2, Sophia Smith Collection, Smith College, Northampton, MA; and *Life*, "Profession of Babysitting," 85.

17. Gwen Elsemore to Mary Weeks, memorandum, 23 October 1958, file Program—Health and Safety—Activities-Babysitting; Minutes, Girl Scouts Archives, New York City, NY.

18. Block, "Code for Sitters," 38. On political activism in 1960, see Mintz, *Huck's Raft*, 311.

19. Block, "Code for Sitters," 38.

20. *New York Times*, "Teen-Agers Demand Data," 27; *New York Times*, "Sitters Lay Down Code for Parents," 27; and Usher, "Bill of Rights," 120.

21. Ibid.

22. *Boston Globe*, "Baby Sitting."

23. Ibid.

24. King and Ryan, *Anybody Who Owns*, 147–48.

25. *Look* cited in Mintz, *Huck's Raft*, 312.

26. Nancy Hana, Personal Communication, October 1998. But then there were those like Eliza Winston: "There was an older son who really liked me, but I was able to control the problems." Eliza Winston, Personal Communication, April 2004.

27. Books include Wyden, *Suburbia's Coddled Kids*; Friedenberg, *Vanishing Adolescent*; and P. Goodman, *Growing Up Absurd*. For articles, see Oppenheim, "Teen-Age Drinking," 80, 186–91.

28. Shupp, "Little Girls," 12–13.

29. Grafton, "Tense Generation," 17–23.

30. Abigail Van Buren, Dear Abby, "What's That about Underpaid Sitters?" 24 December 1969, 27, C3939, box 42, *The San Francisco Chronicle*, The Peter Tamony Collection, Western Historical Manuscripts Collection, Columbia, MO.

31. Loyd, "Baby-Sitters," 82; and *Today's Health*, "Checklist," 83.

32. Sam Lame, Roasted Baby, 1 November 1979, file Legend I, Urban Beliefs, I B3 B3, Folklore Archives, University of California, Berkeley.

33. Ainsworth, *Foktales of America*, 106–7.

34. Wolf, *Promiscuities*, 21; and U.S. Children's Bureau, *Infant Care*, 39. Also see Illick, *American Childhoods*, 112; and "Kits for Baby Sitters," *The San Francisco Examiner*, 6 August, 1965, 26, C3939, box 42, The Peter Tamony Collection, Western Historical Manuscripts Collection, Columbia, MO.

35. Kugelmass, *Complete Child Care*, 202.

36. *New York Times*, "Baby-Sitter Warning," 17:1.

37. Loyd, "Baby-Sitters," 82.

38. Statistic cited in Mintz, *Huck's Raft*, 312.

39. Nash, *American Sweethearts*, 169, 183.

40. On girls, young women, and popular culture in the sixties, see Douglas, *Where the Girls Are*.

41. As documented by Barbara Ehrenreich and Susan Douglas in Bloch and Umansky, *Impossible to Hold*.

42. On girls and rock music see Ehrenreich, Hess, and Jacobs, *Re-Making Love*, chap. 1; Douglas, *Where the Girls Are*, chap. 4; and Mintz, *Huck's Raft*, 283.
43. Luckett, "Girl Watchers," 96.
44. Many thanks to Ilana Nash for sharing this episode and her insights with me. "Babysitters," 30 October 1963.
45. On the girls and *The Patty Duke Show* see Nash, *American Sweethearts*; Douglas, *Where the Girls Are*; and Luckett, "Girl Watchers."
46. Kitt, *Billy Brown*. Margaret B. Ruttenberg, *Princeton Alumni Weekly*, "Photographs." Kraft, *When Teenagers Take Care*, 12.
47. Robertson, *Henry Reed's Babysitting Service*, 25–26, 69.
48. Ibid., 59, 74, 87.
49. Ibid., 112, 145, 162.
50. Ibid., 88, 148. Ibid., 159. Henry was humbled and then only briefly when he feared that the IRS would investigate his business. But after a successful babysitting stint for the child of an IRS agent, Henry confidently informed his uncle, with whom he was spending the summer, that if he ever had any trouble with the Internal Revenue Department he should let him know. "I've got influence there." Ibid., 197.
51. Ibid., 197, 204.
52. *Boston Globe*, "Good Baby-Sitter," 76.
53. *The Babysitter*, 1964. In addition to the tips on babysitting the pamphlet provided others on manners, allowance, sewing, cooking ("Romance at the Range"), smart shopping, and party planning. The art of conversation urged girls to invite their friends over for a "How is your voice?" session. To refresh the tonsils, the pamphlet suggested stocking up with Carnation Conversation Coolers and preparing some postsession recipes. Piper, *Tips for Teens*. 6.
54. Margery Lawrence to Mary Weeks, memorandum, 15 February 1965; Marie Vendouzis to Mary Weeks, memorandum, 17 February 1965; Judy Cook to Mary Weeks, memorandum, 19 February 1965; Mary Weeks to Margery Lawrence, memorandum, 17 February 1965; and Mary Weeks to Mary Miller, memorandum, 23 June 1965, file Program—Health and Safety—Activities—Babysitting, Girl Scouts Archives, New York, NY.
55. AT&T and Associated Companies, *Baby Sitter* (c. 1965).
56. *Girls Beware* (1961).
57. *The ABC's of Baby Sitting* (c. 1965).
58. Ella Stefan, Baby Sitter and the Man Upstairs, File I B3 M2, Folklore Archives, University of California, Berkeley.
59. Levine, "Trickster Tales," 190.
60. Ana Turn, Baby Sitter and the Man Upstairs, File I B3 M2, Folklore Archives, University of California, Berkeley.
61. Inness, *Disco Divas*, 196.
62. Clover, *Men, Women, and Chainsaws*, 44; and Trencansky, "Final Girls," 63–73.

63. E. West, *Growing Up*, 185; and Stearns, *Anxious Parents*, 48, 54–55.

64. Schaller, Scharff, and Schulzinger, *Coming of Age*, 454; and Chafe, *Road to Equality*, 24.

65. Figure cited in Mintz, *Huck's Raft*, 313.

66. Rossio, "No Trapped Housewives Here," 6; *National Business Woman*, "Day Care," 12; and *Parents' Magazine and Better Homemaking*, "Are American Parents?" 62, 82, 84.

67. Chafe, *Road to Equality*, 25.

68. Loyd, "Baby-Sitters," 83.

69. Albrecht, "Stand-in for Mother," 58.

70. See Ladd-Taylor and Umansky, eds., *"Bad" Mothers*.

71. Spock, "When Mothers Work," 140.

72. Viorst, "Who's Minding the Baby?" 70.

73. Albrecht, "Stand-in for Mother," 58; and *Good Housekeeping*, "What Counts Most," 131. On women and popular magazines in the postwar era, see Keller, *Mothers and Work*.

74. On men in postwar America see Ehrenreich, *Hearts of Men*.

75. Griswold, *Fatherhood in America*, 220.

76. Coontz, *Way We Never Were*, 35–36; and Griswold, *Fatherhood in America*, 221.

77. Hoffert, *A History of Gender in America*, 334. For classic sociological works on postwar American men see Riesman, *Lonely Crowd*; Whyte, *Organization Man*; and S. Wilson, *Man in the Gray Flannel Suit*.

78. Coontz, *Way We Never Were*, 35–36; and Griswold, *Fatherhood in America*, 221.

79. Ehrenreich, *Hearts of Men*, 120–21.

80. Rogin, *"Ronald Reagan," The Movie*, xiii, xi.

81. Hoffert, *A History of Gender in America*, 328.

82. McLeer, "Practical Perfection," 89.

83. Griswold, *Fatherhood in America*, 220.

84. Cathy Fogan, file Legend, I B3 M2, Folklore Archives, University of California, Berkeley.

85. Jenkins, "Dennis the Menace," 128.

86. Kris Lamar, BS Legends, BS #10, file LB3M2, Center for Pennsylvania Culture Studies, Penn State University.

87. For examples see BS Legends, BS #10, file LB3M2, Center for Pennsylvania Culture Studies, Penn State University.

88. Douglas, *Where the Girls Are*, 24.

89. Wagner, "The Night," 10.

90. *New York Times*, "Philadelphia Girl Stabbed," 46:1; Coontz, *Way We Never Were*, 24, 25, 88.

91. Kraft, *Teenagers Take Care*, 11. On manuals with a community focus, see Southard, *Baby Sitters*; and Ontario Safety League, *Baby-Sitting Training Course*.

92. Kraft, *Teenagers Take Care*, 11.

93. Ibid., 12.

94. West, *Growing Up*, 263; and Chafe, *Road to Equality*, 24; Laura Tune, file I, B3 M2, Folklore Archives, University of California, Berkeley.

Chapter 6

1. Don Henderson, director, *The Babysitter*, 1979, promotional package, author's collection.

2. Robert Coles, *Children in Crisis*, 1st ed. (Boston: Little, Brown, 1967) cited in Strickland and Ambrose, "The Baby Boom," 558; and Rader, "Television," 1850.

3. *Life*, "Profession of Babysitting," 81.

4. Nan Hancy, Personal Communication, June 1999.

5. *San Francisco Examiner*, "Baby Sitter's Romancer," 62.

6. Hal Boyle, "What Baby-Sitters Must Put Up With," *San Francisco Examiner*, 22 September 1970, 33, C3939, box 42, The Peter Tamony Collection, Western Historical Manuscripts Collection, Columbia, MO.

7. D'Emilio and Freedman, *Intimate Matters*, chap. 14.

8. Between 1957 and 1967, the Warren Court eroded definitions of obscenity. See D'Emilio and Freedman, *Intimate Matters*, 287; Fields, *Baby-Sitter*.

9. Fields, *Baby-Sitter*, front cover.

10. Ibid., back cover.

11. Devlin, "Girlhood," 384; and Griswold, "'Flabby American,'" 340. Even before the publication of these blockbusters, the father-daughter relationship had been eroticized by wartime and postwar writers in an effort to reclaim the paternal authority that was on its last legs. See Devlin, *Relative Intimacy*; and Griswold, "'Flabby American,'" 341.

12. Classic critiques include Whyte, *Organization Man*; and Packard, *Status Seekers*.

13. May, *Homeward Bound*, 177; and Fields, *Baby-Sitter*, 14, 93.

14. Fields, *Baby-Sitter*, 124.

15. Ibid., 75, 112.

16. Rivers, "Promiscuous Babysitter," 16.

17. Ibid.

18. Ibid., 16–17, 66–67.

19. Coover, *Pricksongs*, "Babysitter," 206–39.

20. *Superman's Girlfriend Lois Lane*, "Lois Lane Super-Baby-Sitter!" Vol. 57, May 1965.

21. Clay, *Baby Sitter*.

22. Kerr, "Paul Newman," 34–41, 84–85.

23. D'Emilio and Freedman, *Intimate Matters*, 287–88; Douglas, *Where the Girls Are*, 67; and Brumberg, *Body Project*, 189.

24. Don Henderson, director, *The Babysitter*, 1969, trailer.

25. Stanley Eichelbaum, "'Baby Sitter' Hardly for the Family," *San Francisco Examiner*, 22 May 1969, 29, C3939, box 42, The Peter Tamony Collection, Western Historical Manuscripts Collection, Columbia, MO.

26. Don Henderson, director, *The Babysitter*, 1969, promotional package, author's collection. Also see *The Babysitter* (advertisement), *The San Francisco Examiner*, 2 December 1969, C3939, box 42, Peter Tamony Collection, Western Historical Manuscripts Collection, Columbia, MO; and "Kits for Baby Sitters," *San Francisco Examiner*, 6 August 1965, 26, C3939, box 42, The Peter Tamony Collection, Western Historical Manuscripts Collection, Columbia, MO.

27. Ehrenreich, Hess, and Jacobs, *Re-Making Love*, 6.

28. See Dickstein, *Gates of Eden*; and May, *Homeward Bound*, 15. On the medical profession's response to girls' newfound sexual behavior, see Brumberg, *Body Project*, 168.

29. Don Henderson, director, *The Babysitter*.

30. "An 'Honest' Film on 'Babysitters,'" *San Francisco Chronicle*, 22 May 1969, 44, C3939, box 42, Peter Tamony Collection, Western Historical Manuscripts Collection, Columbia, MO.

31. May, *Homeward Bound*, 15.

32. Nash, *American Sweethearts*, 183.

33. *The Babysitter* (advertisement), *San Francisco Examiner*, 2 December 1969, C3939, box 42, Peter Tamony Collection, Western Historical Manuscripts Collection, Columbia, MO; and "Weekend with the Babysitter," *San Francisco Chronicle*, 21 November 1971, 37, C3939, box 42, Peter Tamony Collection, Western Historical Manuscripts Collection, Columbia, MO.

34. Don Henderson, director, *Weekend with the Baby Sitter*, 1970, trailer.

35. McRobbie and Garber, "Girls and Subcultures," 18. By the 1970s, the expansion of pornography would lead to the production of *Jail Bait* (1976), in which the blonde-haired sitter, who arrived at the home of her employer wearing hot pants, "knew what she had and used it." According to a gushing review in *Flick* magazine, the XX-rated *Jail Bait* introduced to the pornographic world Tina Lynn, "a delicious mouthful of Austrian pastry; has a body that is so f——ing incredible it leaves the viewer stunned. She is every man's FANTASY COME TO LIFE!" John Hayes, director, *Jail Bait*, 1976, movie poster.

36. Evans, *Born for Liberty*, 292; and Chafe, *Road to Equality*, 48.

37. *U.S. News & World Report*, "Jobs and the Young."

38. Hal Boyle, "What Baby-Sitters Must Put Up With," *San Francisco Examiner*, 22 September 1970, 33, C3939 Box 42, The Peter Tamony Collection, Western Historical Manuscripts Collection, Columbia, MO.

39. Shulman, quoted in Susan J. Douglas and Meredith W. Michaels, *The Mommy Myth*, 43.

40. *McCall's*, "New Solutions," 40. Along with their teenage granddaughters, widows influenced by feminist beliefs led their own "grandmothers' rebellion." Few took up residence in the homes of their grown children and babysat around the clock. Ciccone, "Baby-Sitter Role." *Retirement Living* nevertheless suggested that retirees could rescue young parents in need of child care. Carlson, "Summer Child Care," 33–34; and A. Smith, "My Children," 37–38.

41. Glickman and Springer, *Who Cares for the Baby?* 2.

42. *Kansas City Times*, "Baby-Sitting Can Be Taught."

43. Rosati, "Baby-Sitting Isn't Bliss!" 18

44. Ibid.

45. Allen, "Baby-sitter Blues," 48–49; and S. Bailey, "Be Kind," 44–45.

46. Brumberg, *Body Project*, 171.

47. Chafe, *Road to Equality*, 90; and Brumberg, *Body Project*, 171.

48. Ibid.

49. Bowles-Reyer, "Becoming a Woman," 21–48; and Ehrenreich, Hess, and Jacobs, *Re-Making Love*, 2.

50. Bowles-Reyer, "Becoming a Woman."

51. Harry Chapin, "Babysitter," 1975.

52. The Ramones, "Babysitter," 1976. Also see Pulp, "The Babysitter," 1978.

53. Carter Stevens, director, *Jail Bait Babysitter*, 1977.

54. Ibid.

55. Ibid.

56. Chafe, *Road to Equality*, 90. In 1978, Congress passed the Adolescent Health Services and Pregnancy Prevention and Care Act. Solinger, "Teen Pregnancy," 650.

57. Rymph, "Neither Neutral nor Neutralized," 501–7.

58. Bowles-Reyer, "Becoming a Woman."

59. *U.S. News & World Report*, "Who's Raising the Children?" 41.

60. Ibid.

61. Hoffert, *Gender in America*, 335.

62. Inness, *Disco Divas*, 5.

63. Peter Collinson, director, *Fright*, 1971.

64. Saunders, *Franklin Watts Concise Guide*, 42–46.

65. On "final girl," see Clover, *Men, Women, and Chainsaws*. On girls who are "pure of heart," see Williams, *When the Woman Looks*.

66. Brumberg, *Body Project*, 182; and L. Williams, "When the Woman Looks," 27. Alice Fleming, in *Baby-Sitter's Nightmare* (Daniel 1992) is also a good girl whose life will be saved because of her sexual purity.

67. Francke, "Putting Father Back," 54.

68. Hoffert, *Gender in America*, 330.

69. Ibid., 335.

70. Shor, "Father Knows Beast," 70.

71. Luckett, "Girl Watchers," 96.

72. Peter Collinson, director, *Fright*, 1971.

73. According to Nashawaty, "Ghoul's Night Out."

74. Fred Walton, director, *When a Stranger Calls*, 1979, promotional package, author's collection.

75. Polly Mend, personal correspondence, September 2000.

76. Internet Movie Database, "Plot Summary for *When a Stranger Calls*," http://www.us.imdb.com/cache/title-movie/plot+123554 (link now discontinued).

77. Even *McCall's* magazine described the once heralded open-space floor plan that had promoted "togetherness" as a "monstrosity of dullness." Leavitt, *Catharine Beecher*, 193.

78. *U.S. News & World Report*, "Who's Raising the Children?" 41.

79. Hoffert, *Gender in America*, 330.

80. *New York Times*, "Rape Case," 23.

81. *New York Times*, "Protection for Baby Sitters"; *New York Times*, "Jersey Police"; and Corbin, "Did a Mafia Hit Man," 46–49, 76–78.

82. *Better Homes and Gardens*, "Baby-Sitting Co-ops," 124–25; Montee, "With a Little Help," 46, 48; Libien, "Try a Baby-Sitting Co-Op," 32; Moffett, "Baby-Sitting," 24; and Zahner, "Big Treat for Toddlers," 27–29.

83. *The National Locksmith*, "Baby Sitter," 18.

84. Kearney, "Birds on the Wire," 568.

85. Ibid., 568, 589–90.

86. Maslin, "Killer on Little Cat Feet," C14.

87. Norman, "Youths Trained."

88. Hughes, *George the Babysitter*.

89. Tom Solari, director, *Understanding Babysitting*, 1980; Tom Solari, director, *Planning Babysitting*, 1980; and Tom Solari, director, *Handling Emergencies*, 1980.

90. Rosenberg, "Davy Crockett as Trickster," 90.

91. Banning, "Things You Should Ask."

92. Sherri Lapound, personal correspondence, May 1999.

Chapter 7

1. Fitzpatrick, "How to Choose a Good Sitter."

2. Kenny, *Daughters of Suburbia*, 8.

3. Roberts, "Girl Power," 312–15.

4. *Kansas City Star*, "Baby Sitter to Face," npn; *Kansas City Star*, "Baby-sitter Accused," npn; *Kansas City Star*, "Boy Accuses Babysitter," npn; *Kansas City Star*, "Baby Sitter Is Held," npn; *Kansas City Star*, "Angry Babysitter" npn; and *Kansas City Star*, "Fifth Child," npn.

5. "Christine Falling," Separatist/Take No Prisoners.

6. Ibid.

7. *Kansas City Star*, "Death Seems to Follow."

8. *Kansas City Star*, "Baby Sitter Calls," npn; *Kansas City Star*, "Fifth Child"; and *Boston Globe*, "Babysitter Held."

9. *Kansas City Times*, "Grand Jury Indicts," npn; and *Kansas City Star*, "Baby Sitter Enters Plea," npn; and "Christine Falling," Separatist/Take No Prisoners.

10. Douglas, *Where the Girls Are*, 29; and *Kansas City Star*, "Baby Sitter Admits," npn.

11. See Curtis Hanson, director, *The Hand That Rocks the Cradle*, 1992; and William Friedkin, director, *The Guardian*, 1990. About female monsters and male fears about women, see Creed, *Monstrous-Feminine*.

12. Faludi, *Backlash*, 5; Illick, *American Childhoods*, 126; and Chafe, *Road to Equality*, 113.

13. In *Daughters of Suburbia: Growing Up White, Middle-Class, and Female* (2000), 3, Lorraine Kenny argues that white, middle-class teenage girls "occupy an ambivalent and at times contradictory position in relation to the norm."

14. LaBarbera, Kourany, and Martin, "College Students," 25; and B. Benton, *Babysitter's Handbook*, 13.

15. Dysfunctional wives include the one in *The Babysitter* (Ferland, director, 1995), who drinks too much; the heroin-addicted wife in *Weekend with the Babysitter* (Laughlin, director, 1971); and Chloe, a drug-addicted alcoholic, in *Implicated* (Belateche, director, 1999). On this as a broader trend, see Faludi, *Backlash*, 124.

16. Creed, *Monstrous-Feminine*.

17. *Grand Rapids Press*, "Girl Trouble."

18. L. Gordon, *Heroes of Their Lives*, 27. On the origins of the "discovery" of child abuse, see Antler and Antler, "Child Rescue to Family Protection," 177–204.

19. Kourany, Martin, and Armstrong, "Sexual Experimentation," 285.

20. LaBarbera, Kournay, and Martin, "College Students," 25; and Kourany, Martin, and LaBarbara, "Adolescents as Babysitters," 156.

21. "Deviant behavior becomes a 'social problem' when policy makers perceive it as threatening to social order, and generate the widespread conviction that organized social action is necessary to control it," according to Linda Gordon, *Heroes of Their Lives*, 27. L. Gordon, "Child Abuse," 269.

22. Bachemin, "Kid Care," 20; and Sullinger, "Working Mothers."

23. E. West, *Growing Up*, 256; and Johnson, "In Search of Sitters," E1.

24. Bachemin, "Kid Care," 20.

25. Saperstein, "They're Standing in Line," E1.

26. DiObilda, "Super Sitters."

27. Husock, "Times Must Be Good."

28. Pierce, "Structured Courses."

29. Pave, "Hold Out," 122.

30. Saperstein, "New Year's Sitters," E1.

31. LaBarbera, Kourany, and Martin, "College Students," 25. The authors of this study interpreted this finding as evidence of their indifference toward babysitting.

32. Wood, "Frankly Speaking," 67.

33. Ibid.

34. Herzig and Mali, *Oh Boy, Babies!*

35. Timothy Thompson, theme for *Charles in Charge*, 1984.

36. Gash, "Kidsday."

37. Molly Realy, personal correspondence, April 1999; Jeanne Wooster, personal correspondence, April 1999; Ruby Strause, personal correspondence, April 1999; and Danica Tingler, personal correspondence, April 1999. See S. Weiss, "Security Blankets," 3

38. Barlett, "Roxbury."

39. Russell, "Jealously," 1; Weiss, "Security Blankets," 3.
Weiss, "Security Blankets," 3.

40. Kourany, Gwinn, and Martin, "Adolescent Babysitting," 939–45.

41. Norman, "Youths Trained."

42. Weiss, "Security Blankets," 3.

43. Russell, "Jealously," 1.

44. Weiss, "Security Blankets," 3.

45. DiObilda, "Super Sitters."

46. Weiss, "Security Blankets," 3.

47. See E. Goodman, *Close to Home*.

48. U.S. Consumer Product Safety Commission, *Super Sitter*; Bachemin, "Kid Care," 20; *National Geographic World*, "Be a Super Sitter!" 10–13; Salk, "Super Sitters," 69; Levin, "Be a Super Sitter," 23; Metropolitan Life Insurance Company, *Sitting Safely*; Biondi, "Complete Guide," 26, 49; Conroy, "Tips on Successful Babysitting"; and Meyeroff, "Baby Sitter Basics," 237.

49. DiObilda, "Super Sitters."

50. Griswold, *Fatherhood in America*, 222.

51. O'Connell, *Baby-Sitting Safe and Sound*, 1.

52. Litvin and Salk, *How to Be a Super Sitter*; Salk, "Super Sitters," 69–73; and DiObilda, "Super Sitters."

53. U.S. Consumer Product Safety Commission, *Super Sitter*; Bachemin, "Kid Care," 20; *National Geographic World*, "Be a Super Sitter!" 10–13; Salk, "Super Sitters," 69–73; Levin, "Be a Super Sitter," 23; Metropolitan Life Insurance Company, *Sitting Safely*; Biondi, "Complete Guide," 26, 49; Conroy, "Tips on Successful Babysitting"; Meyeroff, "Baby Sitter Basics," 237; Litvin and Salk, *How to Be a Super Sitter*; Salk, "Super Sitters," 69–73; and DiObilda, "Super Sitters."

54. Christelow, *Jerome the Babysitter*.

55. Dayee, *Babysitting*; Litvin and Salk, *How to Be a Super Sitter*; Stuhring, *Kid Sitter Basics*; Barkin and James, *New Complete Babysitter's Handbook*; Marsoli, *Things to Know*, 5; Bachemin, "Kid Care," 20; and Black and Brigandi, *Baby-Sitters Club Notebook*. Using the format of a note, *Dear Babysitter Handbook* served as a substitute for a more personal list of instructions to a girl (one is on the cover) provided by a parent (presumably mothers) who did not have the time to deliver them. Lansky, *Dear Babysitter Handbook*, 7. Teen, "Baby-Sitter's Survival Guide," 64; and Callen, "Baby-Sitter's Guide to Survival," 26. When the *Franklin Watts Concise Guide to Baby-Sitting* (Saunders 1972) was reissued in the 1980s, it was tellingly retitled *Baby-Sitting for Fun and Profit* (Saunders 1984). Also in an effort to provide young people with an accessible education in economics was *Sylvia Porter's Your Own Money: Earning It, Spending It, Saving It, Investing It, and Living on It in Your First Independent Years* (Porter 1983).

56. Marsoli, *Things to Know*, 5; Barkin and James, *New Complete Babysitter's Handbook*; Dayee, *Babysitting*; Litvin and Salk, *How to Be a Super Sitter*; and Stuhring, *Kid Sitter Basics*.

57. Bachemin, "Kid Care," 20; and Shannon, "Be a Better Babysitter," 59–60.

58. *Seventeen*, "Baby-Sitting Pretty," 116; *Teen*, "Quiz: How Do You Rate as a Babysitter?"; and Raffel, "Sitting Smart," 237.

59. *The Babysitter's Business Kit* (Middleton, WC: Pleasant Company Publications, 1999), includes Brown, *Babysitter's Handbook*, 64.

60. Metropolitan Life Insurance Company, *Sitting Safely*.

61. Tom Solari, director, *Understanding Babysitting*, 1980.

62. Litvin and Salk, *Super Sitter*. Barkin and James, *New Complete Babysitter's Handbook*. The pocket or purse-sized *New Complete Babysitter's Handbook* also taught skills and inspired "confidence" for readers ten and older.

63. Barlett, "Roxbury."

64. Franklin, "Everything You Need to Know," npn.

65. Levin, "Be a Super Sitter," 23. Purdy, "Be a Super-Safe Sitter," 30–31; and Fitzpatrick, "How to Choose a Good Sitter"; *New York Times*, "Safety Class," C11; *Good Housekeeping*, "Safe Sitters," 36; and *Newsweek*, "Can You Get a Sitter," 84.

66. "Safe Sitter Fact Sheet."

67. See "Course Content: A Comprehensive Approach," in *We're Spreading Our Wings*, brochure (see "Safe Sitter Fact Sheet").

68. *New York Times*, "Safety Class," C11; and Sullivan, "Certified Sitters," 68.

69. *New York Times*, "Safety Class," C11.

70. Ibid.

71. Ibid.

72. Curran, "Are You Risking?" 23.

73. *U.S. Kids: A Weekly Reader*, "Becoming a Safe Sitter," 12–14.

74. Roberts, "Girls in Black and White," 102.

75. Ibid.

76. Kleinfield, "Children's Books," 42. For example, the *Cherry Ames* series had focused on the exploits of nurses. That it did so during the World War II era was due to the fact that the country faced critical shortages of nurses. The BSC books similarly coincided with a shortage in babysitters. Parry, "You Are Needed," 129–44.

77. Ferraro, "Girl Talk," 86.

78. Atwell, "Special Female Voice," 245.

79. Ferraro, "Girl Talk," 86.

80. Tolles, *Katie's Baby-Sitting Job*, 108, 124. In the more lurid story, *Show Me the Evidence* (Ferguson 1989), a babysitter is suspected of killing three babies. Her friend Lauren, who is also implicated, is the victorious heroine who solves the mystery.

81. Roberts, *Baby-Sitting*.

82. Terris, *Baby-Snatcher*, 4.

83. L. Bailey, *How Can I*.

84. Delton, *Angel in Charge*, 131.

85. On girls and adolescence in literature from the 1980s, see Hubler, "Beyond the Image," 84–99.

86. Martin, *Jessi's Wish*, 24.

87. Ibid., *Claudia*, 71.

88. Kearny, "Girl Friends and Girl Power," 133.

89. On relational feminism see Gilligan, *In a Different Voice*; and Gilligan, *Making Connections*.

90. Quoted in Ferraro, "Girl Talk," 98.

91. Lisieux Huelman, personal correspondence, Dec. 18, 2003.

92. Ferraro, "Girl Talk," 98.

93. Martin, *Kristy's Great Idea*.

94. Henry Jenkins quoted in Storey, *Cultural Studies*, 130.

95. Ferraro, "Girl Talk," 63.

96. Pennebaker, "Why Girls," 92; and Martin, *Truth about Stacey*, back cover.

97. Quoted in Ferraro, "Girl Talk," 98.

98. Ibid., 86.

99. Kleinfield, "Children's Books," 42.

100. Inness, "'Anti-Barbies,'" 167.

101. Ferraro, "Girl Talk," 63. Quote by Kevin Dozier, a buyer for B. Dalton and Barnes and Nobel chains.

102. Kleinfield, "Children's Books," 42.

103. Ibid.

104. *Selling to Kids*, "Scholastic's 3rd Quarter Loss"; and *Educational Marketer*, "Scholastic Corp."

105. Lodge, "Baby-Sitter Birthday," 28.

106. Ibid.

107. Becker and Martin, *Ann M. Martin*, 138.

108. Ferraro, "Girl Talk," 86. Novak, "Baby-Sitters Club," 19.

109. Ferraro, "Girl Talk," 86.

110. Cristaldi, *Baby-Sitters Club*.

111. Lodge, "Baby-Sitter Birthday," 28.

112. Lisieux Huelman, Personal Communication, December 2003.

113. Romalov, "Unearthing the Historical Reader," 99–100.

114. Pennebaker, "Why Girls," 92.

115. Henry Jenkins quoted in Storey, *Cultural Studies*, 127.

116. Romalov, "Unearthing the Historical Reader," 99–100. Many BSC fans were as inspired as eleven-year-old Mariana, who explained that "I just think it's nice that a bunch of girls who are so different can be friends and have a club." Ferraro, "Girl Talk," 62.

117. By 1995, there were an estimated one thousand clubs though most were typically short-lived. Bronston, "Baby-Sitters Series," D1.

118. Lisieux Huelman, Personal Communication, December 2003.

119. Kleinfield, "Children's Books," 42; Lisieux Huelman, Personal Communication, December 2003; and Scheiner, "Deanna Durbin Devotees," 82.

120. Lodge, "Baby-Sitter Birthday," 28–29.

121. "Ann M. Martin: The Baby-sitters Club," The Stacks, Scholastic, Inc., http://www.scholastic.com/annmartin/bsc/.

122. Becker and Martin, *Ann M. Martin*, 8.

123. Motivated by individual achievement, she was described as "capable and determined," "disciplined and self-motivated." Becker and Martin, *Ann M. Martin*, 8.

124. "Ann M. Martin: The Baby-sitters Club," The Stacks, Scholastic, Inc., http://www.scholastic.com/annmartin/bsc/.

125. Pennebaker, "Why Girls," 94.

126. See essays by Nancy Tillman Romalov, Sherrie A. Inness, and others in *Nancy Drew and Company: Culture, Gender, and Girls' Series* (Inness 1997).

127. Ferraro, "Girl Talk," 86.

128. As Nancy Tillman Romalov has demonstrated, "Anyone who has read these books quickly discovers that the girls' adventure series is a genre often at odds with itself, replete with contradictory impulses and convoluted narrative

strategies, meant, it seems, to reconcile greater freedom and fitness for girls with their continued subordination to a patriarchal, genteel order." Romalov, "Mobile and Modern Heroines," 76.

129. Nash, *American Sweethearts*, 30.

130. Romalov, "Mobile and Modern Heroines," 76.

131. Ferraro, "Girl Talk," 62.

132. "Why Girls Can't Get Enough of The Baby-Sitters Club." Quoted in Pennebaker, "Why Girls," 94.

133. Ibid., 86.

134. Hurwitz, *Tough-Luck Karen*.

135. Ferraro, "Girl Talk," 86.

136. Roberts, "Girl Power," 313, 315.

137. Chamberlain, "Gender, Class," 37–58.

138. L. Bailey, *How Can I*, 9.

139. Becker and Martin, *Ann M. Martin*, 53.

140. Martin, *Kristy's Big Idea*, "About the Author."

141. "That's probably what made her such an amazing baby-sitter," explains her authorized biography. Becker and Martin, *Ann M. Martin*, 57.

142. See Hurwitz, *Tough-Luck Karen*.

143. "Safe Sitter Fact Sheet,"

144. Ibid.

145. Curran, "Are You Risking?" 53.

146. Quoted in Ferraro, "Girl Talk," 63.

147. Erin Lester, personal correspondence.

148. Lisieux Huelman, Personal Communication, December 2003.

149. Ferraro, "Girl Talk," 98.

Chapter 8

1. Quoted in Ferraro, "Girl Talk," 98.

2. Biondi, "On the Sitting Scene," 26, 49.

3. *Teen*, "Baby-Sitter's Survival Guide," 64; and Sikes, "Baby-Sitting the Brat," 184.

4. Madeline Kaledin, Personal Communication, November 1998.

5. Kamen, "Sit Snit," A23.

6. As one girl explained, "like money/like kids." Chloe Reap, Personal Communication, June 1998.

7. Ginger Josephson, Personal Communication, June 1999.

8. *Street Cents for Tough Street Cents Consumers*, http://www.halifax.cbc.ca/streetcents/entrepreneur/beef.html (site now discontinued; accessed Jan. 8, 1997).

9. Katie Wright, Personal Communication, April 2002.

10. Neus, "Insider's Guide," 15.

11. Cindy Stuart, Personal Communication, October 2001.

12. Beth Hester, Personal Communication. January 1999.

13. Molly Rearly, Personal Communication, April 1999.

14. Helen Appleson, Personal Communication, November 1999.

15. Neus, "Insider's Guide," 19–20.

16. Jessie Waller, Personal Communication, November 1999.

17. Barbara McLarren, Personal Communication, November 1999.

18. Protesting Worker [pseudo.], letter, Dear Beth, *Boston Globe*, February 22, 1983.

19. Cindy Stuart, Personal Communication, October 2001.

20. Mary Beeker, Personal Communication, November 1999.

21. Fifty-two percent of the babysitters surveyed still left wage-rate decisions up to their employers. Forty-three percent of the sitters did so themselves. Six percent used "another approach." McCurrach, "Kids' Baby-Sitting."

22. Alley Higgins, Personal Communication, April 1998.

23. Wood, "Frankly Speaking," 67.

24. Becky Haas, Personal Communication, June 1999.

25. Debbie Morge, Personal Communication, September 1997.

26. Madeline Kaledin, Personal Communication, November 1998.

27. Neus, "Insider's Guide," 17.

28. Neus, "Insider's Guide," 14; and Dow, "Finding—and Keeping," 28.

29. Neus, "Insider's Guide," 18. Molly Rearly, Personal Communication, April 1999. When Margaret and Tammy were paid by check, they used it as an opportunity to save instead of spend what they earned. Neus, "Insider's Guide," 19.

30. Neus, "Insider's Guide," 20.

31. Amelia's employer paid her "all she had," though it was far less than what she owed. Ibid., 26.

32. Neus, "Insider's Guide," 20.

33. Ibid., 19.

34. Amelia Joy, Personal Communication, May 1998.

35. Essary, "How to Coddle," 40.

36. Katie Schuller, Personal Communication, August 1998; Mary Beeker, Personal Communication, November 1999; Amelia Joy, Personal Communication, May 1998; and Neus, "Insider's Guide," 23.

37. Chira, "'Just like a Mom,'" A17.

38. Hofferth and Sandberg, "Changes," 423–36.

39. Neus, "Insider's Guide," 24–26.

40. Katie Schuller, Personal Communication, August 1998.

41. Neus, "Insider's Guide," 23.

42. Ibid.

43. Ibid., 11.

44. Ibid.

45. Amelia Joy, Personal Communication, May 1998.

46. Lisieux Huelman, Personal Communication, December 2003.

47. "Safe Sitter Fact Sheet."

48. Neus, "Insider's Guide," 70–71.

49. Ibid., 73.

50. Ibid., 72.

51. June Random, Personal Communication, October 1998; and Jane Greer, Personal Communication, June 1999.

52. Lisieux Huelman, Personal Communication, December 2003.

53. Pantiel, "Stalking the Teenage Babysitter," 50–51; and Stapen, "Caring," 148, 150.

54. Molly Rearly, Personal Communication, April 1999.

55. Neus, "Insider's Guide," 15–16.

56. Katie Wright, Personal Communication, April 2002.

57. Julian Gray, Personal Communication, March 1999.

58. Musser, "Sitting Lucrative."

59. Julian Gray, Personal Communication, March 1999.

60. Beth Hester, Personal Communication, January 1999.

61. Neus, "Insider's Guide," 26–27.

62. Chris Rod, Personal Communication, May 1998.

63. Neus, "Insider's Guide," 26.

64. June Random, Personal Communication, October 1998.

65. DeCrow, "Sen. Bob Packwood," 11.

66. Cassidy Rockefeller, Personal Communication, July 1999; and Ginger Josephson, Personal Communication, June 1999.

67. Neus, "Insider's Guide," 10. See also Jo-Jo Lohen, Personal Communication, December 1999.

68. Michelle Greenfield, Personal Communication, February 1999.

69. Amelia Joy, Personal Communication, May 1998.

70. Pearson, "Sitter Accuses Alpharetta Man," 4B.

71. Sherri Lapound, Personal Communication, May 1999.

72. Naomi France, Personal Communication, June 1998; and Julian Gray, Personal Communication, March 1999.

73. Calbert, "Babysitting," 4.

74. Thibodeaux, "Dealing with Molestation Class," B7.

75. Barkin and James, New Complete Babysitter's Handbook, 119.

76. Abigail Glicks, Personal Communication, September 1998.

77. Battiata, "Shepherdess in the Suburbs," 15.

78. Neus, "Insider's Guide," 73.

79. Betty Ryberg, Personal Communication, October 1998. Ury, "The Case."

80. Battiata, "Shepherdess in the Suburbs," 15.

81. Debbie Morge, Personal Communication, September 1997.

82. For examples see University of California Folklore Archive, file I B3 M2, Legend I B3 M2.

83. Pinedo, *Recreational Terror*, 6.

84. For examples see University of California Folklore Archive, file I B3 M2, Legend I B3 M2.

85. Ibid.

86. Ibid.

87. Ibid.

88. Ibid.

89. Neus, "Insider's Guide," 74.

90. Neus, "Insider's Guide," 72.

91. See examples in University of California Folklore Archive.

92. Ibid.

93. Margolin, "Child Abuse by Baby-Sitters," 104; and Callen, "Baby-Sitter's Guide to Survival," 26.

94. Alicia Olive, Personal Communication, May 1998; and M. Smith, "My Adventures," 126, 136.

95. M. Smith, "My Adventures," 126, 136; Mary Beeker, Personal Communication, November 1999; and Amelia Joy, Personal Communication, May 1998. It is twins who are considered the quintessential terrors in babysitting fiction. "Not the terrible Tibble twins!" gasps Prunella in M. Brown, *Arthur Babysits*.

96. Mary Beeker, Personal Communication, November 1999; and Amelia Joy, Personal Communication, May 1998.

97. Mary Mann, Personal Communication, July 1999.

98. Ginger Josephson, Personal Communication, June 1999.

99. Jane Greer, Personal Communication, June 1999.

100. Debbie Morge, Personal Communication, September 1997.

101. Sherry Milner, Personal Communication, April 2000.

102. Julian Gray, Personal Communication, March 1999; and Jo-Jo Lohen, Personal Communication, December 1999.

103. Margolin, "Child Abuse by Baby-Sitters," 104; Betty Ryberg, Personal Communication, October 1998; Jean Ringo, Personal Communication, June 2000.

104. Neus, "Insider's Guide," 79.

105. Ibid., 80.

106. Jackie Osmond, Personal Communication, June 1999.

107. Katie Schuller, Personal Communication, August 1998.

108. Mary Beeker, Personal Communication, November 1999.

109. Sikes, "Baby-Sitting the Brat," 184.

110. Ginger Josephson, Personal Communication, June 1999; and Barbara McLarren, Personal Communication, November 1999.

111. Chloe Reap, Personal Communication, June 1998; Jessie Waller, Personal Communication, November 1999; and Alicia Olive, Personal Communication, May 1998.

112. Mary Mann, Personal Communication, July 1999.

113. Neus, "Insider's Guide," 49.

114. S. Weiss, "Security Blankets," 3.

115. Katie Schuller, Personal Communication, August 1998.

116. Sikes, "Baby-Sitting the Brat," 184. "It would drive me crazy," explained one sitter about the hardships associated with getting children to sleep. Julian Gray, Personal Communication, March 1999.

117. Kraft, *When Teenagers Take Care*, 46.

118. Sikes, "Baby-Sitting the Brat," 184; and Kraft, *Teenagers Take Care*, 46.

119. Callen, "Baby-Sitter's Guide to Survival," 26; and Neus, "Insider's Guide," 61.

120. Barbara McLarren, Personal Communication, November 1999. "My mother always lets us eat these [taco chips] before dinner." Allen, "Baby-Sitter Blues," 49.

121. See Stevens, *Beast and the Babysitter*; and Kingsley, *Sitter for Baby Monster*, 1987.

122. For examples in fiction see Gliori, *Mr. Bear Babysits*; Winthrop, *Bear and Mrs. Duck*; Paterson, *Bun and Mrs. Tubby*; Stine, *Baby-Sitter I*, 56; M. Brown, *Arthur Babysits*; Bethell, *Barbie the Baby Sitter*; and McGill, *Six Little Possums*.

123. Neus, "Insider's Guide," 73–74.

124. Ibid., 70.

125. Ibid., 28–29, 31, 74, 75; Erickson, "Mother for a Week," 122, 124; Jackie Osmond, Personal Communication, June 1999; Katie Wright, Personal Communication, April 2002; and Ginger Josephson, Personal Communication, June 1999.

126. Katie Wright, Personal Communication, April 2002.

127. Jackie Osmond, Personal Communication, June 1999.

128. Ginger Josephson, Personal Communication, June 1999.

129. Neus, "Insider's Guide," 75.

130. LaBarbera, Kourany, and Martin, "College Students," 25.

131. Ibid.

132. Neus, "Insider's Guide," 28–29.

133. Ibid., 31.

134. Sikes, "Baby-Sitting the Brat," 184. Becky did not like it when the kids would hit and bite. See Becky Haas, Personal Communication, June 1999. When Alyssa babysat for one girl, she "pulled out a butter knife and said she was going to stab me. I wasn't too scared by the butter knife, but the look in her eyes made her look so possessed. I tried to kind of hide from her, to avoid her, but she kept following me around the house with that knife." Neus, "Insider's Guide," 30.

135. Tammy Fueller, Personal Communication, October 2002. Also see Neus, "Insider's Guide," 33, 34.

136. See University of California Folklore Archive, file I B3 M2, Legend I B3 M2.

137. For examples, see University of California Folklore Archive, file I B3 M2, Legend I B3 M2.

138. Ibid.

139. Beth Hester, Personal Communication, January 1999.

140. Molly Rearly, Personal Communication, April 1999; Cassidy Rockefeller, Personal Communication, July 1999; and Marianne Minchin, Personal Communication, April 2000.

141. Slatalla, "Learning How to Sit," 12.

142. Neus, "Insider's Guide," 34.

143. Christelow, Jerome the Babysitter; Margolin, "Child Abuse by Baby-Sitters," 103; and M. Brown, Arthur Babysits.

144. Julian Gray, Personal Communication, March 1999.

145. Neus, "Insider's Guide," 31.

146. Mary Beeker, Personal Communication, November 1999; Molly Rearly, Personal Communication, April 1999; and Madeline Kaledin, Personal Communication, November 1998.

147. Neus, "Insider's Guide," 28–29.

148. Ibid., 31.

149. Sikes, "Baby-Sitting the Brat," 187.

150. Michelle Greenfield, Personal Communication, February 1999.

151. LaBarbera, Kourany, and Martin, "College Students," 25; Kourany, Martin, and LaBarbara, "Adolescents as Babysitters," 156; Margolin, "Child Abuse by Baby-Sitters," 97; Margolin, "Deviance on Record," 64; Margolin, "Child Abuse by Baby-Sitters," 100, 102; and Mary Beeker, Personal Communication, November 1999.

152. For example, babysitters accused of child abuse in Iowa explained that before they became violent, they had tried "holding these children, talking to them, feeding them, giving them a bottle, isolating them, putting them in for a nap, moving them to their playpen, and so forth" but nothing would quell their crying. Margolin, "Child Abuse by Baby-Sitters," 100.

153. Margolin, "Child Abuse by Baby-Sitters," 97, 102; and Margolin, "Deviance on Record," 64.

154. Jean Ringo, Personal Communication, June 2000.

155. Alicia Olive, Personal Communication, May 1998.

156. Lisieux Huelman, Personal Communication, December 2003.

157. Cindy Stuart, Personal Communication, October 2001; and Alicia Olive, Personal Communication, May 1998.

158. Margolin and Craft, "Child Abuse by Adolescent Caregivers," 365–73; and Margolin, "Child Abuse by Baby-Sitters," 96.

159. Margolin, "Child Abuse by Baby-Sitters," 97.

160. Ibid., 96, 100, 103; Margolin and Craft, "Child Abuse by Adolescent Care-givers," 365–73.

161. Margolin, "Child Abuse by Baby-Sitters," 103.

162. Ibid., "Deviance on Record," 60.

163. Ibid.

164. Sikes, "Baby-Sitting the Brat," 184.

165. Ibid.

166. Ibid.

167. Ibid.

168. Debbie Morge, Personal Communication, September 1997.

169. Jackie Osmond, Personal Communication, June 1999; and Becky Haas, Personal Communication, June 1999.

170. Sherri Lapound, Personal Communication, May 1999.

171. Neus, "Insider's Guide," 34.

172. Jeff Bennet, Personal Communication, December 2006.

173. *Maclean's*, "Martensville Scandal," 20, 26–28.

174. Stevens, *Beast and the Babysitter*, 4.

175. Ibid.

176. Neus, "Insider's Guide," 33; Sherri Lapound, Personal Communication, May 1999; and Jane Greer, Personal Communication, June 1999.

177. Marianne Minchin, Personal Communication, April 2000.

178. Butler, http://en.wikipedia.org/wiki/Judith_Butler*Gender Trouble*; and Robin Kelley, "Riddle of the Zoot," 147–48.

Chapter 9

1. Leonard, "How We Survived," 97–98, 100; and Satran, "In Search," 88.

2. *People Weekly*, "When the Bough Breaks," 60.

3. Statistic cited in Palladino, *Teenagers*, xi.

4. Coyle, "Quitter Sitters," C1. See also Berger, "Urban Tactics," sec. 14, p. 3; and Herring, "Desperate for Baby Sitters," sec. 4, p. 2.

5. *New York Times*, "Teen-Age Baby Sitter," 9.

6. Amatenstein, "My Babysitter, My Hero."

7. Silbiger, "Desperately Seeking Sitters," 1E.

8. Merolla, "Are Your Kids Safe," 74–75.

9. Chao, "Nannycams Check Out Caretakers," A27. *People Weekly*, "When the Bough Breaks," 60.

10. Kindergaurd, http://www.kinderguard.net/how_to/nannywatch.html (site now discontinued).

11. Homepage, Nannycheckonline.com, http://www.nannycheckonline.com; and Nannysafe, http://www.nannysafe.com (site now discontinued).

12. See Gateward and Pomerance, eds., *Sugar, Spice,* introduction.

13. *Mr. Peeper's Amateur Home Videos 27: The Backdoor Babysitter* (LBO Entertainment, 1991), video box cover.

14. Www.yourbackyard.com/hotpants/nympho/ (site now discontinued).

15. *Back Door Babysitter* (Trent, c. 1995); and *Back Door Baby Sitters* (Cherry Box, 2007).

16. There is no shortage of pornographic videos about baby sitters. *The Babysitters, Part One* (Zane, 1994); *New Baby Sitter* (1996); *Babysitter* (Gourmet Video, 2000); *Boffing the Babysitter* (2000); *Training the Baby Sitter* (Gourmet Video, 2001); and *Mr. Peeper's Amateaur Home Videos no. 27: The Backdoor Babysitter* (LBO Entertainment, 1991). Internet sites provide another avenue into sexual fantasies about babysitters. On *Bianca's Fantasy Forum,* an internet site, fantasies that sexualize baby sitters are posted. *Deja News Newsgroups* similarly features lengthy fantasy narratives with titles such as "Babysitting Can Improve your Sex Life."

17. Jim Powers, director, *The Babysitter 15,* 2003.

18. Jim Powers, director, *The Babysitter 15,* 2003, back cover.

19. Ibid., *The Babysitter 17,* 2003; Jim Powers, director, *The Babysitter 1,* 2000; Jim Powers, director, *The Babysitter 2,* 2000; Jim Powers, director, *The Babysitter 3,* 2000; Jim Powers, director, *The Babysitter 4,* 2000; Jim Powers, director, *The Babysitter 5,* 2000; Jim Powers, director, *The Babysitter 6,* 2001; Jim Powers, director, *The Babysitter 7,* 2001; Jim Powers, director, *The Babysitter 8,* 2001; *The Babysitter 13,* Jim Powers, director, 2002; *The Babysitter 15,* Jim Powers, director, 2003; *The Babysitter 17,* Jim Powers, director, 2003; *The Babysitter,* Jim Powers, director, 2003; *The Babysitter 25,* Jim Powers, director, 2006.

20. Ibid., *The Babysitter 2,* 2000.

21. *My Favorite Babysitter 17,* Jim Powers, director, 2008; *18 and Eager Boffing the Babysitter,* Executive Video, n.d.; *Mr. Peepers Amateur Home Videos, no. 27: The Backdoor Babysitter* (LBO Entertainment, 1991); Roy Karch, director, *New Babysitter,* 1996; and John T. Bone, director, *Perverted 1: The Babysitters,* 1994.

22. Stains, "Nanny Dearest," 26.

23. *People,* "Betrayal in the Family," 46–48; Pearson, "Sitter Accuses Alpharetta Man," 4B; Garrett, "Father Gets 16 Years," 10B; O'Donnell, "Suspect Sought," 16; Lombardi and Sutton, "RFK's Son and Baby-Sitter?" 5; Garcilazo, "Teen Testifies on Rape," 4; *Chicago Sun-Times,* Editorial, "Peter Pan Syndrome,"; Fitzmaurice and Gillerman, "Man Gets Life Term," 1A; *Plain Dealer,* "'Frasier' Star," 2A; Matachan, "Porter Goes on Trial," 15; and Latour, "Man Asked Girls," B7.

24. Jerome the alligator explained to his unsympathetic sister, who operated her own thriving babysitting service, that "I'd be a terrific babysitter." Though his competitive cutthroat of a sister sets Jerome up to fail, he successfully outwitted the ten practical jokers in his charge (which was something even his more experienced sister could not do). Christelow, *Jerome the Babysitter.*

25. Alsberg and Nelson, "Tom, the Babysitter," *Tom and Jerry*, January 3, 1993.

26. Studies that demonstrate the high prevalence of child abuse among male babysitters include Margolin, "Abuse and Neglect," 694–704; Margolin, "Sexual Abuse by Grandparents," 735–41; Margolin, "Child Abuse by Mothers' Boyfriends," 541–51; Margolin, "Child Sexual Abuse by Uncles," 1–10; Margolin, "Beyond Maternal Blame," 410–23; Kourany, Martin, and Armstrong, "Sexual Experimentation by Adolescents," 283–88; deYoung, *Sexual Victimization of Children*; Margolin and Craft, "Child Abuse by Adolescent Caregivers," 450–55; and *Kansas City Star*, "Baby Sitter Is Convicted," 1.

27. Margolin, "In Their Parents' Absence," 1.

28. Research findings like this help us to better understand newspaper articles such as the one that reported the fatal stabbing of an eleven-year-old and the sexual assault of two girls. The "Suspect Called Trusted Sitter" was a male "family friend." R. Kelly, "Suspect Called Trusted Sitter," A1.

29. Finkelhor and Ormrod, *Crimes against Children*, 107.

30. Mattel, "Pixel Chix Babysitter," children's toy.

31. Big Fish Games, "Babysitting Mania," http://www.bigfishgames.com/download-games/2422/babysitting-mania/index.html?afcode=af75120973ae&src=af75120973ae&gclid=CInzyICmuZUCFQEuxwodwV5JQA.

32. Reflecting the shift toward preteens, end-of-the-century handbooks were often illustrated with images more appealing to children than teenagers. This also included preprinted business cards adorned with little hearts and cute babies. See *Babysitter's Business Kit* (Middleton, WI: Pleasant Company Publications, 1999).

33. Hopkins, *Girl Heroes*; and Gateward and Pomerance, eds., *Sugar, Spice*, introduction.

34. Daniel, *Baby-Sitter's Nightmare*.

35. Ibid., *Babysitter's Nightmare Part II*, back cover.

36. Stine, *The Babysitter*, 20.

37. Ibid., 16, 62.

38. Ibid., *Babysitter IV*, 156.

39. The *Baby-Sitter's Nightmares* book series: Parker, *Alone in the Dark*, cover; O'Keane, *Lights Out*, cover; Sumner, *Evil Child*, cover; and Carroll, *Killer in the House*, cover.

40. Nasar, "Baby-Sitting's History, *USA Today*, 40.

41. Liz Wilson, Personal Communication, April 2004.

42. Silbiger, "Desperately Seeking Sitters," 1E.

43. Millner and Blanding, "Annals of Baby-Sitting."

44. Landers, "Give Working Teens Their Due," E5.

45. Van Buren, "Dear Abby," *Newsday*, npn.

46. Ibid.

47. Ibid.

48. Pantiel, "Stalking the Teenage Babysitter," 50–51; and Satran, "In Search of the Perfect Sitter," 83.

49. Sherry Luden, personal correspondence, March 1999.

50. Jane Greer, personal correspondence, March 1999.

51. Tara Fuller, Personal Communication, December 2002.

52. Coyle, "Quitter Sitters," C1; Russell, "Jealously," 1; Charski, Cohen, and Tharp, "Is Susie Free Tonight?" 72; and Wen and Mohl, "Attention Parents," B2.

53. Mintz, Huck's Raft, 348. According to J. Hawes, 80 percent of adolescents in the 1980s held a job at some point during their high school years. Hawes, "Child Labor," 182. Palladino, Teenagers, xi; Mrs. Max West, Infant Care, 290; and Silbiger, "Desperately Seeking Sitters," 1E.

54. S. Weiss, "Security Blankets," 3.

55. See Wen and Mohl, "Attention Parents," B2.

56. Warren, "Labor Market Stratification," 15, 18.

57. Coyle, "Quitter Sitters," C1.

58. Silbiger, "Desperately Seeking Sitters," 1E.

59. Charski, Cohen, and Tharp, "Is Susie Free Tonight?" 72.

60. Silbiger, "Desperately Seeking Sitters," 1E.

61. Johnson, "In Search of Sitters," E.

62. Tsao, "Pied Piper." In advance of their steady sitter's impending departure for college, one mother began training a twelve-year-old to take her place. She hired the preadolescent to watch her three children for short-term stints. Silbiger, "Desperately Seeking Sitters," 1E.

63. Charski, Cohen, and Tharp, "Is Susie Free Tonight?" 72.

64. S. Weiss, "Security Blankets," 3.

65. Kamen, "Sit Snit," A23.

66. Silbiger, "Desperately Seeking Sitters," 1E.

67. Ibid.; and Wen and Mohl, "Attention Parents," B2.

68. In just one year, the Red Cross of Massachusetts Bay (which included seventy-eight towns and cities in the greater Boston region) had issued seven hundred babysitter certificates to students age eleven and older. Rudavksy, "ABCs of Child Care," B5; and Gormly, "Desperately Seeking a Baby Sitter."

69. "About Safe Sitter," Safe Sitter, Inc., http://www.safesitter.org/about-SafeSitter.htm.

70. Kearney, Girls Make Media, 68.

71. On the Third Wave see Baumgardner and Richards, Manifesta; and Gillis, Howie, and Munford, eds., Third Wave Feminism.

72. Dar Williams, "The Babysitter's Here," The Honesty Room, 1995.

73. Kearney, Girls Make Media, 65.

74. Ibid., 83–95.

75. Lunachicks, "Babysitters on Acid, Lyrics by Lunachicks," ActioNext, http://www.actionext.com/names_l/ lunachicks_lyrics/babysitters_on_acid. html.

76. Kirschner, Meltzer, and Berger, "Bad Babysitter."

77. Tucker, "Single White Rapper."

78. Kirschner, Meltzer, and Berger, "Bad Babysitter."

79. On Girl Power, see Roberts, "Pleasures and Problems," chap. 12.

80. Frezza and Putnam, *Babysitter*.

81. McRobbie, "Notes on Postfeminism," 3–14; and Kearney, *Girls Make Media*, 68.

82. KatWen87, "Who Killed the Babysitter?"

83. Roberts, "Pleasures and Problems," chap. 12.

84. Russell, "Jealously," 1.

85. H. Smith, "Hard to Find."

86. Sidepony4evr, "'Real' Babysitters Club."

87. *The Babysitters*, David Ross, director, 2008.

Bibliography

"The ABC's of Baby Sitting." Vocational film, c. 1965.

"About Safe Sitter." Safe Sitter. http://www. safesitter.org/AboutSafeSitter.htm.

Adams, Samuel S. *The Systematic Training of Nursery-Maids*. Chicago: Office of the American Medical Association, July 30, 1887.

"Adolescent Girls: A Nation-Wide Study of Girls 11 and 18 Years of Age," Survey Research Center, Institute for Social Research, University of Michigan, for the Girl Scouts of the U.S.A., 1956.

Ainsworth, Catherine Harris. *Folktales of America*. Buffalo, NY: Clyde, 1981.

Albrecht, Margaret. "Stand-in for Mother." *Parents' Magazine and Better Homemaking*, March 1966, 58, 136–38.

Alexander, Ruth. *The "Girl Problem": Female Sexual Delinquency in New York, 1900–1930*. Ithaca, NY: Cornell University Press, 1995.

Allen, Jennifer. "Baby-Sitter Blues." *Seventeen*, March 1978, 48–49.

Alsberg, Arthur, and Don Nelson. *Tom, the Babysitter*. Cartoon. Turner Communications, January 3, 1993.

Amatenstein, Sherrie. "My Babysitter, My Hero." *Redbook*, July 1995, 164.

Anderson, Karen. *Wartime Women: Sex Roles, Family Relations, and the Status of Women during World War II*. Westport, CT: Greenwood Press, 1981.

Antler, Joyce, and Stephen Antler. "From Child Rescue to Family Protection: The Evolution of the Child Protective Movement in the United States." *Children and Youth Service Review* 1 (1979): 177–204.

Applebaum, Stella B. "She Trains Baby Sitters." *Woman's Home Companion*, February 1949, 52–53.

Archives of Pennsylvania Folklife and Ethnography. Center for Pennsylvania Culture Studies, Penn State University. Harrisburg, Pennsylvania.

Arvilla, Merritt, Ella Hendricks, and Floy Hendricks. "Trend of Child Labor, 1940–1944." *Monthly Labor Review* 60 (1944): 756–75.

Atwell, Mary Welek. "A Special Female Voice: The Heroine in Series Books for Girls." In *Images of the Child*, edited by Harry Eiss, 245–54. Bowling Green, OH: Bowling Green State University Press, 1994.

Austin, Joe, and Michael Willard. *Generations of Youth: Youth Cultures and History in Twentieth-Century America*. New York: New York University Press, 1998.

The Baby Sitter. Cartoon VHS. Directed by Seymour Kneitel. Paramount Studios, 1947.

"The Baby Sitter." *Make Room for Daddy.* ABC. May 1956.

"The Baby Sitter." *Alfred Hitchcock Presents.* CBS. May 6, 1956.

The Baby Sitter. Instructional movie. AT&T and associated companies, c. 1965.

The Babysitter. Vocational film. Directed by Lewis Baer. 1949.

"The Baby-Sitter." *Lassie.* CBS. December 29, 1957.

The Babysitter, Episode 19, Kids' Stuff. Instructional movie. Behren's Company, 1964.

The Babysitter. VHS. Directed by Don Henderson. Beverly Hills, CA: Crown International Pictures, 1969.

The Babysitter. Directed by Peter Medak. Filmways Television,1980.

The Babysitter. Directed by Guy Ferland. Spelling Films International, 1995.

The Babysitter. DVD. Directed by Jim Powers. Gourmet Video, 2000.

The Babysitter, Part One. DVD. Zane, 1994.

The Babysitter 2. VHS. Directed by Jim Powers. Notorious, 2000.

The Babysitter 3. Directed by Jim Powers. Notorious, 2000.

Babysitter 4. Directed by Jim Powers. Notorious, 2000.

Babysitter 5. Directed by Jim Powers. Notorious, 2000.

Babysitter 6. Directed by Jim Powers. Notorious 2001.

Babysitter 7. Directed by Jim Powers. Notorious, 2001.

Babysitter 8. Directed by Jim Powers. Notorious, October 2001.

Babysitter 13. Directed by Jim Powers. Notorious, 2002.

The Babysitter 15. DVD. Directed by Jim Powers. Notorious, 2003.

The Babysitter 17. DVD. Directed by Jim Powers. Notorious, 2003.

The Babysitter 25. DVD. Directed by Jim Powers. Notorious, 2006.

The Babysitter Jitters. Directed by Jules White. Columbia Pictures, 1951.

Babysitter Wanted. Directed by Michael Manasseri and Jonas Barnes. Hollywood, CA: Big Screen Entertainment, 2008.

"The Babysitters." *Patty Duke Show.* ABC. October 30, 1963.

The Babysitters. Movie. Directed by David Ross. PeaceArch Entertainment, 2008.

The Baby-Sitters and the Boy-Sitters. VHS. New York: KidVision (distributor), 1993.

The Babysitter's Business Kit. Middletown, WI: Pleasant Company Publications, 1999.

The Baby-sitters Club Movie. Directed by Melanie Mayron. Columbia Pictures, 1995.

"Baby-Sitters Code." *Journal of the National Education Association* 39 (October 1950): 539.

The Babysitter's Seduction. TVM. Directed by David Burton Morris. Hearst Entertainment Productions, 1996.

"Babysitting." *The Aldrich Family*. NBC. October 21, 1948. On *Old Time Radio Programs: The Collector Series, Comedy Greats Vol. I*. Radio Spirits, Audio CD edition. November 1, 1994.

"Babysitting." *The Fred Allen Show*. NBC. March 22, 1949.

"Babysitting for Money for a Tuxedo." *Archie Andrews* radio program. NBC. May 27, 1951.

"Babysitting for Three." *Our Miss Brooks*. CBS. November 14, 1948.

Bachemin, Mary Ann. "Kid Care: How to Be a Supersitter." *Teen*, December 1982, 20–22.

Back Door Babysitter. VHS. Trent, c. 1995

Back Door Babysitters. DVD. Cherry Box, 2007.

Bailey, Beth. *From Front Porch to Back Seat: Courtship in Twentieth-Century America*. Baltimore, MD: Johns Hopkins University Press, 1989.

Bailey, Linda. *How Can I Be a Detective If I Have to Baby-Sit?* Morton Grove, IL: Albert Whitman, 1993.

Bailey, Suzanne. "Be Kind to Your Babysitter: She May Be My Daughter." *Parents' Magazine and Better Family Living*, August 1970, 44–45.

Baker, M. Joyce. *Images of Women in Film: The War Years, 1941–1945*. Ann Arbor: University of Michigan Research Press, 1980.

Balcomb, Ruth D. "College Days without Men." In *Women of the Homefront: World War II Recollections of 55 Americans*, edited by Pauline E. Parker, 39–41. Jefferson, NC: McFarland, 2002.

Ball, Jennifer. "Mother: The Pushover Baby Sitter." *Good Housekeeping*, September 1953.

Banning, Jane. "Things You Should Ask Your Baby-Sitter." *Boston Globe*, May 3, 1974.

Barclay, Dorothy. "The Boy-Sitter Takes Over." *New York Times*, 26 May 1957, 48.

———. "The Business of Baby-Sitting." *New York Times Magazine*, May 31, 1959, 28.

———. "Child Care 'Co-Ops.'" *New York Times Magazine*, March 1, 1953, 40.

———. "Community Interest in Baby Sitters." *New York Times Magazine*, June 24, 1951, 34.

———."Law Widely Ignored." *New York Times*, April 17, 1958, 34.

———. "Proposing a B.S. for Baby Sitters." *New York Times Magazine*, April 6, 1958, 49.

———. "State Exempts Sitters from Child Labor Laws," *New York Times*, April 17, 1958, 34.

———. "Two Problems: Teen-Agers and Baby-Sitters." *New York Times Magazine*, February 8, 1953, 40.

Barkin, Carol, and Elizabeth James. *The Complete Baby-Sitter's Handbook*. New York: Simon & Schuster, 1980.

Barkin, Carol, and Elizabeth James. *The New Complete Babysitter's Handbook*. New York: Clarion Books, 1995.

Barlett, Ellen J. "Roxbury: The Three R's Give Way to Other Basics: Pupils Get Lesson in Babysitting." *Boston Globe*, May 24, 1987.

Barnes, Kathleen. "Statistics on Babysitting." *Calling All Girls*, November 1948, 30.

Barrie, J. M. *Peter Pan*. New York: Scribner's, 1911. Reprinted Toronto: Bantam, 1985.

Battiata, Mary. "A Shepherdess in the Suburbs: $1.50/hour." *Washington Post Magazine*, June 12, 1983, Final Edition, 15.

Baumgardner, Jennifer, and Amy Richards. *Manifesta: Young Women, Feminism, and the Future*. New York: Farrar, Straus, and Giroux, 2000.

Becker, Margot R., and Ann M. Martin. *Ann M. Martin: The Story of the Author of the Baby-sitters Club*. New York: Scholastic, 1993.

Beeman, Mary A. "Brief Study of the Interests of High School Girls in Home Activities." *Journal of Home Economics* 21 (December 1929): 900–904.

Bell, Louise Price. "Sitters Are Career Girls." *Hygeia* 25 (October 1947): 761.

Benson, Susan Porter. *Counter Cultures: Saleswomen, Managers, and Customers in American Department Stores, 1890–1940*. Champaign: University of Illinois Press, 1988.

Benton, Barbara. *The Babysitter's Handbook*. New York: William Morrow, 1981.

Benton, Frances. *American Hostess Library Book of Etiquette*. New York: Educational Book Guild, 1956.

———. *Etiquette: The Complete Modern Guide for Day-to-Day Living the Correct Way*. New York: Random House, 1956.

Berg, Joel. "Does Your Insurance Cover Your Baby Sitter?" *Parents Magazine*, August 1957, 52, 98–99.

Berger, Leslie. "Urban Tactics: Parents on Their Knees, Begging for Baby Sitters." *New York Times*, December 26, 1999, sec. 14, 3.

Bernard, Will. "Your Baby Sitter Can Sue You." *Coronet*, April 1958, 96–98.

Bethell, Jean. *Barbie the Baby Sitter*. New York: Wonder Books, 1964.

Better Homes and Gardens, "Baby-Sitting Co-ops: A Boon to the Family Budget," March 1973, 124–25.

Bhule, Mari Jo. *Feminism and Its Discontents: A Century of Struggle with Psychoanalysis*. Cambridge, MA: Harvard University Press, 1998.

"Bill the Baby Sitter." *Beulah*. ABC. March 6, 1951.

Biondi, Jenny. "The Complete Guide to Kid Care." *Teen*, October 1980.

———. "On the Sitting Scene: The Complete Guide to Kid Care." *Teen*, October 1980, 26, 49.

Bird, Carolyn, and Barbara Ashby. "Do Working Wives Have Better Marriages?" *Family Circle*, November 1976, 62.

Black, Sonia, and Pat Brigandi. *The Baby-Sitters Club Notebook*. New York: Scholastic, 1987.

Bloch, Avital H., and Lauri Umansky, eds. *Impossible to Hold: Women and Culture in the 1960s*. New York: New York University Press, 2005.

Bloch, Robert. *Psycho*. Mattituck, NY: River City Press, 1959.

Block, Jean Libman. "Code for Sitters, Sittees—and Parents." *New York Times Magazine*, May 22, 1960, 38, 96–97.

The Bobby Soxer and the Bachelor. DVD. Directed by Irving Reis. Los Angeles: RKO Radio Pictures, 1947.

Boffing the Babysitter. Gentlemen's Studio, 2000.

Boston Globe, "Babysitter Held in 2 Deaths," July 22, 1982, Run of Paper sec.

———, "Baby Sitting," October 3, 1965.

———, "Fathers Preferred as Babysitters," September 5, 1956.

———, "42 Girls, 3 Boys Taught 'Professional' Baby-Sitting," December 17, 1947.

———, "Girls, 3 Boys Taught 'Professional' Baby-Sitting," December 17, 1947.

———, "Good Baby-Sitter, Joy to Behold," August 27, 1967.

———, "School Teaches Baby Sitting to Bring Order Out of Chaos," July 5, 1947.

———, "Some Baby Sitters Now Get 75 cents an Hour and Taxi Home," n.d.

———, "303 Girls, 6 Boys, 4 Adults Certified: Babysitters Given Thorough Course in How to Act in Emergencies," December 2, 1956.

Bowles-Reyer, Amy. "Becoming a Woman in the 1970s: Female Adolescent Sexual Identity and Popular Literature." In *Growing Up Girls: Popular Culture and the Construction of Identity*, edited by Sharon R. Mazzarella and Norma Odom Pecora, 21–48. New York: Peter Lang, 1999.

Bowman, Ruth Baker. "All Set for Sitting." *The American Girl*, April 1957.

Boys Beware. DVD. Directed by Sid Davis. Los Angeles: Sidney Davis Productions, 1961.

Breines, Wini. *Young, White, and Miserable: Growing up Female in the Fifties*. Chicago: University of Chicago Press, 1992.

Brendall, Meda Hallyburton. Interview by Harmett Gill, 2001. Video, Veterans History Project, American Folklife Center, Library of Congress. Quoted in Merilee Ransom, "A Face on the Women of World War Two: The Changes They Made While Supporting the War Effort." Unpublished paper, 2006.

Brettell, Caroline B., and Carolyn F. Sargent. *Gender in Cross-Cultural Perspective*, 4th ed.: Upper Saddle River, NJ: Prentice Hall, 2004.

Bridges, Yvonne Rusbridges. Interview by Michael Lloyd Willie. 2001. Video, Veterans History Project, American Folklife Center, Library of Congress. Quoted in Merilee Ransom, "A Face on the Women of World War Two: The Changes They Made While Supporting the War Effort." Unpublished paper, 2006.

Bronston, Barri. "Baby-Sitters Series Has Earned a Place in Teen's Heart." *The Times-Picayune*, June 1, 1996, D1.

Brooks, Lois G. "School for Sitters." *Today's Health*, June 1955, 38–40.

Brown, Benita. "What a Babysitter Needs to Know." *Boston Globe*, November 27, 1955.

Brown, Dorothy M. *Setting a Course: American Women in the 1920s*. Boston: Twayne, 1987.

Brown, Harriet. *The Babysitter's Handbook*. Middleton, WI: American Girl Publishing, 1999.

Brown, Marc. *Arthur Babysits*. New York: Little, Brown Young Readers, 1994.

Brumberg, Joan Jacobs. *The Body Project: An Intimate History of American Girls*. New York: Random House, 1997.

———. "The Emergence of Slenderness in American Culture." In *Women's America: Refocusing the Past*, 5th ed., edited by Linda K. Kerber and Jane Sherron de Hart, 366. New York: Oxford University Press, 2000.

Buell, Marjorie Henderson. "Little Itch Babysits." *Marge's Little Lulu*, October 1957. New York: Dell.

Business Week, "New Field for Insurance: Willie Winkle Registered Sitters Service," September 14, 1947, 88.

———, "Teen-age Market: It's 'Terrif,'" June 8, 1946, 72–76.

Caesar, Sid. "So I'm a Baby Sitter?" *Coronet*, June 1955, 45–52.

Calbert, Cathleen. "Babysitting." *North American Review*, December 29, 1989, 4.

Callen, Kimberly A. "Baby-Sitter's Guide to Survival." *Seventeen*, June 1, 1984.

Campbell, Daniel R. "A Code for Baby Sitters." *Parents' Magazine and Better Homemaking*, August 1964, 54, 80.

Campbell, D'Ann. *Women at Work with America: Private Lives in a Patriotic Era*. Cambridge, MA: Harvard University Press, 1984.

Carlson, Cynthia. "Summer Child Care: Retirees to the Rescue." *Retirement Living*, June 1976, 33–34.

Carlson, Randy, and Kevin Leman. *Parent Talk*. Nashville, TN: Thomas Nelson, 1993.

Carroll, J. H. *A Killer in the House*. New York: HarperCollins, 1995.

Case of the Baby Sitter. Directed by Lambert Hillyer. 1947.

Casey, Esther. "How We Saved Our Marriage." *Parents Magazine*, January 1951, 30–31, 100.

Casper, Lynne E. "Who's minding Our Preschoolers?" *Household Economic Studies*, March 1996. Www.census.gov/prod/ 1/pop/p70-73pdf. Accessed August 2008.

Chafe, William H. *The American Woman: Her Changing Social, Economic, and Political Roles, 1920–1970*. New York: Oxford University Press, 1972.

———. *The Road to Equality: American Women since 1962*. New York: Oxford University Press, 1994.

Chamberlain, Kathleen Reuter. "Gender, Class, and Domesticity in the Isabel Carleton Series." In *Nancy Drew and Company: Culture, Gender, and Girls' Series*, edited by Sherrie A. Inness, 37–58. Bowling Green, OH: Bowling Green Press, 1997.

Chao, Julie. "Nannycams Check Out Caretakers: Worried Parents Use Hidden Cameras to See Baby Sitters' Behavior." *Rocky Mountain News*, November 18, 1997, Ed. F; p. 27A.

Chapin, Harry. *Babysitter*. Elektra Entertainment, 1975.

Charsky, Minky, Warren Cohen, and Mike Tharp. "Is Susie Free Tonight? The Law of Supply and Demand Gives Baby Sitters the Upper Hand." *U.S. News & World Report*, June 22, 1998.

Chicago Sun-Times, editorial, "Peter Pan Syndrome," February 6, 2001, 25.

"Child Labor." *Monthly Labor Review* 60, no. 4 (April 1945).

Chira, Susan. "Just 'Like a Mom,' Baby Sitters Stepped in (and Reaped Fame)," *New York Times*, September 28, 1994, A17.

Christelow, Eileen. *Jerome the Babysitter*. New York: Clarion Books, 1985.

"Christine Falling." Wikipedia. http://en.wikipedia.org/wiki/Christine_Falling.

Church, Phyllis. "If I Were a Parent." *American Magazine*, June 1951, 36–37, 91–94.

Ciccone, Richard. "Baby-Sitter Role Not for Widows." *Kansas City Times*, March 2, 1972.

Clark, Clifford Edward Jr. *The American Family Home, 1800–1960*. Chapel Hill: University of North Carolina Press, 1986.

Clay, Paul. *The Baby Sitter*. New York: Softcover Library, 1968.

Clifford, Buzz. "Baby Sittin' Boogie" (song). Columbia, 1961.

Clover Carol J. *Men, Women, and Chainsaws: Gender in the Modern Horror Film*. Princeton, NJ: Princeton University Press, 1993.

Cohen, Lizbeth. *A Consumers' Republic: The Politics of Mass Consumption in Postwar America*. New York: Knopf, 2003.

Cole, Jeff. "Man Pleads Guilty to Filming Sex with Teens: Ex-Police Officer to Be Sentenced in February in Affair with Baby Sitter, 17." *Milwaukee Journal Sentinel*, December 6, 2000, News, 10B.

Columbia Alumni News, "Lou's Littles," May 1949, 17.

Conroy, Maryellen. "Tips on Successful Babysitting." Canada Safety Council, 1977.

Coontz, Stephanie. *The Way We Never Were: American Families and the Nostalgia Trap*. New York: Basic Books, 2000.

Coover, Robert. *Pricksongs & Descants: Fictions*. New York: New American Library, 1969. See esp. pp. 206–39, "The Babysitter."

Corbin, Channing. "Did a Mafia Hit Man Kidnap and Kill the Pretty Babysitter?" *Inside Detective*, November 1977, 46–49, 76–78.

Coronet, "Hiring That Baby Sitter," February 1953, 18.

Cott, Nancy. *Public Vows: A History of Marriage and the Nation*. Cambridge, MA: Harvard University Press, 2000.

"A Course for Baby-Sitters." *NEA Journal* 55 (September 1966): 60.

Cowan, Ruth Schwartz. *More Work for Mothers: The Ironies of Household Technology from the Open Hearth to the Microwave*. New York: Basic Books, 1983.

Cox, Marcelene. "Homemakers in the Making." *Ladies Home Journal*, May 1944, 152–53.

Coyle, Erin. "Quitter Sitters: Many Teens Have Other Priorities Than Watching the Kids." *Atlanta Journal and Constitution*, August 19, 2000.

Creed, Barbara. *The Monstrous-Feminine: Film, Feminism, and Psychoanalysis*. New York: Routledge, 1993.

Cristaldi, Kathryn. *The Baby-Sitters Club*. New York: Scholastic, 1995.

Curran, Colleen. "Are You Risking?" *Women's World*, 1989.

"Dad Fucks Teen Babysitter—Mom Watches!" http://207.17.118.217/banner2.jpg. (accessed December 28, 1997; site now discontinued).

Dally, Ann. *Inventing Motherhood: The Consequences of an Ideal*. London: Burnett Books, 1982.

Daly, Mary Tinley. "Sitting Pretty." *Parents' Magazine and Family Home Guide*, September 1949, 156–57.

Daniel, Kate. *Baby-Sitter's Nightmare*. New York: HarperCollins, 1992.

———. *Baby-Sitter's Nightmare Part II*. New York: HarperCollins, 1994.

Daufmann, Helen. "From Ragtime to Swing: A Short History of Popular Music." *Scholastic* 32 (30 April 1938): 29–32. Quoted in Kelly Schrum, *Some Wore Bobby Sox: The Emergence of Teenage Girls' Culture, 1920–1945*. New York: Palgrave, 2004, 107.

Davenport, Gwen. *Belvedere: A Novel*. Indianapolis: Bobbs-Merrill, 1947.

Dayee, Frances S. *Babysitting*. New York: F. Watts, 1990.

Debrovner, Diane. "A Good Babysitter Is Hard to Find: Parents Magazine Editor Offers Tips to Find a Responsible Person to Watch Your Kids." Interview by Harry Smith. *CBS Early Show*, July 23, 2007. http://www.cbsnews.com/stories/2007/07/23/earlyshow/living/parenting/main3087781.shtml.

DeCrow, Karen. "Sen. Bob Packwood Is No Villain." *USA Today*, January 4, 1994, A11.

Delston, Ethel. "The Baby Sitters." *Redbook: The Magazine for Young Adults*, March 1972, 86–87, 207–8, 210.

Delton, Judy. *Angel in Charge*. Boston: Houghton Mifflin, 1985.

DeLuzio, Crista. *Female Adolescence in American Scientific Thought, 1830–1930*. Baltimore, MD: Johns Hopkins Press, 2007.

D'Emilio, John, and Estelle B. Freedman. *Intimate Matters: A History of Sexuality in America*. Chicago: University of Chicago Press, 1997.

D'Emilio, John, and Estelle B. Freedman. "The Sexual Revolution." In *The Way We Lived*, vol. 2., 3rd ed., edited by Frederick M. Binder and David M. Reimers, 167–76. Lexington, MA: Heath, 1996.

Detzer, Karl. "My Day with Susan." *Readers Digest*, April 1953, 5–6.

Deutsch, Sarah. *From Ballots to Breadlines: American Women, 1920–1940*. New York: Oxford University Press, 1998.

Devlin, Rachel. "Female Juvenile Delinquency and the Problem of Sexual Authority in America, 1945–1965." In *Delinquents and Debutantes: Twentieth-Century American Girls' Cultures*, edited by Sherrie A. Inness, 83–108. New York: New York University Press, 1998.

———. "Girlhood." In *Encyclopedia of Children and Childhood in History and Society*, vol. 2, edited by Paula S. Fass, 381–85. New York: Macmillan Reference USA, 2004.

———. *Relative Intimacy: Fathers, Adolescent Daughters, and Postwar American Culture*. Chapel Hill: University of North Carolina Press, 2005.

DeVries, Peter. "They Also Sit: Employing a Sitter." *New Yorker*, March 20, 1948.

DeYoung, Mary. *The Sexual Victimization of Children*. Jefferson, NC: McFarland, 1982.

Dickstein, Morris. *Gates of Eden: American Culture in the Sixties*. New York: Basic Books, 1977.

Diller, Phyllis. *Phyllis Diller's Housekeeping Hints*. New York: Doubleday, 1966.

DiObilda, Barbara. "Super Sitters to the Rescue!" *Kansas City Star*, December 17, 1989.

Douglas, Susan. *Where the Girls Are: Growing up Female with the Media*. New York: Three Rivers Press, 1993.

Douglas, Susan, and Meredith Michaels. *The Mommy Myth: The Idealization of Motherhood and How It Has Undermined All Women*. New York: Free Press, 2004.

Douvan, Edith. "The Age of Narcissism, 1963–1982." In *American Childhood: A Research Guide and Historical Handbook*, edited by Joseph M. Hawes and N. Ray Hines, 587–618. Westport, CT: Greenwood, 1985.

Dow, Leslie Smith. "Finding—and Keeping—the Right Babysitter: There's One to Fit Every Family." *Living Safely*, Summer 1993.

Driscoll, Catherine. *Girls: Feminine Adolescence in Popular Culture and Cultural Theory*. New York: Columbia University Press, 2002.

DuBois, Ellen Carol, and Lynn Dumenil. *Through Women's Eyes: An American History with Documents*. Boston: Bedford/St. Martins, 2005.

Dunlop, Richard. "How to Set Up a Baby Sitter Co-Op." *Today's Health*, December 1958, 38–40, 53.

Education for Victory, "Higher Educational Institutions and the War," March 1, 1943, 25–26.

Educational Marketer, "Scholastic Corp. Gets Back-to-Basics with Plan to Refocus on the Core Strength in K–6 Reading," N.d.

Ehrenreich, Barbara. *The Hearts of Men: American Dreams and the Flight from Commitment.* New York: Bantam, 1983.

Ehrenreich, Barbara, Elizabeth Hess, and Gloria Jacobs. *Re-Making Love: The Feminization of Sex.* New York: Anchor Press/Doubleday, 1987.

18 and Eager Boffing the Babysitter. Executive Video, n.d.

El Nasser, Haya. "Baby Boomers in a Baby Sitter Bind." *USA Today* (US), January 18, 1996, D6.

Elder, Glen H. Jr. *Children of the Great Depression: Social Change in Life Experience.* Chicago: University of Chicago Press, 1974.

Electric Light and Power Companies. "Captain of Industry" (advertisement), *Life,* May 10, 1947, 4.

Ellison, Jerome. "Baby Sitting's Big Business Now." *Saturday Evening Post,* November 20, 1948, 36–37, 92, 94, 97.

Emery, Anne. "Baby Sitter's Boy Friend." *National Parent-Teacher* 54 (October 1959): 23, 37.

Erickson, D. C. "Mother for a Week." *Seventeen,* May 1986.

Essary, Sandra. "How to Coddle—and Keep—a Baby Sitter." *Parents' Magazine and Better Family Living,* December 1969, 40–41.

Evans, Sara M. *Born for Liberty: A History of Women in America.* New York: Free Press, 1989.

Faludi, Susan. *Backlash: The Undeclared War on Women.* New York: Anchor, 1992.

Farber, David. *The Age of Great Dreams: America in the 1960s.* New York: Hill and Wang, 1994.

Fass, Paula. "Creating New Identities: Youth and Ethnicity in New York City High Schools in the 1930s and 1940s." In *Generations of Youth: Youth Cultures and History in Twentieth-century America,* edited by Joe Austin and Michael Willard, 95–117. New York: New York University Press, 1998.

———. *Encyclopedia of Children and Childhood: In History and Society.* NY: Macmillan Reference Books, 2003.

———. *Damned and the Beautiful: American Youth in the 1920s.* New York: Oxford University Press, 1970.

Ferguson, Alane. *Show Me the Evidence.* New York: Bradbury Press, 1989.

Ferraro, Susan. "Girl Talk." *New York Times Magazine,* December 6, 1992.

Fields, Vin. *The Baby-Sitter.* New York: Tower, 1964.

Filene, Peter. *Him/Her/Self.* 3rd ed. Baltimore: Johns Hopkins University Press, 1998.

Fillman, Enid. "Dolores Learns to Take Care of the Baby." *Woman's Home Companion,* October 1942, 10.

Finkelhor, David, and Richard Ormrod. *Crimes against Children by Babysitters, Juvenile Justice Bulletin.* Washington, DC: U.S. Department of Justice Office of Justice Programs Office of Juvenile Justice and Delinquency Prevention, September 2001.

Fitzmaurice, Leo, and Margaret Gillerman. "Man Gets Life Term on Slaying of Baby Sitter, Boy: 'Stacy and Tyler Can Sleep Now,' Teen's Mother Says." *St. Louis Post-Dispatch,* October 5, 1991, News, 1A.

Fitzpatrick, James C. "How to Choose a Good Sitter." *Kansas City Times,* March 16, 1979.

Flander, Judy. *Baby-sitters' Handbook.* Chicago: Science Research Associates, 1952.

Folklore Archives, University of California, Berkeley.

Forman-Brunell, Miriam. *Made to Play House: Dolls and the Commercialization of American Girlhood, 1830–1930.* New Haven, CT: Yale University Press, 1993.

Francke, Linda Bird. "Putting Father Back in the Family." *Newsweek,* September 22, 1975, Life/Style sec., 54.

Frank, Lawrence K. "Baby Sitter's Job." *New York Times Magazine,* January 23, 1949, 32.

Franklin, Marie. "Everything You Need to Know about Babysitting." *Boston Globe,* October 12, 1984.

Freedman, Estelle B. *The History of the Family and the History of Sexuality.* Washington, DC: American Historical Association, 1997.

Freeman, Cyril. "Safety Is No Accident." *Good Housekeeping,* October 1952, 150.

Frey, Richard L. "Your Baby Sitter and the Law." *Good Housekeeping,* April 1953, 51, 202–5.

Frezza, Rebecca, and Chris Putnam. *Babysitter.* Big Truck Music. Compact disc. 2003.

Friedenberg, Edgar Zodiag. *The Vanishing Adolescent.* Boston: Beacon, 1959.

Fright. VHS. Directed by Peter Collinson. Allied Artists, 1971.

Frum, David. *How We Got Here: The 70s, The Decade That Brought You Modern Life for Better or Worse.* New York: Basic Books, 2000.

Gang Boy. Instructional movie on DVD. Directed by Arthur Swerdloff. Los Angeles: Sidney Davis Productions, 1954.

Garcilazo, Miguel. "Teen Testifies on Rape." *Daily News,* April 20, 1995, Suburban sec., 4.

Garrett, Amanda. "Father Gets 16 Years for Sex with Baby-Sitter." *Plain Dealer,* January 5, 2001. Metro sec., 10B.

Gash, Cari. "Kidsday How We Feel About: Babysitting." *Newsday,* July 5, 1987.

Gateward, Frances, and Murray Pomerance, eds. *Sugar, Spice, and Everything Nice: Cinemas of Girlhood.* Detroit: Wayne State University Press, 2002.

Gesell, Arnold, and Frances Ilg. *Infant and Child in the Culture of Today.* New York: Harper and Row, 1943.

Gilbert, James. *A Cycle of Outrage: America's Reaction to the Juvenile Delinquent in the 1950s.* New York: Oxford University Press, 1988.

———. *Men in the Middle: Searching for Masculinity in the 1950s.* Chicago: Chicago University Press, 2005.

Gilbert, Nan. *Hanna Barbera's Fred Flintstone's Bewildered Baby-Sitter with Pebbles.* Racine, WI: Whitman Tip-Top Tales Books, 1963.

Gilligan, Carol. *In a Different Voice: Psychological Theory and Women's Development.* Cambridge, MA: Harvard University Press, 1982.

———. *Making Connections: The Relational Worlds of Adolescent Girls at the Emma Willard School.* Cambridge, MA: Harvard University Press, 1990.

Gillis, Stacy, Gillian Howie, and Rebecca Munford, eds. *Third Wave Feminism: A Critical Exploration.* New York: Palgrave, 2007.

Gilmore, Glenda. "Forging Interracial Links in the Jim Crow South." In *Women's America: Refocusing the Past*, 6th ed., edited by Linda K. Kerber and Jane Sherron DeHart, 288. New York: Oxford University Press, 2004.

Girl Scouts of America. *Girl Scout Handbook.* New York: Girl Scouts of America, 1953.

Girls Beware. Vocational movie. Sid Davis Productions, 1961. http://www.youtube.com/watch?v=-fAKo-i4jpQ.

Gitlin, Todd. *The Sixties: Years of Hope, Days of Rage.* New York: Bantam Books, 1987.

Glickman, Beatrice Marden, and Nesha Bass Springer. *Who Cares for the Baby? Choices in Child Care.* New York: Schocken Books, 1978.

Gliori, Debi. *Mr. Bear Babysits.* New York: Golden Books, 1994.

Good Housekeeping, "Entertaining a Baby-Sitter: Leave Something for Nibbling," May 1949, 172–73.

———, "How to Be Absolutely Sure of Getting a Baby Sitter," June 1959, 133.

———, Letters to the Editor, November 1953, 28.

———, "1956 Price List for Baby Sitters," September 1956, 53.

———, "Safe Sitters," July 1990.

———, "Sunday Baby-Sitting at Church," January 1958, 115.

———, "What Counts Most in Hiring a Baby Sitter," January 1965, 131.

Goodman, Ellen. *Close to Home.* New York: Fawcett Crest, 1979.

Goodman, Paul. *Growing Up Absurd: Problems of Youth in the Organized System.* New York: Random House, 1960.

Gordon, James. "Come Over at 7." *American Magazine*, October 1947, 50–51.

Gordon, Linda. "Child Abuse and Child Protection in Boston, 1880–1910." In *Major Problems in the History of American Families and Children*, edited by Anya Jabour, 269. Boston: Houghton Mifflin, 2005.

———. *Heroes of Their Own Lives: The Politics and History of Family Violence.* New York: Viking, 1998.

Gorer, Geoffrey. *The American People: A Study in National Character.* New York: Norton, 1948.

Gormly, Kellie B. "Desperately Seeking a Baby Sitter." *Tribune Review,* September 20, 2005. http://www.pittsburghlive.com/x/pittsburghtrib/s_375749.html.

Gossip. VHS. Directed by Homer O'Donnell and Leonard Clairmont. Los Angeles: Sid Davis Productions, 1953.

Gould, Bruce, and Beatrice Blackmar Gould. "Baby-Sitters: A War Job for Teen-Agers." *Ladies Home Journal,* December 1942, 6.

Gould, Jack. "TV Transforming U.S. Social Scene: Challenges Films." *New York Times,* June 24, 1951.

Graebner, William. *The Age of Doubt: American Thought and Culture in the 1940s.* Boston, MA: 1991.

Grafton, Samuel. "The Tense Generation." *Look,* August 27, 1963, 17–23. Quoted in Ilana Nash, *American Sweethearts: Teen-Age Girls in Twentieth-Century Popular Culture.* Bloomington: Indiana University Press, 2006, 243.

Grand Rapids Press, "Girl Trouble," January 13, 2002.

Grant, Julia. *Raising Baby by the Book.* New Haven, CT: Yale University Press, 1998.

Grear, Isabel Wiley. "An American Custom We're NOT Really Proud of!" *American Home,* June 1941, 102.

Greenberger, Ellen, and Laurence Steinberg. *When Teenagers Work: The Psychological and Social Costs of Adolescent Employment.* New York: Basic Books, 1986.

Greer, Carlotta C., and Ellen P. Gibbs. *Your Home and You.* Boston: Allyn and Bacon, 1965.

Griswold, Robert L. *Fatherhood in America: A History.* New York: Basic Books, 1993.

———. "The 'Flabby American,' the Body, and the Cold War." In *A History of Gender in America: Essays, Documents, and Articles,* edited by Sylvia D. Hoffert, 340–46. Upper Saddle River, NJ: Prentice Hall, 2003.

Gross, Edwin A. "Baby Sitters I Have Known." *Christian Science Monitor Magazine,* April 10, 1948, 5.

Groves, Ernest R., and Gladys Hoagland Groves. *Wholesome Childhood.* Boston: Houghton Mifflin, 1924.

Gruenberg, Sidonie Matsner, ed. *The New Encyclopedia of Child Care and Guidance.* Garden City, NY: Doubleday, 1954.

The Guardian. VHS. Directed by William Friedkin. Universal Pictures, 1990.

Gunn, Stan. *Baby Sitter Boogie.* Ron-Mar. 1958.

Hal "Lone Pine." *I'd Like to Sit with the Baby Sitter.* RCA Victor. 45 RPM, June 1954.

Hall, G. Stanley. *Adolescence: Its Psychology and Its Relations to Physiology, Anthropology, Sociology, Sex, Crime, Religion, and Education.* New York: Appleton, 1904.

Halloween. VHS. Directed by John Carpenter. Compass International Pictures, 1978.

The Hand That Rocks the Cradle. VHS. Directed by Curtis Hanson. Hollywood Pictures, 1992.

Handling Emergencies, Instructional movie. Directed by Tom Solari. North Hollywood: Film Communications, 1980.

Harbison, Helen. "This Baby-Sitting Business." *Bookshelf*, March–April 1957, 4.

Harmetz, Aljean. "Cheap and Profitable Horror Films Are Multiplying." *New York Times*, October 24, 1979.

Harmon, Bob, and Hank Ketcham. *Babysitter's Guide by Dennis the Menace*. New York: Henry Holt, 1959.

Harris, Anita, ed. *All about the Girl: Culture, Power, and Identity*. New York: Routledge, 2004.

Hartmann, Susan. *The Home Front and Beyond: American Women in the 1940s*. Boston: Twayne, 1982.

Hatch, Kristen. "Fille Fatale: Regulating Images of Adolescent Girls, 1962–1992." In *Sugar, Spice, and Everything Nice: Cinemas of Girlhood*, edited by Frances Gateward and Murray Pomerance, 163–82. Detroit: Wayne State University Press, 2002.

Hawes, Joseph. "Child Labor." In *The Family in America: An Encyclopedia*, vol. 1. Santa Barbara, CA: ABC-CLIO, 2001.

Hawes, Joseph, and N. Ray Hiner, eds. *American Childhood: A Research Guide and Historical Handbook*. Westport, CT: Greenwood Press, 1985.

Hayden, Dolores. *Building Suburbia: Green Fields and Urban Growth, 1820–2000*. New York: Vintage, 2004.

Hegarty, Marilyn E. *Victory Girls, Khaki-Wackies, and Patriotutes: The Regulation of Female Sexuality during World War II*. New York: New York University Press, 2008.

Helford, Elyce Rae, ed. *Fantasy Girls: Gender in the New Universe of Science Fiction and Fantasy Television*. New York: Roman & Littlefield, 2000.

Heller, Susan Stampfer. "Why Not Organize a Sitters' Exchange?" *Parents Magazine and Family Home Guide*, March 1956, 52–53, 123–25.

Herring, Hubert B. "Desperate for Baby Sitters." *New York Times*, December 26, 1999.

Herzig, Alison Cragin, and Jane Lawrence Mali. *Oh Boy, Babies!* New York: Little, Brown, 1980.

Hickey, Margaret. "More Free Time for Mothers." *Ladies Home Journal*, July 1956, 29–30, 77.

Hicks, Bob, and the Fenders. *Baby Sittin' All the Time*. Mirasonic, 1959.

Hinant, Mary H. "Paging Miss Bobby Sox." *Library Journal*, September 15, 1945, 803.

Hoffert, Sylvia D. *A History of Gender in America: Essays, Documents, and Articles*. Upper Saddle River, NJ: Prentice Hall, 2003.

Hofferth, Sandra L., and John F. Sandberg. "Changes in Children's Time with Parents: United States, 1981–1997." *Demography* 38, no. 3 (August 2001): 1–27.

Holt, Luther Emmett Jr. *The Good Housekeeping Book of Baby and Child Care*. New York: Appleton-Century-Crofts, 1957.

Hoover, J. Edgar. "How Safe Is Your Daughter?" *American Magazine* 144 (July 1947): 32–33.

Hopkins, Susan. *Girl Heroes: The New Force in Popular Culture*. North Melbourne: Pluto Press Australia, 2002.

Howse, John. "The Martensville Scandal." *Maclean's*, June 1992, 26–30.

Hubler, Angela E. "Beyond the Image: Adolescent Girls, Reading, and Social Reality." *NWSA Journal* 12, no. 1 (Spring 2000): 84–99.

Hudson, Barbara. "Femininity and Adolescence." In *Gender and Generation*, edited by Angela McMurray and Mica Nava, 31–53. London: Macmillan.

Hughes, Shirley. *George the Babysitter*. Englewood Cliffs, NJ: Prentice-Hall, 1977.

Hulbert, Ann. *Raising America: Experts, Parents, and a Century of Advice about Children*. New York: Knopf, 2003.

Hunter, Jane. *How Young Ladies Became Girls: Victorian Origins of American Girlhood*. New Haven, CT: Yale University Press, 2002.

Hurwitz, Johanna. *Tough-Luck Karen*. New York: William Morrow, 1982.

Husock, Howard. "Times Must Be Good: Just Try and Find a Babysitter," *Boston Globe*, October 17, 1986.

I Saw What You Did. VHS. Directed by William Castle. Los Angeles: Universal Pictures, 1988.

Illick, Joseph E. *American Childhoods*. Philadelphia: University of Philadelphia Press, 2002.

Implicated. VHS. Directed by Irving Belateche. Sony Pictures, 1999.

Inness, Sherrie A. "'Anti-Barbies': The American Girls Collection and Political Ideologies." In *Delinquents and Debutantes: Twentieth-Century American Girls' Cultures*. New York: New York University Press, 1998.

———, ed. *Delinquents and Debutantes: Twentieth-Century American Girls' Cultures*. New York: New York University Press, 1998.

———. *Disco Divas: Women and Popular Culture in the 1970s*. Philadelphia: University of Pennsylvania Press, 2003.

———. *Kitchen Culture in American: Popular Representations of Food, Gender, and Race*. Philadelphia: University of Pennsylvania Press, 2002.

———, ed. *Nancy Drew and Company: Culture, Gender, and Girls' Series*. Bowling Green, OH: Popular Press, 1997.

Ireland, Bey, and the Tri-Tone Stardusters. *Sitter's Rock*. N.d.

Jabour, Anya, ed. *Major Problems in the History of American Families and Children*. Boston: Houghton Mifflin, 2004.

Jackson, Kathryn, and Byron Jackson. *The Big Elephant*. New York: Golden Press, 1949.

Jackson, Kenneth. "The Baby Boom and the Age of the Subdivision." In *The Way We Lived*, 3rd ed., edited by Frederick M. Binder and David M. Reimers, 252. Lexington, MA: Heath, 1996.

———. *Crabgrass Frontier: The Suburbanization of the United States*. New York: Oxford University Press, 1987.

Jacobson, Lisa. "Allowance." In *Girlhood in America*, vol. 1, edited by Miriam Forman-Brunell, 34–38. Santa Barbara, CA: ABC-CLIO, 2001.

———. "Consumer Culture." In *Girlhood in America*, vol. 1, edited by Miriam Forman-Brunell, 156. Santa Barbara, CA: ABC-CLIO, 2001.

———. *Raising Consumers: Children and the American Mass Market in the Early Twentieth Century*. New York: Columbia University Press, 2004.

Jail Bait. Movie. Directed by John Hayes. 1976.

Jail Bait Babysitter. VHS. Directed by Carter Stevens. 1977.

James, Jimmy. *Baby Sitter Rock*. Columbia, 1958.

Jenkins, Henry. "Dennis the Menace, 'The All American Handful.'" In *The Revolution Wasn't Televised: Sixties Television and Social Conflict*, edited by Lynn Spigel and Michael Curtin, 119–38. New York: Routledge, 1997.

Jetty, Mark. "Babysitter Impresario." *Nation's Business*, March 1948, 86.

Johnson, John. "In Search of Sitters." *Cincinnati Enquirer*, August 23, 1996, E1.

Johnstone, John, and Elihu Katz. "Youth and Popular Music: A Study in the Sociology of Taste." *American Journal of Sociology* 62, no. 6 (May 1957): 563–68.

Jones, Jacqueline. *Labor of Love, Labor of Sorrow: Black Women, Work, and Family from Slavery to Present*. New York: Basic Books, 1985.

Journal of the National Education Association. "Baby-Sitters' Code." 39 (Oct. 1950): 539.

Julian, Nancy R. *Miss Pickett's Secret*. New York: Holt, Rinehart, and Winston, 1952.

Kahn, E. J. Jr. "Profiles Phenomenon: II. The Fave, the Fans, and the Friends." *New Yorker*, November 2, 1946.

Kahn, Sandy. "Sitting Bull." *Boston Magazine*, December 1997, 56–58.

Kaledin, Eugenia. *Mothers and More: American Women in the 1950s*. Boston: Twayne, 1984.

Kamen, Al. "Sit Snit." *Washington Post*, August 7, 1998, A.

Kansas City Star, "Angry Babysitter Gives Tot to Police," July 2, 1980.

———, "Baby-sitter Accused of Murder and Arson," December 1, 1982.

———, "Baby Sitter Admits All Five Slayings," July 28, 1982.

———, "Baby Sitter Calls Children's Deaths 'Weird,'" July 6, 1982.

———, "Baby Sitter Enters Plea, Gets Life Term in Killings," December 3, 1982.

———, "Baby Sitter Is Convicted," June 11, 1997.

———, "Baby Sitter Is Held in Boy's Death," May 12, 1983.

———, "Baby-Sitting Training," January 30, 1981.

———, "Boy Accuses Babysitter in Death of Younger Sister." November 12, 1982.

Kansas City Star, "Death Seems to Follow 18-Year-old Baby Sitter," July 27, 1981.
———, "Fifth Child Cared for by Baby Sitter Dies," July 5, 1982.
———, "Grand Jury Indicts Florida Baby Sitter," August 10, 1982.
———, "Response Too Great," January 12, 1966.
———, "Suddenly You're Alone with Those Kids," June 6, 1970.
———, "Training for Baby-Sitters," December 30, 1970.
Kansas City Times, "Baby Sitter to Face Hearing in House Fire," November 29, 1982.
———, "Baby-Sitters Can Learn How Job Is Done," October 8, 1966.
———, "Baby-Sitting Can Be Taught," March 25, 1972.
Kasey, Elizabeth. "A City Health Department, Recreation Department, and Library Cooperate in Offering a Baby Sitters' Course for Teen-Agers." *The American Journal of Public Health* 42 (September 1952): 1051.
KatWen87. "Who Killed the Babysitter?" YouTube, http://www.youtube.com/watch?v=YMfoyw_IsG0. September 19, 2006.
Katzman, David M. *Seven Days a Week: Women and Domestic Service in Industrializing America*. New York: Oxford University Press, 1978.
Keane, Ben. "Who Is Baby Sitting for Baby Sitter While Baby Sitter's Baby Sitting?" *The Boston Globe*, May 31, 1953, n.p.n.
Kearney, Mary Celeste. "Birds on the Wire: Troping Teenage Girlhood through Telephony in Mid-Twentieth-Century United States." *Cultural Studies* 19, no. 5 (September 2005): 568–601.
———. "Girl Friends and Girl Power: Female Adolescence in Contemporary Cinema." In *Sugar and Spice: Cinemas of Girlhood*, edited by Frances Gateward and Murray Pomerance, 125–44. Detroit: Wayne State University Press, 2002.
———. *Girls Make Media*. New York: Routledge, 2006.
———. "Recycling Judy and Corliss: Transmedia Exploitation and the First Teen-Girl Production Trend." *Feminist Media Studies* 4, no. 3 (November 2004): 265–95.
———. "Riot Grrrl: It's Not Just Music, It's Not Just Punk," *Spectator* 16, no. 1 (Fall/Winter 1995): 83–95.
Kelder, Robert J. "Know Where You Stand with Your Sitter!" *Better Homes and Gardens*, April 1951, 258–59.
Keller, Kathryn. *Mothers and Work in Popular American Magazines*. Westport, CT: Greenwood, 1994.
Kelly, Robert. "Suspect Called Trusted Sitter." *St. Louis Post-Dispatch*, May 15, 1990, A.
Kelley, Robin D. G. "The Riddle of the Zoot: Malcolm Little and Black Cultural Politics during World War II." In *Generations of Youth: Youth Cultures and History in Twentieth-Century America*, edited by Joe Austin and Michael Willard, 136–56. New York: New York University Press, 1998.

Kenny, Lorraine Delia. *Daughters of Suburbia: Growing Up White, Middle Class, and Female.* New Brunswick, NJ: Rutgers University Press, 2000.

Kenyon, Josephine H. "The Baby Sitter." *Good Housekeeping,* November 1949, 28, 131–32.

Kerber, Linda A. "The Republican Mother and the Woman Citizen: Contradictions and Choices in Revolutionary America." In *Women's America: Refocusing the Past,* 6th ed., edited by Linda A. Kerber and Jane De Hart Mathews, 119–28. New York: Oxford University Press, 2004.

Kerr, Marianne. "Paul Newman: Love Affair with a Babysitter." *Photoplay,* August 1968.

Kett, Joseph. *Rites of Passage: Adolescence in America, 1790 to the Present.* New York: Basic Books, 1979.

King, Allan, and Kathryn Ryan. *Anybody Who Owns His Own Home Deserves It.* New York: E.P. Dutton, 1962.

King, Mary Sarah. "Natick Group Sponsors Baby Sitting Course." *Boston Globe,* April 14, 1968.

Kingsley, Emily Perl. *A Sitter for Baby Monster.* Racine, WI: Western Publishing, 1987.

The Kiplinger Magazine, "Baby-Sitting Co-Ops," September 1960, 13.

Kirk, Robert William. "American Children in the Second World War." In *Childhood in America,* edited by Paula Fass and Mary Mason, 269–71. New York: New York University Press, 2000.

Kirksey, Jim. "Jeffco Babysitter Arrested in Fatal Child-Abuse Case." *Denver Post,* January 23, 1990.

Kirschner, Concetta, E. Meltzer, and M. Berger. *Bad Babysitter.* Performed by Princess Superstar, The High & Mighty, Mr. Eon, and Concetta Kirschner. Rapster, B00005V683. Compact disc. 2002.

Kitt, Tamara. *Billy Brown: The Baby Sitter.* New York: Wonder Books, 1962.

Kleinfield, N. R. "Children's Books: Inside the Baby-Sitters Club." Review of *The Baby-Sitters Club,* by Ann M. Martin. *New York Times,* April 30, 1989.

Koch, Beverly. "Day Care's First Steps." *San Francisco Chronicle,* November 19, 1969, 25.

Kohlmann, Eleanore L. "Teen-Age Interest in Children." *Journal of Home Economics* 43 (January 1951): 23–26.

Kopvillem, Peeter, and Dale Eisler. "The Agony of Martensville." *Maclean's,* June 16, 1992.

Kourany, Ronald F. C., Marta Gwinn, and James E. Martin. "Adolescent Babysitting: A 30-year-old Phenomenon." *Adolescence* 15, no. 60 (Winter 1980): 939–45.

Kourany, Ronald F. C., James E. Martin, and S. H. Armstrong. "Sexual Experimentation by Adolescents While Babysitting." *Adolescence* 14, no. 54 (Summer 1979): 283–88.

Kourany, Ronald F. C., James E. Martin, and Joseph D. LaBarbara. "Adolescents as Babysitters." *Adolescence* 15, no. 57 (Spring 1980): 155–58.

Kraft, Ivor. *When Teenagers Take Care of Children.* Philadelphia: Macrae Smith, 1965.

Kruckemeyer, Kate. "More Than Just a Pretty Face: Feminism, Race, and Popular Culture for Girls, 1955–2001." Ph.D. diss., George Washington University, 2003.

Kugelmass, Isaac Newton. *Complete Child Care in Body and Mind: A Modern Parents' Guide to the Healthy Growth and Development of the Newborn, the Infant, the Child, and the Adolescent.* New York: Twayne, 1959.

Kurtz, David, Michael Jacobs, and Al Burton. "Charles in Charge Theme Song," c. 1985.

LaBarbera, J. D., Ronald F. C. Kournay, and James E. Martin. "College Students as Baby Sitters." *College Student Journal* 14, no. 1 (Spring 1980): 24–26.

Ladd-Taylor, Molly, and Lauri Umansky, eds. *"Bad" Mothers: The Politics of Blame in Twentieth-Century America.* New York: New York University Press, 1998.

Ladies Home Journal, "'We're Telling You,'" December 1944, 20–21.

———, "More Free Time for Mothers," July 1956, 29–30.

Lake, Eleanor. "Trouble on the Street Corners." *Reader's Digest,* May 1943.

Landers, Ann. "Give Working Teens Their Due." *Times-Picayune,* April 16, 1999, E5.

Lansky, Vicki. *Dear Babysitter Handbook.* Toronto: Bantam, 1987.

Lasch, Christopher. *Haven in a Heartless World: The Family Besieged.* New York: Basic Books, 1977.

Latour, Francie. "Man Asked Girls to Pose Nude, Police Say." *Boston Globe,* June 27, 2000, Metro/Region sec., B7.

Lavitt, Wendy. *The Knopf Collector's Guide to American Antiques.* New York: Knopf, 1983.

Leavitt, Sarah. *From Catharine Beecher to Martha Stewart: A Cultural History of Domestic Advice.* Chapel Hill: University of North Carolina Press, 2002.

Lee, Myron. "Baby Sittin'" (song). 1959.

LeFavre, Carrica L. *Mother's Help and Child's Friend.* Chicago: privately printed, 1890.

LeGarde Twins. "Baby Sitter" (song). Liberty, 1960.

Leonard, Joan. "How We Survived Our First Night Out." *Parents Magazine,* November 1989, 97–98, 100.

LeShan, Eda J. "How to Choose a Babysitter." *Parents' Magazine and Better Homemaking,* April 1960, 52–53, 88, 90.

Levin, M. "Be a Super Sitter." *Career World,* November 1992, 23.

Levine, Lawrence, "Trickster Tales." In *A History of Gender in America: Essays, Documents, and Articles,* edited by Sylvia D. Hoffert, 189–94. Upper Saddle River, NJ: Prentice Hall, 2003.

Libien, Lois. "Try a Baby-Sitting Co-Op." *Parents' Magazine and Better Family Living,* July 1971, 32–33, 58–59.

Life, "Baby-Sitting with By-laws," November 23, 1959, 69–71.

———, "Community Sitter," June 7, 1948, 148, 151–52.

———, "Graduate Course in Baby-sitting," April 12, 1954, 107–8.

———, "High-School Fads: The Ever-Changing Fashions and Language of Youth Indicate a Healthy Spirit of Rebellion," May 15, 1944, 65–71.

———, "*Life* Goes to a Slumber Party at Indianapolis' D.A.M.S.E.L. Club," January 4, 1943, 72–75.

———, "A New, $10-Billion Power: the U.S. Teen-age Consumer," August 31, 1959, 78–85.

———, "The Profession of Babysitting: It Is Thriving at the Rate of a Billion Dollars a Year," July 29, 1957.

———, "Sub-Deb Clubs: The Midwest Is Full of Them," April 12, 1945, 87–93.

———, "Subdebs: They Live in a Jolly World of Gangs, Games, Gadding, Movies, Malteds, and Music," January 27, 1941, 74–79.

———, "Teen-Age Girls: They Live in a Wonderful World of Their Own," December 11, 1944, 91–99.

Lilly Library Manuscript Collections, Indiana University, Bloomington.

Lindenmeyer, Kriste. *The Greatest Generation Grows Up: American Childhood in the 1930s.* Chicago: Ivan R. Dee, 2005.

Literary Digest, "The Juvenile Jazz to Jail," March 28, 1925, 31–34.

Little Lulu: The Babysitter. Cartoon. Hollywood, CA: Paramount Pictures, 1947.

Litvin, Jay, and Lee Salk. *How to Be a Super Sitter.* Chicago: VGM Career Horizons, 1991.

Lodge, Sally. "A Baby-Sitter Birthday." *Publishers Weekly,* September 4, 1995.

Lombardi, Frank, and Larry Sutton. "RFK's Son and Baby-Sitter? Accused of Affair with the Teenager." *Daily News,* April 26, 1997, News sec., 5.

Loomis, Christine. *My New Baby-Sitter.* New York: William Morrow, 1991.

Lowndes, Marion S. *A Manual for Babysitters.* Boston: Little, Brown, 1949.

Loyd, F. Glen. "Baby-Sitters: Good Emergency Mothers Are GEMS." *Today's Health,* September 1969, 12–13, 83.

Luckett, Moya. "Girl Watchers: Patty Duke and Teen TV." In *The Revolution Wasn't Televised: Sixties Television and Social Conflict,* edited by Lynn Spigel and Michael Curtin, 95–118. New York: Routledge, 1997.

Lunachicks. "Babysitters on Acid Lyrics." Musicsonglyrics.com. http://www.musicsonglyrics.com/L/lunachickslyrics/lunachicksbabysittersonacidlyrics.htm.

Lynd, Robert, and Helen Lynd. *Middletown: A Study in American Culture.* New York: Harcourt, Brace, and World, 1929.

Mackenzie, Catherine. "Grandmothers Are Needed Again." *New York Times Magazine,* September 27, 1942.

Maclean's, "The Martensville Scandal," June 1992, 26–30.

Mann, Judy. "Trooper Firing a Case of Bad Management." *Washington Post,* January 3, 1979, Metro sec., C1.

Marcin, Marietta. "Part-time Parents." *American Mercury,* November 1955, 103–4.

"Margie Baby-Sits." *My Little Margie.* NBC. February 17, 1954.

Margolin, Leslie. "Abuse and Neglect in Nonparental Child Care: A Risk Assessment." *Journal of Marriage and the Family* 53 (July 1991): 694–704.

———. "Beyond Maternal Blame: Physical Child Abuse as a Phenomenon of Gender." *Journal of Family Issues* 13, no. 3 (September 1992): 410–23.

———. "Child Abuse by Adolescent Caregivers." *Child Abuse & Neglect* 14 (1990): 365–73.

———. "Child Abuse by Baby-Sitters: An Ecological–Interactional Interpretation." *Journal of Family Violence* 5, no. 2 (1990): 95–105.

———. "Child Abuse by Mothers' Boyfriends: Why the Overrepresentation?" *Child Abuse & Neglect* 16 (1992): 541–51.

———. "Child Sexual Abuse by Uncles: A Risk Assessment." *Child Abuse & Neglect* 18 (1994): 1–10.

———. "Deviance on Record: Techniques for Labeling Child Abusers in Official Documents." *Social Problems* 39, no. 1 (February 1992): 58–70.

———. "In Their Parents' Absence: Sexual Abuse in Child Care." *Violence Update* 3, no. 9 (May 1993): 1–2, 4.

———. "Sexual Abuse by Caretakers." *Family Relations* 38 (1989): 450–55.

———. "Sexual Abuse by Grandparents." *Child Abuse & Neglect* 16 (1992): 735–41.

Margolin, Leslie, and J. L. Craft. "Child Abuse by Adolescent Caregivers." *Child Abuse & Neglect* 14 (1990): 365–73.

Marke, David Taylor. "Does Child Know Its Baby Sitter When You Parents Take Night Off?" *Boston Globe,* November 16, 1954.

Marsoli, Lisa Ann. *Things to Know about Babysitting.* Morristown, NJ: Tribeca Communications, 1985.

Martin, Ann M. *Claudia and the Phantom Phone Calls.* New York: Scholastic, 1986.

———. *Jessi's Wish.* New York: Scholastic, 1991.

———. *Kristy's Great Idea.* New York: Scholastic, 1986.

———. *The Truth about Stacey.* New York: Scholastic, 1986.

Maslin, Janet. "Killer on Little Cat Feet" (review). *New York Times,* October 12, 1979.

Matachan, Linda. "Porter Goes on Trial Today: Minn. Baby Sitter Alleges Abuse." *Boston Globe,* December 7, 1992, Metro/Region sec., 15.

Matthews, Glenna. *"Just a Housewife": The Rise and Fall of Domesticity in America.* New York: Oxford University Press, 1987.

Mattel. "Pixel Chix Babysitter" (children's toy). Pixel Chix Shop. http://pixelchix.everythinggirl.com/us/shop/shop.aspx?9. Accessed Aug. 2008.

Matusky, Joy Abbett. "We Solved Our Sitter Problem the Co-Op Way." *Parents' Magazine and Better Homemaking*, December 1961, 60.

May, Elaine Tyler. *Homeward Bound: American Families in the Cold War Era*. New York: Basic Books, 1988.

Mazzarella, Sharon R., and Norma Odom Pecora. *Growing Up Girls: Popular Culture and the Construction of Identity*. New York: Peter Lang, 1999.

———. *Pushing the Limits: American Women, 1940-1961*. New York: Oxford University Press, 1994.

McCall's Magazine, "Live the Life of *McCall's*," May 1954.

———, "New Solutions to the Baby-Sitting Problem," June 1973, 40.

McCurrach, David. "Kids Baby-Sitting: Baby-Sitters' Survey Results." Kids' Money. http://www.kidsmoney.org/babysit.htm. Accessed Jan. 2, 2009.

McElravy, May F. "Grandma Is Drafted." *Parents Magazine*, May 1945, 11–12.

McGill, Marci. *The Six Little Possums and the Baby Sitter*. New York: Golden, 1982.

McIntosh, Edna Mae. "Baby Sitting." *Practical Home Economics* 33 (April 1955): 10–11, 36.

McLeer, Anne. "Practical Perfection? The Nanny Negotiates Gender, Class, and Family Contradictions in 1960s Popular Culture." *NWSA Journal* 14, no. 2 (Summer 2002): 83.

McRobbie, Angela. *Feminism and Youth Culture*. 2nd ed. New York: Routledge, 2000.

———. "Notes on Postfeminism and Popular Culture: Bridget Jones and the New Gender Regime." In *All about the Girl*, edited by Anita Harris, 3–14. New York: Routledge, 2004.

McRobbie, Angela, and Jenny Garber. "Girls and Subcultures." In *Feminism and Youth Culture*, 2nd ed., edited by Angela McRobbie, 12–25. New York: Routledge, 2000.

Mead, Margaret. "Family Life Is Changing." In *The New Encyclopedia of Child Care and Guidance*, edited by Sidonie Matsner Gruenberg, 675–82. Garden City, NY: Doubleday, 1954.

Merolla, Carla. "Are Your Kids Safe with the Sitter?" *Safety and Health*, August 1996, 74–75.

Merrit, Ella Arvilla, and Edith S. Gray. "Child Labor Trends in an Expanding Market." *Monthly Labor Review* 67, no. 6 (December 1948): 589–95.

Merritt, Ella Arvilla, and Floyd Hendricks. "Trends of Child Labor, 1940–1944." *Monthly Labor Review* 60 (1944): 756–75.

Metropolitan Life Insurance Company. *Sitting Safely: A Brief Safety Guide for Teen-Age Baby Sitters*. New York: Metropolitan Life Insurance Company, 1987.

Meyeroff, Wendy J. "Baby Sitter Basics." *Good Housekeeping*, September 1992.

Meyerowitz, Joanne, ed. *Not June Cleaver: Women and Gender in Postwar America, 1945–1960.* Philadelphia: Temple University Press, 1994.

———. "Beyond the Feminine Mystique: A Reassessment of Postwar Mass Culture, 1946–1958." In *Not June Cleaver: Women and Gender in Postwar America, 1945–1960,* edited by Joanne Meyerowitz, 229–62. Philadelphia: Temple University Press, 1994.

Miller, Douglas, and Marion Novak. *The Fifties: The Way We Really Were.* Garden City, NY: Doubleday, 1977.

Miller, Laura. "Graffiti Photos: Expressive Art in Japanese Girls' Culture." *Harvard Asia Quarterly* 7, no. 3 (Summer 2003).

Millner, Caille, and Mike Blanding. "Annals of Baby-Sitting: The Newest Growth Industry." *Jinn Magazine, Pacific News Service,* April 2, 1997. http://www.pacificnews.org/jinn/stories/3.07/970402-babysit.html. Also available on Yo! Youth Outlook, "YOpinion: A Babysitter's Manifesto." http://www.youthoutlook.org/news/view_article.html?article_id=196.

Milner, Sherry. Private Communication, April 2000.

Mintz, Steven. *Huck's Raft: A History of American Childhood.* Cambridge, MA: Belknap Press of Harvard University Press, 2004.

———. "Parenting." In *Encyclopedia of Children and Childhood,* edited by Paula S. Fass, 648–54. New York: Macmillan Library Reference, 2003.

Mintz, Steven, and Susan Kellogg. *Domestic Revolutions: A Social History of American Family Life.* New York: Free Press, 1988.

Miss America, a Quarterly Magazine for Girls, "Baby-Sitting Is Big Business!" Winter 1949.

Moffett, Martha. "Baby-Sitting." *American Home,* July 1976, 24.

Montee, Patricia. "With a Little Help from my Friends, Babysitting Cooperative." *Redbook,* June 1972, 46, 48.

Montgomery, John C., and Margaret Jane Suydam. *America's Baby Book.* New York: Scribner's, 1951.

Moore, Mary Furlong. *The Baby Sitter's Guide.* New York: Merkley, 1953.

Morton, Annie. "Starting a Baby-Sitting Co-op." *Parents' Magazine,* June 1990.

Moscrip, Mary Wright. "Time Off for Mother." *Parents Magazine and Family Home Guide,* March 1946, 42, 174.

Mr. Peepers Amateur Home Videos #27: The Backdoor Babysitter. DVD. LBO Entertainment, 1991.

Mulvey, Laura. "Visual Pleasure and Narrative Cinema." *Screen* 16, no. 3 (Autumn 1975): 6–18.

Musselman, Virginia. "Teen Trouble: What Can Recreation Do about It?" *Recreation,* April 1943, 8.

Musser, R. S. "Sitting Lucrative on New Year's, but Tipsy Parents a Problem." *Kansas City Star,* December 30, 1982.

My Favorite Babysitter 17. Directed by Jim Powers. Multimedia Pictures, 2003.

Nanny Watch, http://www.kinderguard.net/how_to/nannywatch.html (site now discontinued).

"Nannysafe." http://www.nannysafe.com.

Nasar, Haya El. "Baby-Sitting's History." *USA Today*, January 1996, 40.

Nash, Ilana. *American Sweethearts: Teenaged Girls in Twentieth-Century Popular Culture*. Indianapolis: Indiana University Press, 2006.

Nashawaty, Chris. "Ghoul's Night Out." Interview with John Carpenter, Nick Castle, Dean Cundey, Jamie Lee Curtis, and Debra Hill. *Entertainment Weekly*, n.d. http://www.geocities.com/j_nada/carp/interview/ew.html.

National Business Woman, "Day Care for Children of Working Mothers," January 1961, 12.

National Geographic World, "Be a Super Sitter" (Red Cross Course), March 1984, 10–13.

National Locksmith, "The Baby Sitter," June 1977, 18.

National Safety Council. *You're In Charge*. Chicago: National Safety Council, 1946 and 1948.

Neff, Emily. "The Baby Sitter." *Cosmopolitan*, May 1953, 88–91.

Neisser, Edith G. "Standards for Baby-Sitters." 1950. Reprinted from *The Woman's Press: The National Magazine for Young Women's Christian Associations*, March 1947.

Neus, Margaret. "The Insider's Guide to Babysitting: Anecdotes and Advice from Babysitters for Babysitters." Master's thesis, Emerson College, 1990.

New Baby Sitter. DVD. Directed by Roy Karch. Gourmet Video Collection, 1996.

New York Herald Tribune Home Institute. *America's Housekeeping Book*. New York: Scribner's, 1956.

New York Times, "Baby Sitter Is Jailed under Lindbergh Law," November 10, 1953.

———, "Babysitter by the Ton: Dodgers Football Squad to Guard 4-Year-Old on Flight," September 1, 1948.

———, Baby-Sitter, 14, Held in Killing," January 31, 1954.

———, "Baby-Sitter Held in Slaying," February 2, 1952.

———, "Baby-Sitter Warning," December 21, 1959.

———, "Baby Sitters at Dental Clinic," November 20, 1954, 19.

———, "Baby Sitters' Clinic Aids Church," December 13, 1953.

———, "Baby Sitters' Code Proposed," December 13, 1953.

———, "Baby Sitters Now Help Parents Attend Church," November 18, 1950.

———, "Baby Sitters Set Up Working Conditions Code," October 4, 1957.

———, "Baby Sitters to Aid Voters," August 24, 1949.

———, "Baby Sitters to Spur Voting," April 19, 1947.

———, "Baby Sitters Win Pact," January 20, 1947.

———, "Baby-Sitting Guide Mailed in Jersey," October 14, 1952.

New York Times, "Barn Theater's Actress Baby-Sitters Wow Children with Mother Goose Roles," August 8, 1949.

———, "Boy, 4, Liable in Suit," February 28, 1953.

———, "Champs Mother Found," December 28, 1950.

———, "Folder and Film Strip Aid Mother in Instructing Sitter for Junior," October 4, 1955.

———, "Greenbush Summer Theatre, Blauvelt, NY, Provides Unoccupied Actors for Patrons' Children during Shows," August 8, 1949.

———, "Held in Child's Death," November 11, 1952.

———, "'Infant Care' Is Out in Revised Edition," October 14, 1951.

———, "Jersey Police Hunt Suspected Rapist after Two Robberies," October 30, 1977.

———, "Kidnapping Charge Filed," November 8, 1953.

———, "Legal Guide Urged for Teen 'Sitters,'" February 25, 1953.

———, "Measure to License Baby Sitters Is Killed on State House Floor," March 7, 1958.

———, "More Rivalry Due for Baby-Sitters," November 9, 1953.

———, "New Baby-Sitter Bill Goes to Governor: Would Free Parents from Legal Claims," March 25, 1958.

———, "No Discord in This Music: Buffalo Philharmonic Arrange Baby Sitting Service," September 8, 1948, 31.

———, "No Men Are Wanted," August 4, 1947.

———, "N.Y. Young Women's Republican Club to Provide Sitters for Women Registering to Vote," October 8, 1949, 37.

———, "Parents of Babies Warned on Sitters," January 30, 1952.

———, "Philadelphia Girl Stabbed," January 10, 1975.

———, "Protection for Baby Sitters," November 17, 1977.

———, "Rape Case to High Court," October 19, 1977.

———, "Rules for Baby Sitters," October 4, 1947.

———, "Safety Class for Young Sitters," October 11, 1990, C11.

———, "Safety Council Urges Talks on Baby Sitters," March 22, 1956.

———, "Santa Claus Sitters for Hire," March 22, 1956, 30.

———, "Scouts to Aid Voting Mothers," October 19, 1947, 50.

———, "Sitter Seized with Baby in Indiana Kidnap Case," November 9, 1953.

———, "Sitters Lay Down Code for Parents," March 18, 1960.

———, "State Exempts Sitters from Child Labor Laws," April 17, 1958.

———, "Teen-Age Baby Sitter, Unaided, Fends Off Would-Be Kidnapper," March 20, 1995.

———, "Teen-Agers Demand Data on Rates, Number of Babies, and Any Special Care," March 17, 1960, 27.

———, "30 Girls Complete Child Care Study," November 9, 1954.

———, "TV Cuts Baby Sitters," November 20, 1951.

New York Times, "Veteran of 200 Bouts Is Flattened in First Baby-Sitting Engagement," December 26, 1950.

———, "Veterans to Test Exchange 'Sitting,'" January 2, 1947.

———, "Woman Trooper, Lacking a Baby Sitter, Is Dismissed," December 31, 1978.

New York Times Magazine, "What Is a Bobby Sock?" March 5, 1944, 23.

New Yorker, "Ideal Baby-Sitting Service, Columbia," October 29, 1949, 20–21.

Newberry, Clare Turlay. *T-Bone the Babysitter*. New York: HarperCollins, 1950.

Newsweek, "Can you Get a Sitter?" May 1987.

———, "Combating the Victory Girl," March 6, 1944, 88, 91.

———, "Our Billion-Dollar Night Out: Boom in Baby-Sitting," December 3, 1956, 87–88.

———, "Three Smart Girls." October 29, 1951, 38.

Nichols, Sodie. "Teen-Age Parties: New American Headache." *Good Housekeeping*, February 1953, 49.

Norman, Cynthia. "Youths Trained in Babysitting Skills." *Boston Globe*, October 3, 1979.

Norton, Mary Beth, et al. *A People and a Nation: A History of the United States*. 3rd ed. Boston: Houghton Mifflin, 1991.

Novak, Ralph. "The Baby-Sitters Club" (movie review), *People Weekly*, September 4, 1995, 19.

O'Connell, Dorothy R. *Baby-Sitting Safe and Sound*. New York: Fawcett Gold Metal, 1990.

Odem, Mary E. *Delinquent Daughters: Protecting and Policing Adolescent Female Sexuality in the United States, 1885–1920*. Chapel Hill: University of North Carolina Press, 1995.

———. "Female Sexuality and Juvenile Delinquency in Early-Twentieth-Century California." In Major *Problems in the History of American Families and Children*, edited by Anya Jabour, 279–88. Boston: Houghton Mifflin, 2004.

———. "Teenage Girls, Sexuality, and Working-Class Parents." In *Generations of Youth: Youth Cultures and History in Twentieth-Century America*, edited by Joe Austin and Michael Willard, 50–64. New York: New York University Press, 1998.

O'Donnell, Maureen. "Suspect Sought in Girls' Murder: Three Others Held in Baby-Sitter's Death." *Chicago Sun-Times*, March 9, 1998, 16.

Ogren, Kathy. "Nightlife." In *Encyclopedia of American Social History*, edited by Mary Kupiec Cayton, Elliott J. Gorn, and Peter W. Williams, 1:1713–22. New York: Scribner's, 1993.

O'Keane, Bernard. *Lights Out*. New York: HarperCollins, 1995.

Olwine, Margaret. "Baby-Sitter Clinic Draws Nearly 100." *Kansas City Star*, June 17, 1966.

O'Neill, William L. *Coming Apart: An Informal History of America in the 1960s*. New York: Quadrangle, 1971.

Ontario Safety League. *Baby-Sitting Training Course*. Ontario: Ontario Safety League, Ontario Tuberculosis Association, Northumberland-Durham TB and Health Association, 1963.

Opdycke, Sandra. *The Routledge Historical Atlas of Women in America*. New York: Routledge, 2000.

Operation Babysitter. VHS Cartoon. Directed by Steve Grant. 1985.

Oppenheim, Garrret. "Teen-Age Drinking Can Spell Disaster." *Parents Magazine*, May 1961, 80, 186–91.

Oriental Babysitter. VHS. Directed by Anthony Spinelli. 1976.

Packard, Vance. *The Status Seekers*. New York: Pocket Books, 1959.

Palladino, Grace. *Teenagers: An American History*. New York: Basic Books, 1996.

Pantiel, Mindy. "Stalking the Teenage Babysitter." *Working Mother*, July 1991.

Pardini, Jane Crowley. *The Babysitter Book*. Chicago: Contemporary, 2006.

Parents' Magazine and Better Homemaking, "Are American Parents Making Too Much of Chore of Child Care?" December 1961, 62, 82, 84.

———, "The Cosmetic Urge," January 1933, 21–22.

Parents Magazine and Family Home Guide, "Training for Baby Sitters," April 1951, 134.

Parker, Daniel. *Alone in the Dark*. New York: HarperCollins, 1995.

Parker, Johnny. *Baby Sittin' Boogie*. Buzz Clifford (Herb Reiss Music Corp). 1960.

Parry, Sally E. "'You Are Needed, Desperately Needed!': Cherry Ames in World War II." In *Nancy Drew and Company: Culture, Gender, and Girls' Series*, edited by Sherrie A. Inness, 129–44. Bowling Green, OH: Bowling Green Press, 1997.

Passalaqua, Carolyn. "1950s History: Information, Notes." *Boomer's Fifties Teen Idol Magazine*. http://home.att.net/~boomers.fifties.teenmag/1950_history.html. December 2008.

Paterson, Bettina. *Bun and Mrs. Tubby*. New York: Franklin Watts, 1987.

Pave, Irene. "Hold Out for the Best Baby-Sitter." *Business Week*, November 24, 1986.

Pearson, Michael. "Sitter Accuses Alpharetta Man of Sex Assault: His 3-year-old in Bed at Time, Teenager Alleges." *Atlanta Journal-Constitution*, June 5, 2003, Metro News, 4B.

Peiss, Kathy. *Cheap Amusements: The Making of America's Beauty Culture*. New York: Holt, 1999.

———. *Hope in a Jar: The Making of America's Beauty Culture*. New York: Metropolitan Books, 1998.

Pennebaker, Ruth. "Why Girls Can't Get Enough of *The Baby-Sitters Club*." *Parents Magazine*, June 1995.

People, "A Betrayal in the Family," May 12, 1997, 46–48.

People Weekly, "When the Bough Breaks," February 24, 1992, 60.

Perverted #01-Babysitters. Directed by John T. Bone. 1994.

Philbin, Walt. "Boy, 2, Shot to Death: Baby-Sitter Charged." *Times-Picayune*, March 28, 1992, A1.

Pierce, R. Taeza. "Structured Courses Being Offered Babysitting School." *Boston Globe*, August 19, 1985, Living sec., 17.

Pinedo, Isabel Cristina. *Recreational Terror: Women and the Pleasures of Horror Film Viewing*. New York: SUNY Press, 1997.

Pinson, Penelope. "A Pictorial Guide to the Very Special Art of Baby Sitting." *Parents' Magazine and Family Home Guide*, February 1954, 38–40.

———. "What a Baby Sitter Needs to Know." *Boston Globe*, November 8, 1955.

Piper, Virginia. *Tips for Teens from Carnation*. Los Angeles: Carnation Company, 1967.

Plain Dealer, "'Frasier' Star Kelsey Grammer Denies He Had," November 19, 1994, National sec., 2A.

Planning Babysitting. Vocational movie. Directed by Tom Solari, 1980.

Plath, Sylvia. "As a Baby-Sitter Sees It." *Christian Science Monitor*, November 7, 1951.

Pleck, Joseph H. *The Myth of Masculinity*. Cambridge, MA: MIT Press, 1983.

Pollock, Kathryn M. "Helping the Mother-Aides." *Journal of Home Economics* 35 (January 1943): 31–32.

Pollock, Shirley. "Do You Rate with Your Baby Sitter?" *Parents Magazine and Family Home Guide*, April 1957, 44–45, 95.

Porter, Sylvia. *Sylvia Porter's Your Own Money: Earning It, Spending It, Saving It, Investing It, and Living on It in Your First Independent Years*. New York: Avon, 1983.

Postelle, Yvonne. "Baby Sitters Money Can't Buy." *Parents' Magazine and Better Family Living*, August 1969, 56–57, 74, 78.

Princeton Alumni Weekly. "Photographs from Princeton Past and What Our Readers Have to Say about Them." Princeton, http://www.princeton.edu/~paw/web_exclusives/FTA/from_the_archives.html. Accessed April 2008.

"Protesting Worker," letter, "Dear Beth," *Boston Globe*, February 22, 1983.

Psycho. Directed by Alfred Hitchcock. Los Angeles: Paramount Pictures, 1960.

Pulp. *The Babysitter*. Britannia Row Studios, compact disc, 1994.

Purdy, Candy. "Be a Super-Safe Sitter." *Current Health 2: A Weekly Reader Publication*, November 1, 1994.

———. "Think before You (Baby)sit." *Current Health*, November 1989, 22–23.

Quandt, Albert L. *Baby Sitter*. New York: Original Novels, 1952.

Rader, Benjamin G. "Television." In *Encyclopedia of American Social History*, edited by Mary Kupiec Cayton, Elliott J. Gorn, Peter W. Williams. New York: Scribner's, 1993.

Raffel, Dawn. "Sitting Smart." *Seventeen*, August 1983, 237.

The Ramones. Song. *Babysitter*. Sundragon Studios, 1977.

Ransom, Merilee. "A Face on the Women of World War Two: The Changes They Made While Supporting the War Effort" (unpublished paper, 2006).

Recreation, "Some Wartime Programs for Girls," April 1944.

"Red Cross Babysitting Teaches Vital Skills to New Sitters." http://www.infozine.com/z9706/kcr1.html (site now discontinued).

Reed, Ann Rose. "Princeton Alumni Weekly," from the Archives 2000–01 and 2001–02. Princeton. http://www.princeton.edu/~paw/web_exclusives/FTA/from_the_archives.html. Accessed April 2008.

"Report." Placement Office, Wellesley College. 1 July 1946–30 June 1947.

Richards, Virginia. "This Baby-Sitting Business." *Coronet*, April 1949, 101–5.

Riesman, David. *The Lonely Crowd: A Study of the Changing American Character*. New Haven, CT: Yale University Press, 1961.

Riley, Bob. *Baby Sittin* (song). Dot, 1957.

Ritter, Bess. "School for Sitters." *Profitable Hobbies*, October 1955, 25.

Rivers, Donald. "The Promiscuous Babysitter." *Men*, September 1964.

Roberts, Kimberley. "Girl Power." In *Girlhood in America: An Encyclopedia*, vol. 1, edited by Miriam Forman-Brunell, 312–15. Santa Barbara: ABC-CLIO, 2001.

———. "Girls in Black and White: The Iconography of Teenage Girls in Post-Feminist America." Ph.D. diss., University of Virginia, May 2002.

———. "Pleasures and Problems of the 'Angry Girl.'" In *Sugar, Spice, and Everything Nice*, edited by Frances Gateward and Murray Pomerance, chap. 12. Detroit: Wayne State University Press, 2002.

Roberts, Willo Davis. *Baby-Sitting Is a Dangerous Job*. New York: Atheneum, 1985.

Robertson, Keith. *Henry Reed's Babysitting Service*. New York: Random House, 1962.

Rockwell, Norman. *Norman Rockwell's America: Portrait of America*. New York: Crescent Books, 1989, 18.

Rodgers, Mary Augusta. "We Love our Babysitters . . . But Please No Bongo Drums." *Good Housekeeping*, August 1960, 40, 42.

Rogin, Michael. *"Ronald Reagan," The Movie: And Other Episodes of Political Demonology*. Berkeley: University of California Press, 1987.

Romalov, Nancy Tillman. "Mobile and Modern Heroines: Early Twentieth-Century Girls' Automobile Series." In *Nancy Drew & Co.: Culture, Gender, and Girls' Series*, edited by Sherrie A. Inness, 75–88. Bowling Green, OH: Bowling Green State University Popular Press, 1997.

———. "Unearthing the Historical Reader; or, Reading Girls' Reading." In *Pioneers, Passionate Ladies, and Private Eyes: Dime Novels, Series Books, and Paperbacks*, edited by Larry P. Sullivan and Lydia Cushman Schurman, 87–101. Binghamton, NY: Hawthorn Press, 1996.

Romanoff, Gladys. "Big-sister Role." *The American Girl*, December 1951, 22–23.

Rosati, Roberta. "Baby-Sitting Isn't Bliss!" *Seventeen*, February 1973, 18.

Rosen, Ilene S. "Baby-sitter Basics." *Parents*, November 1996, 171–72.

Rosenberg, Carroll Smith. "Davy Crockett as Trickster: Pornography, Liminality, and Symbolic Inversion in Victorian America." Part 2 in *Disorderly Conduct: Visions of Gender in Victorian America*. New York: Oxford University Press, 1985.

Rossio, Joann. "No Trapped Housewives Here: A Neighborhood Baby-Sitting Exchange." *Redbook*, August 1964, 6, 8, 10, 12–13.

Rudavsky, Shari. "ABCs of Child Care: Preteens Are Learning the Basics of Baby-Sitting." *Boston Globe*, February 24, 2002, B5.

Russell, Jenna. "Jealously Guarding the Baby Sitter: Once Found, Mothers Nurture Rare Resource." *Boston Globe*, January 16, 2000, West Weekly sec.

Rymph, Catherine E. "Neither Neutral nor Neutralized: Phyllis Schlafly's Battle against Sexism." In *Women's America: Refocusing the Past*, 5th ed., edited by Linda K. Kerber and Jane Sherron De Hart, 501–7. New York: Oxford University Press, 2000.

"Safe Sitter Fact Sheet." In *We're Spreading Our Wings*, compiled by Safe Sitter Inc. Brochure, 1997.

Salk, Lee. "Super Sitters." *McCall's*, June 1989, 69–73.

San Diego Union-Tribune, "Chmura Ordered to Stand Trial," May 31, 2000, Sports sec., D7.

San Francisco Call-Bulletin, "Club to Popularize Baby Sitting for GI Students," February 17, 1948, 17.

San Francisco Examiner, "Baby Sitter's Romancer Gets a Year in Jail," May 20, 1965, 62.

San Francisco News, "Sitter, Father Jailed," August 22, 1947, 1.

Saperstein, Saundra. "They're Standing in Line for New Year's Sitters." *The Washington Post*, December 29, 1984, Metro sec., E1.

Satran, Pamela Redmond. "In Search of the Perfect Sitter," *Working Mother*, July 1993.

Saturday Evening Post, Cover, "Babysitter," November 8, 1947.

———, Cover, "Babysitter at Beach Stand," August 24, 1954.

———, Cover, "The New Baby Sitter," February 14, 1953.

———, Cover. "New Year's Babysitter," January 4, 1958.

Saunders, Rubie. *Baby-Sitting for Fun and Profit*. New York: Simon & Schuster, 1984.

———. *The Franklin Watts Concise Guide to Baby-Sitting*. New York: Franklin Watts, 1972.

Say No to Strangers! Directed by Sid Davis. Los Angeles: Sidney Davis Productions, 1957.

Schaller, Michael, Virginia Scharff, and Robert D. Schulzinger. *Coming of Age: America in the Twentieth Century.* Boston: Houghton Mifflin, 1998.

Scharf, Lois. *To Work and to Wed: Female Employment, Feminism, and the Great Depression.* Westport, CT: Greenwood, 1980.

Scheiner, Georganne. "The Deanna Durbin Devotees: Fan Clubs and Spectatorship." In *Generations of Youth: Youth Culture and History in Twentieth-Century America,* edited by Joe Austin and Michael Nevin Willard, 81–94. New York: New York University Press, 1998.

———. *Signifying Female Adolescence: Film, Representations, and Fans, 1920–1950.* Westport, CT: Praeger, 2000.

Schulman, Bruce. *The Seventies: The Great Shift in American Culture, Society, and Politics.* New York: Free Press, 2001.

Schrum, Kelly. "Bobby Socks." In *The St. James Encyclopedia of Popular Culture,* edited by Tom Pendergast and Sara Pendergast, 5 vols. Farmington Hills, MI: St. James Press, 1999.

———. *Some Wore Bobby Sox: The Emergence of Teenage Girls' Culture, 1920–1945.* New York: Palgrave, 2004.

———. "'Teena Means Business': Teenage Girls' Culture and *Seventeen* Magazine." In *Delinquents and Debutantes: Twentieth-Century American Girls' Cultures,* edited by Sherrie A. Inness, 134–63. New York: New York University Press, 1998.

Seduction of the Innocent. DVD. Directed by Sid Davis. Los Angeles: Sidney Davis Productions, 1961.

Selling to Kids, "Scholastic's 3rd Quarter Loss Linked to Slump in Popular Kids Books," May 19, 1997.

Seventeen Magazine, "A Baby-Sitter's Guide to Survival," June 1984.

———, "Baby-Sitting Pretty: Focus on Teens in Business," April 1985, 116.

———, "Baby Sitting: Your First Big Job," July 1958, 52.

———, "Jobs Have No Gender," April 1945, 18, 159.

———, Letters to Editor, November 1944.

———, Letters to Editor, January 1945.

Shannon, Jacqueline. "Be a Better Babysitter." *Teen,* November 1984.

Shea, Nancy. *The Army Wife.* 3rd ed. New York: Harper & Brothers, 1954.

Sheldon, Kathleen. "How to Trap and Train a Babysitter." *Parents' Magazine and Better Homemaker,* January 1963, 42–43, 68.

Shor, Francis. "Father Knows Beast: Patriarchal Rage and the Horror Personality Film." *Journal of Criminal Justice and Popular Culture* 3 (1995): 60–73. http://www.albany. edu/scj/jcjpc/vol3is3/beast.html.

Shupp, Cleo. "Little Girls Are Too Sexy Too Soon." *Saturday Evening Post,* June 29, 1963, 12.

Sidepony4evr, "'Real' Babysitters Club," YouTube, http://www.youtube.com/watch?v=VX9f-7Gwgr0. Accessed August 18, 2006.

Sikes, Gini. "Baby-Sitting the Brat." *Seventeen*, March 1987.

Silbiger, Hollace. "Desperately Seeking Sitters: Many Teenagers Prefer Socializing, Sports Activities to Watching Kids." *Plain Dealer* (Cleveland, OH), Family sec., 1E.

The Sitter. Directed by Fred Walton. 1978.

The Sitter. TVM. Directed by Rick Berger. FNM Films, 1991.

Sitting Pretty. VHS. Directed by Walter Lang. Los Angeles: Twentieth Century Fox, 1948.

Sitting Pretty. Final script. Twentieth-Century Fox Film Corporation. October 5, 1947.

Slatalla, Michelle. "Learning How to Sit in for Parents." *Newsday*, June 7, 1985, npn.

Smith, Ann. "My Children Were Using Me," *Ladies Home Journal*, July 1980, 37–38.

Smith, Harry. "A Good Babysitter Is Hard to Find: Parents Magazine Editor Offers Tips to Find a Responsible Person to Watch Your Kids." Interview with Diane Debrovner. *CBS Early Show*, July 23, 2007. Sttp://www.cbsnews.com/ stories/2007/07/23/earlyshow/living/parenting/main3087781.shtml.

Smith, Maureen A. "My Adventures as a Quint Sitter." *Seventeen*, June 1972, 126, 136.

Smith, Sarah Collie. "So Many Children." *The Wellesley Magazine*, April 1943, 222–24.

Social Security Online. "Social Security Handbook." U.S. Social Security Administration. http://www.ssa.gov/OP_Home/handbook/handbook.html.

Solinger, Rickie. "Teen Pregnancy." In *Girlhood in America: An Encyclopedia*, vol. 2, edited by Miriam Forman-Brunell, 645–53. Santa Barbara, CA: ABC-CLIO, 2001.

Sophia Smith Collection, Smith College, Northampton, MA.

Southard, Helen F. *Baby Sitters: A Basic Training Manual for Sitters, Parents, Schools, Community Leaders, and Youth Organizations,* 2nd printing. New York: National Board of the YWCA, 1962.

———. "Early Marriages: Some Young People Speak." Reprinted in *The YWCA Magazine*, December 1955.

Spigel, Lynn. *Make Room for TV: Television and the Family Ideal in Postwar America*. Chicago: University of Chicago Press, 1992.

———. "Seducing the Innocent." In *The Children's Culture Reader*, edited by Henry Jenkins, 117. New York: New York University Press, 1998.

Spock, Benjamin McLane. *Baby and Child Care*. New York: Duell, Sloan, and Pearce, 1944 and 1956.

———. *The Common Sense Book of Baby and Child Care*. New York: Duell, Sloan, and Pearce, 1946.

———. *Infant and Child Care.* 2nd ed. New York: Pocket Books, 1958.

———. "When Mothers Work." *Ladies Home Journal,* March 1963, 140, 142–43.

Spock, Benjamin, Arnold Gesell, Herman N. Bundesen, and Frederick Drimmer. *Every Woman's Standard Guide to Home and Child Care.* New York: Greystone Press/Hawthorn Books, 1959.

Stains, Laurence. "Nanny Dearest." *Men's Health,* September 1993, 26.

Stanton, Barbara. "Baby Sitters United." *Woman's Home Companion,* March 1947, 150–51.

Stapen, Candyce H. "Caring for Your Child-Care Person." *Working Woman,* March 1988.

Stearns, Peter N. *Anxious Parents: A History of Modern Childrearing in America.* New York: New York University Press, 2003.

Steffens, Margaret Crawford. "Mother's Helper: A Few Rules for Each Member of a Mutual Job." *Woman's Home Companion,* October 1937, 56–57.

Stevens, Kathleen. *The Beast and the Babysitter.* Milwaukee, WI: Gareth Stevens Children's Books, 1989.

Stine, R. L. *The Babysitter.* New York: Scholastic, 1989.

———. *The Babysitter II.* New York: Scholastic, 1991.

———. *The Babysitter III.* New York: Scholastic, 1993.

———. *The Babysitter IV.* New York: Scholastic, 1995.

Stinnett, Caskie. "Baby-Sitting Rates." *Look,* April 19, 1955, 132.

Story, John. *Cultural Studies and the Study of Popular Culture: Theories and Methods.* Athens: University of Georgia Press, 1996.

Strasser, Susan. *Never Done: A History of American Housework.* New York: Holt, 2000.

Street Cents. http://www.halifax.cbc.ca/streetcents/entrepreneur/beef/html. Accessed January 8, 1997.

Strickland, Charles E., and Andrew M. Ambrose. "The Baby Boom, Prosperity, and the Changing Worlds of Children, 1945–1963." In *American Childhood: A Research Guide and Historical Handbook,* edited by Joseph M. Hawes and N. Ray Hiner, 533–85. Westport, CT: Greenwood Press, 1985.

Stuhring, Celeste. *Kid Sitter Basics: A Handbook for Babysitters.* Kansas City, MO: Westport, 1994.

Sullinger, James H. "Working Mothers Search Hard for Sitters," *Kansas City Star,* February 12, 1980.

Sullivan, Dana. "Certified Sitters." *Parenting,* June/July 1989.

Summer Girl. TVM. Directed by Robert Michael Lewis. Bruce Lansbury Production Co., 1983.

Superman's Girlfriend Lois Lane. "Lois Lane, Super-Baby-sitter!" Vol. 57, May 1965.

Sumner, M. C. *The Evil Child.* New York: HarperCollins, 1995.

Teen, "Baby-Sitter's Survival Guide," March 1987.

Teen, "Quiz: How Do You Rate as a Babysitter?" January 1982, 64.

"Teenage Girls." Newsreel. *March of Time* 11 no. 11 (1945).

Terris, Susan. *Baby-Snatcher.* New York: Farrar, Straus, Giroux, 1984.

Thiboxeaux, Ron. "Dealing with Molestation Class." *Times–Picayune,* May 24, 1997, B.

Thompson, Margaret. "Boys as Mothers-Helpers." *Parents Magazine,* August 1939, 24, 53–54.

Thompson, Nellie Zetta. "Baby-Sitting Is Growing Up." *Journal of the National Education Association* 40 (November 1951): 565–66.

Thorton-Dill, Bonnie. "'The Means to Put My Children Through': Child-Rearing Goals and Strategies among Black Female Domestic Servants." In *Feminist Frontiers,* edited by Laurel Richardson, et al., 192. New York: McGraw-Hill, 1999.

Time, "Little Women," October 29, 1951, 24.

———, "They Think of the Moment," February 26, 1945. http://www.time.com/time/magazine/article/0,9171,792035-1,00.html.

Today's Health Magazine, "Checklist for Choosing a Baby Sitter," May 1961, 83.

———, "The Fine Art of Baby Sitting," March 1952, 28–30.

Tolles, Martha. *Katie's Baby-Sitting Job.* New York: Scholastic, 1985.

Toms, Agnes. "How We Teach Baby Sitting." *Practical Home Economics* 34 (September 1955): 46–47.

Tooker, Robert N. *All about the Baby and Preparations for Its Advent Together with the Homeopathic Treatment of Its Ordinary Ailments.* Chicago: Rand, McNally, 1896.

Training the Baby Sitter. Gourmet Video, 2001.

"Training High-School Students for Wartime Service to Children," Washington, DC: Government Printing Office, 1943.

Trencansky, Sarah. "Final Girls and Terrible Youth: Transgression in 1980s Slasher Horror." *Journal of Popular Film and Television* 29, no. 2 (Summer 2001): 63–73.

Tsao, Mary. "The Pied Piper of Babysitters." *Mom Writes,* January 17, 2006. http://marytsao.blogspot.com/2006_01_01_marytsao_archive.html.

Tucker, Ian. "Single White Rapper." Interview with Princess Superstar. *The Times Magazine,* February 16, 2002. http://www.princesssuperstar.com/press/features/times_feat.shtml.

Tuttle, William M. *"Daddy's Gone to War": The Second World War in the Lives of America's Children.* New York: Oxford University Press, 1995.

Understanding Babysitting. VHS. Directed by Tom Solari. North Hollywood, CA: Film Communicators, 1980.

University of California Folklore Archive. Berkeley, California.

Ury, Allen B. "The Case of the Very Bad Baby Sitter." In *More Scary Mysteries for Sleep-Overs,* edited by Allen B. Ury, 81–91. New York: Price Stern Sloan, 1996.

U.S. Bureau of the Census. 2001. Tables of Detailed Occupation, 1990. Www.
    census.gov/hhes/www/occupation.html. Retrieved June 21, 2000.

U.S. Children's Bureau. *Infant Care*. Washington, DC: U.S. Government Printing
    Office, 1963, 39.

U.S. Consumer Product Safety Commission. *The Super Sitter*. September 1987.

U.S. Department of the Interior. National Park Service. *The National Register Bul-
    letin, Historic Residential Suburbs*. N.d. http://www.cr.nps.gov/nr/
    publications/bulletins/suburbs/part3.htm.

U.S. Kids: A Weekly Reader Magazine, "Becoming a Safe Sitter," September 1997.

U.S. News & World Report, "As Parents Influence Fades—Who's Raising the Chil-
    dren?" October 27, 1975.

———, "Jobs and the Young: Chances of Finding Work This Summer," May 17,
    1976, Labor sec., 72.

Usher, Ann. "A Bill of Rights—and Wrongs—for Baby-Sitting." *Better Homes &
    Gardens*, October 1960, 120.

Van Buren, Abigail. "Dear Abby." *Newsday*, May 8, 1996.

Vaneck, Joanne. "Time Spent in Housework." In *A Heritage of Her Own: Toward a
    New Social History of American Women*, edited by Nancy Cott and Elizabeth
    Pleck, chap. 21. New York: Toachstone/Simon & Schuster, 1979.

Viorst, Judith. "Who's Minding the Baby?" *Redbook*, June 1970, 70, 176, 178.

Wagner, Esther. "The Night a Sitter Stood Tall." *Better Homes and Gardens*, July
    1962, 10.

Walker, Charles Rumford. *American City*. New York: Farrar & Rinehart, 1937.

Walt Disney's *Donald Duck, Baby Sitter*. Record. New York: Simon & Schuster,
    1950. 45 RPM, Golden Record.

Ward, Ivan. *Baby Sitter* (song). 1961.

Ware, Susan. *Holding Their Own: American Women in the 1930s*. Boston: Twayne,
    1982.

Warner, Judith. *Perfect Madness: Motherhood in the Age of Anxiety*. New York: Riv-
    erhead, 2005.

Warren, John Robert. "Labor Market Stratification among High School Students:
    Evidence from Sound Futures and Tacoma 2000." Unpublished paper cited
    with permission by author, July 2001, 1–24.

Watson, John B. *Behavior: An Introduction to Comparative Psychology*. New York:
    Henry Holt, 1914.

———. *Psychological Care of Infant and Child*. London: Allen, 1928.

Weekend with the Baby Sitter. Trailer and movie. Directed by Don Henderson.
    Crown International Pictures, 1970.

Weiner, Lynn Y. *From Working Girl to Working Mother: The Female Labor Force in
    the United States, 1820–1980*. Chapel Hill: University of North Carolina
    Press, 1985.

Weiss, Jessica. *To Have and to Hold: Marriage, the Baby Boom, and Social Change.* Chicago: University of Chicago Press, 2000.

Weiss, Nancy Pottishman. "Mother, the Invention of Necessity: Dr. Benjamin Spock's Baby and Child Care." In *Growing Up in America: Children in Historical Perspective*, edited by N. Ray Hiner and Joseph M. Hawes, 283–303. Chicago: University of Chicago Press, 1985.

Weiss, Susan Zelvin. "Security Blankets: Baby-Sitting Isn't Children's Play." *Chicago Tribune*, May 24, 1992, final edition, Tempo Lake sec..

The Wellesley Magazine, "So Many Children," April 1943, 224.

Wen, Patricia, and Bruce Mohl. "Attention Parents: Rate for Teenage Baby-Sitting Answered." *Boston Globe*, September 21, 1997, Metro/Region sec., B2.

West, Elliott. *Growing Up in the Twentieth Century: A History and Reference Guide.* Westport, CT: Greenwood Press, 1996.

West, Mrs. Max. *Infant Care.* Care of Children Series 2, Bureau Publication no. 8., U.S. Department of Labor, Children's Bureau. Washington, DC: Government Printing Office, 1914.

What Makes a Good Party? Coronet Instructional Media, 1950.

When a Killer Calls. DVD. Directed by Peter Mervis. Los Angeles, CA: Asylum Home Entertainment, 2006.

When a Stranger Calls. DVD. Directed by Fred Walton. Los Angeles: Columbia Pictures, 1979.

When a Stranger Calls. DVD. Directed by Simon West. Los Angeles: Screen, 2006.

Whitbread, Jane. "Baby-sitting Fathers." *McCall's*, January 1959, 7–8, 10.

White, Barbara A. "Foremothers." In *Ordinary Lessons: Girlhoods of the 1950s*, edited by Susan Douglas Franzosa, 17–46. New York: Peter Lang, 1999.

Whyte, William H. Jr. *The Organization Man.* New York: Simon and Schuster, 1956.

Wikipedia. S.v. "slang," http://en.wikipedia.org/wiki/Slang.

William, Kate. *Beware the Baby-Sitter.* New York: Bantam Books, 1993.

Williams, Dar. *The Babysitter's Here* (song). 1995.

Williams, Linda. "When the Woman Looks." In *The Dread Difference: Gender and the Horror Film*, edited by Barry Keith Grant, 15–34. Austin: University of Texas Press, 1996.

Wilson, Liz. Interview by Dhruv Singh. Winter, 2004.

Wilson, Sloan. *The Man in the Gray Flannel Suit.* New York: Simon & Schuster, 1955.

Winkler, Allan M. *Homefront U.S.A.: America during World War II.* Arlington Heights, IL: Harlan Davidson, 1986.

Winthrop, Elizabeth. *Bear and Mrs. Duck.* New York: Holiday House, 1988.

Wiseman, Bernard. *Morris Is a Cowboy, a Policeman, and a Baby Sitter.* New York: Harper and Row, 1960.

Wolf, Naomi. *Promiscuities: The Secret Struggle for Womanhood.* New York: Random House, 1997.

Woloch, Nancy. *Women and the American Experience.* New York: Knopf, 1984.

Woman's Home Companion, "Dolores Learns to Take Care of the Baby," October 1942, 7–8.

———, "Sitter's Rights," February 1948, 150–53.

Wood, Jennifer. "Frankly Speaking." *Seventeen,* January 1982, 67.

Wrenn, C. Gilbert, and D. L. Harley. "Time on Their Hands." Washington, DC: American Youth Commission, 1940. Cited in "Time on Their Hands," *Recreation,* August 1941, 361.

Wright, Betty. *Baby Sitter.* Atlantic Recording Corp., 1972.

Wright, Gwendolyn. *Building the Dream: A Social History of Housing in America.* Cambridge, MA: MIT Press, 1983.

Wright, Helen Russel. "Children of Wage-Earning Mothers." Washington, DC: Government Printing Office, 1922.

Wyden, Peter. *Suburbia's Coddled Kids.* New York: Doubleday, 1962.

You and Your Family (short). Directed by George Blake. 1946.

Youcha, Geraldine. *Who's Minding the Children: Child Care in America from Colonial Times to the Present.* New York: Scribner's, 1995.

Young, Erma. "Baby Sitters Service." *Kansas City Star,* December 11, 1949.

"Youth in Crisis." Newsreel. *March of Time,* vol. 10, no. 3.

Yourbackyard.com. www.yourbackyard.com/hotpants.nympho/.

YWCA. *Babysitters: A Basic Training Manual for—Sitters, Parents, Schools, Community Leaders, and Youth Organizations.* New York: National Board of the YWCA, 1956/1957.

Zahner, Barbara F. "Big Treat for Toddlers." *Parents' Magazine and Better Homemaking,* June 1976, 27–29.

Zelizer, Viviana A. *Pricing the Priceless Child: The Changing Social Value of Children.* New York: Basic Books, 1985.

Index

182, 183, 184, 191–198, 199, 214,
262n. 134, 263n. 152; on the home
front, 42,43; pet problems, 123,
191–192; responses of girls, 13. *See
also* Children; Household chores;
Payment; Rights; Sexual abuse;
Unions; Work culture

Work culture, 17, 88
Work ethic, 32

Youth culture, 5, 16, 17, 22, 28, 140,
216. *See also* Girls' culture
YWCA, 42, 83, 113, 114, 115, 123,
124

About the Author

MIRIAM FORMAN-BRUNELL is Professor of History at the University of Missouri–Kansas City. She is the editor of *Girlhood in America: An Encyclopedia* and author of *Made to Play House: The Commercialization of American Girlhood*.